# Pindar and the Sublime

NEW DIRECTIONS IN CLASSICS

**New Directions in Classics** is a series of short monographs on Classical antiquity and its reception, covering subjects from across the entire spectrum of ancient Mediterranean culture, including its literature, history, material survivals and their afterlife in diverse media. These volumes move the discipline of Classics forward by breaking new ground, whether in their combination of sources or their method, and by presenting pluralist studies that blend and transcend modes of analysis that have enriched Classics, broadly defined, in recent decades. As fresh and stimulating takes on their topics they are characterized by their dynamism, intellectual energy and interdisciplinary scope, and are accessible without compromising on academic rigour.

*Titles in the series*
*Antiquity and the Meanings of Time: A Philosophy of Ancient and Modern Literature*, Duncan F. Kennedy
*In Search of the Labyrinth: The Cultural Legacy of Minoan Crete*, Nicoletta Momigliano
*The Modernity of Ancient Sculpture: Greek Sculpture and Modern Art from Winckelmann to Picasso*, Elizabeth Prettejohn
*Thucydides and the Idea of History*, Neville Morley

# Pindar and the Sublime

*Greek Myth, Reception, and Lyric Experience*

Robert L. Fowler

BLOOMSBURY ACADEMIC
LONDON • NEW YORK • OXFORD • NEW DELHI • SYDNEY

BLOOMSBURY ACADEMIC
Bloomsbury Publishing Plc
50 Bedford Square, London, WC1B 3DP, UK
1385 Broadway, New York, NY 10018, USA
29 Earlsfort Terrace, Dublin 2, Ireland

BLOOMSBURY, BLOOMSBURY ACADEMIC and the Diana logo are trademarks of
Bloomsbury Publishing Plc

First published in Great Britain 2022

Cover design: Terry Woodley
Cover image © Salvator Rosa's painting, *Pan and Pindar*, by kind permission of
the Palazzo Chigi, Ariccia, Italy.

A catalogue record for this book is available from the British Library.

Library of Congress Cataloging-in-Publication Data
Names: Fowler, Robert L., author.
Title: Pindar and the sublime : Greek myth, reception, and lyric experience /
Robert L. Fowler.
Other titles: New directions in classics.
Description: New York : Bloomsbury Academic, 2022. | Series: New directions in classics |
Includes bibliographical references and index.
Identifiers: LCCN 2021029751 (print) | LCCN 2021029752 (ebook) |
ISBN 9781350198166 (paperback) | ISBN 9781788311144 (hardback) |
ISBN 9781350198135 (ebook) | ISBN 9781350198142 (epub)
Subjects: LCSH: Pindar–Criticism and interpretation. | Greek poetry–History and criticism. |
Sublime, The, in literature.
Classification: LCC PA4276 .F59 2022 (print) | LCC PA4276 (ebook) | DDC 884/.01—dc23
LC record available at https://lccn.loc.gov/2021029751
LC ebook record available at https://lccn.loc.gov/2021029752

ISBN:   HB:      978-1-7883-1114-4
        PB:      978-1-3501-9816-6
        ePDF:    978-1-3501-9813-5
        eBook:   978-1-3501-9814-2

Series: New Directions in Classics

Typeset by RefineCatch Limited, Bungay, Suffolk

To find out more about our authors and books visit www.bloomsbury.com
and sign up for our newsletters.

# Contents

Preface                                                                      vii

Acknowledgements                                                             xiii

1  Sublime Receptions                                                          1
   Ancient perceptions of Pindar                                              1
   Preliminary remarks on early modern receptions                            5
   Abraham Cowley and English receptions                                     7
   Boileau, Perrault and Pindar                                             10
   Herder and the exaltation of genius                                      15
   Edmund Burke                                                             19
   Immanuel Kant                                                            21
   Reaction to Kant: Friedrich Schiller                                     26
   Friedrich Hölderlin                                                      32
   Lyric parataxis                                                          41
   Ancient and modern receptions in conversation                           50

2  Shared Experience                                                         59
   The first *Pythian*                                                      59
   Primary and secondary (and tertiary) audiences                          63
   The lyric 'now' and lyric experience: Being there                       68
   Occasions: The Pindaric *kōmos*                                          73
   Personae, performativity and authors                                    83
   Pindar acting 'Pindar'                                                   94
   'So I too': Pindar's 'I' and us                                         102
   The shadow's dream                                                      116
   On the razor's edge: The poet, the *kairos*, art and politics           123

3  Exceeding Limits                                                         137
   Greek myth, Greek religion                                              137
   Transcendence and immanence                                             144
   Personifications                                                        147
   Probing the boundary of eternity                                        156
   Divine epiphanies                                                       163

In and out of time: Pindaric temporality                         170
'As when': Pindaric metaphor and the limits of language          177

Epilogue                                                         189

Notes                                                            193
Bibliography                                                     225
Index of Passages                                                249
Index of Names and Subjects                                      257

# Preface

For decades now the overwhelming emphasis in Pindaric studies has been on the historical circumstances of the first performance. To understand a poem was to know everything one could about the occasion on which it was performed: purpose, performers, social context. That Pindar's poetry, like all other lyric[1] poetry of the archaic and classical periods (seventh to late fourth centuries BCE), was occasional poetry had always been known, but scholars did not begin fully to explore the implications of this fact until the 1960s. It is hard to overstate the impact of this development; the results were revelatory and transformative. I use them everywhere in this book.

What I missed more and more, however, was discussion of Pindar as a poet, which is, after all, how he had been read for millennia before. We have had large quantities of outstanding work on Pindar and athletics, Pindar and the polis, Pindar and his patrons and so on, but much less on the aesthetics of the poetry. At times, indeed, such discussion seemed actively discouraged, unless it aided understanding of how Pindar delivered his commission on the day of performance. Any hint of a Romantic sensibility in reading Pindar's 'I', for instance, would be denounced as an anachronism, and this was a heresy we had been taught as undergraduates to fear above all others. Now no one would advocate reading Pindar just as if he were Wordsworth (although trying it out might be instructive). Or Wordsworth as if he were Eliot, for that matter. But some of the reasons for which we still read Wordsworth are the same as the reasons for which we still read Pindar, and the methodological challenge is to assess the aesthetics both historically and transhistorically.

Recently, as so often happens in the humanities, the pendulum has started to swing, and people have been addressing themselves to aspects of that issue. My work aligns itself in this respect with the work of scholars such as Felix Budelmann, David Fearn, Boris Maslov, Mark Payne, Tom Phillips, Asya Sigelman, Henry Spelman and Anna Uhlig, different from each other though they are in many ways, and each of whom would doubtless take issue with various parts of the argument. Of non-classicists I have found the work of Wayne Booth, Jonathan Culler and Käte Hamburger particularly congenial. Research on the reperformance of epinician poetry, such as that of Lucia Athanassaki,

Christopher Carey, Bruno Currie and Andrew Morrison, also forms an important contribution to this general picture. Earlier, David Carne-Ross had protested that Pindar was, after all, a poet, a protest implicitly affirmed already by Michael Silk in his 1974 book on poetic imagery, and registered *alta voce* in other publications thereafter.[2]

There are many things one could say under the rubric 'Pindar as poet', but in thinking about my own engagement with him, the notion of the sublime captured most of what I wanted to say. As a topic of interest the sublime too has seen its ebbs and flows. In modern literary and philosophical studies, ennui seemed to set in during the early years of this century, to see a revival in the second decade. In the introduction to his edited collection of 2012, Timothy Costelloe amusingly quotes several authorities who had declared 'in their collective terminology, the sublime anaemic, bourgeois, elitist, feeble, ideological, ineffective, irrelevant, irresponsible, nostalgic, poor, and weak – in a word, dead'.[3] Since then, studies have continued to appear on a regular basis, as a search in any database of scholarly bibliography will reveal. Art historians, film critics, musicologists and others have not been idle, whether looking at sublimity specifically or at beauty more generally (a concept which has also enjoyed a resurgence).[4] The result is a bibliography no one could master in its entirety. In Classics, at no time has there been a lack of work on Longinus, but consideration of the wider topic and how it might provide a touchstone for reading an author is a fairly recent development. Pride of place goes to James Porter's massive and challenging *The Sublime in Antiquity*, an indispensable resource.[5] We have seen studies of the sublime in Lucretius,[6] Virgil,[7] Seneca,[8] Lucan,[9] Silius Italicus,[10] Statius,[11] and Sophocles' *Oedipus at Colonus*.[12]

'After nearly six decades of writing Longinian criticism', concluded Harold Bloom, 'I have learned that the literary Sublime can be exemplified but not defined'.[13] There being no essential, transhistorical sublime, and a myriad of approaches on offer, one must choose those which promise the greatest heuristic return according to one's particular interests. To be sure, some points are common (though not universal): the sublime is uplifting, grand, impassioned and so on. But a quite different conversation results from putting Pindar and Edmund Burke into the same frame as opposed to, say, Jean-François Lyotard. For myself, the story of consuming interest has always been the reception of Longinus and the sublime in the long eighteenth century. This ran along two tracks, literary and philosophical, which were at times parallel and at times diverged. The philosophical track departed most from the literary in Kant, who had real difficulty in finding a place for art and literature in his theory of the sublime. In England, Shakespeare and Milton – each in his own way dubbed the 'English Homer' – were placed upon their sublime pedestals, never to be removed, by literary critics like Dryden, Addison, Pope and Johnson, all inspired by Longinus.[14] Burke found room for both literature and philosophy in his treatise on the sublime. After Kant, the two streams come triumphantly together in Schiller, and, of inestimable importance for Pindar, in the poet and philosopher Friedrich Hölderlin.

In Chapter 1 I have sought to tell this story, concisely in respect of the number of texts and writers but still at some length, in order to bring out the themes that inform my reading of both Hölderlin and Pindar. Hölderlin in this narrative constitutes a kind of telos. After him, undeniably, in both Germany and elsewhere interest in Pindar waned amongst the literati, to recover again in the early twentieth century with the emergence of Hölderlin's unpublished poems and essays. I trust, however, that the narrative will not seem teleological in a hard sense. Hölderlin is just as easily seen as a diversion in a line that leads more directly from Kant to postmodernism (if one is to think in terms of lines at all). Some day I may write about Lyotard and others; apart from problems of representation, the sublimity of objects is a topic on which much more could be said than I have done in this book (though I make a start with the golden lyre of the first *Pythian*).

The second and third chapters explore both literary and philosophical aspects of the sublime in Pindar, following the programme laid out at the end of Chapter 1. Chapter 2 springs from Longinus' remark (*On the Sublime*, ch. 7) about the mind being filled with the sublime, and how we share the writer's passion. Pindar to an extraordinary degree has the ability to draw his reader in, and make us want to be there on that magical first occasion. The occasion, for us, is a matter of the text, and the drawing-in is due entirely to the poet as he presents himself in, and works through, his text. Consequently, since these are two primary drivers of Pindar's sublime, a thorough exploration seemed justified of the persona and the occasion as they exist in the text. Pindar's 'I' has already been the subject of long debate, while the occasion as experienced by audiences after the premiere has been a more recent topic of discussion. By bringing these two together I hope to have added some new considerations to the debate, and more importantly to suggest some new readings of Pindaric passages. I make space in this chapter also briefly to discuss a more general problem in aesthetics, which is whether a purely aesthetic judgement is possible, and how this affects the appreciation of Pindar's sublime, given the antipathy some readers have felt towards his politics.

Chapter 3 brings Pindar the thinker into sharper focus. Emmet Robbins (of lamented memory) said to me when I was an undergraduate that he knew of no better way to learn Greek mythology than by studying Pindar. The truth of this remark has struck me often in the years since, not only with respect to learning the stories but understanding something of their beauty and meaning. For many readers now, I suspect, it is Pindar's myths that would spring to mind first if asked to say how he exemplifies sublimity. At the heart of Greek mythology is a conception of divinity quite different from that of monotheistic religions. I have thought it important at the start of the chapter, particularly for the benefit of anyone new to the subject, to provide an overview of some key aspects of Greek myth and religion, especially those which are relevant to the sublime. As I say there, Greek religion is one of immanence rather than transcendence; that is not a new point, but reading Pindar through Hölderlin has encouraged me to think more than I have done before about what these terms mean. I have sought to show how these notions are manifested in Pindar's poetics, which entails discussion of personifications, time, the possibilities of human immortality, epiphany and metaphor.

My hope is that the book can be profitably read by classicists and non-classicists alike. In the text, all Greek is translated or transliterated. The translations from Greek and other languages are all mine, except where noted. They have no literary pretensions, aiming only at accuracy and readability, though I occasionally attempt to replicate the layout of the Greek verses, so far as possible without doing violence to the English word order. It is arguably impossible to give an adequate sense of Pindar's style in English while remaining faithful to the literal meaning of the Greek, or something like it. Imitations perhaps have a better chance. Some of these are mentioned in Chapter 1,[15] but of all those which have been suggested I would say the poems of Gerard Manley Hopkins come closest, with their fiery sweep, breathless syntax, bold images, and virtuoso invention of compound adjectives.[16] Carne-Ross, it is true, dismissed the comparison: 'Classicists will sometimes pause to show their reading by comparing him to Gerard Hopkins … Certainly he is a strong poet, but his strength is not at all like that of Hopkins, whose thudding hammer-blows are decidedly un-Pindaric; in his massive show of force Hopkins is if anything more Aeschylean.'[17] He himself builds the odd case that Pindar is not a 'sublime, heavy, earnest, Beethovian' but a 'delicate, light-footed, deft Mozartian'. Silk also frequently contrasts Pindar's delicacy with Aeschylus' vigour in his book on interaction in imagery.[18] He documents this in convincing detail, but I would prefer to think in terms of subliminal subtleties born of deep thought about what his images are doing rather than delicacy, since on the surface they are often overwhelming, like much else in the poems. So for my money Hopkins still comes closest, in poems like 'The Wreck of the Deutschland', 'The Windhover' and 'God's Grandeur'.

On any one of my topics whole books have been written, and I am aware that there is much more to be said on all of them, even as they relate to sublimity. For further information I have referred to other studies in the notes; for a general introduction to the poet, as well as excellent remarks on many aspects, I would refer here to Richard Stoneman's *Pindar* (2014). My bibliography is already large enough, but could be extended. For the period 1988–2007, Arlette Neumann-Hartmann's bibliography in *Lustrum* volume 52 (2010) is exhaustive; she refers to earlier compilations. During 2020–21, as readers will understand, I have sometimes been prevented by the pandemic from gaining access to books they might have expected to see cited; fortunately, the digitization of so many works these days has kept such gaps to a minimum. At all events, I hope that what I have provided will be sufficient (and sufficiently persuasive) to encourage further work along similar lines.

I have great pleasure in expressing my gratitude to colleagues who have helped me in many ways in the course of this project. Three friends in particular have read through the whole manuscript and given much sage advice: Bruno Currie, Charles Martindale and Henry Spelman. They have saved me from numerous mistakes and made invaluable suggestions for improvements in the argument and presentation. Michael Silk read a large portion of the manuscript and put his finger on several weaknesses. David Hopkins generously shared his unrivalled knowledge of seventeenth- and eighteenth-century English literature; Rowan Tomlinson provided expert evaluation of the treatment of French literature, while Steffan Davies and Robert Vilain did the same for the German. Jan Bremmer was good enough to read the third chapter on myth and religion, and offered helpful supplements and corrections. For information and assistance of various kinds I am grateful to Felix Budelmann, Chris Carey, Giambattista D'Alessio, Armand D'Angour, Patrick Finglass, Richard Gordon, Jonas Grethlein, Simon Jones, Ahuvia Kahane, Glenn Most, Alex Purves, Richard Stoneman and Philip Young. Parts of this project were presented in talks at Amsterdam and Bristol, where sympathetic audiences gave useful feedback; during a pleasant week at Princeton in 2016 I had the opportunity to discuss the germ of the book with my kind hosts there. I thank Irene de Jong, Andrew Feldherr, Andrew Ford, and Deborah Steiner. Over the years I have benefited hugely from conversations with my colleagues at Bristol on Pindar, myth and other topics in this book: I am thankful for this and for friendship to Joanna Burch-Brown, Richard Buxton, Emma Cole, Duncan Kennedy, Pantelis Michelakis, Ellen O'Gorman, Maria Pavlou, Jessica Romney, Bradley Stephens and Vanda Zajko. I am profoundly in the debt of all these good people.

Coombe Dingle, Bristol

19 May 2021

# Acknowledgements

Salvator Rosa's painting, *Pan and Pindar*, is reproduced on the cover and p. 139 by kind permission of the Palazzo Chigi, Ariccia, Italy.

The excerpt from the translation of Friedrich Hölderlin's poem, 'Brod und Wein', on p. 42 is reprinted by kind permission of Carcanet Press, Manchester, UK, from Michael Hamburger, *Friedrich Hölderlin: Poems and Fragments*, 4th edition (Anvil Press Poetry, London 2004).

# 1

# Sublime Receptions

## Ancient perceptions of Pindar

The warrant for reading Pindar under the sign of sublimity lies, in the first instance, in Pindar himself. In the four books of epinician poetry by which we principally know him today, his business is the exaltation of victors in the Panhellenic games. He speaks of the victors' nobility and honour, of their innate superiority, of their worldwide and even immortal fame. The register is constantly in the superlative degree; he deploys a lavish stock of words for heights, peaks, excellence, boundlessness, enormity, and praise itself. He compares his victors to the great heroes of Greek myth – Achilles, Perseus, Jason, Pelops and above all Heracles – children of the very gods. In the moment of victory these winners are indeed touched by divinity, and reflect its splendour.

If the praise-poet is to do justice to such sublime objects of praise, his performance must be no less exhilarating. Pindar leaves us in no doubt that he is equal to the task. Few ancient poets speak so insistently about their craft. Here too we find ample encouragement to think of sublimity. Images of flight, speed, brilliance abound. The poems have wings; they are arrows, far-sailing ships, whirling javelins, speeding chariots, flowing waters. They are a torch blazing upon the victor and his city; they soak the city with honey. Fame, guaranteed of course by the poems, is like sunlight spreading throughout the world. The poet himself is an archer, a javelineer, a charioteer; he soars as the eagle in the clouds above ravens and jackdaws, who caw raucously far below.[1] The note resounding throughout the epinicians is a thunderous diapason, extolling victors, heroes and gods. Nothing here is pedestrian, ordinary, earthbound.

If we may appeal for the moment to commonplace connotations of sublimity – that is to say, such things as magnificence, awe, elevation – the word's application to Pindar seems justified. Ancient readers endorsed the poet's self-description.[2] The earliest instance, a generation after Pindar's death, is satirical, but of course that in itself confirms the point. Aristophanes in the *Birds* (414 BCE) represents a praise-poet who has come to the newly founded Cloudcuckooland in search of patronage (ll. 904–53); he spouts high-flown eulogy, refers explicitly to Pindar and even quotes some of his lines. Pindar's famous praise of Athens itself (fr. 76) has a similar reputation in other Aristophanic places (*Ach.* 633–40, *Eq.* 1323–30). Among later receptions the most famous and influential is that of Horace, who in *Odes* 4.2 compares Pindar to a mountain river in spate; he is Apollo's laureate, who in his unfettered inspiration springs the bounds of the received lexicon and scorns the rules of metre. (Pindar is indeed full of neologisms, and his complicated versification may seem to conform to no system at all, though it is in fact highly disciplined.) Pindar, continues Horace, is a majestic swan, lifted high in the clouds by mighty poetic winds; the Roman poet, in this poem at least, is but a humble bee flitting from bloom to bloom. Although Pindar does not compare himself to a swan in his surviving poetry, it is an eminently poetical bird in ancient tradition; to cite the most salient example, in *Odes* 2.20 Horace himself claimed to be transformed into a swan and to have earned immortality with his poetry. Neither statement need be taken at face value as far as Horace is concerned, of course, but both presume the same image. More familiar nowadays is Pindar the 'Theban eagle'; the description seems to originate with Thomas Gray in *The Progress of Poesy* (1757), taking his lead from the Pindaric passages cited above. To remain for now with ancient receptions, however, Horace's ancient commentator Porphyry wrote that 'he compared Pindar to a swan on account of his charm (*suavitas*) and sublimity (*sublimitas*)'; here is the very word, used also by Pliny (*Nat. Hist.* 2.54). Similarly at the close of *Odes* 3.1, the Horatian poet wisely declines to build a lofty hall (*sublime atrium*) whose columns would only court envy (*invidendis postibus*; the image recalls the opening of Pindar's sixth *Olympian*, and the risk of envy is a familiar Pindaric theme). Quintilian, whose late first-century manual of rhetoric was widely influential in the early modern West, amplifies Horace's opinion:

Pindar is by far the greatest of the nine lyric poets, with his spirit, magnificence, sentiments, figures, a most felicitous abundance of material and diction, and as it were a kind of river of eloquence: which is why Horace rightly believes that he is beyond imitation by anybody.

Nouem uero lyricorum longe Pindarus princeps spiritu, magnificentia, sententiis, figuris, beatissima rerum uerborumque copia et uelut quodam eloquentiae flumine: propter quae Horatius eum merito nemini credit imitabilem.[3]

Greek writers unsurprisingly subscribed to this image of the grand, overwhelming Pindar. Hellenistic epigrammatists say he 'shouts' or 'roars' (*AP* 9.571, 16.305) and liken his verse to the blare of a trumpet (*AP* 7.34, 16.305 again). The anthologist Athenaeus, writing about 200 CE, twice refers to Pindar as 'most grandiloquent' (*megalophōnotatos*); given that he quotes over 1,200 authors, and that this unusual superlative, which is used elsewhere in this sense only of Homer,[4] comes at opposite ends of the gigantic work (2.13 p. 40f, 13.17 p. 564d), we may infer that it is for Athenaeus a kind of standing epithet of Pindar. An extensive discussion is found in the Augustan writer Dionysius of Halicarnassus, for whom Pindar exemplifies the severe (*austērā*, also translatable 'harsh') style of composition, as opposed to the smooth or polished and the 'mixed' styles (*On the Composition of Words* 22). He compares the arrangement of phrases in this style to buildings made of rough-hewn, undressed blocks of stone, each one sturdy and independent.[5] It prefers words with ponderous, long syllables to those with fussy short ones. Its rhythms are dignified (*axiōmatikos*) and grand (*megaloprepēs*). It avoids the balanced, periodic structures of display rhetoric; its clauses tumble out just as they suggest themselves to a free and noble spirit. The composition seems to be more a matter of nature than of art, says Dionysius (echoing Pindar's hierarchy of those two things: O.2.86, 9.100, N.3.40), and the effect depends on frank emotion rather than a subtle projection of character (*pathos*, that is, rather than *ēthos*, a fundamental distinction in ancient rhetoric). He sums up its qualities thus:

| | |
|---|---|
| Flexible in its use of the cases; varied in its use of figures; sparing of connectives; lacking articles; often unconcerned about natural sequence; not at all florid; high-minded, frank, unadorned: its beauty lies in its patina of antiquity. | ἀγχίστροφός[6] ἐστι περὶ τὰς πτώσεις, ποικίλη περὶ τοὺς σχηματισμοὺς, ὀλιγοσύνδεσμος, ἄναρθρος, ἐν πολλοῖς ὑπεροπτικὴ τῆς ἀκολουθίας, ἥκιστ' ἀνθηρά, μεγαλόφρων, αὐθέκαστος, ἀκόμψευτος, τὸν ἀρχαϊσμὸν καὶ τὸν πίνον ἔχουσα κάλλος.[7] |

He then quotes one of Pindar's dithyrambs, now fragment 75 in the standard edition, and offers an analysis restricted, for the most part, to its aural effects; but he starts with a general comment about the vigour and stateliness of the poem, remarking too that its ruggedness is not such as to be unpleasant, and its harshness is not unrestrained. These words are echoed in another treatise, *On Imitation* (6.2), where he praises Pindar for being harsh in a pleasant way; this sort of cognitive clash is one of the characteristics of the sublime in modern thinking. In this second passage he praises also Pindar's intensity (*tonos*), forcefulness (*dunamis, deinotēs*), density (*puknotēs*), solemnity (*semnotēs*), vividness (*enargeia*) and powers of amplification (*auxēsis*); the poet's fine sentiments are conducive to virtue, piety and ethical grandeur (*megaloprepeia*). This last word, in its adjectival form *megaloprepēs*, was used of Pindar's style in *On Composition*, as we saw; in Demetrius' manual *On Style* (perhaps third or second century BCE), *megaloprepēs* is the name for this style as a whole (§§36–127) – that is, for Demetrius it is 'the grand style' rather than 'the severe style', but it is clearly the same animal (such tweaking of the terminology from authority to authority is common in ancient rhetorical texts). Though he does not cite Pindar, Demetrius offers much material to expand and illustrate Dionysius' analysis, making many of the same points and drawing on a common stock of material.[8]

Then there is the treatise *On the Sublime*.[9] Both author and date are uncertain. The author is given in the principal manuscript as 'Dionysius Longinus' on the page where the treatise begins, but as 'Dionysius or Longinus' in the table of contents. The latter has the appearance of someone making a guess about the author of the anonymously transmitted text he set out to copy: it had to be one of two great critics, either Dionysius of Halicarnassus or the third-century Neoplatonist Cassius Longinus. For myself, I am attracted by Malcolm Heath's vigorous defence of the view that the treatise really is by the latter,[10] but fortunately for present purposes nothing turns on a decision. If the attribution is not correct, scholars are at any rate agreed that the book is not by Dionysius of Halicarnassus, and it is no earlier than the first century CE. For convenience I shall continue to call its author Longinus. As it happens, he quotes Pindar only once (though at ch. 35.4 he does allude to Pindar's famous description of the eruption of Etna, that archetypically sublime event). The single quotation is, however, most telling. In this chapter (33), he is making the point that the sublime writer is rarely faultless, but his greatness makes us overlook his minor blemishes. The surface of an Apollonius or Theocritus may be as smooth as glass, but no one would put them ahead of Homer. In lyric poetry, he asks, would you rather be Bacchylides or Pindar? In tragedy, would you rather be Ion of Chios or Sophocles? Bacchylides and Ion are polished and elegant writers, but Pindar and Sophocles carry all before them like a wildfire. Even if they sometimes fizzle out unaccountably and stumble disastrously, who in their right mind would value all the works of Ion equally with a single play of Sophocles, the *Oedipus*? Longinus' notion of an irresistible forward sweep (*phorā*) is echoed by Horace and others; his image of the fire uses a word Pindar himself applied to his poetry (*epiphlegō* O.9.22, cf. P.5.45).

There is, therefore, a well-documented ancient tradition of Pindar as a sublime poet, in the sense of one who treats a noble subject in a grand manner, and lifts his reader into the ether. The tradition springs from Pindar himself, and ancient readers agreed with his self-assessment (while occasionally noting that he could overdo things).[11] To go further in an assessment of his sublimity, we obviously need to probe more deeply into the meaning (or meanings), or at least the applications, of this slippery word. Longinus' ideas will be crucial, but to get a perspective on them it may be more useful to postpone discussion until we have had a look through the lens of reception.

## Preliminary remarks on early modern receptions

Early modern criticism echoed the ancients' admiration of Pindar, but in time ambivalence and even outright antipathy begin to make themselves heard. In the context of the Enlightenment, the concept of the sublime itself underwent radical transformation whose effects are still with us. Several major cultural trends are relevant to the present project. First, a growing sense of the differences between antiquity and modernity challenged the ancient world's exemplary status, and gave rise to historicism, the belief that each period of history has its own, often radically different, character, which needs to be understood on its own terms. Next, received religion came under increasing pressure, but at the same time most thinkers remained reluctant to abandon some notion of God or of a transcendent reality; the alternative world-view implied by Greek mythology was powerfully attractive (and the flight to Greece gained strength in Protestant lands because of the association of Rome with Catholicism). Third, thinkers, writers and visual artists were profoundly and explicitly concerned with the meaning of art and the role of the artist as an autonomous agent in society; art itself became more and more overtly philosophical. The result of these trends, which themselves played out against the transformative backdrop of two revolutions – the French and the Industrial – was an explosion of philosophical and creative writing about Greece, its poets and artists, as the intellectual elite of Europe rethought the whole of human nature, culture, modernity and nationality from the ground up.

Lyric poetry played a small but typical part in the larger story. As a genre it sought to establish itself on an equal footing with epic and dramatic verse, and thinking lyricists inevitably contemplated the work of their greatest ancient counterpart, Pindar. The idea of the artist as at once visionary, prophet and genius, a soul apart, a mystic hovering on the edge of the infinite and the ineffable, gained force in the second half of the eighteenth century and reached its apogee in Romanticism. In this process the sublime came to be seen not merely as an occasional product of a poet's technique, but as an emblem of his or her mission. As a pointer to what lay beyond ordinary experience and comprehension, the sublime was very easily associated with the eternal, the transcendent and the divine, and particularly in Germany became a subject for metaphysical analysis. In Germany too one finds a more intense and direct engagement with Pindar's poetry and poetics than elsewhere – none more intense than that of Friedrich Hölderlin, who will receive extended discussion below. Though Homer and Greek tragedy received more attention in these enterprises, Pindar was hardly neglected, being as he was one of the richest mythmakers amongst the Greeks. His business too was with eternity, the transcendent and the divine; and according to the ancients themselves, he was the very exemplar of lyric sublimity.

Critical reflection on the sublime in the twentieth and early twenty-first centuries, by contrast, has for the most part been non-metaphysical (and the general decline of the Classics meant that the Greeks ceased to figure centrally in the debates). Since in Pindar the sublime, on any understanding, can hardly be considered apart from his understanding of divinity, atheistical notions of the sublime would seem a less promising place to start. Moreover, more recent theorists (especially Jean-François Lyotard) have often written in explicit reaction to Kant and the idealists. Though such work will not be overlooked here, the earlier thinkers remain the cardinal moment in this history. They wrought a permanent change in the way we think about such matters. For them in their time and place the Greeks were the 'nearest Other', the closest point of reference with sufficient contrast yet also sufficient overlap with their own concerns to serve as a model for self-reflection and self-definition. We need to chart those points of contact and contrast and consider what they might mean for a fruitful reading of Pindar.

Without attempting in so short a space a complete history either of early modern reception of Pindar or of the re-evaluation of the sublime, in what follows I shall attempt to tease out the salient points of these two narratives in order to inform my reading of the poet. To anticipate, and to assist the reader in navigating a somewhat involved exposition, the key themes that will emerge from this survey are: the 'sublime' style ('enthusiasm'); the nature of poetic genius; emotional and cognitive aspects of the sublime (analysis of the observer's mental state); political aspects of the sublime; art and myth as gateways to ultimate truth and transcendent reality; language and the sublime; and lyric's technique of parataxis (juxtaposition). What these suggest specifically for reading Pindar is flagged up briefly as the discussion proceeds, then expounded in greater detail at the end of the chapter as a programme for the remainder of the book.[12]

## Abraham Cowley and English receptions

Pindar was available to the West in Greek from 1513 (published in Venice by Aldus Manutius); five further Greek editions were published in the sixteenth century. The first complete Latin translation of the epinicians was made by Joannes Lonicerus in 1528 (much expanded in 1535), with numerous others following over the next two centuries; complete translations into the vernacular languages appeared in 1617 (French), 1626 (French again), 1631 (Italian), 1770–1 (German) and 1798 (Spanish).[13] Horace and Quintilian, quoted above, were widely known texts (Lonicerus, echoing the latter, calls Pindar on his title page *lyricorum facile princeps*) and their opinions of Pindar were repeatedly cited and elaborated, sometimes with the help of Longinus (available in Latin from 1612). Poets tried their hand at 'Pindaric' odes, writing encomia of great men and celebrations of great events in a grand style; some were composed in triads after Pindar's model, and the metres were irregular. Though not the first such poems to be written, Pierre de Ronsard's four books of French *Odes* (1550) effectively started the trend, one in which Pindar's grand style, neologisms, gnomic utterances, mythical allusions, obscure expressions and abrupt transitions were also imitated.[14]

While these imitators explored such devices, they nonetheless believed that Pindar was in control of his art; they studied his artful rhetoric, and the poet's divine inspiration was not thought incompatible with his sober learning. Early English receptions, particularly those of Ben Jonson, display a similar estimation.[15] Abraham Cowley took a different line and touched off a Pindaric craze in England. In his *Pindarique Odes* of 1656 ('the noblest and highest kind of writing in Verse', he proclaims in the preface) he gave special prominence to the idea of poetic enthusiasm, as for instance in the last stanza of 'The Resurrection':[16]

> Stop, stop, my Muse, allay thy vigorous heat,
>    Kindled at a hint so great.
> Hold thy Pindaric Pegasus closely in,
>    Which does to rage begin,
> And this steep hill would gallop up with violent course.

'Tis an unruly and a hard-mouthed Horse,
    Fierce and unbroken yet,
    Impatient of the spur or bit.
Now prances stately, and anon flies o'er the place,
Disdains the servile law of any settled pace,
Conscious and proud of his own natural force.
    'Twill no unskilful touch endure,
But flings writer and reader too that sits not sure.

The line lengths and rhythms are very irregular, much more so than in Ronsard and his followers, and in the poem as a whole there is no strophic responsion. Though (as will be noticed) Cowley asserts his ability to master the wild Pegasus at the same time as he advertises its unruliness, and though Pindar, too, often checks himself in this overt manner, the image of the insecure poet being tossed violently about, as if he were the Sibyl seized by Apollo, is un-Pindaric. Nor is Pindar at odds with his Muse, if that is the implication of the first line. Nonetheless, the seemingly wild Pindaric style was often dubbed 'dithyrambic', meaning enthused with the spirit of Bacchus like a raging maenad. Almost nothing of Pindar's own dithyrambs was then available on which to base such a judgement. Rather, it derives from the association of the *vates* (the god-possessed prophet) and the poet in Augustan poetry. At the end of the first poem in his first book of *Odes* (1.1.35–6), Horace writes *quod si me lyricis vatibus inseres, / sublimi feriam sidera vertice* ('but should you count me in the number of the lyric *vates*, my exalted head will strike the stars'); *sublimi*, 'exalted', is particularly apt in view of our theme (the ode has more than one Pindaric echo). In the Pindaric *Ode* cited above, Horace associates the Theban's novel diction and irregular rhythms specifically with his dithyrambs (4.2.10), and another well-known poem (3.25) begins *quo me, Bacchus, rapis, tui / plenum* ('whither, Bacchus, do you ravish me, filled with you?'). *Plenum* ('filled with') here reflects an interpretation of *entheos* in Greek: *en-theos*, the god is in you; you are enthused. *Bacchatur vates*, says Virgil of the Sibyl (*Aen.* 6.78), the *vates* is in a Bacchic frenzy (even though it is Apollo who possesses her).[17]

Cowley not only wrote Pindaric odes, he offered translations of the second *Olympian* and the first *Nemean*; by any standard these are exceedingly free, with much expansion, curtailment and creative rewriting. He justified his practice in his notes and his highly interesting preface, which begins with the much-quoted line 'If a man were to undertake to translate Pindar word for word, it would be thought that one mad man had translated another'; he explains that his aim was not so much to convey what Pindar said as 'his way and manner of speaking'.

Dryden, who thought his own Pindaric ode *Alexander's Feast* one of the best things he ever wrote, defended Cowley:

> Pindar is generally known to be a dark writer, to want connection (I mean as to our understanding), to soar out of sight, and leave his reader at a gaze. So wild and ungovernable a poet cannot be translated literally; his genius is too strong to bear a chain, and Samson-like he shakes it off. A genius so elevated and unconfined as Mr. Cowley's, was but necessary to make Pindar speak English, and that was to be performed by no other way than imitation.[18]

For all that Dryden admired Cowley, one detects a tentativeness here; it is unclear whether Dryden thinks we can ever really get at Pindar's own understanding, and 'unconfined' is somewhat backhanded praise (elsewhere Dryden speaks of the need to exercise restraint in the use of 'Pindaric' rhythms, and owns that Cowley's efforts fell short of perfection).[19] Others were less charitable. William Congreve, while praising Cowley's own genius, deplored the trend he started:

> There is nothing more frequent among us than a sort of poems entitled Pindaric Odes, pretending to be written in imitation of the manner and style of Pindar … The character of these late Pindarics is a bundle of rambling incoherent thoughts, expressed in a like parcel of irregular stanzas, which also consist of such another complication of disproportioned, uncertain, and perplexed verses and rhymes … On the contrary, there is nothing more regular than the odes of Pindar, both as to the exact observation of the measures and numbers of his stanzas and verses, and the perpetual coherence of his thoughts. For though his digressions are frequent and his transitions sudden, yet is there ever some secret connection, which though not always appearing to the eye, never fails to communicate itself to the understanding of the reader.[20]

Addison also derided those who availed themselves of this licence to write inferior verses ('[C]an anything be more ridiculous than for men of a sober and moderate fancy to imitate this poet's way of writing in those monstrous compositions which go among us under the name of Pindarics?').[21] Looking back over a century of such stuff, Johnson predictably took a dim view:

> This lax and lawless versification so much concealed the deficiencies of the barren, and flattered the laziness of the idle, that it immediately overspread our books of poetry; all the boys and girls caught the pleasing fashion, and they that could do nothing else could write like Pindar.[22]

In Cowley's defence it should be pointed out that, unlike his imitators, he knew Pindar first-hand, and his adaptations and notes reveal intelligent reflection.[23] In the wake of Congreve's assault, however, the undisciplined Pindaric fell out of favour in England. Thomas Gray's two well-known Pindarics, *The Progress of Poesy* and *The Bard* (both published in 1757), were scrupulously triadic.

In addition to stressing the metrical responsion between Pindar's strophes Congreve speaks of his coherence of thought, which, he says, can seem lacking on a superficial perusal, but which an attentive reading will discover. The idea that if one can only crack the code, the true coherence of a Pindaric ode will emerge, has had enormous traction in the history of his criticism and still influences (bedevils?) scholarship today.[24] Dryden too speaks of Pindar's wildness, but links it expressly to sublimity, when he says that Pindar seems to 'soar out of sight, and leave his reader at a gaze'. Wonder at the grandeur of nature, a sense of its vastness, intimations of the majesty of God and emotional transport are all part of the Longinian sublime (§§1.4, 35.3–4, 36.1), but feeling left behind by the speaker is not; rather the opposite, for according to Longinus the speaker takes the audience with him into these ethereal realms. In this comment of Dryden's we have an early intimation of what was to be a crucial aspect of modern discourse: the sublime as that which exceeds comprehension. How useful (and how legitimate) this idea might be in interpreting Pindar will be an important theme in our study.

## Boileau, Perrault and Pindar

Dryden was writing at a time when the so-called 'Quarrel of the Ancients and Moderns' about the superiority of one over the other was at its height (often 'La Querelle des anciens et modernes', it being an argument that raged mainly, though by no means exclusively, in France). The Quarrel was ignited by Charles Perrault in a series of publications, culminating in the four-volume *Parallèle des Anciens et des Modernes* of 1688–96 (*Comparison of the Ancients and Moderns*; the title gave rise to the punning sobriquet 'La Querelle etc.').[25] Nicolas Boileau-Despréaux, esteemed poet, doyen of critics, friend of Racine and chief advocate for the Ancients, had translated Longinus into French in 1674, the same year as he published his influential poem *Art poétique*. In one satirical scene in Perrault's *Parallèle*, the blinkered provincial Président Morinet, a pedant who champions the ancients, declares Pindar to be 'le plus sublime des Poëtes' ('the most sublime of poets'), and reads aloud the opening of the first *Olympian*. His wife declares that he must be mocking her; this is some gibberish (*galimatias*) he's made up for his own entertainment. The Président indignantly replies that he does not mock at all, and that it is her fault if she is not enraptured by such fine things. The dialogue continues:

*Mme la Présidente.* It is true that good clear water, shining gold and the sun at the height of noon are very fine things; but if water is best and gold gleams like fire in the night, is that a reason to contemplate or not to contemplate any other star but the sun during the day? To sing or not to sing of the contests at the Olympic games? I confess I don't understand a word of it.

Il est vray, reprit la Presidente, que de l'eau bien claire, de l'or bien luisant & le Soleil en plein midy, sont de fort belles choses; mais parce que l'eau est tres-bonne & que l'or brille comme le feu pendant la nuit, est-ce une raison de contempler ou de ne contempler pas un autre astre que le Soleil pendant le jour? De chanter ou de ne chanter pas les combats des jeux Olympiques? Je vous avoüe que je n'y comprens rien.

*M. le Président.* I am not surprised, Madam. Legions of very learned men have understood it no better than you. Should we find that strange? He is a poet carried away by his enthusiasm, who uplifted by the grandeur of his thoughts and expressions rises above the limits of ordinary human reason; and in this state he ecstatically delivers everything that his madness inspires in him. It is a divine place, and people are very far from being able to do anything like it today.

Je ne m'en étonne pas, Madame, dit le President, une infinité de tres-sçavans hommes n'y ont rien compris non plus que vous. Faut-il trouver cela étrange. C'est un Poëte emporté par son enthousiasme qui soûtenu par la grandeur de ses pensées & de ses expressions s'éleve au dessus de la raison ordinaire des hommes, & qui en cet état profere avec transport tout ce que sa fureur luy inspire. Cet endroit est divin & l'on est bien éloigné de rien faire aujourd'huy de semblable.

*Mme la Présidente.* Indeed they are, and they do very well to avoid it.

Assurément, dit la Presidente, & l'on s'en donne bien de garde.[26]

Such heresy was too much for Boileau (whose *Art* was also pilloried in the *Parallèle*). In 1692 he published a brief *Discours sur l'Ode*, written as a preface to his Pindaric *Ode sur la prise de Namur* (*Ode on the Capture of Namur*), and in 1693 *Réflexions critiques sur quelques passages du rhéteur Longin où, par occasion, on répond à quelques objections de Monsieur P\*\*\* contre Homère et contre Pindare* (*Critical Reflections on some Passages of the Rhetor Longinus with occasional responses to some objections of Monsieur P\*\*\* against Homer and Pindar*). In the *Discours* he writes:

Since the beauties of this poet are closely bound up with his language, the author of these dialogues, who apparently knows no Greek and has read Pindar only in quite defective Latin translations, took to be gibberish (*galimatias*) that which the feebleness of his own lights did not allow him to understand. He has particularly ridiculed those marvellous passages where the poet, to mark a spirit entirely outside of itself, breaks by design the train of his discourse, and takes leaves of reason, if one must so express the matter, the better to enter into it, very carefully avoiding that methodical order and those precise connections of sense which deprive lyric poetry of its soul. The critic of whom I speak has not noticed that in attacking Pindar's noble audacity, he was giving cause to believe that he has never understood the sublime in the psalms of David; where, if one may speak of those sacred songs alongside such profane matters, there are many of these interrupted trains of thought, which sometimes even serve to make one sensible of the Divinity. To all appearances this critic is little persuaded of the precept I advanced in my *Art poétique* concerning the lyric ode:

Its impetuous style at random oft
    proceeds,
Through art a fair disorder thus
    achieves.

Comme les beautés de ce poëte son extrêmement renfermées dans sa langue, l'auteur de ces dialogues, qui vraisembablement ne sait point de Grec, et qui n'a lu Pindare que dans des traductions Latines assez défectueuses, a pris pour galimatias tout ce que la foiblesse de ses lumières ne lui permettoit pas de comprendre. Il a surtout traité de ridicules ces endroits merveilleux où le poëte, pour marquer un esprit entièrement hors de soi, rompt quelquefois de dessein formé la suite de son discours ; et afin de mieux entrer dans la raison, sort, s'il faut ainsi parler, de la raison même, évitant avec grand soin cet ordre méthodique et ces exactes liaisons de sens qui ôteroient l'âme à la poésie lyrique. Le censeur dont je parle n'a pas pris garde qu'en attaquant ces nobles hardiesses de Pindare, il donnoit lieu de croire qu'il n'a jamais conçu le sublime des psaumes de David, où, s'il est permis de parler de ces saints cantiques à propos de choses si profanes, il y a beaucoup de ces sens rompus, qui servent même quelquefois à en faire sentir la divinité. Ce critique, selon toutes les apparences, n'est pas fort convaincu du précepte que j'ai avancé dans mon *Art poétique* [Chant II], à propos de l'ode :

« Son style impétueux souvent marche
    au hasard :
Chez elle un beau désordre est un effet
    de l'art. »

Ce prétexte effectivement, qui donne pour règle de ne point garder quelquefois de

Indeed this precept, which gives as a rule that sometimes one should not observe rules at all, is a mystery of art which a man without taste, who thinks that *Clélie* and our operas are the model of the sublime genre, who finds Terence bland, Virgil frigid, and Homer nonsensical, and whom a kind of deformity of spirit renders insensible to all that ordinarily astonishes people, cannot easily be made to understand.

règles, est un mystère de l'art, qu'il n'est pas aisé de faire entendre à un homme sans aucun goût, qui croit que la *Clélie* et nos opéra [sic] sont les modèles du genre sublime ; qui trouve Térence fade, Virgile froid, Homère de mauvais sens, et qu'une espèce de bizarrerie d'esprit rend insensible à tout ce qui frappe ordinairement les hommes.[27]

Boileau goes on to speak of Pindar's 'manner, full of shifts and transports, where the spirit appears to be rather carried away by the daemon of poetry than guided by reason' (*sa manière, c'est-à-dire pleine de mouvements et de transports, où l'esprit parût plutôt entraîné du démon de la poésie que guidé par la raison*).[28] In the *Critical Reflections*, no. VIII, he writes:

Longinus here [ch. 33, paraphrased above p. 4] makes it quite clear that he found things to fault in Pindar. In what author does one not find them? But at the same time he declares that these faults he has noticed cannot properly be called faults; they are nothing but trivial oversights into which Pindar has fallen because of that divine spirit which carries him away, and which it was not in his power to govern as he wished.

Longin donne ici assez à entendre qu'il avoit trouvé des choses à redire dans Pindare. Et dans quel auteur n'en trouve-t-on point? Mais en même temps il déclare que ces fautes qu'il y a remarquées ne peuvent point être appelées proprement fautes, et que ce ne sont que de petites négligences où Pindare est tombé à cause de cet esprit divin dont il est entrainé, et qu'il n'étoit pas en sa puissance de régler comme il vouloit.[29]

There follows much abuse of Perrault (whose ignorance is entirely to blame for Pindar's supposed *galimatias*) and a spirited defence of the beauty, sublimity, majesty, nobility (etc.) of the first *Olympian*'s opening.

This tussle between those who blamed Pindar and those who blamed his translators continued throughout the century (and beyond). Edward Young, for instance, in his 'On Lyrick Poetry' of 1728 states that, as the lyric ode is by nature sublime, so should the lyric poet's genius be; Pindar is his first case in point, 'who has as much logic at the bottom as Aristotle or Euclid, to some critics has appeared as mad; and must appear so to all, who enjoy no portion of his own divine spirit'.[30] Voltaire was in the other camp; his 1766 poem *Galimatias pindarique* sarcastically praised the poet for being one 'who had the talent of speaking much while saying nothing; who ably warbled verses no one understands but which must always be admired' (*Toi qui possédas le talent / De parler beaucoup sans rien dire; / Toi qui modulas savamment / Des vers que personne n'entend / Et qu'il faut toujours qu'on admire*).[31] But Diderot's *Encyclopédie* in its entry 'Pindarique' adopted Boileau's line, quoting his couplet about a 'fair disorder'.[32] In England, Boileau was widely known and respected; the *Art poétique* was translated in 1683 (with English examples inserted by Dryden), and the translation of his complete works appeared in 1711–13 (Longinus was in the first volume). Johnson in his *Dictionary* (1755) described 'the sublime' as a domesticated Gallicism; with his typically sure touch he cites Pope's *Essay on Criticism* (also of 1711), line 680, which refers to Longinus (and owes much to Boileau), and an essay by Addison in the *Guardian* no. 117 (25 July 1713), which refers to Boileau's notes on the same author. Addison was one of the addressees of the 1711 translation, and had even interviewed Boileau in Paris in 1700.[33] Johnson of course was very familiar with Boileau's works, and echoes his 'fair disorder' when he speaks of the 'rules of enthusiasm' (above, n. 22).

Though Longinus was known before Boileau, the prominence of his translation within the context of the Quarrel, and the distinction of its author, made it a decisive moment in the history of the sublime.[34] The Quarrel was no mere literary spat, but tied into larger issues about the sources of authority and knowledge in the world at a time of political and religious upheaval. Boileau's 'fair disorder', whose practical implications must be thought elusive (he says that one needs taste to recognize it), suggests an attempt to find a balance between creative liberty on the one hand and sensible conformity on the other. Text after text addresses this issue. In the article on '*Enthousiasme*' in Diderot's *Encyclopédie*, for instance,[35] the writer explains that the common understanding of enthusiasm as madness is quite mistaken; rather, it consists in reason's *response* to a sudden, overwhelming apparition, and its ability, after the initial shock, to comprehend the totality of the vista, to regulate the emotional excitement thereby engendered, and to communicate this passion to others. Simple madness would look nothing like this. Reason is, in fact, the ultimate source of all great achievement in art, and real enthusiasm is the property of genius. The author of the entry spends some time answering imaginary conservative objectors to his 'metaphysical' explanation, as he calls it, in the course of which he contrasts ordinary, worthy, conventional talent with the unique, rule-shattering productions of genius. He speaks of prejudice as 'the perpetual tyrant of contemporary opinions' and proclaims that, if reason – a brilliant ray of light from the Supreme Being – is supreme, prejudice will fall away, and art will triumph. The revolutionary implications of such talk are plain enough, and of a piece with other articles in the *Encyclopédie*, whose democratization of knowledge and advocacy of free speech and religion led to its suppression by the authorities.

## Herder and the exaltation of genius

In the rules–enthusiasm debate, broadly speaking, one may say that some writers (such as Johnson, Boileau and Pope) inclined more to the rules end, others to the enthusiasm end (such as the 'German Pindar' Friedrich Klopstock in 'To my Friends', a very early poem of 1747, which explicitly evokes Pindar, enthusiasm and sublimity),[36] though the former group neither advocated the blind application of rules nor underestimated the uniqueness of great writing, and Klopstock was as careful and reflective a poet as one could name. The many permutations of views on either side – also about the relative merits of Ancients and Moderns – warn against too schematic a representation of the differences. After 1674 Longinus' dictum that sublime rule-breakers are preferable to correct pedestrians is cited repeatedly even by the most ardent 'Augustans'. Common to all sides in these arguments, however, was the assumption of a conflict between different impulses needing to be resolved in the poet's mind. This psychological and introspective orientation takes modern poetics in a different direction from the ancient. The modern poet's source of inspiration in this understanding is not the Muse but his or her own genius, and the truth the poet divines is not the collective wisdom of society, as in the Greek poetics inherited by Pindar, but a creed or a philosophy. The ancient image of the poet/prophet, the *vates*, so often used by these writers, masks this discontinuity; the modern writers take it literally, because they want the poet to be one who sees into the metaphysical world, and to be the voice of revelation, like, they supposed, David to the Israelites, or Pindar to the Greeks.[37]

Herder's Pindaric ode *Der Genius der Zukunft* (*The Genius of the Future*) of 1769 is an example (this is the third stanza, the epode of the first of two triads):

| | |
|---|---|
| With strokes of fire there shines | Mit Flammenzügen glänzt |
| In the abyss of souls an image of the older world | in der Seelen Abgründen der Vorwelt Bild |
| Which shoots its strong, prophetic arrow far away | und schießt weitüber weissagend starkes Geschoß |

| | |
|---|---|
| Into the heart of the future! Look! There rise up | in das Herz der Zukunft! Siehe! da steigen |
| Midnight's shapes! Like gods, arising from the grave, | der Mitternacht Gestalten empor! wie Götter, aus Gräbern empor |
| From the ashes of youth's glow, the seers! They tear | aus Asche der Jugendglut die Seher! Sie zerreißen |
| The clouds with their lightning swords! They wander | mit Schwerterblitzen das Gewölk! Sie wehn |
| In their gaze through the seven heavens, and leap down again! | im Blick durch die Sieben der Himmel, und schwingen sich herab! |
| Then the spirit reads | Denn liest der Geist in seines Meers |
| In the magic mirror of its sea | Zauberspiegel die Ewigkeit.[38] |
| Eternity! | |

The image of the arrow is Pindaric, as is the reach back to origins to explain the present. But the poets are once again 'seers', i.e. *vates*.[39] They have visited the upper world, like Plato's philosophers leaving the Cave, and have come back to earth to tell us what they saw. The mirror image alludes to Pindar, *Nemean* 7.11–16:

| | |
|---|---|
| If a man succeeds in his endeavours, a pleasing pretext | εἰ δὲ τύχῃ τις ἔρδων, μελίφρον᾽ αἰτίαν |
| Does he impart to the Muses' stream. For great feats of strength | ῥοαῖσι Μοισᾶν ἐνέβαλε. ταὶ μεγάλαι γὰρ ἀλκαί |
| Find deep darkness if they lack hymns of praise; | σκότον πολὺν ὕμνων ἔχοντι δεόμεναι· |
| And of fine deeds we know the mirror in but one way, | ἔργοις δὲ καλοῖς ἔσοπτρον ἴσαμεν ἐνὶ σὺν τρόπῳ, |
| If for Memory's sake, she of the shining chaplet, | εἰ Μναμοσύνας ἕκατι λιπαράμπυκος |
| Recompense of labour is found through famous singing of verse. | εὕρηται ἄποινα μόχθων κλυταῖς ἐπέων ἀοιδαῖς. |

The theme is ubiquitous in Pindar that great deeds, however notable, fall into obscurity without the poet's praise. In this passage, poetry is the Muses' stream (not the poet's); they flow through the poet and his chorus (the 'we' of 'we know'). The image of the mirror (unique in Pindar, strengthening the supposition of allusion here) represents the poet as a passive reflector of the honorands' deeds, however indispensable his services may be. These are performed for the sake of the Muses' mother Mnemosyne (Memory); in this one way can the record shine forth, famous and immortal, into the future. All of this is orthodox Greek poetics. In Herder, by contrast, the 'spirit' (*Geist*; also 'mind') looks into its own sea and reads eternity in that magic mirror. The sea is established at the outset of the poem as a metaphor for the entirety of past experience. From it arises a shadowy image in the soul (called a 'daemon', Plato's term in the *Symposium* for Eros, the divinity within that leads us to beauty and knowledge); it is transformed into a torch which kindles the song, and leads the singer forth into the future. In the quoted stanza, seers rise as if by resurrection from the past. They make it possible for the *Geist* to grasp eternity; but if at this point they seem to be different from the poet, the poet's capacity to be a seer has been stressed from the start. With their help, he becomes one in a temporal perspective, but in the perspective of eternity he has always been one. Just as sky and sea meld into a single element on a dark night at sea (and the poem was in fact written at sea), the line between internal conscience and external world is effaced. Thus the *Geist* which reads the mirror is that of the individual poet, the seers all together, and the spirit of the world in general: they are all ultimately one in this pantheistic vision. The genius of the title is a Latin word for the divine element in each individual, like Plato's mediating daemon. The unities in the poem include past and future, light and darkness, heaven and sea, one poet and all poets, *Geist* and soul, divine and human knowledge, and ultimately god and human when at the end of the poem, after long travails at sea, the poet reaches the promised land of immortality, and all becomes clear. The poet here is at the centre of the cosmos, and at the end of his journey, all mortal doubts now resolved, he triumphs over life and death.

The Pindaric poet is at the centre of things in many ways too; he understands, recognizes and captures for posterity the decisive moment (the *kairos*) when everything comes together – god, human, victory, celebration; he too seeks to collapse past, present and future. But he does not *see* the future, except insofar as he can confidently predict that his poetry will be part of it, and he sometimes hazards the prediction that his celebrand will win more victories. (In this respect Gray's *The Bard* – which is one long prophecy – departs radically from the Pindaric model.) Pindar is not himself on a spiritual journey; nor does he display any doubts about meaning, values or truth. Ostensibly, the poem is about him only insofar as his god-given ability is needed if the honorand is to receive due praise.

The poet's genius in Herder and other writers of the period entailed a heightened sensitivity to the divine and the sublime. This was not just a passive capacity; the poet was an active agent seeking knowledge and spiritual fulfilment.

But the divine inspiration was seen as troubling, and its impulses needed to be mastered through understanding and self-control. As we have seen in the case of Cowley, this inner conflict was then retrospectively diagnosed in the ancient poets. Another example is Boileau's Reflection quoted above: '… oversights into which Pindar has fallen because of that divine spirit which carries him away, and *which it was not in his power to govern as he wished*'. The words I have emphasized are more literally 'which it is difficult to bring under the rule of law'; 'as he wished' is Boileau's addition and implies an inner struggle not in the original.[40] Or consider the way the young Goethe described his first encounter with Pindar in a celebrated letter to Herder of July 1772, which echoes the poem quoted above:

When he shoots his arrows one after the other at his target in the clouds, I stand there and gawk, of course, yet at the same time I feel what Horace expressed and Quintilian extols, and that which is active in me springs to life, for I sense nobility and recognize ends. *Knows by nature, Obscure man, Tastes a thousand excellences with unfulfilled intention, Never treads with sure foot, Learned* etc.[41] These words pierced my soul like swords … everything is still horribly confused with me. And the Good Spirit finally revealed to me the reason for my woodpecker nature. It became clear through Pindar's words *to be able to control*. When you stand bravely in your chariot, and four new horses, wild and disorderly, rear beneath your reins, you guide their strength, ply your whip to bring the one who steps out back in line and the one who rears up back down, you drive and steer and turn, whip, stop, and drive again until all sixteen hooves are moving in one rhythm towards the goal: that is mastery, *control*, virtuosity.

Wenn er die Pfeile ein übern anderen nach dem Wolkenziel schiest steh ich freylich noch da und gaffe; doch fühl ich indess, was Horaz aussprechen konnte, was Quintilian rühmt, und was tätiges an mir ist lebt auf da ich Adel fühle und Zwecke kenne. Ειδως φυα, ψεφηνος ανηρ, μυριαν αρεταν ατελει νοω γευεται, ουποτ ατρεκει κατεβα ποδι, μαθοντες pp. Diese Worte sind mir wie Schwerdter durch die Seele gangen … es geht bey mir noch alles entsetzlich durch einander. Auch hat mir endlich der gute Geist den Grund meines spechtischen Wesens entdeckt. Über den Worten Pindars επικρατειν δυνασθαι ist mirs aufgegangen. Wenn du kühn im Wagen stehst, und vier neue Pferde wild unordentlich an deinen Zügeln bäumen, du ihre Krafft lenckst, den austretenden herbey, den aufbäumenden hinabpeitschest, und iagst und lenckst und wendest, peitschest, hältst, und wieder ausjagst biss alle sechzehn Füsse in einem Tackt ans Ziel tragen. Das ist Meisterschaft, επικρατειν, Virtuosität.[42]

The poet as charioteer is Pindaric, but Goethe's horses are as unruly as Cowley's. The quotation 'to be able to control' comes from the eighth *Nemean* (line 5), but there are no horses there; Pindar speaks of controlling *erotic* passion, and there is no reason at all to read the passage metapoetically. On the other hand, the poet's prowess – his *sophiā* – is a prominent theme in Pindar, and the poetic persona in the odes has a very strong personality. These critics were not responding to nothing, and the character of poetic inspiration and the poet's 'I' in Pindar will be a central consideration in Chapter 2.

# Edmund Burke

The preoccupation with bringing emotion under the control of reason finds a close parallel in contemporary philosophical discussion of the sublime. It is a concern very much of its age. The two most significant eighteenth-century texts are Edmund Burke, *A Philosophical Enquiry into the Origin of our Ideas of the Sublime and Beautiful* (1757; second edition 1759), and Immanuel Kant, *Critique of the Power of Judgement* (1790; second edition 1793).[43] The larger problem of how one analyses the operations of sensory perception and the imagination, the moral content of art, and the objective validity of statements about beauty received more and more attention in this period, and acquired its modern name of 'aesthetics' as a branch of philosophy.[44]

Burke's emphasis, as indicated already in the title, is on the human subject's reaction to sublime objects. As a committed empiricist, he argues stoutly that all our ideas originate in sensory perception; he has much to say about the material qualities of objects and the different impacts they have on the senses; he also has a detailed explanation (in the Introduction) of why people can judge the same sensory experience differently (e.g. finding it agreeable or disagreeable, impressive or negligible), in spite of the experience operating mechanically in exactly the same way on everyone. Nevertheless, his detailed analysis and taxonomy of what goes on inside the mind set his treatise apart from previous discussions. Burke sharply distinguished the beautiful from the sublime, arguing that the former was a judgement based on the positive pleasure we feel when looking at certain things, while the latter resulted from a different kind of pleasure, which he called 'delight', defined as 'the sensation which accompanies the removal of pain or danger'.[45] The sublime is the feeling we have when we are in the presence of something terrible but realize that we are not in any actual danger (in which case we would feel simple fear). 'Now whatever whether upon good or upon bad grounds tends to raise a man in his own opinion,' he writes, 'produces a sort of swelling and triumph that is extremely grateful to the human mind; and this swelling is never more perceived, nor operates with more force, than when without danger we are conversant with terrible objects, the mind always claiming to itself some part of the dignity and importance of the things which it contemplates.'[46]

All sublimity proceeds from terror, and all terror is a form of power. The passions relating to our own self-preservation are always in play in the sublime, whereas the social passions, such as love or sympathy, generate the beautiful. Love, if it contains no element of lust, has beauty as its object, 'which is a name I shall apply to all such qualities as induce in us a sense of affection and tenderness, or some other passion the most nearly resembling these.'[47] Ignorance and obscurity heighten the sense of the sublime, since familiarity diminishes the fear of terrible things. Language therefore achieves its most sublime effects by being indistinct rather than clear, by evocative suggestion rather than accurate description.

In Part V, 'Of Words', in many ways the most far-sighted part of the essay, Burke explores the character of language itself, and argues that the power of words lies precisely in their ability to conjure concepts that have no direct counterpart in what we see. He seems here almost to take us into structuralist and poststructuralist territory in their concern with the working of signs. Since Longinus the rhetorical tradition had explored how language can create sublime effects, but here we have the argument that language can create hitherto unknown concepts and make us 'see' what cannot literally be seen. As Ashfield and de Bolla remark, this move not only has wider significance for progress in theoretical enquiry (particularly in epistemology), it resonates with postmodern work such as that of Lyotard foregrounding the problem of presentability as essential to the sublime.[48] Also implied in Burke's scheme is the status of language and art as autonomous realms in human cognition,[49] an implication that will be important for the Romantics.

Of course there are difficulties in Burke's analysis. In general a rationalist would find much to challenge in his empiricist explanation of concepts and their working. His theory of the sublime is deliberately secular, but believing as he does in God as author of all creation and a sublime being, he cannot avoid speaking of Him. He expects objections from theologians when he says that our experience of God is primarily one of terror, yet he does not seem to notice (in these pages, anyway) that God is not sublime in terms of his own system: He is all terror and no delight.[50] The crassly sexist scheme – not only is beauty feminine and sublimity masculine, but women are not really capable of appreciating the sublime – earned a withering rebuke already from Mary Wollstonecraft.[51] The list of criticisms could be extended, but more important for our purposes are the positive contributions of this great work: the role of fear and astonishment in the sublime, which make it different from the beautiful; the relation of language to imagination; the autonomy of art; the connection between the sublime and the obscure; and the way that the mind appropriates 'some part of the dignity and importance of the things which it contemplates'. These will all come into play one way or another in reading Pindar.

I said above that bringing emotion under the control of reason was a central preoccupation of eighteenth-century philosophical writing on the sublime. It might be thought that in Burke conflict is not much in evidence; he speaks mostly of feelings, and in the second passage quoted above emotion seems to win. Yet the whole experience of the sublime to him is one of survival and self-affirmation, and the crucial sensation of delight following upon terror implies a detached contemplation of the situation. Also, to take possession of the 'dignity and importance' of the sublime is to assert control. So the point is there, if less in the foreground given Burke's preoccupations.

# Immanuel Kant

In Kant, conflict and control play a central role. His analytic of the beautiful in the *Critique of the Power of Judgement* is chiefly concerned with the validity of judgements of taste (i.e. judgements of what is beautiful), to which he argues we rightly impute universal validity, if they are made without any kind of interest. His examples are mostly drawn from nature, and the disinterest[52] means that we find something beautiful because of our aesthetic response to the object in and of itself without considering whether there might be some purpose or benefit in it. Such usefulness might increase our pleasure, but the judgement would then become partly teleological rather than aesthetic, and our approval would necessarily be governed by a general concept of some kind. The judgement of taste cannot be governed by such a concept, or its validity would be demonstrable by reason rather than by appeal to the similar constitution of human beings, whom we expect to share our judgement of the beautiful if it is truly disinterested (even though in practice we may not find such agreement). Neither is the judgement of taste a judgement of the senses – that I find something agreeable to the touch, for instance, or to my taste buds – since we could not reasonably expect such a judgement to be held by other, disinterested people.

A difference between the beautiful and the sublime is that the latter is a property of objects with limits, whereas the sublime is a property of objects or ideas without comprehensible limits (such as vast seas or mountains, or the concept of infinity itself). Kant divides the sublime into two types, the dynamic and the mathematical. The former is occasioned by overwhelming power, the latter by quantities which are beyond our capacity to imagine. The sublime is *entirely* a matter of the mind's efforts to deal with such phenomena; it has nothing to do with anything inherent in the phenomena themselves. Unlike the beautiful, our response to the sublime does not take the form of a single judgement, but requires a further step after the initial sense experience, which may terrify us (the dynamic sublime), or disorient, confuse and frustrate us in our inability to comprehend the limits of what we are perceiving (the mathematical sublime). In the first case, the realization, after the first frightful shock, that we are in fact safe

> reveals a capacity for judging ourselves as independent of [our physical powerlessness] and a superiority over nature on which is grounded a self-preservation of quite another kind than that which can be threatened and endangered by nature outside us, whereby the humanity in our person remains undemeaned even though the human being must submit to that dominion.[53]

Astronomical phenomena, a prime example of the mathematical sublime, may be measurable in one sense by scientific models, but aesthetically, as we stare up at the night sky, our ability to comprehend the magnitude of such phenomena rapidly gives out. Yet – the second step – the experience is pleasurable precisely because we then *understand* what is happening, and can affirm through it the existence of our rational powers, i.e. that we are able to have such a concept as infinity in the first place. It creates 'an enlargement of the mind which feels itself empowered to overstep the limits of sensibility'.[54] Nature is 'called sublime merely because it raises the imagination to the point of presenting those cases in which the mind can make palpable to itself the sublimity of its own vocation even over nature'.[55]

The pleasure of the sublime is not a stable one; upon taking the second step of realization, we do not relax into a smug complacency about our superiority. The experience is a vacillation of pleasure and displeasure, a 'rapidly alternating repulsion from and attraction to one and the same object';[56] 'the object is taken up as sublime with a pleasure that is possible only by means of a displeasure'.[57] Kant's dynamic sublime has much in common with Burke's sublime, as his reference to self-preservation shows, and in some respects his two forms of the sublime overlap.[58] In an experience of the dynamic sublime – a great waterfall, for instance – we not only sense the danger of annihilation, we attempt, however vainly, to imagine the extent of the power (the mathematical sublime). Standing at the very edge of Niagara Falls, mere metres from where the stupendous waters plunge over the cliff – a very scary (and truly sublime) experience, as I can tell you – one tries to comprehend, to *feel*, the extent of that gargantuan force (what would it be like to be *in* the river, one asks oneself with a shudder). The force can be measured, to be sure, but it means little to the understanding to be told that 160,000 cubic metres of water are passing by every minute. Here the dynamic sublime shades into the mathematical. Conversely, in contemplating infinity, an element of fear might creep in if we pause to think of our own puniness, and wonder what overwhelming power inhabits that other realm. The architects of the great medieval cathedrals understood this; when standing dwarfed at the foot of the mighty spires in Cologne, craning upwards, unable to see their summits, one is meant to feel the fear of God. Yet the distinction is useful, for it allows Kant to analyse as sublime those experiences in which fear, if present at all, must often be very attenuated, such as, precisely, in the contemplation of infinity, which for Burke was sublime only because it is a form of power. More importantly for Kant, the analysis allows him to explain the sublime in terms of his transcendental philosophy, that is to say, to identify the *a priori* principles upon which the experience of the sublime is grounded, and thence to link the critique of judgement to the critiques of pure and practical reason in the overarching system. Empiricism could not in his view account for the operation of concepts, or explain the commonalities of human understanding.[59] For our purposes, simultaneous attraction and fear as part of the sublime experience will prove fruitful in reading Pindar, especially when he has to do with gods.

Apart from the challenge to the whole Enlightenment project mounted in the twentieth century, many criticisms have been advanced of Kant's aesthetic theory (a mark of its importance, of course). I will here pick out two. The first is the relation of the sublime to morality. Kant's remarks in the *Critique* remain at a general level, linking the sublime to morality insofar as the former confirms, and makes us aware, that we possess the sovereign freedom (in practice if not in metaphysical theory) which is the ground of the latter.[60] But a specific moral judgement must always have some end in view and cannot be disinterested. At one point Kant asserts that 'even war, if it is conducted with order and reverence for the rights of civilians, has something sublime about it' and that it makes the 'mentality of the people who conduct it in this way all the more sublime, the more dangers it has been exposed to and before which it has been able to assert its courage'.[61] Kant is clear that 'satisfaction in the sublime, just like that in the beautiful, must be represented … as without interest in its quality'.[62] Yet his caveat about war being sublime if it is properly conducted makes it hard to regard this as a purely aesthetic judgement. Indeed one cannot think about any aspect of war without presupposing the concept of an end, except by occlusion; appreciation of its sublimity – of magnificent sacrifice, selfless courage and so on – must suppress awareness of the context in which such things are happening, or argue that they serve a good purpose in spite of the loss of life. The issue had bite in the wake of the French Revolution, which Burke's theory would commit him to regard as a sublime event, because he himself was safe from the terror. As the appalling events unfolded, the distressing implications of his theory caused him considerable discomfort. The First World War, the Holocaust or 9/11: by such criteria one could regard these too as sublime, as Karlheinz Stockhausen appeared to assert of the last atrocity, to near universal outrage.[63]

Kant explicitly confronts this point neither in the *Critique of the Power of Judgement* nor in his subsequent writings on law and political rights, which evince a complicated attitude towards revolution.[64] One could, as with Burke on God, put arguments in his mouth: the utopian sublime of the revolutionary he would surely regard as *Schwärmerei* – fanaticism, a rapturous vision which makes you think you can see things that aren't there (whereas sublimity is a negative intuition of what lies beyond sensibility, intimately linked to our rational powers).[65] Such good as revolutions produced came in his opinion from the uses made of their outcomes by enlightened leaders. In the pre-Revolution writings on morality, however, his focus is strongly on the virtue of people as individuals, not as social beings, just as in his aesthetics his strong preference is to dwell on the sublimity of nature and the individual's reaction to it, rather than on society and what people do in it. Surely there can be sublimity in collective human action, such as the overthrow of a tyrant; but that is by definition political, and interested. Individual actions too can rarely be separated from their social context.

This particular problem in the theory of the sublime is still with us. In any ascription of sublimity to a human action, there is bound to be occlusion of some kind. Human suffering too alters the case. If while marvelling at the Niagara River I chance to see a boatload of children swept over the falls, it ceases at once to be a sublime spectacle. On the other hand, long-ago suffering can be contemplated much more abstractly, enabling sublimity to return; an example might be Thucydides' description of the Sicilian disaster in Book 7 of *The*

*Peloponnesian War.* The problem then is, however, to say at one point in the passage of time the suffering becomes sufficiently abstract; and even for Thucydides an individual observer might be so overcome by the grim death toll as to feel only outrage at the folly of war.

Whenever the sublime object has propositional content, as in literature, or implies it, as in political action, there will be morality. In Pindar, a strongly aristocratic ideology underpins the celebration of competitive achievement by leading families in the Greek city-states. The rivalries between aristocratic clans, or tensions between such clans and the ordinary people, are not concealed, but neither is their true extent revealed. Pindar has various strategies to counter the ever-present threat of envy (*phthonos*), and to promote unity and harmony in the city. These have been studied intensely by scholars for some decades now.[66] My concern in this book is not to analyse them *qua* ideology, but to ask how these moments of ideological occlusion operate aesthetically in the poems. Not all readers have been able to suppress their dislike of Pindar's politics or his flattery of power. If such qualms can be bracketed, however, then one can ask what contribution the very common theme of envy makes to the experience of the sublime in the poems.

Another point on which Kant's aesthetics have exercised critics, not unrelated to the first, is his treatment of art. He is very clear that beauty in art is inferior to beauty in nature, and that, since art merely imitated nature – a rather Platonic outlook, this – one's judgement of it would inevitably include some opinion on how well that imitation was done. One could declare a work of art to be beautiful, but it would not be a pure judgement of taste.[67] He seems to think that one can find sublimity in art, but does not tell us how, and on his account representational art must face a severe handicap in creating sublime effects in and of itself rather than indirectly through what it represents.[68] Concerning poetry, sublimity is hovering round the edges of these fine remarks:

> It expands the mind by setting the imagination free and presenting, within the limits of a given concept and among the unbounded manifold of forms possibly agreeing with it, the one that connects its presentation with a fullness of thought to which no linguistic expression is fully adequate, and thus elevates itself aesthetically to the level of ideas. It strengthens the mind by letting it feel its capacity to consider and judge of nature, as appearance, freely, self-actively, and independently of determination by nature, in accordance with points of view that nature does not present by itself in experience either for sense or for the understanding, and thus to use it for the sake of and as it were as the schema of the supersensible. It plays with the illusion which is produces at will, yet without thereby being deceitful; for

it itself declares its occupation to be mere play, which can nevertheless be purposively employed by the understanding for its own business.[69]

There is so much in common here with his description of sublimity that one wonders that he did not point it out. The limits of language are a central topic in any discussion of poetic sublimity, not least for Pindar. For Pindar too one could almost adopt the phrase 'the schema of the supersensible' (*das Schema des Übersinnlichen*) to describe his myths. On the whole, however, Kant's downplaying of art ('mere play'!) must have dismayed his contemporaries. His remarks on genius also seemed inadequate to them: for Kant, genius was merely 'a talent for producing that for which no determinate rule can be given, not a predisposition of skill for that which can be learned in accordance with some rule', whose owner 'does not know himself how the ideas for [his product] come to him, and also does not have it in his power to think up such things at will or according to plan, and to communicate to others precepts that would put them in a position to produce similar products'.[70] Plato had dismissed poets' claims to know truth on identical grounds. About enthusiasm Kant was at best ambivalent. He acknowledges that it can be 'aesthetically sublime, because it is a stretching of the powers through ideas, which gives the mind a momentum that acts far more powerfully and persistently than the impetus given by sensory representations',[71] but goes on immediately to say that as an emotional affect it is inferior to affectless, reasoned assessment of aesthetic experience (which should produce continuous admiration rather than astonishment); a little later on enthusiasm is only one degree better than *Schwärmerei*.[72] In his brief comments on the topic it is notable that he does not use the common German word *Begeisterung*, but prefers the English loanword *Enthusiasm* (not even the Greek-derived German *Enthusiasmus*), commonly applied in English of the period to excesses of religious or political passion. He would have known the etymology, of course; implicitly he ridicules the idea that God speaks directly to the artist. If he knew the explanation of enthusiasm offered by Diderot's encyclopaedist quoted above (p. 14), who actually anticipates Kant's own idea of the sublime in some ways, he was not accepting of it.

## Reaction to Kant: Friedrich Schiller

Kant would certainly have had robust responses to offer his critics, but it was their recentring of art that set the tone for the nineteenth-century attitude to the sublime. Friedrich Schiller, in most respects a devout Kantian, nevertheless was the first to effect this shift of emphasis.[73] In his essay 'On the Sublime' (published in 1801), as in his earlier essay 'Of the Sublime: On the Further Elaboration of Certain Kantian Ideas' (1793), he accepts Kant's distinction of the beautiful and the sublime, and the two kinds of the latter (though substituting, rather usefully, the terms 'theoretical' and 'practical' for 'mathematical' and 'dynamic'). As in Kant the emphasis is on the relationship between perception and reason, and feelings of the sublime arise from a clash between the two, awaking awareness of our rational powers and superiority. Like Kant, but more clearly and forcefully, he equates the freedom of which we become aware with the freedom to determine moral law (that we possess true freedom, not just freedom in practical terms, was a point of deep disagreement with Kant for Schiller and his successors). He draws back, however, from the view that the sublime resides only in the mind; what is in the mind is an innate sensitivity to both the beautiful and the sublime. Both of these begin in nature, and end in the mind, according to whether the phenomena are in harmony with or clash with our ability to comprehend them. To develop that sensitivity is to be morally educated; only such a person is truly free. And crucially, it is art which develops our capacity for appreciation of beauty, sublimity, truth and morality:

The sublime, like the beautiful, is dispensed profligately throughout all nature. The capacity to sense both resides in everyone; but its seed grows unequally, and needs the help of Art. Nature's purpose entails from the start that we first hasten to greet beauty while we yet flee the sublime; for beauty is the nurse of our childhood, and ought to lead us from the raw state of nature to greater refinement. But though beauty is our first love, and our capacity to sense it develops first, Nature has nonetheless taken care that it matures but slowly, and for its complete development awaits the education of the understanding and the heart. If taste reaches its fullest maturity before truth and morality have been planted in our hearts upon a better path

Das Erhabene, wie das Schöne, ist durch die ganze Natur verschwenderisch ausgegossen, und die Empfindungsfähigkeit für beides in allen Menschen gelegt; aber der Keim dazu entwickelt sich ungleich, und durch die Kunst muß ihm nachgeholfen werden. Schon der Zweck der Natur bringt es mit sich, daß wir der Schönheit zuerst entgegeneilen, wenn wir noch vor dem Erhabenen fliehn; denn die Schönheit ist unsre Wärterinn im kindischen Alter, und soll uns ja aus der rohem Naturstand zur Verfeinerung führen. Aber ob sie gleich unsre erste Liebe ist, und unsre Empindungsfähigkeit für dieselbe zuerst sich entfaltet, so hat die Natur doch dafür gesorgt, daß sie langsamer reif wird, und zu ihrer völligen Entwicklung

than is possible through its agency, then
the sensual world will forever remain the
limit of our exertions.

erst die Ausbildung des Verstandes und
Herzens abwartet. Erreichte der
Geschmack seine völlige Reife, ehe
Wahrheit und Sittlichkeit auf einem
bessern Weg, als durch ihn geschehen
kann, in unser Herz gepflanzt wären, so
würde die Sinnenwelt ewig die Grenze
unsrer Bestrebungen bleiben.[74]

In imitating nature art makes our task of free contemplation easier, by
removing the inessential and the irrelevant:

Now to be sure, Nature of itself affords a
plenitude of objects upon which the
sensibility for the sublime and the
beautiful may practise; but the human
being here, as in other cases, is better
served by the second hand than by the
first, and prefers to receive matter
prepared and selected by Art, than to
draw laboriously and poorly from the
impure spring of Nature. Our instinct for
mimetic representation, which can
experience no impression without at
once striving for a vivid expression of it,
and sees in every beautiful or grand form
in Nature a challenge to compete with it,
has the great advantage over the same
that it can treat as a principal end and a
self-contained whole what Nature (if it
does not just unthinkingly toss it aside)
can take in only *en passant*, as it pursues
its immediate purpose.

Nun stellt zwar schon die Natur für sich
allein Objekte in Menge auf, an denen
sich die Empfindungsfähigkeit für das
Schöne und Erhabene üben könnte; aber
der Mensch ist, wie in anderen Fällen. so
auch hier, von der zweiten Hand besser
bedient, als von der Ersten, und will
lieber einen zubereiteten und
auserlesenen Stoff von der Kunst
empfangen, als an der unreinen Quelle
der Natur mühsam und dürftig schöpfen.
Der nachahmende Bildungstrieb, der
keinen *Eindruck* erleiden kann, ohne
zugleich nach einem lebendigen
*Ausdruck* zu streben, und in jeder
schönen oder großen Form der Natur
eine Ausforderung erblickt, mit ihr zu
ringen, hat vor derselben den großen
Vorteil voraus, dasjenige als
Hauptzweck und als ein eigenes Ganzes
behandeln zu dürfen, was die Natur –
wenn sie es nicht gar absichtslos
hinwirft – bei Verfolgung eines ihr näher
liegenden Zwecks bloß im Vorbeigehen
mitnimmt.[75]

Both the beautiful and the sublime are necessary for the complete education, but the sublime 'fashions for us an exit from the world of the senses, where the beautiful would be happy to keep us imprisoned forever' (*Das Erhabene verschafft uns also einen Ausgang aus der sinnlichen Welt, worin uns das Schöne gern immer gefangen halten möchte*).[76] This sounds quite Platonic, and one naturally assumes that, as in Plato, the opposite of the sensible world is the world of ideas, i.e. ultimate reality, but in this close reader of Kant one cannot make such an assumption, since for Kant the human intellect has no access to that world. The sublime would then take us away from the sensuous and to the world of transcendent human reason, but no further. These two passages, however, push us towards the first interpretation:

So long as man was merely a slave of physical necessity, had found no exit yet from the narrow circle of need, and did not yet divine the high *daemonic* freedom in his breast, so could *incomprehensible* nature only remind him of the limits of his conceptual power, and *destructive* nature only of his physical impotence.

So lange der Mensch bloß Sklave der physischen Notwendigkeit war, aus dem engen Kreis der Bedürfnisse noch keinen Ausgang gefunden hatte, und die hohe *dämonische* Freiheit in seiner Brust noch nicht ahnte, so konnte ihn die *unfaßbare* Natur nur an die Schranken seiner Vorstellungskraft und die *verderbende* Natur [these are Kant's mathematical and dynamic sublime] nur an seine physische Ohnmacht erinnern.[77]

The beautiful is of use only to the *person*, whereas the sublime addresses the *pure daemon* within; and since it is our destiny, in spite of all the limitations of our senses, to steer our course according to the lawcode of pure souls, so must the sublime join with the beautiful to make our *aesthetic education* complete and whole, and to expand the sensibility of the human heart to encompass the whole range of its destiny, and thus reach beyond the world of senses.

Das Schöne macht sich bloß verdient um den *Menschen*, das Erhabene um den *reinen Dämon* in ihm; und, weil es einmal unsre Bestimmung ist, auch bei allen sinnlichen Schranken uns nach dem Gesetzbuch reiner Geister zu richten, so muß das Erhabene zu dem Schönen hinzukommen, um die *ästhetiche Erziehung* zu einem vollständigen Ganzen zu machen, und die Empfindunsfähigkeit des menschlichen Herzens nach dem ganzen Umfang unsrer Bestimmung, und also auch über die Sinnenwelt hinaus, zu erweitern.[78]

This language strongly suggests the Platonic daemon we have already met in Herder, the divine element in us that links to absolute reality. Even if he declares allegiance to Kant's metaphysics and epistemology, he was not quite as rigorous as Kant in keeping ultimate reality separate from our cognitive world, often seeming to suggest, as in the passages above, that now and then we catch a glimpse of it. At any rate, it is towards the absolute Being that all our spiritual striving is, or ought to be, directed, even if we do not attain it in this life. This too is Platonic, or perhaps one should say Socratic, echoing as it does to the stance of the early dialogues.

Decidedly un-Platonic, however, is the idea that art can yield true insight. Here and in his longer work *On the Aesthetic Education of Man in a Series of Letters* (1795), Schiller argues that aesthetic experience can mediate between our rational and sensual selves. In the *Aesthetic Letters*, he also identified the instinct to play as essentially human: it is play – our free, creative imagination – that brings sense and reason together; it is the very engine of art; and only in the reconciliation of matter and form, body and spirit, can we be fully human, and achieve our greatest insights.[79] So much for Kant's 'mere play'.

Schiller's ideas on art exerted huge influence on subsequent thinkers and writers, including the Idealists Georg Wilhelm Friedrich Hegel and Friedrich Schelling, and the poet, philosopher and visionary Friedrich Hölderlin. All three were students together in the theological seminary of Tübingen, where Hegel and Hölderlin graduated in 1793, and Schelling in 1795. A document dating from about 1797, and dubbed the 'Oldest Systematic Programme of German Idealism' upon its publication in 1917, shows the influence very clearly.[80] The authorship is much debated, but it is written in Hegel's hand (and in the first person), and most critics accept that it was composed by him, with input, direct or indirect, from Schelling and Hölderlin. The document opens by declaring Kant's ethics to be an incomplete system. It asserts the 'absolute' freedom of the individual, whose autonomy and self-consciousness create a world out of nothing, the only world that can be said to be so created. There is no Idea of a state, which is nothing more than a mechanism: only what is the object of freedom can be an Idea; so the state must be superseded, with the goal of uniting all humanity. The document renounces the Church, and declares that all absolutely free minds 'carry within them the intellectual world, and need seek neither God nor immortality *outside themselves*' (*absolute Freiheit aller Geister, die die intellektuelle Welt in sich tragen, und weder Gott noch Unsterblichkeit ausser sich suchen dürfen*). The idea that unites all ideas is that of Beauty. The highest act of reason is an aesthetic act; Truth and the Good are related to each other only through Beauty. Philosophy must become as aesthetic as poetry, and in the new world poetry will become again what it once was, the teacher of humanity. Ordinary people and philosophers alike need a sensual religion; we need 'monotheism of the reason and heart, polytheism of the imagination and art' (*Monotheismus der Vernunft und des Herzens, Polytheismus der Einbildungskraft und der Kunst*). A new mythology is required – the mythology of reason. The people will not be interested in ideas unless they are made aesthetic, i.e. made into mythology, and the philosophers will despise mythology unless it is made reasonable. When this is achieved, the uneducated and the educated will join hands; there will be eternal peace, freedom, and unity of all spirits (*Geister*). 'A higher spirit sent from Heaven must found this religion among us, and it will be the last, greatest work of humanity' (*Ein höherer Geist vom Himmel gesandt, muß diese neue Religion unter uns stiften, sie wird das lezte, gröste Werk der Menschheit seyn*).

This wonderful example of youthful idealism (in the non-technical sense), while short on argument and long on assertion, nevertheless flags up important issues that its putative authors would later develop in profound ways. At bottom is a dissatisfaction with Kant's doctrine that we have no access to the absolute world-in-itself; consistently with that dissatisfaction, the document rejects Kant's view of personal freedom, that its existence cannot be justified theoretically, though there are powerful practical arguments for its existence. In general, the distance between this document and the mature philosophies of its authors is greatest in the case of Hegel, and least in the case of Hölderlin (who was to lose his sanity within a decade of its writing). While Hegel and Schelling, against Kant, both looked for an absolute ground to existence, thought and knowledge, Hölderlin denied the possibility of such systematic foundationalism. But unlike Kant, and even more clearly than Schiller, he did think we could have insight into the world of absolute being. Such insights were gained by intuition rather than methodical thought; they were not subsumed by any concept, but were essentially aesthetic in character. Schelling too continued to assign a central role to aesthetic experience, but the principal focus of his philosophy was to find a way to overcome Kant's dualism of subject and object altogether. Important though Hegel and Schelling were and are for the history of aesthetics, at this point we shall turn our attention exclusively to Hölderlin, since it was he who brought all of his artistic powers to bear on Pindar.

## Friedrich Hölderlin

Hölderlin was an enthusiast if ever there was one. *Schwärmer* ('dreamer'), other characters call his alter ego in his philosophical novel *Hyperion, or the Hermit in Greece*, in which *Begeisterung, Geist* and the like also occur very frequently. Schiller found it necessary to warn Hölderlin against too much *Begeisterung* in the verses he submitted to his journal.[81] He also warned him against being too philosophical in his poetry. Both warnings, one may think, were in vain, for *Hyperion* was already well advanced, the first volume appearing in 1797, the second in 1799. The deeply philosophical verses on which Hölderlin's claim to greatness now chiefly rests were written after 1800. These rhythmically free, triadic poems would have been recognized by contemporaries as Pindaric and thus 'enthusiastic' for that reason alone, but even more so for their (as it seemed) weirdly cryptic contents. The nine 'Night-Songs' (*Nachtgesänge*) published in 1804 met with derision (even if some of them were in regular Alcaic stanzas and Asclepiadean metre); one reviewer called them 'versified gibberish' (*versificierte Rodottagen*, a fine German equivalent of *galimatias*).[82]

Hölderlin, however, would have agreed with Johnson that enthusiasm had its rules. Those in *Hyperion* who call him a *Schwärmer* do so as a gentle rebuke. However important it might be as the source of inspiration, *Begeisterung*, the link with divinity ('be-spiriting'; 'inspiration' sometimes serves as a translation), was only one ingredient in art, alongside others like feeling (*Gefühl* or *Empfindung*), passion (*Leidenschaft*), reflection (*Besinnung*), awareness (*Bewußtsein*), imagination (*Phantasie*), drive (*Streben*) and intuition (*Anschauung*, sometimes accompanied by the adjective *intellektuelle*; the concept, rejected by Kant, derives from Neoplatonism, a philosophy with which Hölderlin sympathized deeply).[83] The artist struggles to marshal these at times warring impulses in pursuit of union with all of being, and truth. In one of the series of reflections written in the late 1790s (dubbed 'Frankfurt Aphorisms' by Michael Knaupp), Hölderlin writes:

| | |
|---|---|
| There are degrees of enthusiasm. From merriment, probably the lowest degree, up to the enthusiasm of the general who, with composure in the midst of battle, maintains powerful control of his genius, there is an infinite ladder. It is the calling and joy of the poet to ascend and descend this ladder. | Es giebt Grade der Begeisterung. Von der Lustigkeit an, die wohl der unterste ist, bis zur Begeisterung des Feldherrn der mitten in der Schlacht unter Besonnenheit den Genius mächtig erhält, giebt es eine unendliche Stufenleiter. Auf dieser auf- und abzusteigen ist Beruf und Wonne des Dichters.[84] |

The note of control, which we have heard sounded before, is loud here, and reinforced by the military metaphor. Another of the 'aphorisms', a short essay probably written in response to Schiller's letter, begins:

| | |
|---|---|
| Everyone is given their own measure of enthusiasm; one person preserves their deliberation (*Besinnung*) in the necessary degree through a greater fire, the other only through a weaker. Where your sobriety leaves you, there is the boundary of your enthusiasm. The great poet is never abandoned by himself, however far he may wish to raise himself above himself. | Das ist das Maas Begeisterung, das jedem Einzelnen gegeben ist, daß der eine bei größerem, der andere nur bei schwächerem Feuer die Besinnung noch im nöthigen Grade behält. Da wo die Nüchternheit dich verläßt, da ist die Gränze deiner Begeisterung. Der große Dichter ist niemals von sich selbst verlassen, er mag sich so weit über sich selbst erheben als er will.[85] |

He goes on to say how the right kind of feeling (*Gefühl*) warms and stimulates reflection (*Besinnung*) and the *Geist*, and sets the limit of enthusiasm; feeling, he declares, is at once both will and understanding. In his scheme, then, one retains self-possession even at the height of enthusiasm.

The longest of the so-called 'poetological' essays, known by its opening words 'When the poet gains mastery of his spirit' (*Wenn der Dichter einmal des Geistes mächtig ist*), written about 1800, reaches a climax in a rapturous description of *Empfindung*, 'feeling' or 'sensation'. The word is often indistinguishable from *Gefühl*, but it is doing particular work here. Hölderlin assumes Kant's distinction in the *Critique of Judgement* (§3) according to which *Empfindung* relates to representations of external objects in sensation, whereas *Gefühl* relates to feelings within the subject.[86] *Empfindung* for Hölderlin, however, carries further connotations of the capacity to receive such sensations; moreover, it can perceive not only the visible but the ideal world. It has much in common with *Begeisterung*, of which as we saw each person is given their due measure. In 'When the poet ...', Hölderlin argues that we can only achieve the full measure of our being as humans (which entails the recognition of the outer world as a unity within us, and ourselves as a unity within the outer world) through an *Empfindung* which is 'beautiful, holy, divine' (*schön, heilig, göttlich*); a feeling which is the perfect balance of subjectivity and objectivity, of reflection, striving and intuition, of calmness and sublimity; which harbours an excess of no one emotion or perspective, but the due presence and reciprocal connection of all at once.

This state is obviously an ideal. Until it is achieved, life is an unending effort to reconcile opposites. The key point is that only aesthetic experience creates the possibility of unity. As in Plato's *Symposium*, the beauty we see in this world shows us the way to perfection. The ultimate unity is that of all humans with each other and of all humans with nature; the oneness of absolute Being entails the end of the subject–object distinction. The emergence of culture marked the beginning of dissolution; art, being mimetic, implies a subject and object. But since conceptual, cognizable knowledge of the world also implies a subject–object distinction, it is only through art – understanding that is not subsumable under concepts – that we can work back to the original unity. One might think such unity could happen only in heaven, but for Hölderlin the process applied not only to individuals but to societies (of whom poets must be the teachers, as in the 'Oldest Systematic Programme'). He held a cyclical view of history, according to which periods of unity dissolve into periods of strife (consistently figured in his poems as day and night), until resolved again into a period of unity (he owes much here to the pre-Socratic philosopher Empedocles). Ancient Greece had achieved this perfection; about the prospects of modern Germany Hölderlin was less certain.[87]

Hölderlin's novel is an extended and passionate hymn to these ideas. His poetics reflect them, explicitly in the poetological essays and implicitly in his poetic practice. To analyse these in detail here would take us too far afield, but a few key points may be highlighted which will lead us to his engagement with Pindar.

Each of the three principal genres – lyric, epic, tragedy – has a natural 'tone' – naive, heroic and idealistic respectively – and, at the same time, a contrasting superficial appearance – respectively idealistic, naive and heroic. The theory, as adumbrated in these unpublished, sketchy and sometimes inconsistent essays, explains how the appearances and tones interact with each other, with subject matter, feeling (both *Empfindung* and *Gefühl*), intuition, imagination and style.

Although each genre has its basic tone, it need not always adopt it; but if it does not, compensatory moves are made. The different tones are always present in a poem in some way, whatever the genre. Furthermore, they must modulate in the course of the poem: the 'change of tones' (*Wechsel der Töne*) was for Hölderlin fundamental to poetry, as reflecting life. The literary analysis is also a metaphysical one; these tones are the essential, but tentative and shifting modes through which art engages with nature. Nature's original purity is nowhere directly visible to us; it makes itself known, or rather felt and intuited, through its very imperfection, through dissolution, fragmentation, signs. This negative representation, the gesturing to the ineffable beyond, is precisely the sphere of the sublime, as Hölderlin well knew. It is therefore of great interest that he speaks of *Erhebung* – elevation, etymologically from the same root as *erhaben*, sublime – only in connection with lyric, not epic or tragedy. Why should this be?

A lyric poem, according to Hölderlin, is a combination of naive, unreflective expression of feeling and idealization. The former is its most basic impulse, and tempts the poet to become lost in the particulars of the sensible world. Aware of this risk, the poet reaches for the ideal. One must distinguish what is going on here from the absolute idealism of Schelling and Hegel, and relate it to Hölderlin's views on the relationship between the sensible and the absolute, which as we saw was a modified version of Kant's transcendental idealism. The section of the essay on tragedy, whose basic tone is idealistic, opens by declaring that underlying all tragedies is the intellectual intuition of the unity of all life. In fact, the 'idealistic' is not opposed to the 'naive' in the way the ideal and the real are opposed. The drive for unity is and must be oriented in the first instance towards this world, which is cognized, understood and judged in a Kantian manner (except that the aesthetic assumes supremacy). For Hölderlin the idealistic is an understanding of *real* life from a certain perspective: it is to understand the mode of *instantiation* of the totality in the particulars of our historical circumstances; it is not to understand some Platonic form of life residing in the absolute (though, as intellectual intuition, the idealistic tone provides insight into the totality). The idealistic is therefore diffused through the other basic tones and not entirely separate from them, though it can predominate should the poet choose to emphasize it.

The lyric poet responds to this world and expresses a feeling in a particular moment, but at the same time, assisted by intellectual intuition, tries to understand what is signified thereby in an ideal perspective. These impulses (feeling vs intellectual intuition) have opposing orientations, but often co-exist in mental experience. Hence the reason why the sublime makes its appearance only in connection with lyric: the archetypal sublime arises from intense *personal* experience of the sensible world, one which produces feelings of the marvellous and inexplicable, of what lies beyond the senses, of ultimate meaning imperfectly grasped. As in Kant, the sublime is an internal mental state. Tragedy and epic may afford many opportunities to experience the sublime, but lyric exists to re-present the whole process.

Hölderlin also says that, in lyric, the heroic mediates between the naive and the idealistic. One way it can do this is through the use of myth, which prevents the lyric poet from becoming lost in sensual particulars on the one hand, and on the other connects that experience to the universally meaningful. In a tantalizingly brief discussion of myth at the end of 'Fragment of Philosophical Letters,'[88] Hölderlin asks how 'religious relationships' differ both from 'intellectual, moral and legal' relationships (i.e. idealistic ones) and from 'physical, mechanical and historical' ones (i.e. those anchored in the sensible environment). The answer is that religious relationships are both at once; they are 'intellectual-historical, i.e. *mythical*' (his emphasis). They contain neither ideas and characters alone nor events and facts alone but both together. 'Thus, all religion would be in its essence poetic' (*So wäre alle Religion ihrem Wesen nach poëtisch*), a much-quoted remark. Religion, myth and poetry are all engaged in the same enterprise of connecting ideal and real, the totality of life and its particular manifestations. Hölderlin's metaphysics, epistemology, philosophy of history and poetics are all devoted to working out this relationship.

The world for Hölderlin is a symphony perpetually struggling between harmony and dissonance. The 'change of tones' was not only a matter of theory; he found fault with poetry that was too monotonous.[89] Pindar's multivocal verse surely set the pattern of his late poems, whose style he forged in the furnace of his translations. His engagement with Pindar began early, however; his poem 'My resolve' (*Mein Vorsatz*), written in 1787 at age 17, declares his allegiance to Pindar and Klopstock.[90] This could be a conventional gesture, but there are Pindaric echoes scattered throughout the poems of the 1790s. *Hyperion* offers some prominent allusions. In one of the novel's moments of despair, he admonishes the 'children of the moment' (*Kinder des Augenbliks*) not to aspire to heaven's heights;[91] these are the 'creatures of a day' (*epāmeroi*) at the close of the eighth *Pythian*. This is, to be sure, a passage everybody knew; so too was the opening of the first *Pythian*, the famous image of Zeus's eagle slumbering as the lyre plays. But Hölderlin puts it to telling use. His spirits restored, Hyperion writes to Bellarmin:

> As Jupiter's eagle hearkens to the song of the Muses, so I hearken to the wondrous, infinite euphony within me … I play in spirit with destiny and with the three sisters, the holy Parcae. Full of divine youth, my whole being rejoices in itself, in everything. Like the starry heavens, I am serene and moved.[92]

Here a link is drawn to the central philosophical tenets of the novel ('everything' receives full emphasis; this is the universe's totality). The Muses' song is the emblem of inner and outer harmony. Even more emphatic is a passage close to the end of the novel, in a letter from Diotima to Hyperion, in which she says:

> The stars have chosen constancy, they shine unceasingly in silent fullness of life and do not know age. We represent perfection in flux; we divide the great chords of joy into ever-changing melodies. Like harp players among the thrones of the most ancient, we live, ourselves divine, among the silent gods of the world; with the fleeting song of life we temper the blessed seriousness of the sun-god and the others.[93]

The constant harmony of the heavens dissolves into the modulating chords of this world (the 'change of tones'). 'We' – Diotima means poets, as opposed to those who scorn genius, do not know nature, fear death and choose servitude – are the divine ones, representing the heavenly perfection on earth. Without exception, I think, every reference to lyres or harps in Hölderlin's verse occurs in a context where this relationship is thematized.[94]

Hölderlin's really intense engagement with Greek literature began in the late 1790s, and transformed him as a writer. His earlier verse was powerfully shaped by the example of Schiller, whom he worshipped, but whose influence he had to shake off if he was to find his own way. So much he frankly admitted to him in a remarkable letter of 30 June 1798.[95] In this period too the passionate affair with Susette Gontard took place, whose husband had hired Hölderlin to tutor their children. This is the Diotima of *Hyperion*, named for the heroine of Plato's *Symposium* who showed Socrates the path from earthly to heavenly beauty. As Diotima she is also the subject of various poems, and a number of their letters survive. There must have been many conversations about Hölderlin's philosophy and radical new poetics, and she was clearly a huge inspiration; it is a pity that the letters have so little to say on such matters.

The famous Pindar translations were probably made in 1800; those of Sophocles, perhaps in 1802.[96] Hölderlin's debt to Pindar in his late poems is massive. Apart from free (but carefully modulated) rhythms and strophic structure, one can list such things as neologisms; asymmetry in syntax, rhythm, register, content (description, historical and mythological references, apostrophe and personal relationships, gnomic reflection); daring hyperbata; jarring asyndeta; abrupt transitions; frequent appositions, especially of nouns; abundant, powerfully resonant metaphors; personifications of abstract notions; imagery of light; brilliant openings and quiet endings; special effects achieved across strophic boundaries; and lapidary pronouncements.[97] Hölderlin adapts Pindar's technique of ring-composition, and his movements backward and forward in time; and there are many dense allusions to the odes.[98]

Hölderlin's involvement with Pindar was thus as finely grained as it could possibly be. The translations are notoriously literal, taking the Greek words in order as they came, and transposing them into German. I give here a sample from the fourth *Pythian*; the English renders the German much as the German renders the Greek, and attempts to capture its effect. The Greek is from the edition used by Hölderlin, that of Christian Gottlob Heyne, which predates the now standard division of verses (these are verses 180–92 in Heyne, 102–8 in editions since Böckh's of 1811–1821).

|  |  |
|---|---|
| φαμὶ διδασκαλίαν | Ich sage die Lehre |
| Χείρωνος οἴσειν. ἄντροθε γὰρ νέομαι | Chirons zu bringen. Von der Grotte |
|  | nemlich komm' ich |
| Πὰρ Χαρικλοῦς καὶ Φιλύρας, ἵνα Κεν- | Bei Charikloe und Philyra, wo des Ken- |
| ταύρου με κοῦραι θρέψαν ἁγναί. | tauren mich die Töchter gezogen die |
|  | heilgen. |
| Εἴκοσι δ᾽ ἐκτελέσαις | Zwanzig aber vollendend |
| Ἐνιαυτοὺς, οὔτε ἔργον | Der Jahre, nachdem ich weder ein Werk |
| Οὔτ᾽ ἔπος εὐτράπελον | Noch Wort gesprächig |
| Κείνοισιν εἰπὼν, ἱκόμαν | In jenen gesagt, bin ich gekommen |
| Οἴκαδ᾽, ἀρχαίαν κομίζων | Nach Haus, der alten mich annehmend |
| Πατρὸς ἐμοῦ, βασιλευομέναν | Des Vaters mein, die beherrschet wird |
| Οὐ κατ᾽ αἶσαν, τάν ποτε | Nicht nach Fug, die einst |
| Ζεὺς ὤπασεν λαγέτᾳ | Zeus hat ertheilt dem Fürsten |
| Αἰόλῳ καὶ παισὶ, τιμάν. | Aeolos und den Kindern die Ehre.[99] |

I say the teaching
Of Chiron to bring. From the cave, that is, come I
By Charikloe and Philyra, where of the Cen-
taur me the daughters raised the holy.
Twenty however completing
Of years, after I neither a deed
Nor word loquacious
Among them said, have I come
Home, of the old looking after
Of my father, which is ruled
Not rightly, which once
Zeus had bestowed upon the prince
Aeolos and his children, the honour.

Prosaically, the Greek may be rendered thus:

I claim to bring the teaching of Chiron, since I come from his cave, where Philyra
and Chariclo, the pure daughters of the Centaur, raised me. Having completed
twenty years, without any impertinent[100] deed or word to them, I have come
home to reclaim my father's ancient royal prerogative, now unjustly ruled, which
Zeus once bestowed upon Aeolus, leader of the people, and his sons.

Extreme faithfulness even leads Hölderlin to write *Ken-tauren* because the
word is thus divided in Heyne's text. The view prevailed for a time that Hölderlin
made these translations only as a private guide to the Greek, and never meant to

publish them. As translations in an ordinary sense they would certainly seem to labour under a disadvantage if one sometimes needs to consult the Greek in order to understand them. But the Sophocles versions also occupy a place towards the same end of the slavishly literal – free imitation spectrum of translation possibilities, and Hölderlin published those. Predictably, they baffled or amused early readers (Schiller and Goethe thought them hilarious).[101] But this reaction utterly missed the point, and later readers have realized that they raise far-reaching questions about the nature and purpose of translation.

Merely on a practical level, Hölderlin's procedures make one face up to oddities that a normal translation smooths over. Five lines before the end, *der alten* translates the adjective ἀρχαίαν ('old'). We must wait four lines for the noun 'Ehre' (τιμάν, 'honour'). The effect of the hyperbaton in both German and English is beyond strange; but in fact it is unusual in Greek too. So what *is* its actual force in the original? In translating, one too easily ducks such questions by substituting the 'natural' order; in time one hardly notices the occlusion, and nurtures the illusion that one is really thinking like a Greek. Hölderlin's method brutally forces one to confront these matters.

On the theoretical level, for Hölderlin translation was a means of discovering the *vaterländisch* or *nationell*, the 'national'. By this he does not refer to national characteristics in an ordinary political or ethnic sense. Every period has its own culture resulting from the particular form that the constant elements of the human experience assumed in the historical circumstances. Paradoxically, however, what is one's own is hardest to identify, isolate and freely employ. In the case of the Greeks, Hölderlin believed that what was *vaterländisch* to them was not their calm rationality and clarity of form, as ordinarily thought – Winckelmann's 'noble simplicity and quiet grandeur' (*edle Einfalt und stille Größe*) – but just the opposite: their native tendency was to irrationality, lack of control and formlessness. That is precisely why they became so good at the other. Hölderlin figured these two impulses as Oriental and Hesperian, Dionysian and 'Junonian'.[102] With Germans it was the other way around: their natural tendency was to sobriety and orderly calm. In his verse he symbolized them respectively by the sun (Helios) and the brilliant open sky (Aither, a favourite word) and the dark earth, deploying a trope that became ubiquitous in the nineteenth century (hot, passionate Mediterraneans vs cold, forest-dwelling northerners).[103]

However one interprets the sometimes incomprehensible thoughts on language appended to 'When the poet …',[104] it is clear that for Hölderlin language, knowledge and inspiration were intimately linked in the unending effort to reach back to Nature and the original unity. In translation one should confront the other's *Vaterland* in the starkest possible form, doing violence to one's own language and thought processes in order to understand them better. The ultimate purpose was not, however, to be able to write pure *vaterländisch*, triumphantly bringing to light what had been hidden; that would be a crude kind of nationalism indeed.[105] Hölderlin thought the Germans would never be able to compete with the Greeks in *edle Einfalt* and there was no point trying (thus he flatly rejects the traditional reason for imitating them, to emulate their *Einfalt*: not only is that to misread the Greeks, it stultifies one's own artistic efforts). Rather, the purpose was to find common ground and reconcile opposites (as often in Hölderlin's philosophy). By smashing the languages together, one tries to break through to the universal language beyond either. Hölderlin's translations are neither German nor Greek, but a third, transcendental language, or more accurately a gesture towards such a language. There are times when Hölderlin uses *vaterländisch* in a way that emphasizes not the instantiation of the infinite in some particular finitude, but the underlying process of instantiation itself, which is the same throughout history. A conventional translation – one that a German could read as if it were German – would conceal rather than reveal meaning. Translation enables access to both the particular and the universal *Vaterland*. This notion of the eternal *Vaterland* allowed Hölderlin to 'correct' Sophocles, as he put it in a letter to his publisher, because in retrospect he could see more clearly what was *vaterländisch* than Sophocles could himself. He felt free to make him more 'lively' by bringing out the 'Oriental' in a way the public were not accustomed to when reading their Greeks.[106] Though Hölderlin versions sometimes badly misunderstand the Greek, and can be (frankly) unreadable, there are times when they bring unsuspected essences to the fore in a most arresting manner. These translations pulse with a direct energy few others have achieved. And philological accuracy was actually irrelevant to Hölderlin's enterprise.

In Hölderlin's renderings, minute aspects of technique merge with spiritual vision. They shatter the language into a thousand sherds, inviting the reader to put them back together. Words are liberated from grammatical shackles, encouraging new associations from their paradigmatic fields and/or from elsewhere in the poem. They stand out, sharp as needles. Meaning hovers between and around them. Uncertainty about where the syntax is going forces multiple close readings and careful reflection. Outright grammatical ambiguities forbid closure. Symbols – fire, ether, earth, water – serve as pointers to the ineffable. Small wonder that the late poems had a profound impact on modernist poetry when they began to appear in the 1910s. They transformed Hölderlin's reputation. After being regarded as no more than a worthy imitator of Schiller throughout the nineteenth century, he was now placed on a par with Schiller, Goethe and the greatest poets anywhere.

## Lyric parataxis

Apposition and parataxis lie at the foundation of both poets' style, and well illustrate the fusion of technique and meaning. This is a topic worth dwelling on at some length for the purposes of this book. When Norbert von Hellingrath published the Pindar translations in 1911, he instantly drew the link between Hölderlin's late poems, Pindar and Dionysius of Halicarnassus' severe style (*harte Fügung*, as he translated it).[107] Hellingrath was also engaged at the time in the first publication of the complete works from the manuscripts (he managed two volumes before he was killed at the Battle of Verdun in December 1916). Thus he was aware that what he was seeing in the translations went to the heart of the late poetry (and enabled a re-evaluation of such poems of this period as had been published before). Hölderlin makes no reference in his works to Dionysius except for a passing mention of his *Roman Antiquities* in a student dissertation;[108] the treatise on composition may, however, be lurking behind the second 'Frankfurt Aphorism':

| | |
|---|---|
| In periods there are inversions of words. Greater and more effective then must be the inversion of periods themselves. The logical arrangement of periods, where the foundation (the foundation period) is followed by the development, the development by the goal, the goal by the purpose, and the subordinate clauses are only ever appended to the principal clauses to which they refer in the first instance, – is certainly only very rarely of use to the poet. | Man hat Inversionen der Worte in der Periode. Größer und wirksamer muß aber dann auch die Inversion der Perioden selbst seyn. Die logische Stellung der Perioden, wo dem Grunde (der Grundperiode) das Werden, dem Werden das Ziel, dem Ziele der Zwek folgt, und die Nebensäze immer nur hinten an gehängt sind an die Hauptsäze worauf sie sich zunächst beziehen, – ist dem Dichter gewiß nur höchst selten brauchbar.[109] |

In his comments on the severe style, Dionysius says bluntly that it has little use for periods. More immediately in view, however, may be Aristotle's *Rhetoric* (book 3, chapter 9), which lays down the basic distinction between periodic or syntactic style and non-periodic, paratactic style. The latter is unpleasant, says Aristotle, because one cannot see where the sentence is going; there is no obvious end (*telos*), and one thing just follows another (Aristotle's name for parataxis is actually 'the strung-on style', *lexis eiromenē*).[110] A period, on the other hand, has a beginning and predictable end according to a logical plan. Hölderlin extends this description of the periodic sentence to longer successions of periods – paragraphs, say. A foundation is laid; the thought develops; it finishes at an end-point (*Ziel / telos*) which is predetermined by the overarching goal. 'Effective' suggests he is describing something of which he approves, until we learn at the end of the aphorism that, like Dionysius, he has little use for such things.

Ancient critics tended to prefer the periodic style to the paratactic, and saw the history of prose as a development from one to the other. Longinus' fifth source of sublimity is composition, by which he means the careful, harmonious (periodic) arrangement of words (§§39–42), including due attention to their rhythmical patterns (also part of the periodic style in Aristotle). But he knows that too much of this sort of thing is frigid, and inimical to sublimity. He knows too, as we have seen, that early authors such as Pindar can achieve sublimity by other means. Dionysius agrees.

In Hölderlin's proto-Romantic aesthetic periodicity is suspect. To impose artificial patterns on the data of experience is to proceed the wrong way around; it is to hobble *Empfindung* before it can do its work. The aesthesis of the world should be taken as it is given, in all its jumble; the clash of different perspectives, the messiness of data, is to be welcomed, not thwarted. In this collocation of incommensurables, the individual, struggling to become one again with nature, experiences a gap in understanding, a clash between non-linguistic intuition and articulating reason. In this gap the sublime may reside.

Theodor Adorno, in his essay 'Parataxis: On Hölderlin's Late Lyric', deserves the credit for seeing this. In his analysis, periodicity for Hölderlin is a kind of violence done to language, the result of a deluded belief that one's subjectivity is unmediated, primary and ultimate, and of privileging culture over nature. He cites these lines from 'Bread and Wine':

> Why are they silent too, the theatres, ancient and hallowed?
> Why not now does the dance celebrate, consecrate joy?
> Why no more does a god imprint on the brow of a mortal
> Struck, as by lightning, the mark, brand him, as once he would do?
> Else he would come himself, assuming a shape that was human,
> And, consoling the guests, crowned and concluded the feast.[111]

> Warum schweigen auch sie, die alten heilgen Theater?
> Warum freuet sich denn nicht der geweihete Tanz?

Warum zeichnet, wie sonst, die Stirne des Mannes ein Gott nicht,
    Drükt den Stempel, wie sonst, nicht dem Getroffenen auf?
Oder er kam auch selbst und nahm des Menschen Gestalt an
    Und vollendet' und schloß tröstend das himmlische Fest.[112]

He comments:

Such constructions [i.e. paratactic, giving form primacy over articulated content], straining away from what fetters them, are to be found in Hölderlin's most elevated [i.e. sublime?] passages, including passages in poems from the time preceding his crisis, as for example the caesura in 'Brot und Wein' [quotation as above] … The historico-philosophical rhythm that joins the fall of antiquity with the appearance of Christ is marked, in an interruption, by the word 'oder' [or]; at the point where what is most specific, the catastrophe, is named, that specification is put forth as something preartistic, mere conceptual content, not asserted in fixed propositional form but rather suggested, like a possibility.[113]

This technique of juxtaposition is not confined to Pindar amongst Greek lyric poets; parataxis is in fact the rule. An earlier generation of scholars advanced a psychological explanation for the style, linking it to the supposed 'discovery of the self' in the so-called Lyric Age of Greece (early seventh to early fifth centuries BCE). In this period the notion of an integral human subject was first articulated (claimed to be absent from the preceding 'Epic Age', i.e. Homer and Hesiod). Lyric poets revelled in this new-found internal world, exploring their reactions to external stimuli. Lacking the mental maturity and detachment necessary to the periodic style, they were bound to follow their impulses wherever they might lead. Mesmerized by the glittering world around them, they flitted from one brilliant impression to another. The theory was ruthlessly teleological, and lyric poets could be held up as examples of 'primitive' or childlike mentality. More sensitive critics like Fränkel were anxious to point out the positive charms of the strung-on style, but these could never outweigh the burden it carried of being forever not yet periodic.[114]

Though their explanation of the phenomenon would not now (I hope) find agreement, these scholars were not wrong to observe it. Adorno spoke of Hölderlin's 'docility' and his concept of subjectivity, but he explicitly disavowed naive psychologizing, and explained Hölderlin's style by reference to his philosophical poetics. In archaic Greek lyric, whose earliest surviving writers are already sophisticated in ways too many to list (but one could mention at least the manipulation of the poetic persona, a subtly allusive relationship with epic, a fine sense of stylistic register, and masterful deployment of myth; and one could recall that some ancient critics ranked Archilochus with Homer), we should look to the genre, and the poets' understanding of its possibilities. In epic we expect the grand sweep and stirring eloquence. Greek epic was a solemn performance, often on an international stage at the great Panhellenic festivals. It could last for hours if not days. Master singers in splendid robes portrayed the doings of the gods and the great heroes, passing on received wisdom to coming generations. The singer himself was by convention anonymous in his poetry, a mere instantiation of ageless tradition. The poem could be performed virtually anywhere. Lyric poems, by contrast, were in the first instance composed for and performed on particular occasions. There were songs for everything: to accompany a procession, praise a god, mourn the deceased, adorn a symposium, celebrate a wedding or a victory. Poems prayed, exhorted, mocked, grieved, moralized, shamed, congratulated, remembered. There were solo performances, and there were choral ones for children, youths and adults; the choral odes had both song and dance, a fine spectacle. The poet's task was to capture the mood of the occasion, heighten the sense of it, and reflect on its meaning. Intense focus on the present in all its vivid energy is to be expected in such circumstances. Significant details work as synecdoches. Foregrounding the poetic persona, in which the performative 'I' means 'I, like all of you' (who share the excitement), follows naturally from this stance. The personal gaze picks out the details. Convoluted syntax is out of place. Even in poems of sombre reflection, simple assertion is more apt, suggestive selectivity more effective than dense argument. The speaker is as much led by, as leading the audience; he or she is not persuading the unconvinced, but giving voice to thoughts hanging in the air.

Parataxis, then, is the rule from the beginning in Greek lyric, and the poets knew how to exploit its evocative juxtapositions. These invite the hearer to fill in the gaps, and to be part of a conversation. The power of suggestion was well understood; much remains unsaid. Variations in the approach of individual poets reveal that this is a matter of artistic choice. Simonides is so regular that Schadewaldt dubbed him a 'logistician',[115] whereas Pindar's ellipses lumbered him with a reputation for obscurity. The choice has nothing to do with mental deficiencies, and the more concentrated the effects in a text, the more purely literary it becomes: the experience is as much that of the text (particularly in its subsequent circulation) as it is of the occasion it relates to. Hölderlin saw that Pindar was a master of the style, and given his ideas about how reality is apprehended in fragments, signs, dissolution, and gaps, one sees why he put parataxis at the heart of his poetics.

Pindar was building on an already long tradition. To illustrate these points let us consider an outstanding example. Here is Sappho fr. 16:[116]

Some say a force of cavalry, others of
    infantry,
Others say one of ships is fairest
Upon the black earth, but I say:
    It's what you love.

5 It's very easy to make everybody
    Understand this. The woman who far
      exceeded
    All others in beauty, Helen, her man –
    Her excellent man –

Abandoned, and went off a-sailing to
    Troy.
10 Neither her child nor dear parents
    Entered her thoughts at all. Led astray
    [         ]

        ] thought
[      ] lightly [    ] think
15 Which] brings to my mind Anactoria
    now –
    Absent she is;

Her lovely walk I would rather see
And the bright sparkle of her face
Than the Lydians' chariots and in their
    armour
20 Soldiers of foot.

ο]ἰ μὲν ἰππήων cτρότον, οἰ δὲ πέcδων
οἰ δὲ νάων φαῖc' ἐπὶ γᾶν μέλαιναν
ἔ]μμεναι κάλλιcτον, ἔγω δὲ κῆν' ὄτ-
    τω τιc ἔραται·

5 πά]γχυ δ' εὔμαρεc cύνετον πόηcαι
π]άντι τ[ο]ῦτ', ἀ γὰρ πόλυ περcκέθοιcα
κάλλοc [ἀνθ]ρώπων Ἐλένα [τὸ]ν ἄνδρα
τὸγ [   αρ]ιcτον

καλλ[ίποι]c' ἔβα 'c Τροΐαν πλέοι[cα
10 κωὐδ[ὲ παῖ]δοc οὐδὲ φίλων το[κ]ήων
πά[μπαν] ἐμνάcθ<η> ἀλλὰ παράγαγ'
    αὔταν]
    caν

....... ]αμπτον γὰρ [.....] νόημμα
....] ... κούφωc τ[......] γοήcηι
15 .. ]με νῦν Ἀνακτορί[αc ὀ]νέμναι-
    c' οὐ] παρεοίcαc,

τᾶ]c <κ>ε βολλοίμαν ἐρατόν τε βᾶμα
κἀμάρυχμα λάμπρον ἴδην προcώπω
ἢ τὰ Λύδων ἄρματα κἀν ὄπλοιcι
20    πεcδομ]άχενταc.

The first stanza is a textbook example of the paratactic construction known as a priamel.[117] It throws the final item in the list, which will be the topic of what follows in the poem, into relief (not this, nor this, nor this, but *that*). The first items are, however, more than mere foil. Much depends on the selection, and the nature of the contrast. In this case, another military contingent of some kind might have been expected; 'what you love' is a surprise. The splendid horsemen (infanteers, sailors) present a fine sight; 'what you love' shifts the focus from the external qualities of what is seen to the internal quality of what is felt.

Who the others are with whom the speaker is contrasted are not identified – nameless groups as opposed to the feeling, speaking person in front of you. But, since we know it is Sappho who wrote the poem, we presume a contrast between groups of men (grammatically the pronouns are masculine) arrayed, like the military hosts and probably just as numerous, against a lonely, defiant Sappho. (But note she has set the men against each other: some like cavalry, but others ...)

Simply putting these different items on the table, as it were, invites a discussion about criteria of value, and about who does the judging. The implications are subtly explored in the following stanzas. To prove her point, the poet instances Helen, who abandoned her home and family to follow Paris to Troy. Sappho then expresses her feelings for the absent Anactoria, whose lovely step (*eraton* is the adjective, cognate with *erōs*) and sparkling face she would rather gaze upon than Lydian chariots and footsoldiers in their panoplies. The 'sparkle' of Anactoria's face is described by another erotic word (*amaruchma*);[118] she has appropriated the dazzle of the shining armour, and external sight and internal feeling here merge. The poem sets up a series of contrasts, between men who like military things and a woman preferring her beloved; between nameless hordes and a named individual; between public and private worlds. And there is another contrast: when Sappho says 'upon the black earth', she employs an expression instantly recognizable as epic (where *gaia melaina*, 'black earth', is a formula). The items in the first stanza are the subject of epic poetry; what follows – love, personal feeling – is the province of lyric. So the poem also says 'others prefer epic; I prefer my sort of song'. The listener may be influenced by the immediate environment (the lyric performance of the poem itself) to assent to this hierarchy; the speaker probably counts on this, and offers a masterful song to clinch the point. Of course, the listener may choose to resist the steer.

In sum, the poem places demands on the listener much subtler than they seem at first (and this is far from the most complicated example in Sappho's poetry). At the same time, the whole thing is done in Sappho's crystalline, simple diction, every word in its everyday place, yet effortlessly shaping the Sapphic stanza. There is also a modulation of tones that would have appealed to Hölderlin: terse, formal and argumentative in the first stanza; matter-of-fact at the start of the next (perhaps with a touch of humour, as Budelmann notes); a longer sentence of connected principal clauses lending cumulative force to the proof; then intimate, personal thoughts and a soft tone; then reversion to the opening theme (giving a 'ring-composition' pattern) and a sharpish tone to close.

We are not done with juxtapositions, however. As part of her proof, Sappho says that Helen was more beautiful than anyone else in the world (she does not say 'the most beautiful of women', incidentally, but of all people: the beauty of love is gender-neutral). But if the argument is that Helen gave up everything to be with Paris, whom (we infer) she found beautiful, logically it doesn't matter that she herself is beautiful. By inserting this additional point, Sappho complicates matters, and starts a conversation that is still going on (there's a large bibliography on this).[119] She could mean many things. For instance, as one who is most beautiful, Helen could expect to be the object of love (and indeed all the champions of Greece paid suit before she was married to Menelaus); so the point is that the power of love reverses expectations, cancels agency, and makes what is 'most beautiful' yearn for something even more beautiful. Or we might be encouraged to think of things from Menelaus' point of view, who stands in relation to Helen as Sappho to Anactoria; perhaps he has similar feelings and is motivated by more than bruised masculine honour. Or perhaps we are led to ponder whether beauty is objective or subjective; on the surface, the argument is that it's subjective (the beautiful is whatever you love), but Helen is said to be most beautiful, as if it's an objective quality. It is, after all, her defining attribute in the epic tradition. Yet if she is objectively 'most beautiful' there is nothing else she could find more beautiful; an element of subjectivity is unavoidable. In spite of being 'most beautiful', she finds something else 'most beautiful'. Sappho does concede that some people find other things most beautiful (horsemen, for instance); does she mean to imply, only in the absence of love? Probably; the thrust of her argument is that the emotional involvement of the lover makes all the difference. Ultimately, we are left with the question, what *is* the relation of love and beauty, between subjective and objective perspectives? Anactoria is, it seems, objectively beautiful (like Helen), but cannot something not beautiful be loved too (in which case the love creates the beauty, not the other way around)? These and many other questions arise from the simple addition (juxtaposition) of one datum, Helen's beauty.

We are not done with complications, either. The natural assumption is that the masculine pronouns of the first lines denote biological men, who are contrasted with a female speaker. This is indeed the obvious and standard reading, but it is not the only possible one. Difficulties in the transmission of this poem prevent us from knowing certainly where and how it ended, but in the surviving bits down to line 20, which could very well be where the poem ends, there is nothing to identify the speaker's gender.[120] Though we know that Sappho composed the song, it was quite possible for a male listener or performer to inhabit the 'I' (especially if the poem ended at line 20, but even if it did not): Sappho's poems *were* in fact performed at men's symposia.[121] And the rules of Greek grammar mean that the masculine 'some' and 'others' of the first stanza could also include women. Asking 'what is best' was a traditional game at the symposium. Even on the easy reading (men and armies vs women and love), the poem boldly challenges men's ideas of what is best; but if we entertain the possibility of a performing male 'I', matters become more complicated, since the challenge can now include gender roles (what do 'I' as a man really think?). And might not a speaker or listener of any gender entertain a fond thought for the lovely Anactoria? (I hear my traditional reader object: but Sappho did not intend such a reading! And the original occasion, for which the poem was composed, determines the meaning! Well, both points are open to challenge: the lyric 'I' is neither the same as nor different from the historical woman of Lesbos, and has built into it this flexible potential; and, as I said above, the poems were composed *in the first instance* for specific occasions. I shall return to these points in the next chapter.)

One of the many marvellous things about Sappho is the tension between the limpid surface and the complicated depths. These poems set up a cognitive gap which can never quite be bridged; and this is sublime. Longinus (ch. 10) singles out as a prime instance the famous poem (fr. 31) in which Sappho contrasts her physical and mental paralysis with the Olympic calm of a man sitting unperturbed beside a beautiful woman ('my tongue is fixed in silence; a subtle fire straightway runs under my skin; my eyes see nothing; my ears are roaring; the sweat pours down me; I am all a-tremble; I am paler than grass; I think I shall be very near to dying').[122] He notes the paradox that, in spite of all this, Sappho is nevertheless able to speak about it; she looks at herself from inside and outside simultaneously. He admires her ability to unite contradictions ('she freezes, she burns; she is mad, she is sane; she is either terrified [? the text may be corrupt here] or nearly dead'); he praises her canny selection of details, and their combination into a powerful whole. Whoever, indeed, takes no delight in a well-constructed list should get their poetic ears checked. Longinus here is especially interested in the workings of the list, but also notes the importance of the list's framing. Jonathan Culler, who in *Theory of the Lyric* repeatedly turns to Sappho for illustrations of transhistorical commonalities, comments on this poem (with acknowledgement of Longinus): 'The articulation of what dramatically happens whenever I catch a glimpse of you produces a striking effect: cast in the present tense, an account of what happens repeatedly, it nonetheless impresses us as something happening now, in the performance temporality of the lyric.'[123] The 'Hymn to Aphrodite', with which Culler begins his book, offers a similar clash of temporal perspectives, between something that has happened repeatedly (Aphrodite helping Sappho in a matter of love) and something happening now (her affections are not returned, so she prays for the goddess's help). The past moment is represented mimetically as the goddess speaking in the present tense, making promises for the future. The moment is described simultaneously from without – poor Sappho, says Aphrodite, here you go again – and within, as the agony of the current passion returns, and Sappho prays urgently to Aphrodite to come *now*. Past and present 'nows' coincide not only with themselves but with the future 'now' of reperformance, and of our reading: an arresting sequence, which no sensitive reader can resist attempting to understand, yet which always eludes fully expressible understanding.

Whereas Sappho conveys complex emotions and relationships that seem to overflow the limits of her plain language, in Pindar it is the other way around: the surface of the language is turbulent, while underneath there is a rock-solid aristocratic world-view. The turbulence consists, most obviously, in his well-known habit of variation (*variatio* or *poikiliā* in ancient rhetorical terminology): his constant search for novel ways to say familiar things, and his evident aversion to saying the same thing twice in the same way. Since some sentiments recur many times in the poems, his powers of invention are much on display. We could illustrate the point here by quoting his own most famous priamel, the opening of *Olympian* 1 ('water is best; gold, like blazing fire, stands out at night, best of a noble man's wealth; but if, my heart, you wish to sing of games, mark by day no other bright star warmer than the sun in the empty aether, and let us speak of no contest superior to Olympia'),[124] which offers several points of comparison and contrast with Sappho's priamel both in respect of parataxis and variation. Such linguistic fireworks can indeed have their sublime effects. But a better illustration of Pindaric variation and irregularity as they link to a world-view would be his habit of introducing the mythical section of the epinician by means of a relative pronoun.[125] These sections are (usually, though not always) clearly demarcated from the rest of the poem, but the point in the poem at which the section begins (if there is one; not every poem has a myth) varies considerably; the myth is sprung on you quite suddenly, very often (but not always!) by means of a relative pronoun acting as a hinge. In the first *Olympian*, for instance, Pindar says that Hieron's 'fame shines in the settlement of Lydian Pelops, *whom* Poseidon loved …' (23–5), and therewith we are launched into the tale about the young Pelops, Poseidon's love of him, his winning his bride Hippodameia (a foundation myth of the Olympic Games), and the crime of his father Tantalus against the gods. That 'whom', and dozens of others like it in the odes, function like Adorno's 'or' in Hölderlin's *Bread and Wine*: two worlds – the contemporary world of the victory, and the world of heroic legend – are brought into contact with each other through a single word: a momentous juxtaposition indeed. The irruption of the divine is sudden and unpredictable, in the odes as in life. Gods lie everywhere behind the phenomena; in special circumstances, they come into view. It is for the poet to tell us how and when.

This is one example of what may be termed Pindar's aesthetics of surprise – which, as Longinus well knew, is a common aspect of the sublime moment (it hits 'like a thunderbolt', 1.4). As well as the myth, there are other recurring elements in the epinicians, what Schadewaldt called their programme: praise of the victor, his family and his city; the victory itself, and others won in the past; gnomic reflection; prayers to the gods.[126] Interwoven among these elements are favourite themes such as the problem of envy, the essence of nobility, the virtues of hospitality, the proper use of wealth, the demands of piety and the role of the poet. One can never know in advance how many of these will be found in an ode, in what order, to what extent or how expressed. Although there is a stable overall framework (the programme), as in the world at large the phenomena within the frame are kaleidoscopic. It is essential to Pindar's poetic strategy to suggest this disorder while at the same time bringing it under control and elucidating its meaning. The moment of victory is one of supreme happiness, the height of human achievement, an all-too-brief illumination by the gods; it is the rare combination of fortune and effort, the *kairos*. This elusive coherence comes into being once again with the performance of the ode, where the poet, aided by the Muse, judges the *kairos* of what to say (neither too much nor too little, always the right words), reviving the exhilaration of the first moment and, paradoxically, making it permanent by means of the ode itself.[127] Although Hölderlin owes Pindar much, it would not be right to say that Pindar's juxtapositions are 'pre-artistic', in Adorno's terms; on the contrary, Pindar is the master of these ceremonies.

## Ancient and modern receptions in conversation

Let me now return to Longinus with these various receptions and considerations in mind, and conclude by mapping out the programme for the remainder of the book.

Since (says Longinus) his dedicatee already knows well what the sublime is, he gives no definition other than that it is 'a certain excellence and distinction of discourse' (1.3), followed by some remarks on its effects (how it carries the audience away, strikes them like a thunderbolt and so on). As Porter stresses, his primary interest is rhetoric; he is not a Romantic out of time.[128] But the lines between thought and expression are not always clear, and Longinus himself says the two are intertwined (30.1). He states memorably that sublimity is 'the echo of a noble mind' (*megalophrosunēs apēchēma*, 9.2), and of his five sources of sublimity the first and most important is grandeur of conception (8.1). The second source, moreover, is 'strong and inspired [or 'enthusiastic'] passion' (*to sphodron kai enthousiastikon pathos*), while the remaining three are (finally) 'matters of art' (*technē*: these are figures of thought and speech, noble diction, and composition). His best-known examples of the sublime are about qualities of mind and character. Everyone remembers his citation (itself sublime; he aims to exemplify his own principles) of Ajax's silence in *Odyssey* 11 ('more sublime than words'; that is, words alone cannot get us there). The quotation (9.9) of *Genesis* 1:3 ('and God said "Let there be light"; and there was light') is memorable, of course, just for being a startling appearance of the *Septuagint* in pagan literature, but Longinus praises it because the author has formed a suitably grand conception of God; he has just praised lines of the *Iliad* for the same reason. He prefers Pindar and Sophocles to Bacchylides and Ion because of their innate character (*phusis*, 33.2), and in spite of their stylistic shortcomings. Demosthenes' overwhelming powers derive from his 'heaven-sent' talents (34.4); 'for it would not be right to call them human'. Such remarks make it hard to think that his sublime is a matter of style alone.

In his description of the *effects* of sublime style on the mind, Longinus comes even closer to our modern writers. That he repeatedly stresses astonishment is not so remarkable, but coupling that with a feeling of transport or ecstasy (*ekstasis* 1.4), not (or not only) in the enthusiastic writer but in the audience, points to a cognitive understanding of the sublime.[129] More than that, he says that the truly sublime lifts the mind (or soul: *psūchē*) and fills it with joy and boasting, 'as if it itself had created what it heard' (7.2); this strongly calls to mind the passage from Burke quoted above (p. 20: 'the mind always claiming to itself some part of the dignity and importance of the things which it contemplates'), though as we shall see in a moment there is an important difference too. In chapter 35, the great writers achieve their effects because of humanity's inborn love of what is greater than the merely mortal. The entire universe does not suffice for our inquiry and thought; our intuitions perpetually transgress the boundaries of our environment. The gods, indeed, created us to be thus ambitious. We are led naturally to admire not the small but the great – the Danube, the Nile, the Rhine, and even more the Ocean; or the stupendous eruptions of Etna. The qualities of a Homer or a Demosthenes raise them 'close to the greatness of God' (36.1: *megalophrosunē* is the word, as in 9.2 quoted above). These remarks are suggestive of Kant's essential idea that in the sublime the mind becomes aware of its own capacities. In some ways Longinus' most startling remark, however, is that, whereas in plastic art we expect productions that resemble their human subjects as accurately as possible, in discourse (*logos*) we expect something that transcends the human (*huperairon ta anthrōpina*, 36.3). What amazes us in art (*technē*) is accuracy, but in nature it is grandeur; and language is humankind's distinctive natural gift. It is what makes Homer and the others divine. So Longinus means to say more than that language can arouse visions of the divine; statues can do that too. Just as the human soul is immortal, language adumbrates the divine *in itself*; through its very nature it speaks what lies beyond its words. Language and its limits: Longinus is close here to Hölderlin's idea of the sublime as an attempt to express the ineffable, or represent what can never be wholly represented.

This cognitive orientation has understandably appealed to modern readers, but the differences should not be overlooked. First of all, in spite of the passages highlighted above, the technical side of his analysis is very important. For Longinus neither nature nor art alone is sufficient to produce sublimity; they must work together (36.4). Longinus thrills to stylistic minutiae like any other ancient rhetorician, and would have thought Boileau's idea of a *beau désordre* unhelpful, to say the least.

Longinus' understanding of the cognitive side of the sublime also has its differences. As Stephen Halliwell puts it:

> In contrast to [Kantian] and other modern notions of the sublime as entailing a degree of cognitive failure or inadequacy, Longinian *hupsos* infallibly brings with it the promise of a fulfilment and enlargement of the mind's own potential. It operates through a sense of the removal or transcendence of limits, not a confrontation with impediments placed in the path of thought.[130]

Consistent with this difference is the absence of any notion of claiming control or superiority, which as we saw was a central element in Burkean and Kantian thought. It is in any case a highly gendered notion, as critics have pointed out.[131] For Longinus, natural wonders inspire astonishment at their grandeur, not fear at the prospect of annihilation. In oratory, the sublime for him does not entail a contest between speaker and audience, as if the former is trying to intimidate the latter; the sublime is rather a sharing of emotion, whereby the audience, or reader, is brought into the writer's mental world. For all the similarity of language between Longinus and Burke noted above, the crucial difference is that the boasting in Longinus does not involve usurping the orator's place. He is still there with you, exulting on the mountain-top, but to have the experience one must fully internalize the force of his words, which is a kind of co-ownership. There is no smug, Burkean contemplation from a distance.

Longinus does recognize that fear can be aroused by descriptions of frightening events (10.5). He also acknowledges that a powerful orator can frighten his auditors; one would more readily withstand a thunderbolt than the passion of Demosthenes, he says, whereas 'nobody is afraid when they read Hyperides' (34.4). Dionysius (*Dem.* 22) and Demetrius (*Eloc.* 100, 283) also found Demosthenes quite overwhelming. But the sublime experience is not to be had by resisting the fear, it is to be had by giving in to it. Descriptions of aesthetic responses in Greek texts from Homer onwards stress the emotional involvement of the listener and viewer.[132] For Longinus, sublimity means exhilaration, uplift and, wherever possible, moral edification. In this regard Halliwell aptly notes the difference between Longinus' discussion of *Iliad* 17.645–7 and the treatment of the same passage in Burke. The Greeks on the battlefield are enveloped in darkness, and Ajax cries out in despair to Zeus that, if he means to destroy them, at least let him do so in the light. Of this passage Longinus says:

> This is the true attitude of an Ajax. He does not pray for life, for such a petition would have ill beseemed a hero. But since in the hopeless darkness he can turn his valour to no noble end, he chafes at his slackness in the fray and craves the boon of immediate light, resolved to find a death worthy of his bravery, even though Zeus should fight in the ranks against him.[133]

For Burke, by contrast, the darkness is here the source of the sublime, because it is terrible. In darkness 'the boldest are staggered, and he who would pray for nothing else towards his defence, is forced to pray for light: [quotation of *Iliad* 17.645–7]'.[134] We are afraid only by proxy, and can look upon the passage as sublime because we are not actually there.

Yet there *is* a way in which fear-at-a-distance can profitably be related to the sublime in Pindar: in a nutshell, it is that for Pindar, however glorious human success and happiness may be, they are fragile matters, lasting but a moment, and prevented or undone by chance, malice and envy. These are ever-present threats, truly fearful when they materialize; in the poems, we experience that fear by proxy. If the origin of the malice or envy is divine, the threat is even more terrifying. The most earnest piety is needed to avert it, and even so there is no guarantee of success. If the poet has done his job, however, we should understand that these dangers provide the necessary context for the greatest human joy and the thrill of victory, like flashes of lightning in the darkness. The Hyperboreans of the tenth *Pythian*, the residents of the Blessed Isles in the second *Olympian*, and the gods themselves in heaven may live in eternal bliss; but in those places there can be no epinician poetry.

Envy in the odes is sometimes divine, coming from gods who resent any presumption in humans of greater than mortal status, but more often it is human, coming from people who resent the victor's success. Its negativity provides a foil to the proper attitude of praise and celebration. As I noted in discussing Kant (p. 25), the theme of envy leads directly to Pindar's politics and occlusions. Some of the victors were monarchs or tyrants, facing the constant threat of revolution which in the case of Cyrene and Syracuse actually came about not long after Pindar praised the previous rulers. Even without knowing the history one can guess from the odes themselves that his plea for civic harmony could be disingenuous or deluded. But if one is willing to go along with Pindar – and not to be willing is simply to refuse the poem[135] – then the envious hatred which an ancient or modern democrat, or disgruntled oligarch, might well feel towards Hieron in ordinary life becomes *in the world of the poem* a generalized, uncontextualized potential, comparable to the jealousy of the gods and equally to be deprecated. One hopes that it never strikes, but the fact that it could sets up an equilibrium between fear and joy that can create a sublime effect. It is a choice between oblivion and immortal fame not unlike the sublime, paradoxical co-existence of death and eternal glory in the *Iliad* (most famously in the speech of Sarpedon, 12.322–8).

In the case of fear, then, one of many topics that recur in ways both similar and different in modern and ancient writers, we may have found a new way to look at familiar passages and ask about their aesthetics, specifically about how they may be considered sublime; conversely, consideration of such passages may feed back into the general theory of the sublime (particularly in relation to morality and politics). Language is another recurring theme. Style is a central concern of ancient rhetoricians like Longinus and Dionysius, but language acquires overtly metaphysical implications in the modern writers we have examined, particularly the German ones. The working of language in Pindar and its relation to meaning, so central to Hölderlin, obviously demand our attention; metaphysical implications seem unlikely, but a fresh look may yield surprises. Other topics include the experience of the cognitive subject, the role of the poet and poetic genius, and (related to that) the whole notion of enthusiasm and its rules (or lack thereof). Though these may be thought of as particularly modern, they have congeners in Longinus as we have just seen. Conversely, topics whose ancient and modern treatments may seem to have more in common, such as the place of wonder in the sublime or the relation of the sublime to the transcendent, may turn out on closer inspection to be rather different. How we negotiate these similarities and differences is of central importance. The readings of the long eighteenth century are not to be dismissed because the early twenty-first century finds them anachronistic (or uncongenial). These were intelligent critics who knew their classical texts profoundly well. One should ask what it is that led them to read Pindar as they did, and why we read Pindar as we do, especially on topics where a view seems beyond dispute to most contemporary critics (for instance, that the Pindaric 'I' has nothing to do with the expression of personal feeling). It is not a matter (obviously) of teasing out some timeless essence of the sublime, which does not exist. Rather, reflecting on such matters may provide greater clarity on the grounds for choosing one reading over another, and shake the critic out of unfounded complacency.

To focus discussion in subsequent chapters I propose to gather these many topics under two broad headings. The first is captured by Longinus' remark in chapter 7 about the mind being filled with the sublime, and seeming to share in the writer's creation. This joyous sense of expansion, exhilaration and fellow-feeling has struck a chord of recognition in modern readers since Boileau.[136] I shall call it 'shared experience' (Chapter 2). Since the experience is created by the poet, this is where we may consider Pindar's persona (his 'I'), his relation to the Muse and inspiration, his direction of the text's reception, and his metapoetic remarks, such as about the *kairos* (above, pp. 17, 50), which is a central part of the sublime for Longinus.[137] Under this heading too naturally falls consideration of the audiences, not just the primary (those present at the first performance) but the secondary (other, contemporary ancient Greeks) and the tertiary (later readers, including us). The primary audience has been studied intensively for fifty years or more, with relentless focus on the occasion of the first performance. Much of the discussion has revolved around the epinician genre and its social conventions (also relevant, obviously, to the poet's 'I'); these will come into our purview. Secondary and tertiary audiences have started to come to the fore in more recent criticism. This is an important development, and opens the way to considering how textual anticipations of the secondary audience (and, by extension, the tertiary) help to create the experience of the sublime.

The second broad area may be dubbed 'exceeding limits' (Chapter 3): the sublime is what lies beyond. First of all, the limits of language, theorized in similar-but-different ways by Longinus and Hölderlin. Pindar's constant invention of new words suggests that he found the existing resources of language insufficient, and raises the question of whether the meaning has been fully captured. His metaphors, astonishing in range and quantity, gesture continually to an unstated *tertium quid*. His boast that he always chooses the right thing to say, and the right number of words to say it, might discourage one from putting further words into his mouth or reading between the lines; yet he tells us (*O*.2.85) that interpreters are needed to understand his poetry, and his virtuoso parataxis leaves much unsaid. In these silences may lie the sublime.

As we have seen, for Longinus language is one of the things that make us like gods, but, as in everything else, we fall far short of their perfection. The Muse needs no outside assistance, and on Olympus there can be no mismatch between what is said and what is signified. One of the things human language can never say, Pindar's or anyone else's, is what the future holds. In Greek thinking our time-limited mortality separates us absolutely from divinity. Yet human tradition and memory can offer a substitute for immortality. As Pindar is acutely aware, poets create and sustain such traditions. He repeatedly invokes the past as foreshadowing the present, and the present as instantiating the past. By writing himself emphatically into tradition, he anticipates the future efficacy of his memorialization. To be collapsed, temporal perspectives must also be differentiated; the sudden moment in the poem when they all come together in a god's-eye view becomes thereby all the more paradoxical and sublime.

Imperfect language and imprisonment in time are two ways in which humans are inferior to the gods; there are many others. Yet, says Pindar, humans and gods are one race, sprung from the same mother (Earth, *N*.6.1–2). This simultaneous stress on human insignificance and on our divine affinities is a deep-running theme in Greek mythology. The whole class of heroes – demigods – is the most distinctive thing about it in a comparative perspective, and the stories tell how they repeatedly test the limits of their mortality; their punishment by death is as predictable as their determination to defy it. But after death, they receive timeless heroic honours in cult and song. The greatest of their number did become a god: Heracles, a particular favourite of Pindar (and how congenial it was to him that he was Theban). At the same time as he spurs his hearers on to greater and greater heights, and denounces the evil of envy, Pindar warns us never to try to exceed the limits, to go beyond the Pillars of Heracles and seek to be a god. Those limits we must approach with trembling, since, unlike the edge of the lethal river, we often do not know where they are. The quivering oscillation of desire and terror, this fragile balance can be, like Blake's fearful symmetry, sublime.

Hölderlin might have agreed that gods and humans are one race, and as we saw the divine spark of human genius played a central role in early Romantic notions of the sublime. Yet however much they tried to revive a pagan world-view, Hölderlin and others did not quite shake free of the notion that God is ultimate, transcendent reality. Greek religion, by contrast, is one of immanence. Its many gods were born into the world; they did not create it, and there are limits to what they can do. On the other hand, it would be wrong to dismiss early Romantic views as still overly Christianized, as if we have now seen through the historical encrustations to the true nature of Greek religion. This historical dialogue encourages us to look more closely at these terms 'immanent' and 'transcendent' and ask what they might mean for the Pindaric sublime. I said above that Kant's 'schema of the supersensible' was a rather good description of Pindaric myth. Where does *his* supersensible reside?

My two general areas can, of course, shade into each other. The shared experience might include an experience of exceeding limits; a passage probing such limits might draw the reader imaginatively into its scenario. The persona of the poet is never long out of sight in the telling of myth. So this is only a guiding schema. Certainly I am not looking for some mechanical calculus, a list of characteristics of which a given number would allow one to say that this passage is sublime, whereas that one is not. That would be both futile and boring. Apart from the deluded essentialism of such a procedure, there must be room for disagreement; an aesthetic judgement in Kantian terms is offered for universal assent, but in practice there are many obstacles to agreement. Not everyone is impressed by Niagara Falls,[138] and Mary Wollstonecraft was 'sick of hearing of the sublimity of Milton'.[139] It is a matter of reading a passage in a certain light, with a range of considerations in mind, and seeing if others can be induced to read it in the same way.

# 2

# Shared Experience

## The first *Pythian*

The opening of the first *Pythian* is one of the two passages in Pindar – the other being the close of the eighth – most frequently dubbed sublime:

Golden lyre, own champion[1] of Apollo and the violet-tressed Muses! The dancers' steps heed you to start the gleaming celebration, and singers follow your cue when your quivering strings set up the choral preludes. (5) You extinguish even the piercing lightning-bolt of ever-flowing fire. On Zeus's sceptre the eagle sleeps, swift wings drooping on either side,

Χρυσέα φόρμιγξ, Ἀπόλλωνος καὶ
  ἰοπλοκάμων
σύνδικον Μοισᾶν κτέανον· τᾶς
  ἀκούει μὲν βάσις ἀγλαΐας ἀρχά,
πείθονται δ' ἀοιδοὶ σάμασιν
ἀγησιχόρων ὁπόταν προοιμίων
  ἀμβολὰς τεύχῃς ἐλελιζομένα.
5 καὶ τὸν αἰχματὰν κεραυνὸν
  σβεννύεις
αἰενάου πυρός. εὕδει δ' ἀνὰ σκάπτῳ
  Διὸς αἰετός, ὠκεῖαν πτέρυγ'
  ἀμφοτέρωθεν χαλάξαις,

King of birds; you poured upon his curved head a murky cloud, a sweet key to lock the eyelids. Slumbering in the grip of your casts he gently heaves his lissome back. (10) Even mighty Ares leaves his cruelly barbed spears outside and warms his heart with sleep; your darts enchant the minds even of the gods, through the art of Lato's son and the deep-robed Muses.

ἀρχὸς οἰωνῶν, κελαινῶπιν δ' ἐπί οἱ
  νεφέλαν
ἀγκύλῳ κρατί, γλεφάρων ἁδὺ
  κλάϊθρον, κατέχευας· ὁ δὲ
  κνώσσων
ὑγρὸν νῶτον αἰωτεῖ, τεαῖς
10 ῥιπαῖσι κατασχόμενος. καὶ γὰρ
  βιατὰς Ἄρης, τραχεῖαν ἄνευθε
  λιπών
ἐγχέων ἀκμάν, ἰαίνει καρδίαν
κώματι, κῆλα δὲ καὶ δαιμόνων
  θέλγει φρένας ἀμφί τε Λατοΐδα
  σοφίᾳ βαθυκόλπων τε Μοισᾶν.

But those who are not loved of
Zeus are stricken with terror to
hear the cry of the Pierides, by
land and unyielding sea, (15) and
he who lies in dread Tartarus,
enemy of the gods, Typhos of the
hundred heads. A famous Cilician
cave once reared him, but now the
cliffs above Cymae, fencing the sea,
and Sicily crush his shaggy breast;
a towering pillar pins him, (20)
snowy Etna, year-round nurse of
bitter snow.

ὅσσα δὲ μὴ πεφίληκε Ζεύς,
  ἀτύζονται βοάν
Πιερίδων ἀΐοντα, γᾶν τε καὶ πόντον
  κατ' ἀμαιμάκετον,
15 ὅς τ' ἐν αἰνᾷ Ταρτάρῳ κεῖται, θεῶν
  πολέμιος,
Τυφὼς ἑκατοντακάρανος· τόν ποτε
  Κιλίκιον θρέψεν πολώνυμον
  ἄντρον· νῦν γε μάν
ταί θ' ὑπὲρ Κύμας ἁλιέρκεες ὄχθαι
  Σικελία τ' αὐτοῦ πιέζει στέρνα
  λαχνάεντα· κίων δ' οὐρανία
  συνέχει,
20 νιφόεσσ' Αἴτνα, πάνετες χιόνος
  ὀξείας τιθηνά·

From its depths purest flows of
unapproachable fire belch forth. By
day its rivers pour out a shining
stream of smoke, but in the
darkness a rolling red flame brings
boulders with a crash to the deep
flat of the sea. (25) That creature
sends aloft terrifying fountains of
Hephaestus; a wondrous prodigy
to behold, a wonder even to hear of
from those who were there.

τᾶς ἐρεύγονται μὲν ἀπλάτου πυρὸς
  ἁγνόταται
ἐκ μυχῶν παγαί· ποταμοὶ δ'
  ἀμέραισιν μὲν πρόχεοντι ῥόον
  καπνοῦ
αἴθων'· ἀλλ' ἐν ὄρφναισιν πέτρας
  φοίνισσα κυλινδομένα φλὸξ ἐς
  βαθεῖαν φέρει πόντου πλάκα συν
  πατάγῳ.
25 κεῖνο δ' Ἀφαίστοιο κρουνοὺς
  ἑρπετόν
δεινοτάτους ἀναπέμπει· τέρας μὲν
  θαυμάσιον προσιδέσθαι, θαῦμα
  δὲ καὶ παρεόντων ἀκοῦσαι.

There is geographical, even cosmic vastness in the canvas: from Cilicia in the east to Sicily in the west, practically the outer edges of the Greek world; from Typhos' prison in Tartarus to the heights of heaven; and on the third axis, Typhos' monstrous body, stretching from Sicily north to the Bay of Naples. 'Once' and 'now' in lines 16–17 capture in two words the whole of cosmological time. The description of the eruption of Etna was famous in antiquity,[2] and the volcano comes readily to Longinus' mind as an example of the sublime in nature (35.4, alluding to Pindar). Zeus's sleeping eagle is an unforgettable image, a stroke of mythological genius. The passage easily meets Longinus' first and greatest requirement, grandeur of conception, and the keynote of wonder, ubiquitous aspect of the sublime, is emphatically sounded at the end.

Our concern at the moment, however, is with shared experience, and in this respect too the passage offers much to admire. The poem opens with a hymn to the power of music (inherently self-reflexive as often in Pindar). The point is much more than the communal pleasure people feel at a concert. In Greek culture music had powerful ethical associations. Music was overwhelmingly heard not in solo recital but to accompany song, whose mood and ethical import the musical style reflected – the tumultuous dithyramb, as it might be, the dismal lament, the joyous paean, the spine-stiffening martial elegy. Choral celebrations for the gods were ubiquitous, and it was a vital part of young people's education that they should learn how to participate in them. Music and dance fostered personal and civic virtue, which explains why Plato spends so much time in the *Republic* and the *Laws* regulating them, and why conservative persons were so worried about musical innovations.[3] Different tunings of the lyre – *harmoniai* – did more than promote the ethical qualities associated with different performances; they embodied them. A moralizing attitude to music is hardly confined to antiquity, of course; think of the riot at the premier of *The Rite of Spring*, the symbolism of twelve-tone music in Thomas Mann's *Doctor Faustus*, or the hysterical denunciations of rock and roll (the devil's music) in the 1950s.

The lyre in particular, as opposed to the raucous aulos (the double pipe, a reed instrument), was felt to induce a sense of calm serenity. Longinus says (39.2) that, by the consonance (*sumphōniā*) of its sounds, the lyre exerts a 'wonderful enchantment' (*thaumaston thelgētron*) upon its audience. The language he uses suggests a physical intervention of the sound in the listener's constitution. He goes on to say that well-composed oratory has an even more powerful impact of this sort, because the words convey not only sound but meaning, and through the ideas and images they conjure up the speaker brings the audience to share his emotion and feel a sense of 'swelling, dignity and sublimity' (*ogkon te kai axiōma kai hupsos*, 39.3). Pindar also has this physical conception of sound, and he too speaks of enchantment (*thelgei*, line 12). His 'darts' (*kēla*) are only partly metaphorical, and there is a pun on *kēlei*, a synonym of *thelgei*. That poetry, and subsequently oratory, had this power of enchantment was a deeply embedded notion in archaic Greece.[4]

The poem celebrates Hieron of Syracuse's victory in the Pythian games of 470 BCE; it was performed in the city of Aetna, which Hieron had founded only a few years before. The celebration of the victory was at the same time a celebration of the new city – a grand occasion. The opening lines evoke choral performance; we may imagine, if we wish, a crowd of onlookers, with the Syracusan tyrant and his son Deinomenes, ruler of Aetna, prominently ensconced. The harmony of the music reflects the civic harmony; the music and dance in themselves would have helped create a feeling of bonding in the audience, whatever theme the poet had chosen, but his deployment of music itself both thematically and to reflect on the actual proceedings (the lyre having performed the very action described in the opening lines) redoubles the effect, surely creating in any well-disposed recipient the mood identified by Longinus.

The suggestion that the whole scene is mirrored in heaven then greatly amplifies the sublime uplift. Here too peace and concord prevail; Ares has left his weapons outside, and Zeus's thunderbolts are idle. The mighty eagle sleeps. The verb used of Ares, who warms or cheers his heart (*iainei*, 11), is used elsewhere of both gods and humans delighting in music at a celebration or symposium.[5] The divine scene in the first *Pythian* does indeed seem more like a symposium than a public choral performance; it is a quieter, indoor gathering of friends and relations (*philoi*). That companionable atmosphere may be read back onto the celebration on the ground below, however (whatever form it took), since both groups are emphatically contrasted with those who are *not* loved of Zeus, i.e. those who are not his *philoi* but his enemies (*echthroi*). In Greek mythology Typhos (also called Typhon, Typhaon and Typhoeus) posed a mortal threat to the dominion of Zeus; had Zeus lost the battle, chaos and lawlessness would have reigned instead of his justice and good order. This cosmic victory was celebrated by Greek poets from Hesiod onwards.[6] For the audience of this ode, the story had particular relevance owing to the proximity of the monster himself under the dangerous volcano (which had spectacularly erupted a few years before) – an excellent example of the Burkean sublime. Furthermore, the mythological victory parallels that of Hieron over the Etruscans at Cymae in 474, and of his brother Gelon over the Carthaginians at Himera in 480. These barbarous enemies, like Typhos, threatened to destroy the Greek order; they represent violence, *hvbris*, slavery (72–80). Finally, Hieron is contrasted with the wicked ruler Phalaris of Acragas; *his* memory will not be celebrated in symposia (95–8). From Homer on, the justice of wise human kings is underpinned by, and reflects, the justice of Zeus. Immediately after the description of Typhos, the chorus prays that they may please the king of gods (29); throughout the rest of the ode they pray for good fortune, glory, victory and euphonious celebrations like the one they are enjoying now (*euphōnoi thaliai*, 38). With Zeus's help, they say, Hieron and his son will lead the people to a harmonious peace, all voices sounding together (*sumphōnos hēsuchiā*, 70, like the *sumphōniā* of the lyre). Good cheer, good order, respectful dealings with fellows, devotion to the common weal: poem after poem in the archaic corpus praises these as the ideals both of the symposium and of public life. They all coincide in the first *Pythian*.[7]

We can well imagine the euphoria of the first audience. That we *can* do so is of course Pindar's doing. Naturally, at so far a remove, we have to elucidate the text's meaning by research, bringing other texts to bear (to grasp the significance of *sumphōniā*, for instance). We may be considered a tertiary audience. The first, primary audience needed far less assistance (though one should never forget that that audience was not homogeneous, and consisted of people with different levels of knowledge and poetic aptitude). Other Greeks living at the time of the first performance (the secondary audiences) would also have needed little assistance. As the ancient commentaries preserved in the scholia show, ancient readers eventually did need help, becoming themselves tertiary audiences. But everything I have said in my explication above is information that would have been available to the original secondary audiences. The careful engagement of these audiences is, in fact, a distinctive characteristic of Pindaric poetics and, as we shall see, of the experience of his sublimity. Consideration of this point will bring some matters of central importance to light.

## Primary and secondary (and tertiary) audiences

As Spelman has argued, Pindar's odes occupy a space between primary and secondary audiences.[8] Dozens of passages demonstrate Pindar's awareness of the latter, and indeed his mission of spreading fame absolutely requires him to reach it. At the same time, Pindar was writing on commission for particular patrons in particular circumstances, which means the poems will have local detail. While the primary audience is made fully aware of the future reception, the poems also convey to the secondary audience the fact of the first performance and its general character. Crucially, however, the secondary audience will not be prevented from appreciating the ode by lack of information. If, for instance, family members are mentioned, and it is important to know how they are related to the victor, Pindar tells us. As Spelman states, 'There is no place in the epinicians where further knowledge of the victor's personal circumstances would render an unclear text clear.'[9] While the odes often give an impression of the performative environment, they contain no deictic gestures or puzzling references that only the local audience could have understood. As Slater pointedly remarks:

[T]o find unassailable evidence in Pindar for the context of the triumph is not easy, not just because he is so miserly with detail. One tends to discover that even apparent detail is vague enough to belong to the whole symbolism of triumph and can be or is metaphorical, thereby plunging all similar detail into a no-man's land between image and reality. The word *kômos* is a song or procession with song, but when led by the Muse in her chariot, its outlines become understandably imprecise. The victory crater, the mitra, the victor's crown all turn out to be a song, which like a large metaphorical sponge absorbs to itself all the other associations of triumph, whether they are present or not.[10]

Spelman wryly comments that 'I would wager that there has been no actual occasion on which a performer of *Olympian* 1 took his lyre from its peg *after* beginning his song' (*à propos* lines 17–18), thus putting his finger on the weakness of readings that presume a close mimetic relationship of text and performance.[11] Such transparent fictionality obliges us, not to try to recover lost realities but to interpret the texts; to assess not the real world, but the kind of world the texts create. Apart from the circularity of many statements about the original context (projected as they are from the text which they are then used to read), an exclusive focus on first performances misses much of what is actually happening in the poems.

Spelman formulates the principle that 'when puzzled by Pindar's train of thought, we should work towards an understanding using knowledge that would have been available to his contemporary secondary audiences'.[12] If matters remain obscure, the reason is that we, a tertiary audience (whom Pindar hoped would exist, but about whose nature and experience he could have no knowledge), lack the information available to the secondary audience. Our access to that information has been steadily growing since Hölderlin's time, owing to new finds and patient analysis of epinician language, motifs, conventions and so on. These topics have often become clearer by bearing the original performative context in mind. But to insist that the primary audience at the first performance is the only or final arbiter of meaning is to misunderstand and underestimate the Pindaric ode.

When modern scholars attempt to recreate the experience of the first audience, in fact they do so on the basis of information also available to the *secondary* audience. Such information (about Cymae and Himera, for instance, or about lyres and symposia) might be deducible from the poem itself, or we might glean it from other ancient sources. If we now can discover such data, so could members of the secondary audience. One can object that much local knowledge, about persons in the poem, cults, myths, landmarks and so on, would in practice be available to very few members of the secondary audience, whereas modern research into, say, the archaeology of the local sanctuaries can bring such matters to light. We can never really gauge the extent of this difficulty for the secondary audience, of course; some items might in fact have been widely known to foreigners. More importantly, we must in the end revert to the text itself to determine the relevance of such knowledge to interpretation. The point at issue, therefore, is whether its absence damages or even prevents understanding of the poem, or whether it merely changes it. I shall argue for the second alternative, and that Pindar's technique creates an equally valid experience for his future audiences.

There are certainly times when acquiring new information can correct *mis*understanding: we may learn, for instance, that a certain poem is not by Pindar, or has been wrongly dated. Such philological work goes on to this day for poets of all ages. As tertiary audiences, modern readers are more exposed to that kind of error. At the most basic level, there are no native speakers of ancient Greek left in the world, and many nuances must be lost forever; we reconstruct the ancient *langue* as best we can, but our knowledge will never be more than an accumulation of *paroles*, and vital gaps in such knowledge there are bound to be. Yet even in this respect one can ask: who was the typical native Greek speaker? How many of them could compare, and study at leisure as we can, a sizeable body of Greek poetry from Pindar's day – epic, lyric, dramatic? Was their grasp of epinician convention as fine-grained as ours can be by analysing dozens of Pindaric and Bacchylidean odes? Could they ponder translations into different languages and assess the implications for Greek? It is easy to underestimate how much we do know, and the advantages conferred by our viewpoint.

Of course we will not and should not stop trying to learn more about the first occasion, but by inquiring instead or also about how we apprehend that occasion as represented in the text we may arrive at new readings and appreciation of Pindar's craft. This change in perspective can be liberating. There are many questions about the context of the first performance which the text might raise in our minds but which we cannot answer. Scholars deploy much effort and admirable learning in suggesting possible answers, making discoveries along the way, but there will come a point when one has to say 'the first audience knew, but we will never know', and throw up one's hands in defeat. If the limit of inquiry is the first audience's perspective (which, to repeat, was not unitary anyway), then indeed you are defeated. But if the ode is constructed in such a way as to be appreciated in satisfying ways by primary and secondary audiences, one can focus instead on the experience of the text as we have it without the sense of failure.

Closely linked to this stress on the original audience is the preoccupation of Hellenists during the last fifty years or so on the orality of Greek culture.[13] This approach has also produced a superabundance of lasting insights. But like any other perspective it involves its occlusions, and opens up some lines of inquiry at the expense of others. Among other things it tends to underestimate the high degree of literacy amongst a small elite in Greece, and the role of literacy in cultural communication. The international circulation of specific poems by named authors had been a feature of Greek culture for some time. Precisely how far back it goes remains a matter of intense debate (all the way to Homer and Hesiod? only as far as Sappho?), but it was certainly a feature of the late archaic cultural landscape, when Pindar was young. Solon (fr. 20) quotes Mimnermus (fr. 6), for instance; Homer 'springs into life' in the late sixth century with quotation after quotation, the invention of a biography, and even a book of allegorical interpretation by Theagenes of Rhegium;[14] Simonides (fr. 273 Poltera) quotes Stesichorus; Hecataeus (fr. 19 *EGM*) cites Hesiod. The very survival of so many poems must have depended on archaic originals – they cannot be later distillations of oral transmission. Contemporary reperformance of poems such as Pindar's would also depend, at a minimum, on a text memorized word for word; that is, ultimately on a written version. So the circulation of poems as fixed texts was nothing new.

Modern studies of orality vs literacy tend to drive a harder line between them than Pindar himself would have perceived. Society did not move from one all-embracing condition (orality) to another because of the advent of literacy (which always works in conjunction with many other cultural factors). Pindar clearly envisages future reception as reperformance, not reading, and he and Bacchylides alike speak again and again of fame delivered by resounding voices.[15] Yet he could not have thought that worldwide fame of his poems could be guaranteed by poets like himself travelling to the four corners of the world and instructing local performers. There was no global network of epinician singers as there was of epic bards perpetuating an inherited encyclopedic tradition. Each epinician was a one-off, fixed text. The written text was not at odds with its performed version; it was an enabler opening up new possibilities of circulation and engagement.

In this enriched atmosphere Pindar's interventions were of a different order from those of his predecessors. Apart from references to named poets, there are many general references to older poets and poetic practices, and close intertextual relationships with earlier poems.[16] He is intensely conscious of poetic history, and inscribes himself into it with a clear implication that he, or rather his texts, will be part of it in the future. He reads the older poets as he expects to be read. All of this looks very much like a literary experience. Accordingly, scholars have begun to consider the ways in which Pindar's odes deserve to be called literature in a strong sense, with all due attention to what that term might mean in a transcultural context.[17] To quote Maslov: 'The distinctiveness of literary discourse lies in a pervasive, obsessive awareness of its own historicity, of its own nature as a trans-national and trans-lingual tradition that reaches far back into the past'; and again: 'Pindaric poetics participates in the historical in a way that would be inconceivable in earlier literary forms.'[18]

Actually being present at the premiere was of course a unique experience. But the difference in Pindar is that being in the secondary audience does not create an inferior one. Contrast again his predecessors. Some of them evince awareness of a posterity that clearly goes beyond being an anonymous link in an endless tradition (as is the convention in epic poetry). That is, the poets presume the survival of their texts, with their names attached (see e.g. Alcman *PMGF* 39, Sappho frr. 58A,[19] 65,147, Theognis 22). At the same time, however, texts such as those of Alcman and Sappho contain impenetrable references to local matters, and leave us (and ancient readers) utterly baffled as to the meaning, and the original performative context. Though anticipating future fame, these poets did not always take into account the changed perspective of the secondary audience. Perhaps they thought that their poems would continue to be used in contexts like the ones for which they were composed, and would be comprehensible to a similarly constituted primary audience. Pindar's technique is differently oriented from conception onwards: he assumes both the primary audience and a wide, Panhellenic range of secondary audiences.

Moreover, a poem so conceived – anchored in, but transcending the particular occasion – becomes a textualized experience. This is self-evidently true upon reperformance, but it is true also in an important sense of the first performance. The text was prepared in advance, and its purpose was to bring out the occasion's meaning, not to record the proceedings. The premiere was thus not only the first performance but already the first reception. Some poems, indeed, advertise the fact that they *are* being received from an author who was unable to attend.[20] For all audiences the key to understanding the text must be its manner of representation. By its nature, this text has removed the primacy of any one point of view for interpretation.

Attic tragedy offers an instructive parallel. The plays, already circulating by means of reperformance and texts, were a prominent part of Pindar's contemporary literary landscape. They were easily detached from their original production context, the Dionysiac festivals of ancient Athens, and offered profound explorations of ethical, political and philosophical questions, in poetry of great beauty and power. Every reader or viewer would have had a different interpretation. Pindar's poetry offers equally rich matter for contemplation. It too was detachable from its occasion. Yet it differs from tragedy in retaining a relationship, even after being put into circulation, with that first occasion. This is a natural entailment of the lyric genres. But for epinicians in particular, the link to the occasion is what creates the opportunity for the sublime moment, as we shall see.

## The lyric 'now' and lyric experience: Being there

For all the difficulties of the terms 'lyric' in a Greek context,[21] the quest for transhistorical similarities is not deluded. Pindar's injunction to 'take the Dorian lyre from its peg' in the first *Olympian* perfectly illustrates the trope of apostrophe explored by Culler in *Theory of the Lyric*. The command is ostensibly directed at somebody in the same room as the poet, but, as he already holds the lyre in his hand, it is obviously a statement about the *sort* of thing that one does on these occasions, just as modern songs exhort their listeners to 'strike up the band' or the like. 'Dorian', moreover, does not (so far as we know) refer to any specific type of lyre; it is an epithet transferred from the Doric literary dialect of the *poem*, and/or the ethics and values the Dorian Greeks espoused (cf. *O*.3.5, fr. 191). Apostrophes 'often tell the addressee something the addressee presumably already knows' (in this case, that the lyre is already off the peg); the poem 'thus acquires a ritual character', because the apostrophe's generic nature makes it iterable and paradigmatic.[22] The notionally deictic 'you' is anyone and everyone, every time the poem is read or performed. The technique means that the poem 'presents itself as an event in time that repeats', creating 'an effect of presence'.[23] The poem is 'not the fictional representation of an experience or event so much as an attempt to be itself an event';[24] and that event is a property of the text.

The apostrophe of the lyre presumes that in some sense you think it hears you (otherwise why address it?). In the first *Pythian*, it not only hears you; it gives commands, which singers and dancers obey. The apostrophe has magically transformed it. The trope entails a gesture to what is beyond the lyre, to what it instantiates, to what is not visible in the inanimate object. In other words, apostrophes render objects potentially sublime, since – however successful the process of signification seems to be – there must always be a residue of meaning that escapes signification; yet at the same time, given the meaningfulness of the object, the urge to pin down and articulate the surplus meaning is irresistible, if perpetually frustrated.

That sublime potential is fully realized in the first *Pythian*. This is not just any lyre, it is a golden one (material of the gods), and it is 'own champion of Apollo and the ivy-tressed Muses'. How does that work, exactly, in relation to the instrument actually in Pindar's hand? Note the choice of the word *kteanon*, possession; what I have translated as 'own champion' is literally 'champion-possession' ('champion' is grammatically an adjective in the Greek): Pindar is very focused on the lyre as an object. Now is he really saying that *this* lyre is theirs? Does *this* lyre quench the thunderbolt? Where precisely is the lyre's advocacy occurring? Within five lines we are transported to Olympus – or are the gods already with us here? Pindar is like Apollo, his choruses are like the Muses; how deep can that comparison run without blasphemy?

We cannot answer. In fact it would be fatal to the sublime experience if we *could* capture the excess of meaning. Culler offers this delectable quotation from Stephen Booth:

> What does the human mind ordinarily want most? It wants to understand what it does not understand. And what does the human mind customarily do to achieve that goal? It works away—sometimes only for a second or two, sometimes for years—until it understands. What does the mind have then? What it wanted? No. What it has is an understanding of something that it now understands. What it wanted was to understand what it did not understand.[25]

Readers of Plato's *Symposium* will be reminded of Diotima's description of love as that which always desires, but never attains, its object. Lyric apostrophe is as much an address to the audience as it is to the object or person,[26] and the apostrophe of the lyre brings all audiences – primary or otherwise – into an immediate three-way affective relationship with it and the poet.

The lyric 'now', the 'now' implicit in the apostrophe, is a special kind of time, an endlessly repeatable (but not timeless) present in which we participate as others have participated before and will participate after.[27] The first word of the fourth *Pythian* is 'today'; that 'today' did not end at sunset of the first performance, as Pindar well knew when he put the poem into circulation. For any subsequent audience or reader, that 'today' becomes their today. In some respects Pindar's procedure was not new; it partly replicates the experience of every symposium, when the guests recited sympotic poems of Alcaeus, Anacreon or Theognis, which are replete with transferable deixis (if only in the imagination) and subjects easily figured as typical (to appreciate Theognis it is not necessary for the historical addressee Kyrnos to be there with you: you understand his function in the poems). The lyric 'now' ensures that the experience can be repeated an infinite number of times in the future.

Pindar did not invent this 'now', but he invested it with such energy that it becomes a source of sublimity, raising questions that can neither be avoided nor answered. Scholars' determined pursuit of the first occasion is in fact a testimony to his success. In what I wrote above about the first *Pythian*, I tried to imagine what it was like to *be there*, and watch Pindar playing the golden lyre. But of course I cannot be there. Here it is useful to invoke Frank Ankersmit's 'sublime historical experience': the awareness that something has been lost forever, combined with the irresistible desire to bridge the gap and repair the loss; it is a 'paradoxical union of the feelings of love and loss, that is, the combination of pain and pleasure in how we relate to the past' – a Kantian oscillation.[28] Great historians bring the past to life again; they create an illusion of actually being there. But the sublime experience arises not from forgetting that it is an illusion, but from the background awareness that it is. The closer we think we get to that reality, the greater the sense that we cannot bridge that last gap and erase time. The otherness of the past is absolute and irreducible; its similarity, on the other hand, unmistakable and seductive. The relationship with the past is affective, even erotic, but can never be consummated. The fascination of modern scholars with the first occasion looks very much like the same phenomenon; it is their 'known unknown', as Keats's Psyche was to Cupid (*Endymion* ii.739). We know there *was* a real occasion, a 'there' at which to be – nothing purely fictional as in, say, Theocritus' *Idylls* – but its precise nature lies out of reach.

Pindar's text urgently invites the reader to imagine the 'now' of the first performance. It brings the reader into its world. It does so through vivid but *generic* evocation of the event, which ancient readers could elaborate from their own experience. What it does not and must not do is provide overly specific detail, since that would frustrate and discourage such an engagement, and defeat the strategy. The strategy is to create a sense of the first occasion sufficiently seductive to make us want the physical experience of being there, and wonder what it was like, even though we can never have it.

It is time to consider an example. I offer the third *Olympian*, not hitherto on many lists of great Pindaric moments.[29] The opening lines identify the occasion as a theoxenia for the Dioscuri, that is a feast at which Castor and Polydeuces were welcomed as invisible guests (though sometimes represented by statues).[30] Theron of Acragas has arranged it to celebrate his Olympic victory (the same as is celebrated in the second *Olympian*). The twins are called 'hospitable'; they reflect the salient quality of the feast itself. Pindar (or the speaking 'I' of the poem; line 5 mentions dance, suggesting a choral execution) vows to please them and their sister Helen (a regular guest at their theoxenia). He has set up a song of praise for Theron (the implication is that this is how he pleases them), and the Muse has stood by him in his invention of a shiny new (*neosīgalos*) way of fitting the song of the splendid revel (*aglaokōmos*) to the Dorian sandal (i.e. as accompaniment to the dance, which is already under way); this he is required to do by the wreaths upon his hair, commingling the many-voiced (*poikilogārus*) lyre, the shrill cry of the auloi and the ordered words in fitting praise of the son of Aenesidamus. Pisa too requires this (line 9), host city of the Olympic games, whence divine songs emanate all over the world for anyone who receives upon his locks the ornament of the olive tree (the prize for an Olympic victory): 'which' Heracles first brought from the land of the Hyperboreans when he established the games (the relative pronoun is, as often, the pivot into the myth).[31]

These self-references reflect the glitter of the occasion and draw attention to the art of the poet, as in the opening of the first *Pythian*; among other things demonstrating his craft are three neologisms in five lines (the three words I have transliterated above, which occur nowhere else in surviving Greek). This ode is itself one of the songs emanating from Pisa all over the world; Pindar thus indicates the existence of the secondary audience, and includes them in the poem for the benefit of both audiences. The mention of Pisa is a paratactic shock; its clause is seemingly tacked on to the end of a lengthy sentence, and its verb has already receded into the distance. It is placed thus to fashion the transition to the myth, anything but casually, but the syntax imitates uncontrolled excitement, in the aesthetics of surprise. The unexpected, seemingly stream-of-consciousness intrusion of Pisa collapses the distance between Pisa and Acragas: Pisa is right here, exacting its due.

The image of the festival having been firmly planted in our minds, the ode turns to the myth of Heracles and the olive tree, which he fetches from the land of the Hyperboreans to provide welcome shade at Olympia. These legendary folk 'beyond the North Wind' inhabit a kind of paradise, which only the most privileged of mortals may visit – Heracles, for instance, and Perseus (see *P.*10.45). Theron is told here that, with his victory, fame and prosperity, he has reached the limit of human achievement, metaphorically expressed as the Pillars of Heracles (see line 44 below); the world beyond the Pillars is in the same conceptual space as the land of the Hyperboreans, and not accessible. Yet although Theron cannot go there like Heracles or Perseus, a piece of their land can come to him, in the form of the olive wreath. The relative pronoun 'which' elides the difference between the present-day tree and the primeval tree. Not coincidentally the wreaths adorning the chorus have just been mentioned. As mediators between human and divine these wreaths are comparable to the lyre of the first *Pythian*. It is a synecdoche for the poem itself; the inference is encouraged that the poem hails from that remote land, or is somehow in touch with it. Certainly it comes from the Muses on Olympus.

After basking for some time in the pleasant warmth of the myth, we return of a sudden to the present:

| | |
|---|---|
| Now too to this festival | καί νυν ἐς ταύταν ἑορτὰν ἵλαος |
|     graciously he comes |     ἀντιθέοισιν νίσεται |
| 35 With the godlike twin sons of deep- | 35 σὺν βαθυζώνοιο διδύμοις παισὶ |
|     robed Leda. |     Λήδας. |
| | |
| For to them on his ascent to Olympus | τοῖς γὰρ ἐπέτραπεν Οὔλυμπόνδ' ἰὼν |
|     he gave stewardship of the |     θαητὸν ἀγῶνα νέμειν |
|     wonderful contest | ἀνδρῶν τ' ἀρετᾶς πέρι καὶ ῥιμφαρμάτου |
| Of men for their skill and driving the | διφρηλασίας. ἐμὲ δ' ὦν πᾳ θυμὸς ὀτρύνει |
|     dashing chariots. |     φάμεν Ἐμμενίδαις |
| But I feel somehow urged to say that | Θήρωνί τ' ἐλθεῖν κῦδος εὐίππων |
|     glory has come to the Emmenids | διδόντων Τυνδαριδᾶν, ὅτι πλείσταισι |
| And to Theron as a gift of the |     βροτῶν |
|     Tyndarids, fine cavaliers, | 40 ξεινίαις αὐτοὺς ἐποίχονται τραπέζαις, |
| 40 Because they approach them with | |
|     hospitable boards exceeding all | |
|     others, | |
| | |
| And piously keep the rites of the blessed | εὐσεβεῖ γνώμᾳ φυλάσσοντες μακάρων |
|     ones. |     τελετάς. |
| If water is best, and of possessions gold | εἰ δ' ἀριστεύει μὲν ὕδωρ, κτεάνων δὲ |
|     most reverend, |     χρυσὸς αἰδοιέστατος, |
| Now Theron in his excellence has | νῦν δὲ πρὸς ἐσχατιὰν Θήρων ἀρεταῖσιν |
|     reached the extremity |     ἱκάνων ἅπτεται |
| And from his native home lays hands | οἴκοθεν Ἡρακλέος σταλᾶν. τὸ πόρσω δ' |
|     on the pillars of Heracles. Beyond |     ἐστὶ σοφοῖς ἄβατον |
|     them | 45 κἀσόφοις. οὔ νιν διώξω· κεινὸς εἴην. |
| 45 No person wise or foolish may tread. I | |
|     shall not pursue it; vain were I then. | |

'Now too to this festival he (Heracles) graciously (*hīlaos*) comes', just as he came to the Games long ago. *Hīlaos* is the word used of deities who join in the exultation of their worshippers, smile benignly on them and grant their wishes; and the proverbially gluttonous Heracles was very fond of theoxenia. The Dioscuri are here, for it is their theoxenia, but Heracles comes too, because he entrusted the oversight of the Olympic Games to the twins. That he did so seems to be a personal inspiration of Pindar's; it is not attested elsewhere. The Dioscuri competed in Heracles' first Games, however, and such a role for them makes eminent sense, exemplary young men as they are (and they are stewards of games at *N*.10.52).[32] Pindar goes on to suggest that the Dioscuri have granted glory to Theron and his clan *because* they approach them with guest-welcoming hospitality more than any other mortals, piously observing the rites of the blessed ones (*makares*) – that is, in feasts like this one. The Hyperboreans are called *makares* in *Pythian* 10.46, and in *Olympian* 2.70, the companion ode to this one, the word is applied to those humans who live three pious lives and finally reach paradise. Theron would have considered himself a candidate.

In this closing triad, the world of myth merges with the world of the present. 'Now too to this festival':[33] the closing pivot is as sudden as the opening 'which', a surprise perhaps mirroring the just-mentioned wonder of Heracles, struck by the beauty of the olive trees. At any rate, the sequel is brimming with wonder. For those who were there at the theoxenia, the full meaning becomes clear in this sublime moment: Heracles and the Dioscuri are here, now, just as they were at the Games in the beginning; the Dioscuri, guardians of the Games, have granted Theron his victory; they have crowned him with the Hyperborean wreath (that one, there!), like the ones we are wearing; they did so because of the many theoxenia, this one and others before (and surely more to come). We who come after cannot feel the physical excitement in the same way, but we can imagine what it was like to be there; and we have what they did not, the luxury of contemplating it as a literary experience, by virtue of the lyric 'now'. The repeated deixis works not because Pindar points to anything specific to Acragas, but rather to generic features familiar to every Greek. 'This' festival happens every time the poem is performed, wherever it is performed (or read); and it must be an impoverished imagination that cannot still see the young twin riders there on the couches.

## Occasions: The Pindaric *kōmos*

Let us look more closely at the Pindaric occasion we are so urgently invited to attend. In the third *Olympian*, as we have just seen, the poet leads us to think of a well-known kind of festival, a theoxenia, as the setting. Similarly the fifth *Pythian* suggests performance at Apollo's festival of the Carneia (80), the ninth *Olympian* at the festival of the Locrian Ajax (112), the tenth *Nemean* at the Heraea in Argos (23), and the fourth *Isthmian* during the Heraclea at Thebes (62). Other odes suggest performance at a sanctuary (whether or not as part of a regular festival is less clear: *O*.14 at a shrine of the Graces in Orchomenus, *P*.11 at the Ismenion in Thebes, *N*.8 at the heroon of Aeacus).[34] Conversely, the language and themes of some poems such as the second *Isthmian* suggest a symposium, which was a more private affair. But in most cases there are no such pointers, or they are ambiguous. Significantly, most of the locations mentioned above for public performance are merely inferences from Pindar's verbal gestures of supplication, arrival and the like, and are by no means certain. 'Suggest' is the key word here. Some of the poems that bring a symposium to mind do so through the use of sympotic imagery, which will certainly be doing other work in the first place and does not oblige us to infer that this was the setting. Of course there *was* a first occasion, but because of this flexibility the poems could often work in various settings, on first performance and even more on reperformance. Believing that the real first occasion determines meaning, scholars have argued about the possibilities for a long time, wishing to find that one true occasion for each poem; but the argument was always doomed to be inconclusive.[35] I do not say that the question should not be asked, because we must still work out how texts relate to occasions, in general; I say only that for epinicians the relationship is less direct than has sometimes been thought, and more interesting for that. Some readers may suspect me of being anti-historicist, but the opposite is true: the received view about the primacy of the first audience is not consistent with the evidence of the poems themselves for their composition and functioning.[36]

The performance setting Pindar most often evokes in the epinicians is neither public feast nor less public symposium, but the *kōmos*; he seems even to designate his productions as 'songs of the *kōmos*'.[37] The *kōmos* was a band of revellers, parading through the streets with torches, music and song; it could take various forms ranging from a formalized ritual for Dionysus to an impromptu celebration of friends. The most notorious manifestation, inevitably, lies at the riotous end of the spectrum, a *kōmos* in which inebriated young men might pick fights with bystanders as they bowled along, call upon friends' houses demanding entry and drink, or stop at a courtesan's house in the hope of admission. In Plato's *Symposium*, there are two *kōmoi*: the first, though led by an already intoxicated Alcibiades, is relatively well behaved, asking the host's permission to enter, while the second simply crashes into the house at the end of the dialogue, and all order breaks down. There are many references also in comedy (which genre too was popularly understood to be the 'song of the *kōmos*', *kōmōidia*); of particular relevance to Pindar is the joyful and on the whole decorous *kōmos* associated with victory, which included songs in praise.[38] Both Pindar and Bacchylides refer to revels at the site of the games immediately after the victories,[39] while the odes often figure themselves as part of a *kōmos* happening later in the victor's city.[40] Though the odes are self-evidently prepared texts, they aim to evoke the *kōmos*' exuberance and spontaneity. So here we have what appears to be an important clue to the original context of at least some, perhaps many, of the poems. On examination, however, Pindar's references turn out to be less helpful than one might have hoped, if looking for a window onto the first performance. But that very elusiveness will prove to be the point.

The relationship of the texts to their performance is oblique; they are not scripts for or transcripts of ritual action. Of course the poems *could* in many cases have been performed as part of a *kōmos*, perhaps at a waystation along the route of a formal procession. However, even if we could know for certain that a given ode really was performed during a *kōmos*, it would hardly begin to be explained by this fact.[41] In the case of the fifth *Pythian*, for instance, Ferrari has shown that the geographical pointers – the grove of Aphrodite (24), the tombs of Battos and the Battiads (93–8) – do not accord at all well with Cyrenean topography, if we take them as marking the route of an actual procession. We are dealing with an 'ideal, rather than a factual journey focused on the foundation and history of the Libyan town'.[42]

In the first *Nemean* (19–22), the speaker says he has come to a halt in the victor's forecourt, and that a feast is prepared for him within. The arrival of the procession and subsequent hospitality is a well-documented phenomenon in Greek life, especially in association with celebrations. One imagines the group moving through the streets, singing this very ode, which is indeed called an *enkōmion melos* (a song in the *kōmos*) in line 7. But only the most literal-minded (and unpoetic) reader would argue that this group *must* have timed its arrival at the door to coincide with line 19. The lines are significantly placed at the point in the ode where the poet turns to praise the victor directly. The verses here tie into a carefully spun web of important themes in the ode.[43] Note that Chromius' hospitality explicitly encompasses foreigners (22), among whom of course is Pindar. The point stresses the international dimension of the events, and allows Pindar to underscore his own pivotal role as the poet.[44] So when the speaker says 'I have taken my stand in hospitable Chromius' forecourt' it is a metaphorical arrival in the first place, a real one only incidentally and not necessarily. The trope states in effect 'I bring you this ode, and immortalize your largesse.' 'I have taken my stand' is an example of the 'arrival' motif and should be compared with passages like 'My heart tastes hymns, not without the Aeacidae [= Aeginetans, but so designating them reminds one of the mythological relationship of Thebes and Aegina through Aeacus]; I have come with the Graces to the sons of Lampon and this well-ordered city' (*I*.5.21–2), or 'And now with [lyre and pipes] I have landed with Diagoras, hymning Rhodes' (*O*.7.13–14).[45] 'I have taken my stand in Chromius' forecourt' works like 'take the lyre off the peg' in *Olympian* 1.17: an emblematic statement, indefinitely repeatable.

Another example is the sixth *Olympian* for Hagesias of Syracuse. In line 99 Pindar asks Hieron to welcome Hagesias' *kōmos*, in effect this poem, which has travelled from Stymphalus in Arcadia (where Hagesias still had citizenship) to his home in Syracuse; some scholars therefore conclude that the poem was performed in Stymphalus. Probably it was (at a festival of Hera? line 88), but there is nothing to tell us this until the end of the poem, and references to Syracuse at the beginning (6, 18) create a presumption that we are in Sicily. At line 22, the speaker exhorts Phintis, the winning driver – one assumes he is being roused from his home in Syracuse – to yoke up the mules and take us all to Pitana in Laconia. This metaphorical cart-ride is the pivot to the myth, since the eponymous nymph Pitana was mother of Evadna, mother of Iamos, the ancestor of Hagesias' clan of prophets based in Olympia at the time of the ode. Evadna for her part dwelled in Arcadia, whence Hagesias' maternal ancestors came (77–81). All these locales are tied together in the metaphorical journeys of mule-cart and *kōmos*, which in turn are identical with the poem. To these locations, with some emphasis, Pindar adds his own Thebes (85), whence he entrusts the poem to one Aeneas (the chorus-master) to deliver. Performances in both Stymphalus and Syracuse are plausible, but do not explain the ode's imaginative strategy. Pindar has taken Hagesias' 'two anchors' (101), i.e. his two homes, as an opportunity to create a Panhellenic panorama.[46] The two primary audiences are made aware of each other, and of themselves as part of a very big picture. The closing lines pray for 'famous fortune' for both peoples (Arcadian and Syracusan), for a trouble-free voyage, and to 'swell the joyous flower of my hymns'. Following as it does on 'famous fortune', the real voyage (Stymphalus to Syracuse) has shaded into a metaphor for life's voyage, to whose fame (if granted) the poet links his own. There is temporal legerdemain too: from a Stymphalian point of view, the closing lines look forward, hoping for more good fortune, and underscoring the role of poetry in securing worldwide fame; for the Syracusans, listening to the ode after its arrival, the prayer for the safe literal voyage has manifestly been granted, so they can be confident about the rest. The prayer is addressed to Poseidon, whose element the sea binds the Greek world together. We as the secondary or tertiary audience share his god's-eye view (which is identical with the poet's), seeing both ends at once; and we are the proof that the poet's hymns have prospered.

The space created by the poem, its real locus of meaning, is conceptual and atemporal.

So the outlines of the *kōmos* are, as Slater put it, imprecise.[47] Agócs's apt term is 'Protean'.[48] The one led by the Muses to which Slater refers is that at the opening of the ninth *Nemean*, where Pindar says to the goddesses 'let us go in a *kōmos* from Sicyon [site of the games] to Aetna, where wide-open doors are overrun with guests, to Chromius' happy home', then exhorts them to start the song (i.e. this poem). It is not too much to say that every reference to the *kōmos* has metapoetic implications. In the sixth *Isthmian* (57), for instance, the poet has 'come as steward of the *kōmoi* for Phylacidas, Pytheas and Euthymenes'; the next lines summarize the achievements of this illustrious family (the present ode celebrates the most recent one of Phylacidas). So these *kōmoi* are past, present and future: in other words, they stand for the poem's act of memorialization and could happen at any time. In the third *Pythian* (73), Pindar says that, had he come in person to Syracuse bringing a *kōmos* to Hieron, he would have 'added lustre to the wreaths of Pythian contests' and outshone the very stars. The *kōmos* here is one that cannot actually happen; it is shorthand for the entirety of the poet's contribution, in this instance curtailed by circumstances (though he nonetheless delivers an immortal *pis aller*). The extratextual *kōmos* is in effect appropriated by the odes even on first performance. In reception, there is no *kōmos* but the ode itself, which invites us to share its experience. The more successfully the poet enables us to be there, the more sublime the experience will be.

The melding of the two *kōmoi*, extra- and intratextual, is particularly clear in some cases. In the closing lines of the second *Nemean*, the citizens are exhorted to 'celebrate (*kōmaxate*) Zeus [god of the Nemean games] for Timodemus with his glorious homecoming; begin (*exarchete*) with melodious voice'. The verb *exarchete* is actually a technical term for leading off or starting;[49] the ode ends by asking the *kōmos* (which is notional first, real second) to do what it has itself just done. The end of the ninth *Nemean* is similar: the poet sketches the lively scene of a symposium, 'sweet harbinger of the *kōmos*', and in his last words prays that he will be able to sing his victor's praises better than anybody else. The final line of the fourth *Isthmian* announces 'I will celebrate (*kōmaxomai*) him, anointing him with delightful song (*charis*)'. (The *Charites* are the Graces, symbolizing the reciprocal goodwill and civilized joy of such occasions; Pindar associates them regularly with song, specifically that of the *kōmos* at O.4.9 and I.3.8, and at *Nem.* 9.54, just discussed.) Such futures, variously dubbed 'epinician', 'encomiastic' or 'performative', refer predominantly in the odes to what is being done on the present occasion, not a future one.[50] When such a future occupies the very last line, however, it must escape the bounds of the poem. These closing exhortations and future tenses look forward to the continuation of praise, in whatever form that might take. When any future audience hears or reads the poem, it become the *kōmos*.

Pindar's lexical usage confirms these points about the *kōmos*. If Pindar speaks of *epikōmios humnos* (song of praise on the occasion of, *epi-*, a *kōmos*: *N*.8.50), or of the *enkōmion melos* (a song in the *kōmos*: *O*.2.47, *N*.1.7), *enkōmioi humnoi* (*P*.10.53), or just *epikōmia* (*N*.6.32), this seems straightforward: the song is only one part of the *kōmos*. But then there are passages where he blurs the difference and quite significantly uses *kōmos* to refer to the song itself.[51] Most interesting is *N*.4.11, where the first strophe of the ode is called the *humnou prokōmion*, the pre-*kōmos* part of the hymn. What follows might then be considered the *enkōmios humnos*, the in-*kōmos* part of the hymn, so that *prokōmion* means no more than 'prelude'. Yet this overlooks the fact that *prokōmion* occurs nowhere else in Greek and is very likely Pindar's coinage. It should be doing special work. Note the subtle genitive (*humnou*) which reverses the hierarchy: it makes the *prokōmion* belong to the hymn ('my hymn's pre-*kōmos* part'), whereas in the expression *enkōmios humnos* the hymn belongs to the *kōmos* ('[my poem is] the *kōmos*'s hymn-part'). Pindar's song has taken over. His word *prokōmion* does not oblige us to think of the rest of the poem as an *en-kōmion*, i.e. part of something external to it; indeed, it rather discourages it: logically, one just drops the *pro-*, and the rest *is* the *kōmos*.

Pindar's prefaces are often the most carefully wrought part of the poem; 'may this be my *prokōmion*' has obvious metapoetic force. This is much more than an example of lyric's seemingly universal habit of referring to itself and the circumstances of its performance. One of Alcman's *Partheneia* (*PMGF* 3) provides a useful contrast to illustrate the point. The speaker at the beginning of the poem anticipates going to the festival, while later on she is there and describes what is going on. Alcman sets up then executes the song and, as often in lyric of all ages, dramatizes its coming-into-being as if it is happening before our very eyes. Pindar also sets up then executes the song, but his *prokōmion* has a quite different character. There is no anticipation, and no deixis. The proem says that *euphrosunā* (good cheer, joy; in context, a metonymy for *kōmos*) is the best healer of *ponoi* (pains and troubles, often used by Pindar to denote the athlete's arduous efforts) after they are done; songs charm them away; praise accompanied by the lyre soothes the limbs more than the warm bath; and the word lasts longer than the deed, if drawn deep from the mind with the favour of the Charites. One would not know from any of this that the poem *was* composed for a specific occasion. So where Alcman's poem looks consistently outwards to its context of performance, Pindar begins with inward-looking metapoetic remarks about memorialization. Note too the role of the Muses: in Homer, the poet ostensibly passes on what they tell him; whereas Pindar's poetry, though dependent on divine favour, is now also the product of his own deep thought. The whole argument is of a piece: *euphrosunā*, the *kōmos* and Pindar's song are equated.[52]

Though we can see how quickly the epinician genre developed conventions, it was still young and feeling its way when Pindar took it over. Like Greek tragedy, it fed omnivorously on everything it could find in Greek cultural tradition: sympotic poetry, choral poetry of all kinds, epic, myth, prayer, fable, wisdom-literature. This self-conscious hybridity provides Maslov with one of his central arguments for claiming that literature emerges with Pindar.[53] It is therefore unsurprising to find Pindar foregrounding his thought about the genre in which he was writing. His coinage *prokōmion* reflects such meditations. *Aglaokōmos* in O.3.6, also a unique word (above, p. 71), is another example.

The difference from Bacchylides' practice is instructive, and shows that even if we regard all of this as somehow (merely?) conventional, individual poets can handle matters differently. Bacchylides makes far fewer references to *kōmoi*, and never uses the so-called '*dexai*-motif', in which the poet asks someone to 'receive' (*dexai*) the *kōmos*.[54] Pindar uses it five times in the epinicians, usually accompanied by a deictic adjective: 'receive this *kōmos*'.[55] This expression has often been taken as a 'here and now' (*hic et nunc*) deictic reference to the poem itself, being performed at that moment by *kōmastai*. Again, yes, that could well be the case, but it doesn't tell us what is going on in the poem. Notice that in the eighth *Olympian* it is the sanctuary of Pisa being asked to receive the *kōmos*; the speaker is, needless to say, not in Pisa but in Aegina. In the fourth *Nemean* it is the 'seat of the Aeacidae', i.e. the entire island of Aegina, which welcomes the band. This request follows immediately on 'may this be the *prokōmion* of my hymn', which sequence further confirms the equation of *kōmos* and poem I argued for above. In the thirteenth *Olympian* the 'institution of the *kōmos*' has supposedly travelled all the way from Olympia (where the victory was won) to Corinth (where the victor lives). The receivers in real life were gods or hosts; they can be that in the poems too, but these instances show that the purpose of such references is to establish an affective and symbolic relationship between giver (poet) and receiver (victor and compatriots), with metapoetic implications. Moreover, the *dexai*-motif is one example among many of how Pindar's poems are full of restless energy and movement. They are always leaving, arriving, being sent, being received, taking shape, being finished, flying around the world: perpetual events.

Because the space of the *kōmos* is notional, the poet can range across its spectrum of associations at will, sometimes within the confines of a single ode, without being obliged merely to echo the circumstances of a particular performance. At one end of the spectrum there is the symposium. Any symposium, if it took to the streets, became a *kōmos*, and any *kōmos*, if admitted indoors, became a symposium. At such intimate gatherings of friends, individuals sang or recited many kinds of poetry, including songs of praise. This was the cradle of aristocratic culture and the context of a large percentage of surviving Greek lyric poetry. At the other end of the spectrum the *kōmos* could be part of a formal public event (such as the Carneia at Cyrene), strongly resembling a *choros*, the group of singers and dancers performing in state-sponsored rites for the gods. In between are other possibilities like the large outdoor banquet that is the theoxenia in the third *Olympian*, where Pindar calls his song *aglaokōmos* (6), a song of the splendid revel.[56]

Of the shifting modes within the same poem there are ready examples. In the first *Olympian*, though there are no overt indicators of a performance venue, it is 'inherently implausible', as Carey puts it, 'that a grand song of praise like this was squandered on an informal gathering',[57] especially one funded by the tyrant of Syracuse (who also paid for a grand ode by Bacchylides for the same victory, his epinician 5). Yet in line 14 we read '(Hieron) glories also in the finest of the Muses' art, such as we men often sing around the table. Take the Dorian lyre off its peg ...': we are in the world of the symposium. Hieron's court is here flatteringly portrayed as cosy and amicable, his door always open to cultivated persons and foreign guests. It is an image burnished for public consumption.[58] The sixth *Pythian* opens with the suggestion of a procession approaching the temple of Apollo at Delphi, but closes by complimenting the victor's son and charioteer on his social graces in the symposium.[59] The poem itself is called a treasury, but one which, unlike the city-treasuries at Delphi, will be impervious to the elements and last forever. A public monument, therefore; but the procession that leads the way does so in the name of Aphrodite and the Graces, goddesses of love and song, who are at home in the symposium. The close of *Olympian* 7 evokes public feasts hosted by the clan of the Eratidae,[60] and this ode which celebrates so memorably the foundations myths of the island was, we are told, publicly displayed by the Rhodians in an inscription with gold letters. Yet it opens with a homely image of the bride's father toasting his new son-in-law at a symposium: so too does Pindar offer this poem to Diagoras. The ninth *Nemean* opens with a metaphorical *kōmos* travelling from Sicyon to Aetna, arriving ultimately at Chromius' house; at the end of the poem we have extended sympotic language: 'peace loves the symposium; a fresh victory is exalted with a gentle song; the voice grows bold by the wine krater. Let somebody mix it now, sweet harbinger of the *kōmos*; and let him serve the mighty son of the vine in the silver dishes Chromius' horses won for him [at Sicyon]'. In the course of the poem, however, we hear of the hospitality of the whole city (2) and public feasting (31).

We saw at the outset of this chapter how sympotic imagery coexists with the language of public celebration also in the first *Pythian*. In my remarks there I was non-committal about the form of the first performance, and said only that the opening lines 'evoke' that of a chorus. Scholars have used these lines, and lines 97–8 (where Pindar says that Phalaris will not be sung of 'under the roof' as Hieron will), to support the hypothesis of solo singing by the poet; they suppose that the chorus of the opening lines merely danced while the poet sang, or alternatively the reference there is to what lyres do in general (so no chorus at all, and performed at a symposium). Others have said that the dancers of line 2 and the singers of line 3 are one and the same and the natural assumption is a reference to the actual execution. The language of the poem is in fact consistent with all of these scenarios. I was non-committal because the poem does not commit. A related point is whether in the very first lines we are already on Olympus, in which case the chorus is a heavenly one and tells us nothing about the form of earthly execution. Most scholars seem to think we are, but in fact the poet is non-committal about this too.[61] Not until line 5 are we certainly there. Without further specification one would assume the lyre of line 1 to be Pindar's. 'Own champion of Apollo and the violet-tressed Muses' does not provide such specification; that describes earthly lyres too. 'Golden' has force whether it is metaphorical or literal.

Now my historicist reader may be thinking that these ambiguities would have been resolved if we had been there on the day, and, whatever the situation was, that would determine the meaning. Since we weren't there, we shall never know for sure. Starting from such a premise, one can only develop criteria for deciding the nature of the first performance from passages one thinks are certain (emphasis on 'thinks'), and in somewhat circular fashion use these to judge uncertain cases. From the point of view of reception, a decision is not needed; but *even for the first occasion this was also the case*. The poems were emphatically not mimetic. It is impossible to overstate the importance of this innovation. It entails that Pindar's strategy for his primary audience works also for the secondary audience. Suppose the first performance was at a symposium, and solo. The language encourages any symposiast to think of a traditional chorus and its rich associations. For the Greeks, choral worship of the gods was a chance to be close to them and to escape the dreary hardships of mortal life (see Plato *Laws* 653c–d); even if the chorus is present only in the imagination, Pindar's imagery perfectly reflects this life-restoring symbiosis.[62] Suppose, on the other hand, it was a chorus singing and dancing. The poet amplifies the mood with sympotic language, through the theme of *harmonia*. The entire assembly becomes one large symposium. We might even suppose (why not?) that there were private performances for Hieron and his circle as well as public ones for the whole city on this famous occasion when the great Pindar arrived with his new masterpiece. The *potential* of the poem is its meaning, which could be (partly) actualized in different performance situations; as I said above (p. 67), every performance, including the first, is a reception. And that lyre again: whether metaphorically or literally golden, the meaning lies beyond the physical object, even at the first occasion.

Because the *kōmos* can link either way – to symposium or chorus – it suits this creative ambiguity perfectly. It is telling that the crossover sometimes created difficulties for the Alexandrian scholars who classified Pindar's poems by genre in their complete edition. Praise poems not associated with victories were put among the 'encomia' (according to contemporary usage of that term; the development from Pindaric usage had taken place in the fourth century); poems praising victors were put among the epinicians. Wherever we can tell, the context of the encomia is sympotic, as one would expect. However, there are epinicians, such as the second *Olympian*, the eleventh *Nemean* or the second *Isthmian*, which might better have been placed among the encomia, and encomia which, though obviously performed at a symposium, mention victories. We have encomia and epinicians commissioned for the same event.[63]

Because encomia were often solo performances, one obviously cannot infer that the epinicians were too. There are passages in the epinicians which an unprejudiced reading would take to imply that the ode is being performed by a chorus.[64] Just as Pindar wants the symposium to be an active presence in his poems, he also wants to activate the associations of public choral celebration. Yet it is significant, as supporters of the solo hypothesis have pointed out, that Pindar rarely if ever uses the word *choros* or derivatives to describe what he is doing in the epinicians.[65] By contrast, in other genres it is no surprise at all to find an expression like 'Come join the *choros*, ye Olympian gods' (fr. 75.1, first line of a dithyramb) or 'Apollo Musagete bids me dance (*choreusai*)' (fr. 94c, first line of a daphnephorikon). The word was closely associated with the worship of the gods and not to be used lightly. Though the epinicians are shot through and through with religious language (like all Greek institutions), and draw heavily on myth, they are not in themselves religious productions. They praise men, not gods. They may be performed alongside the main proceedings of a religious festival;

they are not themselves the ritual. The performers, though having obvious similarities to a chorus, are not a *choros*.[66] But by laying claim to the *kōmos* as its distinctive property, the young genre can stake out its own new ground.

The notional symposium of the epinician includes among its guests everybody in the implied audience; the experience is shared. Real symposia were exclusive. Poets like Alcaeus or Theognis evince a strong sense of who is in their group and who is not.[67] Their poems were born of violent political struggle, and their fellow symposiasts were members of a faction. The poets work to reinforce their sense of unity and purpose. They extol the good qualities of the in-group and execrate the vices of the enemy. Betrayal of the fellowship, of which Pittacus was guilty according to Alcaeus, was the worst possible crime, and brought down the wrath of Zeus upon those who had broken the oath of loyalty. The epinician 'symposium' is not like this. Although there is certainly an out-group – people who prefer blame to praise, people who jealously begrudge the victor his glory – these are not named contemporaries like Pittacus. They exist as a shadowy rabble of malignant evil-wishers out there somewhere, whose one virtue is that they teach us how not to behave. The poet wants us, his Panhellenic, global audience, to think that *of course* we are not one of *them*. We are all in this together.

## Personae, performativity and authors

'Pindar' is a continuous and powerful presence in Pindar's text, and an integral part of the textual occasion. The persona presents itself as an heir to a complex tradition, which it distils, focuses and applies to the task at hand. The poet is in his turn a generator of tradition. He adopts a future perfect perspective, looking back at himself through the eyes of audiences everywhere who complete his task through their agency. The persona makes it clear that the athlete's achievement will be lost to time and memory without commemoration. Poet and athlete are equal partners in a joint enterprise.

But it is not just any poet: it is *this* poet, this Pindar of Thebes, this aristocrat with his biddable Muse. The enormous amount of critical effort devoted to interpreting Pindar's 'I' shows just how dominant the voice is. At the beginning of the debate in the late 1980s, there was a polarization between scholars who argued that the 'I' is always to be understood as the poet, and those who argued that it is always the chorus.[68] Either position requires some hard, not to say special pleading to explain away certain passages which seem unambiguously to denote one or the other. More recently the consensus has been that the 'I' is flexible: sometimes it is the poet, sometimes the chorus, sometimes the two together, sometimes a quite indeterminate 'I', and sometimes perhaps even the athlete. But there remains considerable disagreement about how this flexibility works in practice. Does the 'I' simply switch from one to the other of these functions (and, while in one guise or the other, is wholly in that guise until it switches again)? By no means impossible in theory, but it threatens to undermine any consistency we might wish to attach to the Pindaric 'I'. If this position seems unattractive, then one will have to say that the 'I' is composite: if the chorus speaks, the poet's voice is part of theirs; if the poet speaks, the chorus is his amplifier. Something like this is, I think, the position of most critics nowadays, but there is still a tendency to privilege that first performance, and decide whether it was choral or solo. 'Choral' is the favoured answer, but in my view there is then a danger of underestimating the true extent of the poet's presence in the text, and of misrepresenting its character.

I am in favour of univocality, in the sense that the mix is unmistakably Pindar's and no one else's. And I give primacy in the mix to the poet's voice, not the chorus's. But the mix is itself suited to multiple performance contexts and multiple receptions. One is rarely, perhaps never, forced to make an exclusive choice. The poet's 'I' can be involved sympathetically even in passages where the text points strongly to a chorus (which, in such a case, was probably the form of the premiere). Conversely, the poet's 'I' often reads like that of a chorus-leader (the *chorēgos*), or lends itself easily to that role. This wonderful malleability depends, however, on the poet's continual presence in background or foreground; he cannot disappear entirely.

In all of this, when we refer to the poet's 'I', we must unpack the relationship of the extratextual poet to the intratextual one. This is a knotty theoretical problem to which it is necessary to devote careful attention here, since our relation to either of these 'I's is part of the shared experience of the Pindaric ode.

The circumstances of production are relevant first of all. In all choral genres the authority and impact of the chorus derived not only from the choristers' status as worthy representatives of their city, but from the prestige and ability of the poet. An additional factor in the epinician is the personal relationship between poet and patron. The worthiness of the person praised stands in direct proportion to the worth of the praiser. Furthermore, apart from his skill as a poet, the praiser is living proof of the virtues of the praised: of his hospitality (*xeniā*) towards friends near and far, and his correct use of wealth to advance the good of this city. Exemplary *xeniā* is presumptive proof that the host possesses *all* the virtues, exhibiting correct behaviour in relation to fellow citizens, foreigners and above all the gods (stressed repeatedly in the odes). This correctness in turn demonstrates his innate excellence, his *aretā*.[69] This frame of reference cannot be forgotten; but it is only a starting point in the problem of how the historical Pindar – the extratextual guest-friend, great Theban poet – relates to the 'I' of his poems.

I see the flexibility of the first person in Pindar as precisely analogous to the vagueness of the occasion discussed in the last section, in that audiences everywhere can inhabit that 'I' in different ways while remaining faithful to the text – just as they can inhabit the lyric 'now'. What we have in Pindar is an excellent example of the transferable lyric subject as understood by the critic Käte Hamburger.[70] At bottom, the transferability is possible because the pronoun exemplifies a kind of performativity. Unlike the actual performance, the quality of performativity has been somewhat understudied by critics of Greek lyric.

The modern study of performativity is generally agreed to start with J. L. Austin's famous book *How to Do Things with Words*, based on his William James lectures at Harvard in 1955.[71] He defined performative utterances as ones that make no actual statement about the world, but effect an action or situation in it merely by being uttered: 'I declare the meeting closed', 'I pronounce you husband and wife', 'I guarantee I am telling the truth', 'Let the Games begin'. The analysis of how such statements work in practice raises all manner of general considerations, enabling philosophers, sociologists, anthropologists, gender theorists, literary critics and others to extend the concept of performativity into areas never dreamed of by Austin, but which demonstrate the power of this extraordinarily simple, yet brilliant, insight about the pragmatics of human communication.[72] Theorists in performance studies, among others, have argued that performativity goes a very long way down in the human being. Everything we do can be understood as a performance. Performativity, in this broader sense, is not a quality that pertains to some kinds of language or behaviour but not to others. The process begins in infancy: we learn by imitating our parents and siblings, and in the very doing we create our understanding of the world and our place (role) in it. Cognition and action work together to develop our ability to function as social beings. The evolutionary processes behind this must be very old, and are clearly not confined to humans.

'All the world's a stage / and all the men and women merely players'. The boundary between the stage and real life can be very thin, as theatre practitioners and theorists alike have been demonstrating since the early twentieth century. Phenomenological and psychological approaches analyse the state of mind – the embodied state of mind – of the individual performer, in whom there is a complex interplay between the actor as a real person, the actor in their stage role, and the actor responding to the audience in performance. If ordinary life roles are mimetic, theatrical ones are doubly so: a role-player playing a role. This play-acting, this cognitive awareness of mimesis and the mimetic projection of it, is uniquely and universally human. The spectators, inveterate role-players themselves, require little or no effort to grasp the actors' points of view, and enjoy (in a very particular sense; the experience can, of course, be deeply disturbing) a space in which there is the possibility of both contemplative distance and absorbing proximity (though this distinction too can be put under pressure in some kinds of performance).

When a lyric poem offers or implies a speaking 'I' (the commonest implied form being an apostrophized 'you'), a persona springs into being, and there is a greater or lesser degree of theatricality ('persona' – Latin for 'mask' – is itself a theatrical metaphor). The relationship between the 'I' of the poem and the biographical poet is a long-standing problem in modern criticism, with solutions ranging from an exaggerated belief in direct self-expression to a construct existing *only* on the page, with no relationship at all to its creator's ideas or character. In Pindaric studies, the first extreme had its best-known exponent in the person of Ulrich von Wilamowitz-Moellendorff (1848–1931), who read every first-person statement in the poems as an unmediated statement by Pindar of Thebes. Not exactly at the other extreme, but very much reacting against Wilamowitz was Elroy Bundy (1920–1975), who insisted that first-person statements were not those of the biographical Pindar but of the laudator (eulogist) working within the conventions of the genre, whose primary purpose was praise.[73] Bundy succeeded in showing that many statements that might seem to be irrelevant interventions of a poet settling scores (and ignoring the job he was paid to do by his patrons) in fact served the function of praise. Ironically for this lover of poetry, however, his Pindar seems at times to be more automaton than poet. For his part Wilamowitz, greatest of Greek scholars though he was, cannot escape a charge of philistinism in his treatment of Pindar.

The middle ground is more fruitful. Although the relationship between the 'I' of the poem and the biographical poet must always remain indeterminate, we must read the poem as the statement of a human being, not a machine. There must always be a circumstance of production, and a producer. The inherent theatricality of the 'I' implies an extratextual actor. In practice critics of all persuasions routinely take external circumstances into account. The world outside the poem conditions the text and the language it uses to make statements about that world.

When I say that the lyric presentation of the 'I' is performative, I do not have in mind cases where the poet overtly adopts a role, such as Archilochus (fr. 19), in which he speaks in the character of a carpenter named Charon, or cases where the poet is dramatizing a scene and represents characters in direct speech, as in epic (though these are part of the same larger phenomenon). Nor am I thinking of choral odes in which the chorus may be of a different age, gender etc. from the poet who has written their words for them. Rather, I have in mind the much more interesting case where the 'I' appears to be neutral: just the poet (though of course *that* 'I' lies behind the others just mentioned). 'Performativity' in this context is not the Austinian sense of 'capacity to do things with words'; it means the capacity of something, such as the first-person pronoun, to be performed or to be considered as a performance. We need to ask what kind of shift in perspective takes place to allow the biographical 'I' to become the performative 'I'; what qualities the latter has that the former lacks.

Let us consider a helpful example. Culler draws attention to the advantage of English in having progressive and non-progressive (simple) forms of the present tense.[74] He instances Auden's 'September 1, 1939', which begins 'I sit in one of the dives / On Fifty-second street, / Uncertain and afraid'. The non-progressive 'I sit', without further qualification (e.g. 'I often sit'), alerts us to the fact that this is a poetic utterance. If the text read instead 'I am sitting', we might think we are dealing with a letter, perhaps, or a newspaper report, or the opening of a short story. If we received such a letter, we could of course visualize the scene, but we do not relate to the 'I' in the same way: it would always be us seeing things in the way our correspondent is seeing them, in a particular moment in the past. With the 'I' of 'I sit', however, we identify not with W. H. Auden, but with the poetic persona, and the identification is always in the special temporality of the lyric present.

Greek does not have a non-progressive present, but translators often adopt it, sometimes perhaps inappropriately but hardly always so. Whether one translates κατεύδω in Sappho fr. 168B 4 as 'I sleep' (the usual choice) or 'I am sleeping' ('The moon has set, and the Pleiades are mid-heaven; night-time passes by; and I κατεύδω alone') it is a performative statement, for Sappho is obviously neither asleep nor alone.[75] We have no idea what the historical Sappho was really like, but we can all inhabit the 'I' of this poem. We can do so even with our radically different notions of subjectivity, and our radically different historical circumstances; we can do so whatever our gender (the feminine form of the adjective 'alone' is not an obstacle). We do so with hardly a thought; no question arises that the sharing of that space with 'Sappho' might not be legitimate. Had we presented ourselves at the first performance of this poem, the historical

Sappho might have turned us away. Auden might have resented us sitting down beside him uninvited in the dive. But the poems of 'Sappho' and 'Auden' are common ground where we all may tread, should we choose to do so. And further exploration, description and criticism of the inhabited territory are legitimized in a way they cannot be with our friend's letter; we become authors in our turn, and write our results on the shared map.

What is distinctive about the lyric performative 'I' is precisely this desire and move to meet in a shared space. Every person you meet in the street is a performing 'I' in one sense, but their performance is not meant to create an identity for you to share. This performer relies upon common expectations to claim a position in a social nexus and project an identity (among other things), but much of their personality remains necessarily out of view. In a poetic performative communication, the layers of meaning and hidden depths can be just as complex or even more so (entailing everything in ordinary communication *plus* literary interactions), but the performative 'I' wants you to find out everything about itself *qua* performing persona. It need not be an easy discovery; poetic statements can be obscure for many good reasons. But they are pointless if written in private code, or hide things that can never be discovered.

The performativity of the Greek lyric 'I' is naturally enhanced by the fact that the poems *were* composed to be performed. The performativity ought then to be plainer to see. One frank acknowledgement of theatricality in Greek (and other) lyric is the way it constantly calls attention to the circumstances of its own performance. Another is the speaker's common habit of self-address, which parades its own 'I' as if it were somebody else.[76] Another common form of the performing 'I' has been called the 'exemplary I', in which the 'I' means 'I as representative or typical'.[77] In Greek poetry, given its common task of expressing received wisdom, the exemplary 'I' often expresses ethical maxims; there are many examples in the lyric genres, as well as in the lyric choruses of drama. One could say that in the 'exemplary I', the speaker has gone the maximum distance towards meeting the listener, all but effacing their own individuality. There is not much to find out here about the persona. Yet the 'I' in such statements is not quite identical with 'one', which can usually be substituted without changing the surface sense; pragmatically, it does make a difference, since the 'I', however typical it attempts to be, implies a speaker who subscribes to the view expressed, makes their commitment plain and lends it such authority as they can.

If even in the 'exemplary I' there must be some degree of individuality in the pragmatic situation, all the more must there be a sense of a real person behind the persona when personal opinions are expressed.[78] On the one hand, in the ancient context the poet speaks as a member of the group for which the poem is composed, on the occasion for which it is composed. Any opinion will be about matters of common interest, not a Wordsworthian overheard introspection. This situation does not, however, require the suppression of the biographical personality. Everyone has their own take on matters of common interest, and the poet can challenge as much as confirm received wisdom. Here a paradoxical dynamic comes into play between historical author and the author represented in the text. The real author both is and is not there. I said above that the performative persona wants you to know everything about itself *qua* performative persona. We may have only the evidence of the performance to work out who is being performed, yet we know from the fact of performance that the personality is a projection coming from an author. We inevitably read the text in the light of personality we infer.

In Wayne Booth's terminology, that projection is the implied author: the person who wrote the text in a particular way, with all its choices of style, plot, characterization, ethics and so on. It is a version of the real author – whom Booth calls the 'flesh-and-blood person', the FBP – but, although there are ways in which facts about the FBP might be relevant to an appreciation of the implied author, the FBP did not write the book.[79] A different and perhaps commoner use of the term denotes the elements in a text that mark an authorial act, much like what narratologists call the primary narrator-focalizer.[80] This implied author remains entirely with the text, and the relationship with the real author is of no interest – banished from discussion, indeed, lest some version of the supposed intentionalist fallacy sneak in, whereby one thinks one can determine the text's meaning by reference to what the (real) author intended.

One advantage of Booth's approach, apart from recognizing that readers do in fact project his kind of implied author, is that it accounts for some differences between the two kinds of implied author. A narrator can behave in wildly inconsistent ways. One can leave these contradictions to stand unreconciled, and analyse what they are doing in the text. Not so with Booth's implied author; we must posit a writer whose predilections include this kind of trick as a narrator. We can also look across the whole of an implied author's oeuvre, which might be extremely varied, and modify our image of him or her accordingly. 'Pindar' is not primarily a narrator, but similar considerations apply. For instance, he cannot be both Theban and non-Theban; since we know he is Theban, if the first person in a poem speaks as an Aeginetan, say, we approach the interpretation of the latter statement with that difference in mind. In doing so we preserve the ontological consistency of the implied author, while enriching our understanding of the text.

In one sense the only thing we can say for sure about Pindar is that he created 'Pindar'. Of course other points can be conceded: it is vanishingly unlikely that Pindar was not a paid-up member of the Theban elite, and that he was not personally committed to the aristocratic ethos of the poems. Indeed it would be absurd to think otherwise. But one can do something even with this hypersceptical minimal formulation. Pindar was not hired by the Aleuads of Thessaly as a twenty-year-old from far-away Thebes to write the tenth *Pythian* because he knew the aristocratic code pretty well; they did not hire him to write a choral ode in which the 'I' was the chorus and the voice was like that of any other competent versifier (who might as well be anonymous). They knew Pindar was a poetic genius and wanted to see 'Pindar' in action. The celebration of the victory was the thing, and at its heart was an aesthetic experience. They cast their net far afield to find the best.[81]

So what is Pindar to 'Pindar'? To anticipate, I will want to argue that one of the latter's most distinctive characteristics is how hard it works to make us think we are dealing with the former, and that this is part of the poetry's sublimity. But first let me consider some responses to this question from antiquity. Ancient readers tended to conflate the two, inferring biographical details from poetic statements sometimes in the most literal-minded way.[82] An early example of this attitude is the Athenian politician, poet and philosopher Critias (uncle of Plato, and one of the murderous thirty tyrants of 404–3 BCE), who scolded Archilochus for revealing disreputable facts about himself in his poetry (that he was son of a slave woman, that he was an adulterer, that he threw away his shield in battle). Modern scholars have tended to interpret such statements as a pose deriving from the conventions of Archilochus' iambic genre and its social role. For instance, his mother's name 'Enipo' is derived from *enīpē*, 'abuse', so when Archilochus says he is 'son of Enipo/Abuse' he means that he is by nature suited to the task of publicly shaming society's miscreants. Enipo is a slave because for a community leader (inevitably aristocratic) to be denounced by a low-born outcast (even a pretend one) represented a complete humiliation.

Critias, it seems, has taken 'Archilochus' to be Archilochus. But although he may in theory have misunderstood Archilochus' genre (changed somewhat by his day), or creatively misread him for some ulterior motive,[83] a better way of bringing ancient and modern readings into a single frame of reference is to say that, for Critias, the Archilochus who created 'Archilochus' had to be the *kind* of person who would willingly do so. That is surely a reasonable assumption; Pindar makes it too in the second *Pythian* (52–6). Ancient audiences tended to hold poets morally responsible for what they said; this is a basic premise in

Aristophanes' *Frogs*, for instance (404 BCE, contemporary with Critias), in his poetic competition between Aeschylus and Euripides. Even if (or precisely because) he sends it up, his comedy presumes the attitude was a familiar one.[84] Moderns too would have little sympathy with a poet whose poems appeared to advocate, say, white supremacy, and who then took refuge in the disconnect between the real author and the one in the text. In turning the biographical 'I' into the performative 'I', the performer must meet the audience in the middle; but some part of the first 'I' remains invested in the second. This investment is what prevents me as a reader from wholly *appropriating* the 'I' and making it identical with me, the biographical reader. Otherwise Auden would turn into Sappho (and Pindar, and every other poet). The space is shared, not surrendered.

Should we, however, conclude from ancient reactions like Critias' that we ought not to speak of implied authors at all in relation to Greek literary history? This view has been maintained. To abandon the concept would seem to leave us with two unsavoury alternatives, either full-on biographical interpretation at one extreme ('Archilochus' is nothing more or less than Archilochus), or at the other extreme reading the persona as a bundle of generic conventions, a selfless transmitter of cultural heritage (Archilochus is nothing more or less than 'Archilochus').

One way of coming at the issue is to consider it in terms of Foucault's author-function.[85] The author-function is a 'characteristic of the mode of existence, circulation, and functioning of certain discourses within a society'. The creator of texts acquires an identity and a name; a notion of author's ownership of the text comes into being; the author can therefore be called to account for what the text says; the author's identity is a complex product of all that society associates with a particular kind of discourse; the author is the place where all the contradictions and complexities of the texts can, one way or another, be reconciled (Pindar is created out of 'Pindar'); and, famously, 'The author is the principle of thrift in the proliferation of meaning': the author is that which allows us to restrict the infinite range of possible meanings of a text to a manageable compass, by appealing to the underlying, controlling, psychologized creator. Several of these characteristics are readily instanced from archaic poetry. Archaic poets fault each other for wayward opinions or poor artistry, while bragging about their own superiority and immortality.[86] Already Hesiod (*c.* 700 BCE) names himself in the proem to the *Theogony* and tells us that the Muses (i.e. other poets) can lie (27). In the *Works and Days*, a strong, bluff personality emerges, which is, however, flexible according to need: now scolding, now cajoling, now indignant, now preachy, and many other colours besides.[87] Theognis of Megara claims (19–

23) that his verses will always be recognized as his; while it is not clear how he thinks this integrity can be guaranteed in practice (or how it relates to the poems in the preserved corpus of Theognidea), the claim to ownership is unambiguous: 'Kyrnos, let me, poet that I am, place a seal upon these verses. No theft of them will go undetected, and nobody will exchange better for worse; but everyone will say "These verses are by the world-famous Theognis of Megara!"'.[88] Bakker rightly emphasizes that 'Let me place a seal' is an Austinian performative utterance: the saying is the doing. Given that point; given the following stress on the poetry's unique excellence (20–1) and the prominence of the powerful word *sophisdomenōi* (immediately after the opening address of Kyrnos); given also the present tense of this participle, which underscores the performativity (literally, 'let me, as I practise my craft as a poet') – given all this, I side with those who see the seal as consisting simply in the quality of the poetry: Theognis', and Theognis' alone.[89] His boast at 237–54 that his verses have made Kyrnos world-famous and immortal bears a similar implication.

By the second half of the sixth century, clear evidence emerges for the social context of authored texts. In this period we start finding vases with named figures of poets on them; apparently there was a market.[90] To this period we can trace the habit of wealthy patrons like Polycrates of Samos, Peisistratus of Athens, or Scopas of Thessaly enticing international poetic stars (Ibycus, Anacreon, Simonides) to perform at their courts. Of course, epic poets had long relied on noble patronage, and these patrons would be looking out for top performers. But the poet's personal fame was not built into the poetry, and what they performed was figured as pure tradition. Traditional texts of this kind (and many others, such as sacred texts, folk songs, public inscriptions etc.) cannot have an author-function.

The history of 'Homer' is actually a further confirmation of the author-function. There is no 'Homer' in the *Iliad* or the *Odyssey*. We can compare these texts with others and identify many unique features of their poetic practice, but this is not the same thing as there being a 'Homer'. Indeed, most scholars nowadays accept that these poems are by different authors; so we need to find two 'Homers'. That the thesis is difficult to prove and still not universally accepted shows how far below the surface any putative 'Homer' is buried. Oralists disallow the very term 'author' in connection with what they suppose was the state of the poems before their fixed redaction. 'Homer' is a creation of the late sixth century. It is at this time that the Panathenaic festival established rhapsodic competitions for the performance of the *Iliad* and the *Odyssey*, and no others (the author-function is 'characteristic of the mode of existence, circulation, and functioning of certain discourses within a society'). The Homeridae, guardians of the Homeric tradition and notional descendants of Homer, come into historical view now. The performer of the *Homeric Hymn to Apollo* poses as the living incarnation of Homer himself (166–73). Other epic poems, hitherto anonymous, get attributed to Homer – or to other bards; so in these other early poems too there was no 'Homer' (or 'Creophylus', or 'Stasinus', 'Arctinus', 'Lesches' etc.). But they have become discrete poems, and people thought there had to *be* an author; hence the competing suggestions. At this time too Theagenes of Rhegium inaugurated the long tradition of Homeric criticism with a book defending supposedly impious passages by means of allegorical interpretation; he also gave a biography of the poet. Simonides twice quotes Homer by name, and a third time refers to him indirectly (frr. 11.15–18, 19 IEG[2] and fr. 273 Poltera, in the last of which he also cites Stesichorus).[91]

The evidence from the mid sixth century onwards is widely accepted as proving a concept of authorship. The earlier texts cited above point in the same direction, and it seems needless to deny that we are dealing with the same phenomenon. It is not confined to lyric (witness Hesiod), and it is not necessarily an overnight or universal transformation; Stesichorus (first half of sixth century), with his speaking name ('he who sets up the chorus'), could still be operating along traditional lines. Certainly there is little sign of a 'Stesichorus' in his poems. Interestingly, Homer names the bards he depicts in the *Odyssey* (Demodocus and Phemius); at 8.74, it is remarked that the fame of Demodocus' song had reached high heaven, and at 8.497–8, Odysseus promises to spread his reputation far abroad. Does this reflect an emerging trend of de-anonymization? In any case, the desire of individual poets to emerge from such anonymity and assert their personal claim to fame must derive from wider cultural forces, whose strength accelerated with the advent of the international power-brokers like Polycrates, Peisistratus and Hieron in the late archaic and early classical periods. It is in all probability to such figures as these that we owe the birth of the epinician genre, as they sought to enhance their international cultural capital by immortalizing their achievements in verse.[92]

It is not, then, a modern fancy that imagines Archilochus behind 'Archilochus'. This does not of course mean we can move in any simple way from one to the other. Foucault, however, disallowed the move altogether, and here one might choose to disagree. Foucault's point that the author is the function of a particular historical discourse continues to be fruitful, but since the 1990s the historical author has been returning to life.[93] To elide the historical author altogether is to overlook a dynamic tension in the way texts are produced and read. As Maslov writes, 'For the literary persona – the "I" – to take part in an ideological conflict, one must have a literary system in place in which authority has already been minimally individuated', i.e. in which authority derives from biographical individuals.[94] The persona as a mere embodiment of group values cannot perform this function. Foucault rejected any appeal to the absent writer as being 'a simple repetition, in transcendental terms, of both the religious principle of inalterable and yet never fulfilled tradition, and the aesthetic principle of the work's survival, its perpetuation beyond the author's death, and its enigmatic *excess* in relation to him'.[95] Many critics would now dispute both points. There is such a thing as a tradition, not just a series of disconnected moments, as extreme historicism seems to entail; the question is how that tradition relates to the individual moments, without its being transcendental in a metaphysical, quasi-religious or essentialist sense. And analysing aesthetic experience solely as a matter of discourse is effectively to deny that there is such a thing as aesthetic experience at all.

## Pindar acting 'Pindar'

So what (to repeat the question) is Pindar to 'Pindar'? How do we (should we) make the move from one to the other? One must admit at the outset that, however strong our sense might be of the real Pindar in the text, it is a purely textual effect. One could say that part of 'Pindar's' role-playing is to pretend to be the real Pindar, to convince us of his personal commitment. Perhaps this is too convoluted and sceptical a formula for some tastes: why not just say a given pointer to a real Pindar in the text is simply Pindar (no inverted commas)? Is it not needlessly purist to insist on the inaccessibility of the real author? Quite apart from the difficulties posed by ambiguous pointers, that position would mean that such first-person references are not literary performing 'I's which in principle allow you to find out everything you need to know about the persona. They are instead masks adopted for the moment by a real person, and to really understand the mask you need to understand the person. The text will soon fail to answer your questions about this person; if you insist on answers you will have to make guesses that rely on biographical criticism.

Hamburger's position is that the lyric subject both is and is not the author. The author is inaccessible, but the statements made by the lyric subject only have force because of that relationship, however indeterminate it is. We take the lyric subject to be a real subject in a way that we do not read the subject in fictional and mimetic genres. Relevant too is the highly developed human cognitive ability to 'mentalize', that is to understand other people's state of mind, and engage with their motives and emotions, which is well brought to bear on this discussion by Felix Budelmann;[96] part of this cognitive apparatus is our strong propensity to detect intentions behind statements, actions and events, as cause to effect (the origin of the 'intentionalist fallacy'). Because lyric poetry tends to be selective and paratactic, shining an intense light on short-lived, often emotional moments of a speaking 'I' – in other words bears within it the marks of some person's cognitive and emotional investment – the urge to mentalize the author is that much the stronger. This complements Hamburger's point that we take the lyric subject to be a real subject.

If, in addition, one accepts that the lyric subject is inherently performative, that audiences and readers immediately recognize that performativity, and that the performative 'I' by its nature is a shared space, then one sees how it is that the lyric reader inhabits the 'I'. It might be more accurate, indeed, to say that the 'I' inhabits us. 'I wandered lonely as a cloud', says Wordsworth; as soon as you read that, 'Wordsworth' starts taking you over. Roland Greene endorses Hamburger's point that reading lyric is to re-experience within ourselves statements, feelings and ideas in the poem, not as fictional or illusory, as in a novel or drama, but as part of reality. '[S]uch an imaginative operation', he writes, 'precedes any interpretation, in fact creates the conditions for interpretation, and presumably allows us to expand the experiential dimensions of ourselves by adding to a store of domesticated memories'. He goes on amusingly to point out that this appropriation is what 'prompts lovers to quote each other poems not written by themselves, adopting the poems as their own utterances in the real world' and to ask, 'Has anyone ever quoted a complete utterance from *Pride and Prejudice* to a loved one as though it were his or her own speech?'[97]

So, even if 'Pindar' is a purely textual effect, we must keep Pindar in play as well as 'Pindar'. It helps that Pindar has put so many pointers in the text, as we shall see in detail a moment. I said above (p. 85) that his treatment of the persona in the poems is analogous to his treatment of the occasion. Like the representation of the occasion, that of the poet make us feel as if we are led beyond the text to the real Pindar, inaccessible though we know him to be (another moment in the historical sublime). Another way of putting it is to say that the sense of occasion-in-the-text includes the living, performing poet. Both the occasion and the persona create and feed off their real counterparts in a way that is unique to this poet. The poems create an illusion of unmediated access to both. The mask hardly seems to be a mask. Although all aspects of Pindar's 'I' find antecedents and parallels in other Greek poets, none presents so intense a combination or achieves the same effect. Among Roman poets, one thinks perhaps of Catullus first, then Horace, whose characteristic self-ironizing adds an extra layer of complexity.

The most straightforward pointer to a real Pindar in the text is of course where a Theban poet is speaking, which happens seven times in the epinicians.[98] Also straightforward are passages where the poet differentiates himself from the chorus.[99] Then there are references to the author's personal relationship with the patron who commissioned the ode. Praising his hospitality is one form this may take, but such hospitality could include many others besides Pindar; being one of the aristocratic virtues, it is a general theme in the odes. There are, however, eight passages where the reference clearly applies to the poet personally.[100] In two poems Pindar indicates that he was unable to come in person for the performance, so he has sent the poem separately (*I*.2.47, *P*.3.68–77; probably also *O*.6.90, *P*.4.299); elsewhere the 'sending motif' need not carry this literal implication (the verb can also mean 'escort'), but it has the same effect of bringing (a sense of) the real Pindar into the text.[101] The converse of the 'sending motif' is the 'arrival motif', some examples of which, again, identify the poet as the one arriving.[102] Pindar opens the tenth *Olympian* with an acknowledgement that he is late with the ode, a lapse which he has cleverly turned to advantage by the time the poem ends. At the end of the ninth *Nemean* the speaker states that he has celebrated Chromius better than many another poet; we find the same competitive motif in the thirteenth *Olympian* (44–6) and the fourth *Nemean* (36–8). In the thirteenth *Olympian* the speaker who describes himself as a private person with a public commission (49) is most naturally understood as the poet.

This is already a substantial total, but there is another, more significant way in which the external poet inserts himself in the text. I refer to the use of the word *sophiā* and its cognates. It is worth laying out the details in order to appreciate the true extent and impact of this strategy.[103] 'Wisdom' is the one-word dictionary equivalent, but it denotes intellectual skills of all kinds. Where the context indicates, it denotes poetry; it is, indeed, the *mot juste* for poetic skill. The adjective is *sophos*, which can also serve as a noun; we also find the noun *sophistās* (one who has and practises *sophiā*), and the verb *sophisdomai* (to practise or exhibit *sophiā*, as in Theognis 19, quoted above n. 88). Whenever Pindar uses a word from this family, and poetic skill is indicated by the context, it is a kind of signature. It highlights the excellence of the commissioned poet, and his status as the worthy representative of a venerable cultural institution. Poetic *sophiā* is not a property of the chorus, either in Pindar or arguably anywhere else in archaic or classical Greek literature.

The association between *sophiā* and poetry is well established in the archaic period, as numerous passages show.[104] In Pindar, it is a favourite word; excluding passages where the context is unclear, I count twenty-one references to poetic skill in Slater's lexicon, and forty-four for all other kinds of knowledge or wisdom. In the final words of the first *Olympian*, when the speaker expresses the hope that Hieron may win more victories and he may celebrate them, and describes himself as 'conspicuous for *sophiā* among the Greeks', the reference is obviously to the poet. Apart from the word *sophiā*, the anonymous citizens chosen to perform the song could not be called internationally famous, and they are not the guarantors of Hieron's renown. In the second *Dithyramb*, the speaker announces, 'The Muse has appointed me their chosen herald of *sopha* verses (*epea*) to Greece with its fair dancing-grounds' (23–5); the reference to international fame, and a personal commission from the Muse, indicate the poet, even as the choral execution is reflected in the description given to Greece. At the close of the third *Pythian*, the speaker says that we know about the Homeric heroes Nestor and Sarpedon through poetry (*epea*), 'such as *sophoi* craftsmen fashioned'; this is the role of poets as stewards of tradition, and of course the point here is that Pindar is immortalizing Hieron. The poem is cast as a personal missive to the Syracusan ruler. We find the same function at *I*.7.18 (people forget 'whatever does not appear conjoined with renowned outpourings of verse, the very best of *sophiā*; therefore celebrate Strepsiades with a melodious song', which follows on a catalogue of ancient Theban exploits) and in *I*.5.28, where the heroes of legend have been, and still are, celebrated 'for time beyond measure' by *sophistai*. The young Achilles' feats were announced to an astonished world by the mouths of *sophoi* (i.e. in epics known to Pindar's audience, *I*.8.47). Pindar rebukes Homer for misusing his *sophiā* to overrate Odysseus (*N*.7.23), and turns his back on a theme threatening to become blasphemous because it is 'hateful *sophiā*' (*O*.9.38). In the seventh *Paean* the speaker declines to follow Homer's well-worn path, choosing to strike out in new directions; he prays to Mnemosyne and her daughters the Muses to give him *eumāchaniā*, facility (a metapoetic word in Pindar, denoting the easy flow of words for the poet, and the happy opportunities for the blessed that flow from good fortune and divine favour; the opposite is *amāchaniā*, paralysis, helplessness, such as that of Archilochus);[105] 'for the wits of men are blind, who seek the deep path of *sophiā* without the Helikoniades (Muses)'. With this passage we may compare Bacchylides fr. 5, also from a paean: 'One *sophos* becomes so from another such, both in olden times and now; for it is not the easiest task to discover the gateway to secret verses', which figures poetic tradition as a mystery religion and the poet as one who initiates the devotees.[106]

Among Pindar's most famous passages is this one towards the end of the second *Olympian* (83–8):

| | |
|---|---|
| Many swift darts have I under my arm | πολλά μοι ὑπ' ἀγκῶνος ὠκέα βέλη |
| Within my quiver | ἔνδον ἐντὶ φαρέτρας |
| That speak to those who understand | φωνάεντα συνετοῖσιν· ἐς δὲ τὸ πᾶν |
| (*sunetoi*); but as regards the whole[107] | ἑρμανέων |
| They need interpreters. Wise (*sophos*) is | χατίζει. σοφὸς ὁ πολλὰ εἰδὼς φυᾷ· |
| he who knows much by nature | μαθόντες δὲ λάβροι |
| (*phuā*); but those who have it by | παγγλωσσίᾳ κόρακες ὣς ἄκραντα |
| learning | γαρύετον[108] |
| Gabble uselessly like a pair of furious | Διὸς πρὸς ὄρνιχα θεῖον. |
| crows | |
| At Zeus's divine bird. | |

In itself 'Wise is he who knows much by nature' would refer to wisdom generally (Slater classifies this example amongst the forty-four with this meaning), but we have poetry before and poetry after (the sequel asks 'whom shall we pelt with our fame-bringing arrows?' – it is the poet, not the chorus, who bestows fame – before resuming the praise of Theron). The passage is all about those who truly understand poetry and its ethical import. Bacchylides certainly thought so in his imitation of Pindar at the end of his third *Epinician* (either he imitates Pindar, or they both imitate some lost poem of Simonides; either way the point here is the same):[109] 'I speak what the knowing man understands' (*phroneonti suneta gāruō ~ phōnāenta sunetoisin*), leading up to the 'grace of the honey-tongued Cean' (i.e. Bacchylides, the poem's last words) with a mention of immortalization by the Muse (i.e. poet) in between. The wise understand Pindar's verse; others need to have it explained to them. The *sunetoi* are *sophoi* only if they have their understanding by *phuā*. The poetry of the gabbling crows is a prolix and confused chatter, nothing to the point like Pindar's sharp arrows. All of this effects a typically metapoetic transition after the myth ('I have many arrows; the right sort of person knows whereof I speak; others are babblers'), and throws the following question ('whom then shall we pelt with these arrows?') and its answer ('Theron!') into sharp relief. The quality of *sophiā* is extended to include not only poets but those who are equipped by *phuā* to understand them; similarly in the first *Olympian* the *sophoi* join in the hymn of praise to Zeus at Hieron's hearth (8–11),[110] and in the ninth *Pythian* artful elaboration of a few points among many is the kind of poetry the *sophoi* like to hear (76–8). Pindar's inclusive *sophos* is another way to praise Theron. He is not the only one included: Pindar's general meaning is actually quite clear, and therefore all of us in the audience can consider ourselves amongst the wise. We need no interpreter.[111]

Remaining references to poetic *sophiā* also refer to the poet's skill on a straightforward reading.[112] Bacchylides' usage is the same.[113] The practice of dramatic choruses further underscores the point. In tragedy the choruses can talk about their singing and dancing, and such passages have been read as metacommentary.[114] But, even if so read, the comment is about the singing and dancing – their *choreia*, i.e. what a *choros* does – in the context of the Dionysia festival where the plays were produced, or with wider reference to religion in general. Three times a chorus lays claim to *sophiā*, once in Sophocles (*Electra* 474) and twice in Euripides (*Medea* 1086, *Alcestis* 962); the first refers to skill in prophecy, the second and third to wisdom generally, and in the third the chorus says they have what they know from others. Comic choruses behave the same way as tragic ones, when they are in character; I find no instances where they claim *sophiā* in their own name. In the parabases, however, where they come out of character and speak directly to the audience, they brag about how good the play is – giving explicit credit to the poet (who is *sophos*, e.g. *Peace* 799).[115] In the great debate between Aeschylus and Euripides in the *Frogs*, a 'competition in *sophiā*' (882) to find out which poet is more *sophos* (780), we meet a deluge of *soph-* words. We can conclude that in the mimetic mode the poet must recede into the background; in non-mimetic modes, he is allowed to step forward, and so we find *sophiā*. Since in the epinician so much depends on the excellence of the poet, the theme is more marked than in other genres, but it occurs there too in spite of the greater urgency of ritual requirements. Above I quoted Pindar's second *Dithyramb* and seventh *Paean*; though not using a *soph*-word, the opening of the sixth *Paean*, where the speaker calls himself a 'spokesman (*prophātas*), famous in song, of the Pierides', refers to the poet in the opinion of many (though not all) scholars.[116] Similarly, Bacchylides opens his fifth *Epinician* with a personal signature (he is the *xenos*, foreign guest, and the 'famous servant of gold-veiled Ourania [the Muse]' in 11–14).

In sum, thematizing poetic *sophiā* in an ode is a self-advertisement. Every poem of Pindar refers in some way, often effusively, to the elements of the performance – the music, the dance, the praise – and these can be read metapoetically; but they are for the most part collaborations between poet and chorus, while *sophiā* is his alone. It immediately creates in the text a sense of the external poet – the *sophos*, the cultural icon. Between the *sophiā*-theme and other personal markers we have discussed, about two-thirds of the epinicians are represented, often with multiple occurrences in the same ode. That is a remarkable proportion. To these we may reasonably add other markers which are slightly less explicit but no less unmistakable: the many references to poetic predecessors, which figure the speaker as a poet in a long tradition of poets,[117] and displays of mythological learning in nearly every ode (an important part of a poet's *sophiā*). Linguistic virtuosity and Pindar's very distinctive style also bespeak the poet. When one adds the sheer number of first-person pronouns in the poems, forcefully keeping some kind of 'I' in view, one might feel some sympathy for our scholarly forebears who read the pronoun in a straightforwardly biographical way. This implied author has an exceptionally strong personality.

It is, indeed, difficult to read for very long in the epinicians without encountering some form of the first-person pronoun, whether singular or plural (we shall come back to this alternation below, p. 109). Some poems offer a blizzard of them; in the seventh *Nemean*, for instance, there is one every 4.8 lines on average, and counts in the range of one every six to ten lines are common. Bacchylides, by contrast, does not have this insistence, whether measured by quantity, distribution or variety of his self-references. His intrusions, typically at the beginnings and ends of the epinicians, can indeed be lengthy, and in such passages he shouts even louder than Pindar.[118] In general, however, Pindar's ability to surprise, unsettle and delight by turns throughout his poems contrast sharply with Bacchylides' more consistent tone and restricted range of effects.

These observations are not intended to reinstate the view that the 'I' of the poems is always Pindar, except in a few places where it must be the chorus (a binary choice). Instead I consider that Pindar's omnipresent 'I' acts as a ground bass for all the other voices in the odes, underpinning and sounding through them, while capable of carrying the tune itself at any time. This flexibility opens up multiple and interesting possibilities of reading. For instance, at the end of the fourth *Pythian*, Pindar relies on his standing with both parties to make his case for a rapprochement. We can choose to admire his evident international esteem and skill as a diplomat. If a chorus of worthy citizens performed the ode, however, we also have a grand public display of civic unity. A spectator at the original performance might have been impressed by that – or by both. Conversely, a passage often cited as choral is the close of the eighth *Pythian*, a highly emotional context where the speaker addresses 'dear mother Aegina' and prays for continued freedom. Pindar was not Aeginetan, the argument goes, so this is the chorus speaking. But why cannot he – and we – momentarily share the point of view of the inhabitants? We, his later readers, happen to know from his many other poems for Aeginetans how personally attached Pindar was to the island,

and can well imagine how heartfelt these words were for him.[119] We might have the advantage in that respect over some of the younger members of the original audience! On the other hand, few of them could have been unaware of the mortal threat hanging over their heads, realized only fifteen years later in 431 BCE when the Athenians forcibly expelled the entire population. This external fact lends considerable urgency to the prayer for (permanent) liberation. Those of us who have studied Greek history know this from other sources; not all of us have done so, nor would all ancient readers have known about it. None of these engagements with the text is necessarily inferior to the other. All readings entail occlusions. No one can ever know everything about a poem, and even if one did it would not mean one 'fully' understood it, since understanding poetry is about understanding one's relationship to it.

Another example is the fifth *Pythian* (companion to the fourth), where the speaker tells how the 'Aegeidae, my fathers' came from Sparta to Thera, whence they emigrated to found Cyrene (72–81). The Aegeidae clan of Sparta came originally from Thebes, and those who want the 'I' always to be Pindar lean on this mythological fact. But we do not know if Pindar was an Aegeid, and even if he were he cannot be claiming that the Aegeidae of *Sparta* were his ancestors; nor can 'fathers' mean anything so vague as 'relatives on my father's side'.[120] So, yes, the voice carrying the melody here is the chorus's, but Pindar is in the harmony. His voice does not disappear. Anyone listening (or reading) can focus, if they choose, on the civic pride of the Cyreneans here; and/or they can be charmed by how Pindar affectionately adopts a Cyrenean voice (as if speaking within quotation marks).[121] The performativity of 'Pindar' is what enables this imaginative 'I' to be created and recognized. A similar analysis pertains in the seventh *Nemean*, where the speaker says that Aeacus is the leader of 'my' country (85), which should be the Aeginetan chorus, whereas at line 61 the person who says 'I am foreign guest' must be Pindar. Some scholars want to emend the second passage, but there is no need; one can read it as Pindar momentarily assuming an Aeginetan identity alongside the chorus.[122]

This wonderful mixing of voices in different proportions is only possible, however, because Pindar shares his voice with the chorus; the chorus cannot share its voice with him, for it has no voice other than that which he creates. To use another musical metaphor, it is the sense of a great conductor on the podium (himself the composer) that gives the Pindaric 'I' its distinctive force. The orchestral (choral) fireworks dazzle and absorb the listener; at the same time, a more detached admiration of the craft, the *sophiā*, is in play, boosting the impulse to inhabit the 'I', especially among those able to appreciate the skill (the *sunetoi*).

So let us take a closer look at the composer-conductor in action, and our relationship with him.

## 'So I too': Pindar's 'I' and us

Pindar's openings are often elaborate affairs; he himself lays it down as a principle that a 'far-shining façade' (*prosōpon tēlauges*) is the way to start a poem (*O*.6.3–4). One great opening among many is that of the seventh *Olympian*:[123]

| | |
|---|---|
| As a man takes a drinking-bowl | Φιάλαν ὡς εἴ τις ἀφνειᾶς ἀπὸ |
| Bubbling within with the dew of | χειρὸς ἑλών |
| the vine, and from his wealthy | ἔνδον ἀμπέλου καχλάζοισαν |
| hand | δρόσῳ |
| Presents it (*dōrēsetai*) | δωρήσεται |
| To his young son-in-law, with a | νεανίᾳ γαμβρῷ προπίνων |
| toast from house to house – | οἴκοθεν οἴκαδε, πάγχρυσον |
| all-golden summit of his | κορυφὰν κτεάνων, |
| possessions – | 5 συμποσίου τε χάριν κᾶδός τε |
| 5 In honour of the symposium's | τιμάσαις ‹ν›έον, ἐν δὲ φίλων |
| grace (*charis*) and his new | παρεόντων θῆκέ νιν ζαλωτὸν |
| relation; and has made him | ὁμόφρονος εὐνᾶς· |
| The envy of his gathered friends | |
| for his harmonious marriage, | |
| | |
| So I too send the liquid nectar, | καὶ ἐγὼ νέκταρ χυτόν, Μοισᾶν |
| gift of the Muses, to prize- | δόσιν, ἀεθλοφόροις |
| winning | ἀνδράσιν πέμπων, γλυκὺν |
| Men, sweet fruit of the mind, | καρπὸν φρενός, |
| And pray good cheer | ἱλάσκομαι |
| (*hīlaskomai*) | 10 Ὀλυμπίᾳ Πυθοῖ τε νικώντεσσιν. |
| 10 For the champions at Olympia | ὁ δ' ὄλβιος, ὃν φᾶμαι |
| and Delphi. Happy is he whom | κατέχωντ' ἀγαθαί· |
| good reports embrace; | ἄλλοτε δ' ἄλλον ἐποπτεύει Χάρις |
| Now upon one, now upon | ζωθάλμιος ἁδυμελεῖ |
| another does life-nourishing | θαμὰ μὲν φόρμιγγι παμφώνοισί |
| (*zōthalmios*) Charis smile | τ' ἐν ἔντεσι αὐλῶν. |
| Oft with melodious lyre and the | |
| pipe's many voices. | |

| | |
|---|---|
| And so to the sound of both I | καί νυν ὑπ' ἀμφοτέρων σὺν |
|   have arrived with Diagoras, | Διαγόρᾳ κατέβαν, τὰν ποντίαν |
|   hymning | ὑμνέων, παῖδ' Ἀφροδίτας |
| Her of the sea, child of Aphrodite | Ἀελίοιό τε νύμφαν, Ῥόδον … |
|   and bride of Helios, Rhodes … | |

I draw attention first to the beautiful verb *hīlaskomai* in line 9, whose unusual application here has challenged commentators. It is used predominantly in religious contexts, where one is asking a god to be *hīlaos*, that is propitious and kind, but it can also be used of humans (e.g. Hdt. 8.112.3). Gods are notoriously capricious and often angry; consequently, 'appease' is the first equivalent one finds in the dictionary. The religious use is so prevalent, in fact, that some commentators have thought that 'gods' is the unexpressed object here. That is very difficult, and the idea of resentful gods is clearly not appropriate in the context. And sometimes the gods will be predisposed to be kindly, as for instance Sappho believes that a smiling Aphrodite will join her and her friends in their gathering, even pouring the wine herself (fr. 2.13–16). In fact, and quite unusually, no object is expressed here for the verb, and to supply one would unduly restrict its application. 'Appease' is an adventitious meaning; the root meaning is doing or saying something to produce good cheer and grace. *Hīlaos* is a word entirely at home in feasts and symposia; we have noted it above (p. 72) in discussing the third *Olympian*, and Alcaeus exhorts his fellows to drink with cheery hearts (in his dialect, *illāenti thūmōi*, fr. 58.19). Pindar seeks to spread joy amongst gods and men alike, replicating the spirit of the simile's happy symposium in the victory celebrations. The parallel between his gift and that of the father-in-law is reinforced metrically: *dōrēsetai* and *hīlaskomai* are two extremely short verses, in the same part of each stanza. The religious overtones of the word need not be discarded, but rather than the gods being addressed directly, they are part of the wider scene that Pindar addresses. They meld with the people, just as the Muse merges with Pindar's talent in lines 7–8. In the same way *charis* – grace, civility, goodwill and, personified as Charis (in our poor way of thinking and writing; ancient Greek did not distinguish upper- and lower-case letters), the goddess who bestows all these qualities on festive occasions with her songs and dances – is both the spirit honoured by the father-in-law at the symposium (5), and partner of the Muse in Pindar's celebration (11).[124] She makes life burgeon; Pindar's neologism *zōthalmios* occurs only here in Greek.

The opening tableau is so captivating that one almost forgets it is the vehicle, not the tenor, of the simile. Literal-minded critics have even thought it signals sympotic performance of the ode (possible, of course, but not necessary). But then the bliss of this scene is smoothly redirected to the victory celebration, and Pindar reveals himself as the master both of the proceedings on the ground and of the poem's beautifully integrated ethics and aesthetics. 'So I too' is twice explicit in this proem (lines 7 and 13), and occurs again at *I*.8.5; but it is implicit in any poem with a first-person pronoun, and it is the fundamental dynamic of the epinician's reception. The poet joins in, and so do we; the 'I' guides (though it does not dictate) our response.

Consider how this dynamic works. Already before the first word of any ode, we know there existed a background situation: the victory and its celebration. One cannot forget that it is an extratextual matter, but the poem transfigures the occasion, and it is only through the text that a sense is created of what we are joining. Pindar inscribes his role as mediator so forcefully and so inventively that poet and occasion become one. We have seen too that his visualization is evocative rather than photographic;[125] both it and the 'I' are performative and exemplary. Exemplarity distinguishes this 'I' from the first-person narrator of a novel, who can also bring a scene vividly before the reader's eyes. The novel's visualization tends towards the photographic, and the exemplarity is not typically overt or integral to the speaker's persona.

Exemplarity allows the poet to bridge the gap between the real occasion he has textualized and the future. We can invoke here Mark Payne's striking analysis of 'fidelity' and 'farewell': on the one hand the poet must faithfully reflect the occasion and its ethics, which are anchored in time, yet he also wants to escape the temporal constraint, and gesture towards the transcendent; to go beyond the Pillars of Hercules.[126] Exemplarity stakes a claim to permanence by suggesting that the particular occasion instantiates timeless truths. A sense of tradition is inscribed in the poems, so that the celebration is both part of and not part of the moment. In the absence of an age-old ritual tradition, the epinician must be parasitic upon other forms such as the hymn, but it can also, by virtue of its wide-ranging appropriations from other genres, give its new-made tradition an especially literary character. In such a scenario the poet's exemplary 'I' is the signature of the demiurge. It belongs to both present and future: for the original audience, by being typical and representative; for later audiences, by foregrounding the poet's role as mediator, and by contriving to make us part of the same unbroken tradition as he. Later audiences are the living proof that he has escaped the temporal straitjacket. From Pindar's point of view we live beyond the Pillars. The gesture of farewell speaks more directly to us, but it only works in conjunction with the gesture of fidelity. From our point of view, we oscillate between losing ourselves in the moment (the fidelity) – being there – and standing back to marvel at how this is accomplished (the farewell). For us, the proem's enchanting imagery, elegant structure and affective relationships must stand in for the *charis* that was the first occasion; but this is the secret of the transfiguration, which in some ways creates a superior experience: the poem looks both ways, from text to occasion and from occasion to text. We seem to witness the transfiguration happening before our very eyes. Event and art meld. This simultaneous absorption and distancing is of course the hallmark of sublime historical and literary experience. Charis has worked her magic very well in these lines.

The endings of odes are another place where gestures of fidelity and farewell, enacted by the 'I', are apt to cluster. Here are the closing lines of the tenth *Olympian*:

| | |
|---|---|
| But on you the lyre's delightful words | τὶν δ' ἁδυεπής τε λύρα |
| and the sweet flute sprinkle their grace, | γλυκύς τ' αὐλὸς ἀναπάσσει χάριν· |
| and Zeus's Pierian daughters nurture 95 | τρέφοντι δ' εὐρὺ κλέος |
| your spreading fame; and I, lending them | κόραι Πιερίδες Διός. |
| an eager hand, have embraced the | |
| Lokrians' famous folk, drenching in | ἐγὼ δὲ συνεφαπτόμενος σπουδᾷ, |
| honey this city with its goodly men; and I | κλυτὸν ἔθνος |
| have praised the lovely son of | Λοκρῶν ἀμφέπεσον, μέλιτι |
| Archestratos, whom I saw as he won by | εὐάνορα πόλιν καταβρέχων· παῖδ' |
| strength of hand by the Olympian altar on | ἐρατὸν <δ'> Ἀρχεστράτου |
| that day – fair in his form and blended 100 | αἴνησα, τὸν εἶδον κρατέοντα χερὸς |
| with youth – youth that once kept | ἀλκᾷ |
| ruthless death from Ganymedes with the | βωμὸν παρ' Ὀλύμπιον |
| Cyprian's aid. | κεῖνον κατὰ χρόνον |
| | ἰδέᾳ τε καλόν |
| | ὥρᾳ τε κεκραμένον, ἅ ποτε |
| | 105 ἀναιδέα Γανυμήδει θάνατον ἄλαλκε[127] |
| | σὺν Κυπρογενεῖ. |

This moving translation is by W.S. (Spencer) Barrett (1914–2001), in a posthumously published discussion of the tenth and eleventh *Olympians*.[128] Barrett is the author of the standard commentary on Euripides' *Hippolytus*, a masterpiece of traditional philology but, as one reviewer put it, not a book that would 'inspire the reader with delight in the *Hippolytus* as a work of art'.[129] I attended his lectures and seminars on Pindar in the late 1970s, from which I learned a great deal about manuscripts, metre, Greek usage and so on, but not much about literary criticism (which, to be fair, he did not consider to be part of his job). Here, after the usual sort of philological discussion, Barrett says that 'to finish the paper, I will confine myself to poetry'. He offers translations with brief comments of lines 73 to the end. On lines 91–3 ('So when a man does noble things and then comes without a song, Hagesidamos, to the steading of Hades, he has panted in vain and has given his labour but a brief delight') he writes:

> The same point that we had in *O*.11: without a song, men forget; the victor's glory perishes with him. But with a song it endures. As indeed it does endure: when we now, eighty generations later, on a winter evening in a barbarian island, can still picture the young Hagesidamos in the flush of victory on that hot day in Greece.

Then the translation of the final lines, with which the paper ends. Barrett's comment nicely confirms what I have been saying about the effect Pindar has on readers, even hardened philologists. He inhabits the 'I' and marvels at how it is done, both at the same time; a sublime experience. There is a nested temporality in the lines: the ode was performed long after the Games, but Pindar says that he was there and saw Hagesidamus win: Barrett, from the standpoint of eternity which is also thematized in the passage, zooms past the occasion of the ode to the victory ('we can still picture'). Pindar's comment is indeed arresting, and seizes the imagination (he was actually there!). This is extreme fidelity. So too are his comments about how faithfully he has executed his commission.

Pindar also mentions the lyre and 'flute' (traditional mistranslation of *aulos* or *auloi*, the double pipe), which is a reference to the musical execution of the ode, i.e. a gesture of fidelity. Here, though, we can bridge to the gesture of farewell by way of exemplarity: the instruments are a metonymy for all that the celebration represents. They 'sprinkle their grace' upon Hagesidamus (note the tense: here surely 'are sprinkling' would be wrong). 'Grace' is *charis*, which we have met already in the seventh *Olympian*, keeping company there too with the lyre and pipe (where note the typifying 'oft' in line 12, followed by the instantiation of the general practice in line 13). We have several other references to the two instruments together; sometimes Pindar mentions the lyre alone, and twice the aulos alone.[130] These references can of course indicate how the first performance was accompanied, but it is a mistake to think they were merely prescriptive (and that not even inflexibly: just as Pindar's epinicians could be performed either by chorus or soloist, so they could be accompanied by whatever instrument(s) or musician(s) were available). The main function of the references in the poems is as symbols, and they can do their work even if you have no aulete to go with your lyre-player on the day (or are just reading it).[131]

Other aspects of fidelity in this passage are the variations on the idea of sweetness, which is part of *charis*, and the bonds of affection uniting the participants; but equally, by their exemplarity, these feelings are readily accessed in repeated receptions. They are tied to the gesture of farewell very inventively by way of Ganymede(s), the youth taken up to Olympus to be cup-bearer to the gods and lover of Zeus. Hagesidamus won in the youths' boxing competition, and Pindar casts an intensely erotic gaze on him here. Like Ganymede he is preserved forever in this moment of perfection, which not even death can touch. The poem ends with the vision of Ganymede in our minds, that is to say upon Olympus, and eternity. But his rapture took place at a specific moment in time in the past, just as Pindar saw Hagesidamus 'on that day' at Olympus. From that moment on, through Pindar's present to the unending future of the last line, the boy lives. His 'spreading fame' is identical with the poem. Temporality and eternity here occupy the same place, and the incommensurability creates a characteristically sublime moment.

To return to openings, here are a few that illuminate further aspects of the topic. We shall find that the 'I' is expansive; it spreads its arms to embrace 'we', 'you', 'one' and even a goddess.

1. O.1.1–7:

   | | |
   |---|---|
   | Water is best; gold, like blazing fire, | Ἄριστον μὲν ὕδωρ, ὁ δὲ χρυσὸς αἰθόμενον πῦρ |
   | Stands out at night, best of a noble man's wealth; | ἄτε διαπρέπει νυκτὶ μεγάνορος ἔξοχα πλούτου· |
   | But if, dear heart, you wish To sing of games, | εἰ δ' ἄεθλα γαρύεν ἔλδεαι, φίλον ἦτορ, |
   | 5  Mark by day no other bright star Warmer than the sun in the empty aether, | 5  μηκέτ' ἀελίου σκόπει ἄλλο θαλπνότερον ἐν ἀμέρᾳ φαεννὸν ἄστρον ἐρήμας δι' αἰθέρος, |
   | And let us speak of no contest superior to Olympia | μηδ' Ὀλυμπίας ἀγῶνα φέρτερον αὐδάσομεν· |

2. O.2.1–2:

   | | |
   |---|---|
   | Songs of praise, lords of the lyre, Which god, which hero, which man shall we celebrate? | Ἀναξιφόρμιγγες ὕμνοι, τίνα θεόν, τίν' ἥρωα, τίνα δ' ἄνδρα κελαδήσομεν; |

3. *O*.10.1–6:

Read to me where in my mind
Archestratus' son is written!
I have forgotten that I owe him a sweet
    song. But Muse! You and Zeus's
    daughter Truth, with your upright
    hand
5  Fend off the lying
    Charge that I slight my friends.

Τὸν Ὀλυμπιονίκαν ἀνάγνωτέ μοι
Ἀρχεστράτου παῖδα, πόθι φρενὸς
ἐμᾶς γέγραπται· γλυκὺ γὰρ αὐτῷ
    μέλος ὀφείλων ἐπιλέλαθ'· ὦ
    Μοῖσ', ἀλλὰ σὺ καὶ θυγάτηρ
Ἀλάθεια Διός, ὀρθᾷ χερί
5  ἐρύκετον ψευδέων
    ἐνιπὰν ἀλιτόξενον.

4. *P*.3.1–3:

I could wish that Chiron son of
    Philyra –
If our tongue should express this prayer
    for everyone –
Yet lived, gone though he is

Ἤθελον Χείρωνά κε Φιλλυρίδαν,
εἰ χρεὼν ἁμετέρας ἀπὸ γλώσσας
    κοινὸν εὔξασθαι ἔπος,
ζώειν τὸν ἀποιχόμενον

5. *N*.5.1–5:

I am no maker of statues, working
    images that stand stock-still upon
    their very bases;
No, go sweet song on every ship and
    every packet
And take the news from Aegina
That Lampon's sturdy son Pytheas
5  Has won the crown for the pankration
    in the Nemea

Οὐκ ἀνδριαντοποιός εἰμ', ὥστ'
    ἐλινύσοντα ἐργάζεσθαι
    ἀγάλματ' ἐπ' αὐτᾶς βαθμίδος
ἑστάοτ'· ἀλλ' ἐπὶ πάσας ὁλκάδος ἔν
    τ' ἀκάτῳ, γλυκεῖ' ἀοιδά,
στεῖχ' ἀπ' Αἰγίνας διαγγέλλοισ' ὅτι
Λάμπωνος υἱὸς Πυθέας εὐρυσθενής
5  νίκη Νεμείοις παγκρατίου στέφανον

Much could be, and has been, said about the imagery, themes and language of these wonderfully creative proems. Here we concentrate on the workings of the first person. The singular is explicit in nos 3, 4 and 5. As it happens, no. 4 is a poem that stresses the poet's personal relationship with the dedicatee Hieron, who is seriously ill; it is a prayer that his health may be restored, but it offers too a moving consolation in case the prayer is not answered. That relationship might be thought sufficient to explain the 'I' of the first line; it is Pindar, full stop. But already in line 2 matters become complicated. 'Our tongue' might be an author's 'we', plural for singular, so still Pindar; there are some clear cases of that in the odes.[132] On the other hand, we could be dealing with an alternation familiar from other choral poetry, where the chorus can refer to itself either in the singular or the plural; in that case, the 'I could wish' would refer to the chorus, not Pindar. Then we have the prayer that is spoken 'for everyone' (*koinon*, literally 'shared' or 'common'). The poet's task is to express the thoughts and feelings of the community, which would suit the singular interpretation well; but a chorus actually embodies the community, and they could equally well say this.

Of course it can be both. A chorus could be thought of as simply ventriloquizing Pindar, but one would assume that they endorse the sentiment.[133] A solo performer would also be a ventriloquist in this case, since (as we learn later in the poem) Pindar couldn't be there in person; but a solo performance might have the effect of emphasizing a little more strongly the author's personal relationship with Hieron. In the later passage (63–9), which loops back to the opening by ring-composition (repeating the wish about Chiron), we have the same alternation of 'I' and 'we', although there it is very clear that both are Pindar. Pindar's language, as often, makes provision for flexible performance contexts and flexible receptions. But if we consider further the force of the prayer 'for everyone', we realize another aspect of the flexibility. 'Everyone' obviously means not 'everyone in the chorus' (if the performance is choral) but 'everyone in the community'. The 'we' turns out to be very capacious. 'Our tongue' could just as well belong to everybody listening.

In a non-mimetic genre such as the epinician, 'we' can much more easily include the audience than it does in drama. Already in Homer we find this phenomenon, as the great Swiss linguist Jacob Wackernagel observed a century ago: the *Odyssey* begins 'tell me, Muse, of the man of many turns', and nine lines later rounds off the proem with 'of these matters, from where you will, daughter of Zeus, tell us too': 'us' is the poet and his audience.[134] The first line of Hesiod's *Theogony* says 'let us begin'. Once the narrative gets under way, however, such references in epic become scarce. In the lyric genres, 'we' can shift easily from 'we who are performing this song' to 'we who are members of this community' (or be both at once). Furthermore, if the 'I' is choral, it can often become 'we' by the conventions of choral poetry; or, if it is the poet's 'I', because that pronoun is performative or exemplary (or both at once), 'we' can quite easily take its place. In all cases the effect is to draw the audience into the poem.

There are distinctions within the lyric genres, however, and between poets. One finds more first-person plurals in epinician poetry than in other genres, and more in Pindar than in Bacchylides. In drama, although the alternation of 'I' and 'we' is common, it is not totally random or unlimited. The singular predominates. Plurals are apt to occur when emphasis on the chorus's character as a group is wanted (for instance when they are praying for their community); they are especially likely if the chorus is a group with a stake in the action (thus in Aeschylus' *Suppliant Women*, about the daughters of Danaus avoiding marriage to their cousins, we find many more first-person plurals than in other plays).[135] In genres such as the paean or the dithyramb, undoubtedly choral performances, first-person plurals are scarce.[136] They are not especially common in Bacchylides' epinicians, either.[137] In Pindar's, however, we find a significant number. These can include not only performers, but the audience too;[138] many denote 'people in general' or 'the human race as a whole' (e.g. O.2.31–4, 'for mortals no end of death is fixed, nor when we might complete our peaceful day, child of the sun, with blessings undiminished').[139] The difference from Bacchylides' practice must be the result of poetic choice. As the 'I' shades into 'we' in Pindar's odes, a sense of collaboration is built into the text between speaker and listener, or rather reinforced, since the 'I', as we have seen, already invites inhabitation. Even where this 'we' is explicitly the primary audience (e.g. 'we here in Thebes'), the deft and economical evocation of the scene brings it effortlessly to the imagination of future audiences, who are drawn in as much as the original one, if in a different way.

Pindar's use of the second person points in the same direction. Number 3 above begins 'Read to me where in my mind Archestratus' son is written!' I take the command 'read', second-person plural, to be addressed to the audience, who are invited to help Pindar find his mislaid song, and absolve his debt (it must be his, not the chorus's). The sixth *Pythian* opens with a peremptory 'Listen!', using a verb (*akousate*) which may echo the 'hear ye!' formula of public assemblies.[140] Much more common in Pindar (and wholly absent in Bacchylides) are second-person singular commands addressed to no one in particular, and thus to everyone – a generic or exemplary 'you' to complement the exemplary 'I'. This device is found in Greek choral poetry from the beginning; in Alcman's first *Partheneion* the chorus sings of the beautiful Agido, 'Do you (sing.) not see? The courser is Venetian!' (*PMGF* 1.50–1). Technically they may be supposed to be addressing one another, but anyone listening would turn at once to look at Agido, just as we readers do in our mind's eye. (The singular is in any case patently mannered, and performative; it cannot be taken literally as referring to one individual.) The device is in Homer too (e.g. *Il.* 15.697), Herodotus (e.g. 2.29) and many others; Longinus quotes these passages, and points out how they engage the listener's imagination and emotions.[141] But, as often, Pindar takes an inherited resource and greatly expands its use. I count fully thirty-two examples in the epinicians.[142] In the ninth *Olympian* (36–48) there is a remarkable series of seven commands which are nominally addressed to the speaker's 'mouth', which is admittedly an instance of self-address rather than an address to no one in particular; but of course, when one addresses oneself, one is pretending to address a second person, so there is some overlap. There are four more such addresses in the epinicians, that in no. 1 above plus *O.2.89*, *P.3.61*, and *N.3.31*, and two in the other genres (frr. 123.2, 127.4). All in all, this is a remarkable total of imperatives.[143]

Some of these are gnomic (e.g. *O.5.24* 'do not seek to be a god'), but like all apostrophes these too serve to buttonhole the listener. A much larger number are either exhortations to praise the victor, or form a class of comment especially associated with Pindar, about what is being (or should be) said or done, or not said or done in the poem. Such remarks are frequently found at 'break-off points', for instance to draw the myth to a close and move on to other items in the epinician programme; they are inherently metapoetic. Their very frequency provides Pindar with an opportunity to display his fabled *poikiliā* (variation); metaphors abound: 'you' are variously invited to shoot arrows at Delphi, hold the oar and plant the anchor, sow splendour, spread sails, whirl a murmuring of praise, drown boasting in silence, swim away with light feet (i.e. end the poem), and so on.[144] Such apostrophes encourage reflection on the poet's craft (Pindar's raising the pitch of inventiveness at such moments is predictable). Then there are apostrophes not of people, but of things; in our passages above, songs of praise (or hymns, *hymnoi*) are addressed in no. 2, and the song in no. 5.[145] The poem in these two passages is figured as something apart from its composer, to be interrogated, commanded, enlisted in support. In no. 2, the poem is even asked to specify its own subject, as if the poet didn't know already; the 'we' of the next line is formally 'you hymns and we' (or 'you hymns and I'). Culler's thesis that apostrophes even of objects are inherently collaborative, forming a triangular relationship of speaker, addressee and audience, is well confirmed by these passages, since both of the apostrophes are integrally linked to an 'I/we' in the text. We have here a dramatization of the poem's coming-into-being, and the projection of the poet's own persona – performativity, in other words. In presenting the song as different from himself, the poet poses as merely an equal partner in the production, or perhaps even the junior partner, awaiting instructions. But by highlighting the fact that there *is* both a poet and a song, the trope actually emphasizes the process of creation and advertises the creator, thus revealing the true hierarchy.

A momentary disjunction between performer and text can be diagnosed also in the so-called 'performative future', examples of which abound in Pindar (e.g.

O.6.21 'I shall bear witness', O.13.91 'I shall not speak of his death', or N.9.10 'I shall exalt [Adrastus]', with reference to the present performance).[146] The figure implies a notional shift backwards in time, when the speaker had asked himself 'what shall I say?', and answers 'I will say ...', followed by execution of the decision. The rhetorical effect depends on this separation, however minimal, of decision and performance.[147] It is inherently self-reflective, and advertises the presence and agency of the 'I' as distinct from what is being performed.

Pindar is fully alive to the rhetorical potential of a temporal gap, as D'Alessio in particular has highlighted.[148] Some passages are written as if from the perspective of the time of composition ('coding time'); their future coincides with the actual performance ('receiving time'). At the opening of the third *Nemean*, for instance, the poet asks the Muse to communicate a song to him, which he 'will' in turn communicate to the singers, who are awaiting it. Of course the performance has already begun. No. 3 above is similar (one can count the imperative as the equivalent of a future). There is no cognitive difficulty for the audience in notionally rewinding the clock in such passages, and starting up again a moment later in the present. Openings are perhaps an unsurprising place to find this ploy, given lyric's propensity to begin by setting a scene, or explaining why there is a song in the first place; above I mentioned Alcman *PMGF* 3, also cited by D'Alessio.[149] Less expected are passages after the poem is well under way, and in some of these the gap between coding and receiving time is substantial (as they are inscribed in the text, of course, not as they might have been in reality), as in the ninth *Pythian* where the speaker anticipates the victor's welcome (i.e. this song) upon his return from Delphi.[150]

Most interesting of all are futures or equivalents at the very end of an ode, which happens eight times.[151] Take the ending of the eleventh *Olympian*, which Bundy made the polemical centrepiece of his discussion of these futures. In his opinion they never refer to anything outside the ode. The speaker asserts, 'I will celebrate Hegesidamus' victory, heeding the race of the Western Locrians [the victor's city]; where join the revel! I will guarantee, Muses, that you will find no inhospitable host'. Bundy was concerned to refute the thesis that these words promised a future ode to be performed in Locri (to wit, O.10), while this one was performed in Olympia; also that Pindar subsequently forgot his promise, creating the need for the elaborate apology in the later poem (whose opening is no. 3 above). Now it does seem that Pindar was late with the tenth *Olympian*, as not only the beginning (which could be interpreted less literally, as an example of the 'debt-motif' found elsewhere in Pindar) but also the ending (85–90), with its talk of the poem appearing 'eventually' and its simile of a late-born son bringing joy to an aged father, indicate.[152] Bundy is right, however, that there is no need to connect the ending of *O.*11 with this situation. On the other hand, that passage cannot refer *only* to the present performance. There are two points to make. First, an injunction like 'join the revel', whether at the end of a poem or not, works like 'take the lyre from the peg' in the first *Olympian* (above, p. 68); it is a timeless exhortation. (Even if grammatically this command is addressed to the Muses – which is not agreed by everyone – that means the audience too, whether contemporary or future.) Second, since Pindar's 'performative future' does not in itself execute the action, but dramatizes a gap between decision and performance, then it must create a special situation when the future comes at the end of the poem, and the execution does not in fact follow in the text. The second *Nemean*'s very last words are 'make a start with sweet song!' Clearly this command lingers on. It *might* have been literally realized by further celebrations on the day, and/or by subsequent reperformance of the poems. But these can be no more than guesses, however plausible. More important, and verifiable, is the non-literal realization of the command: it expresses what any right-minded person's response should be to the situation, now or at any time, and therefore as we read we instinctively enact the command. These expressions, where the gap is opened but not closed, effect a *suspension* of temporality, taking the exemplary 'you' into the realm of the lyric 'now'. The sweet song starts, and never ends. The suspension is comparable to that achieved when a poem ends in mythical time, about which I shall have more to say in the next chapter.

The performative disjunction between speaker and text is of course very obvious in the trope of self-address. The sequence in no. 1 above ('But if, dear heart, you wish to sing of games … let us speak') is formally like that in no. 2 ('songs of praise … which man shall we celebrate?'); later on in the second *Olympian* (ll. 89–90), we find 'Come, my spirit (*thūmos*), whom shall we bombard once more, loosing our famous arrows from a gentle temper (*phrēn*)?' In Pindar as in other Greek texts from Homer onwards, the self-address is normally made not to 'you' but to some part of the speaker: in Pindar we find the heart (*ētor*), the spirit (*thūmos*), the soul (*psūchā*), the mouth (*stoma*).[153] The figure's mannered formality confines it unsurprisingly to elevated speech, so that it is an easy target for Aristophanes' parody (e.g. *Ach.* 480–8), which is good native evidence of how the trope was perceived: it is pose-striking, i.e. (once again) performative. Owing to the sometimes quite different and uncertain force of Greek words and concepts for emotions, bodily organs and their capacities, it is unwise to be too dogmatic about the reasons for these different choices in Pindar. But we can at least say the words for heart and spirit denote some kind of emotional impulse or desire, which can be followed or resisted, questioned or commanded. As one might expect, these conversations-with-self frequently address the theme of what should or should not be said in the poem, ineluctably evoking the figure of the poet in the text. Because 'we' stand alongside the poet in the conversation, we and he together become imaginatively involved in what the poem is going to do next.

The same relationship pertains in another category of utterance, which is in effect a variant of the self-address or the generic 'you' command but not a formal apostrophe: the poet often refers to what 'it is necessary' to do or what 'one' must or should do (e.g. *O*.6.1–4, 6.27, *I*.1.41–6, 3.7–8), often adding a first-person pronoun to the impersonal Greek verb as in no. 4 above ('if our tongue should express', literally 'if it is necessary that our tongue express'). At *O*.1.100–3 he writes 'I must crown him'; at *O*.8.74 'I must express the victorious work of their hands'; at *P*.2.52 'I must shun the violent bite of slander', and so on. In fact he has a myriad of ways to express impulse, obligation or principle as driving his poetic course; perhaps the best-known such intervention is in the first *Olympian* (52), where he denounces the traditional tale that Pelops was cut up and eaten by the gods: 'Impossible for me to say that any of the blessed ones is such a glutton: I stand back! Profitless is the lot of evil-speakers', followed by the rest of his alternative version.[154] Many of these statements, both personal and impersonal, are linked to other markers of the poet's presence in the text, and many serve as dividers between elements of the programme (e.g. acting as so-called 'break-off' formulae), for which he is responsible. As D'Alessio has put it, 'The performers were obviously there, but it was clear to everybody that the poet, present or not, was hiding behind their voices.'[155]

Taken together, these devices and tropes represent an astounding variety of ways in which Pindar brings his audience into the poems. And perhaps the most impressive one is yet to mention: his relationship to the Muse (or the Muses; no pattern can be detected in when Pindar thinks of them as a singular or a multi-faceted entity).[156] In no. 3 above, he asks the Muse and Truth to fend off the charge of neglecting his friends. Since he is the defendant, and the defence will consist in the poem he is about to offer, one can read the Muse as a projection of himself, yet another variant of the self-address. The same close collaboration is seen at the end of *Olympian* 10, quoted above (p. 105), where the Muses nurture spreading fame, and Pindar lends a willing hand. On several occasions the two of them head off together in their chariot (*O*.9.81; cf. *P*.10.65, *I*.2.2, 8.61, *Paean* 7b.13–14). At *I*.6.57, he addresses her in passing as he breaks off the myth and announces what he will do next; similarly at *P*.11.38–41 he announces that he has gone off track, then tells the Muse to get on with the praise, 'since you have contracted to provide your silvered voice for recompense'. At *N*.3.28, another break-off passage, he tells his *thūmos* to deliver the Muse to Aeacus. Like self-addresses, these metapoetic mini-dramas sharpen the focus on the poem's workings, and intensify the relationship of audience to speaking persona and the text.

Yet these are not exactly self-addresses, if one means by that that the Muses are ultimately just Pindar in disguise, an alter ego. They are at one, but they are not one. A traditional narrative about poets and Muses in the archaic period holds that the poets increasingly asserted their independence as time passed. In Homer, the bard is a passive recipient of what the Muses have to say. He knows nothing himself; he is merely their mouthpiece. At the other end of this supposed development stands Pindar, who thinks that he is the principal contributor to the poetic enterprise. A passage that could support such a reading is *Pythian* 4.71–2, where the myth is initiated with Homeric-sounding questions 'What beginning of the voyage [of the *Argo*] awaited them? What danger gripped them with adamantine spikes?': no Muses here (they are mentioned in line 67, but there Pindar says he will give his song to *them*!). We find the same omission at *O*.10.60, where Pindar asks who won the prizes at the first Games; also at *O*.13.18–22 and *I*.5.39-42.[157] But Homer too can neglect to mention her (e.g. *Il.* 5.703, 8.273), and no one thinks to charge *him* with hybris.

Rather, the greater complexity of the social contexts of poetry, and the birth of the wholly new genre of the epinician, resulted in a more overtly theoretical reflection on poetics, which naturally enough gets inscribed in the poems. Awareness of collaboration replaces a sense of passive inspiration. The traditional narrative reflects the outsider's perspective, and to talk of increased independence is to impose a false opposition between human being and motivating divinity, as Greeks thought of such matters; in effect, it denies the divinity. These are the goddesses who, for Pindar, sang at the weddings of Peleus and Thetis, of Cadmus and Harmonia (*P*.3.90, *N*.5.23), and they work in and through him. If one surveys his references, one cannot fail to be struck by the depth of his attachment. Except for Sappho and her Aphrodite, there is nothing remotely like it in Greek literature. The Muses nurture his poetic arrows. They stood by him when he found new music for the Dorian dance. They trust him to bear witness; conversely, he can guarantee to them what they will find. He can summon the Muse; he can bid her to be persuaded, to take a stand by the celebrand, or to send a 'breeze' of words. He prays that he may find them willing, and that they will swell the flourishing of his song. He is their ally, their messenger, their herald; his chorus-leader is their 'message-stick'. They are a target for him to aim at. They send up the holy spring of Dirce in Thebes, from which he will drink. They are engravers; they are archers; their gift is liquid nectar; their poets are ploughmen.[158] I have not listed all the passages; these may suffice. Odysseus was not closer to Athena than Pindar was to his Muse.

## The shadow's dream

I mentioned at the beginning of the chapter that, besides the opening of the first *Pythian*, the close of the eighth is the other Pindaric passage most often deemed sublime.

|  | But when one attains a fresh success |  | ὁ δὲ καλόν τι νέον λαχών |
|--|--|--|--|
|  | Amid great prosperity, |  | ἁβρότατος ἔπι μεγάλας |
| 90 | Hope makes one soar | 90 | ἐξ ἐλπίδος πέταται |
|  | On wings of manly prowess |  | ὑποπτέροις ἀνορέαις, ἔχων |
|  | With ambition greater than wealth. |  | κρέσσονα πλούτου μέριμναν. ἐν δ᾽ |
|  | But the flourishing |  | ὀλίγῳ βροτῶν |
|  | Of human joy is brief; and so it falls to the ground, |  | τὸ τερπνὸν αὔξεται· οὕτω δὲ καὶ πίτνει χαμαί, |
|  | Shaken by an adverse judgement. |  | ἀποτρόπῳ γνώμᾳ σεσεισμένον. |
| 95 | Creatures of a day! What are we? What are we not? | 95 | ἐπάμεροι· τί δέ τις; τί δ᾽ οὔ τις; σκιᾶς ὄναρ |
|  | We are the dream of a shadow. Yet when the gleam of Zeus descends, |  | ἄνθρωπος.[159] ἀλλ᾽ ὅταν αἴγλα Διόσδοτος ἔλθῃ, |
|  | The light shines bright around us, and our time is sweet. |  | λαμπρὸν φέγγος ἔπεστιν ἀνδρῶν καὶ μείλιχος αἰών. |
|  | Dear mother Aegina! In a course of freedom |  | Αἴγινα φίλα μᾶτερ, ἐλευθέρῳ στόλῳ |
|  | Bring this city home, with Zeus, mighty Aeacus, |  | πόλιν τάνδε κόμιζε Δὶ καὶ κρέοντι συν Αἰάκῳ |
| 100 | Peleus and good Telamon, and with Achilles. | 100 | Πηλεῖ τε κἀγαθῷ Τελαμῶνι σύν τ᾽ Ἀχιλλεῖ. |

The poem is the latest datable in the corpus (446 BCE), fifty-two years after the earliest (*Pythian* 10, 498 BCE); Pindar would have been in his seventies. Generations of readers have sensed a world-weariness about these closing lines. For those who know about them, it is hard not to think of the grim struggles the people of Aegina had borne and the threats that still faced them under the yoke of the Athenian empire (above, p. 101). Even if one does not, it is easy to infer that the prayer ('In a course of freedom / Bring this city home') is no mere formula. The general point – the insecurity of human fortune, our dependence upon gods for our brief moments of glory – is one Pindar had expressed many times, but the poignancy and power here are unsurpassed.

Stylistic and imagistic virtuosity both contribute. The first stanza is fulsome in its language and leisurely in its pace; the opening of the second, 'Creatures of a day!', then strikes like a thunderbolt. It is a single word in Greek (*epāmeroi*). Longinus would surely call this sublime. There follows a machine-gun run of six monosyllables: *ti de tis ti d'ou tis* ('what are we? what are we not?'); then the famous 'we are the dream of a shadow'.[160] This is a sentence consisting of three nouns without a verb expressed (*skiās onar anthrōpos*), a syntactical structure for which there is no precise parallel in surviving classical Greek.[161] The next words, 'But when the gleam of Zeus …', revert to a statelier rhythm; all is serene, warm, resplendent. But the calm is at once dispelled by 'Dear mother Aegina!', another wholly unexpected, thunderclap moment. After the *cri de coeur*, a parade of venerable Aeginetan heroes, Zeus at their head, closes the poem; a solemn catalogue. The clash of registers and rhythms bespeaks a surfeit of nervous energy, and the quiver of strong emotion. There is an undercurrent of terror, and throughout a sublime oscillation of darkness and light, despair and hope.

The central image is unique. In Homer, the souls of the dead can be a dream or a shadow (*Od.* 10.495, 11.222, 11.207). Tragedy compares living people, particularly old men, to dreams or shadows. But we do not find the two together quite like this.[162] Also unique are the famous and arresting questions that precede them. The continuous debate about their precise meaning among scholars both ancient and modern shows that Pindar has here stretched his language to the limits. I have translated them as I would estimate the majority of translators have done. There is undeniably an existentialist tinge to this version, as if, in defiance of Parmenides, Pindar is thinking of something that is not: there is being, and there is non-being; which are we? The first question asks, what attribute can we positively assign to a person; the second seems to ask, not 'is there some attribute we cannot assign?' (as if we were to say, for example, that person is a scholar, but not a soldier), nor 'is there *any* attribute we cannot assign?' (as if we were to say, 'what are they, you ask? well, what *aren't* they?'), but 'what is a not-one?' As a representative of the alternative translation, we may cite Gentili, who translates '*che cosa è mai qualcuno / che cosa è mai nessuno?*', 'what is a somebody, and what is a nobody?': 'nobody' in the sense of 'a person of no significance'.[163] In the accompanying commentary we read that this was how the passage was understood up to and including Dissen (1830), and that the ancient scholia understood it thus too. The implicit charge is anachronism. The first part of this statement is not quite true, since Heyne translated '*Quidnam est quis? quid non est quis?*' (1774), Böckh '*Quid tandem est quis? quid non quis?* (1821) and Hölderlin '*Was aber ist einer? was aber ist einer nicht?*' (c. 1800); in English, I find that P.E. Laurent translated exactly as I do (with 'we') in 1824. Earlier translations I have consulted do bear out the claim (e.g. H. Stephanus '*quidnam est aliquis? quid vero nullus?*', 1566), so Romantic egocentrism could be responsible for the change.

The scholia also lend support, but their explanation shows that matters are not so black and white. They understand the questions as Gentili does, paraphrasing Pindar 'who is it that seems to be both great and wealthy? And who is considered to be nobody and lowly?', which gives Dissen his '*quid est magnus? quid est parvus?*' ('what is a great person? what is a little one?'). The context in Pindar provides warrant for this, up to a point. The preceding stanza is all about the inconstancy of human fortune. The rapid rhythm of the two antithetical questions itself reflects the blink-of-an-eye oscillation (now this, now not this). The word *ep(h)āmeroi* in Greek ('ephemeral') means 'subject to the day', i.e. changeable, not 'short-lived' (at least not in the first instance; it can come to that in various contexts).[164] But in glossing 'dream of a shadow' the scholia comment 'as if one were to say "what is weaker than weakness"': that is, the phrase denotes the utmost feebleness imaginable. The idea of feebleness leads quickly to that of insubstantiality. The being who has no positive attributes (a 'nobody') is easily looked on as a non-being. In the Greek *imaginaire* a *skiā*, a shade of Hades, is as close to non-being as you can get, as Odysseus discovers when three times he tries to embrace his mother's ghost in the Underworld: thrice she 'flew from my arms like to a shadow or a dream' – the very line Pindar alludes to (*Od.* 11.207). A similar point is made by the chorus of the *Prometheus Bound* (roughly contemporary with this poem) when they tell the Titan he can expect no aid from feeble, blind, dream-like mortals (545–52). The whole play raises existential questions about humanity. Two lines from an unknown play by Aeschylus (fr. 399) use language very similar to Pindar's:

| | |
|---|---|
| The race of humankind has but flighty thoughts (*ephēmera*); | τὸ γὰρ βρότειον σπέρμ' ἐφήμερα φρονεῖ |
| It is no more constant than the shadow of smoke | καὶ πιστὸν οὐδέν μᾶλλον ἢ καπνοῦ σκιά |

Even clearer are these famous lines from Sophocles' *Ajax* (also possibly contemporary), where Odysseus contemplates the wreckage of his former enemy Ajax, humiliated and destroyed by Athena (125–6):

| | |
|---|---|
| I see that we who live are nothing (*ouden*) other than | ὁρῶ γὰρ ἡμᾶς οὐδὲν ὄντας ἄλλο πλὴν |
| Phantoms or an empty shade. | εἴδωλ᾽ ὅσοιπερ ζῶμεν ἢ κούφην σκιάν. |

On this passage an ancient commentator remarked:

| | |
|---|---|
| With reference to Pindar's 'What are we? what are we not? We are the dream of a shadow': what is unreal [or 'nonexistent'] is denoted by what is even more unreal. In this passage Sophocles' language is closer to the truth than Pindar's; Pindar has constructed his hyperbole in terms of insubstantiality, whereas Sophocles does so in terms of what seems and appears to be, but in fact does not exist. | πρὸς τὸ Πινδαρικόν· "τί δέ τις, τί δ᾽ οὔ τις; σκιᾶς ὄναρ ἄνθρωποι." ἀντὶ τοῦ ἀνυπάρκτου τὸ ἀνυπαρκτότερον. ἐνταῦθα μέντοι ἐστὶν ὁ λόγος ἐγγυτέρω τῆς ἀληθείας ἤπερ τὸ Πινδαρικόν· ὁ μὲν γὰρ Πίνδαρος ἐν τοῖς ἀσυστάτοις πεποίηται τὴν ὑπερβολήν, ὁ δὲ ἐν τοῖς φαινομένοις μὲν καὶ δοκοῦσιν οὐχ ὑπάρχουσιν δὲ κατ᾽ ἀλήθειαν.[165] |

And then there is Heraclitus (a generation or so older than Pindar):

| | |
|---|---|
| We step into the same rivers and we do not step into them. We are and we are not. | ποταμοῖς τοῖς αὐτοῖς ἐμβαίνομέν τε καὶ οὐκ ἐμβαίνοιμεν, εἶμέν τε καὶ οὐκ εἶμεν |
| The same thing is therein, living and dead, awake and asleep, young and old. | ταὐτό τ᾽ ἔνι ζῶν καὶ τεθνηκὸς καὶ ἐγρηγορὸς καὶ καθεῦδον καὶ νέον καὶ γηραιόν.[166] |

The authenticity and the interpretation of the second part of the first quotation are disputed, but in the light of the second quotation above an existentialist interpretation can hardly be ruled out.[167]

It is thus no modern fancy that takes Pindar's questions to have such implications. And in the background lies the most famous Nobody of all, the Outis who blinds the Cyclops. Everybody remembers Odysseus' famous trick of telling Polyphemus that his name is 'Nobody' (*Outis*), so that when the other Cyclopes come running in response to Polyphemus' cries, and ask, 'Is somebody trying to kill you by treachery or force?' he answers, 'Nobody is trying to kill me by treachery nor by force', meaning 'by treachery and not by force'; but they hear '... either by treachery or by force', and take their leave (*Od.* 9.408). Later Polyphemus speaks of 'the worthless (*outidanos*) Outis' (460, 515); *that* word does mean a 'nobody'. If Homer is alive to the ambiguities of negatives plus *tis* (and there is more to be said about him than I have here),[168] Pindar is too. So I stick to my translation, and continue to believe that Pindar here not only confronts the stability of our fortune but questions the very grounds of our existence.

As final confirmation I cite the opening of the sixth *Nemean*:

| | |
|---|---|
| One – the race of men[169] and gods is<br>  one; from one | Ἓν ἀνδρῶν, ἓν θεῶν γένος· ἐκ μιᾶς δὲ<br>  πνέομεν |
| Mother we both draw breath. But every<br>  distinction | ματρὸς ἀμφότεροι· διείργει δὲ πᾶσα<br>  κεκριμένα |
| Of power separates us: one is nothing<br>  (*ouden*), for the other the bronze | δύναμις, ὡς τὸ μὲν οὐδέν, ὁ δὲ χάλκεος<br>  ἀσφαλὲς αἰὲν ἕδος |
| heaven endures, an ever unshaken<br>  abode. Nonetheless | μένει οὐρανός. ἀλλά τι προσφέρομεν<br>  ἔμπαν ἢ μέγαν |
| 5  We bear a modicum of resemblance to  5<br>  the immortals | νόον ἤτοι φύσιν ἀθανάτοις, |
| Whether in greatness of thought or<br>  bodily form | καίπερ ἐπαμερίαν οὐκ εἰδότες οὐδὲ<br>  μετὰ νύκτας |
| Even if day by day (*epāmeriān*) and<br>  night by night we know not | ἄμμε πότμος |
| What course fate has inscribed for us to<br>  run. | ἄντιν' ἔγραψε δραμεῖν ποτὶ στάθμαν. |

Here the two ideas are thoroughly commingled. Human inconstancy is emphasized by the contrast with the steadfastness of heaven and by our permanent ignorance of what tomorrow will bring. But the divine attribute we lack – power – is not adventitious or changeable (like wealth, social pre-eminence or human political power). It is the very essence of divine nature – not an attribute at all in a technical Aristotelian sense. To be the opposite of this is to be so feeble as to hardly exist. That the very essence of our being is a theme here is further evident from the reference to the origin of the species in primeval mythological time. The qualification too is revealing: 'nonetheless' we have *something* in common with the gods, in both the way we think and the way we look. What are we? What are we not? Perhaps the most terrifying implication of these questions is that we just don't know.

I will return to the remarkable theology of this passage in the next chapter. For now, continuing with the eighth *Pythian*, I draw attention to the way these reflections are worked into the poem. The excerpt above is preceded by the list of victories won by Aristomenes, including four times at Delphi; the losers, says Pindar memorably, met with no sweet laughter from their mothers upon returning home, and had to sneak through the back alleys to avoid the derision of enemies. The catalogue is a standard element in the epinician programme (creatively varied, as ever); its latest entry is anchored in the specific circumstances of the year 446. The focus then broadens with the general reflections of the next strophe, warning against confidence in the durability of good fortune which a fresh success, in this case an athletic victory, can foster. This leads to the existential anguish of the shadow-dream, which in its turn leads to existential anxiety in a concrete, life-or-death sense for the people of Aegina. We move in a few lines from the joy of a famous victory to a comical vignette of the hapless loser to the grandeur of Zeus to the threat of political annihilation to prayer. So pregnant with meaning is the single moment.

Now the mutability of human fortune is a commonplace in Greek literature, starting with the great scene in *Iliad* 24 (527–33) where Achilles tells of Zeus's two jars, one with evils, one with blessings: sometimes he dispenses from the jar of evils alone, sometimes from both, but never from the jar of blessings alone. It is the central theme of Herodotus' *Histories*, flagged up by the programmatic story of Solon and Croesus in Book One (29–33): 'count no one happy until they are dead' is the moral, for until they are, disaster can befall at any time. The sentiment is echoed many times in tragedy (e.g. Aesch. *Agam.* 928, and the last lines of Sophocles' *Oedipus the King*).[170] In the lyric tradition, Archilochus speaks of life's 'pattern' of woe and happiness (fr. 128), and remarks that our *thūmos*, our spirit, changes according to the day Zeus brings (*eph' hēmerēn agei*, fr. 131: compare Pindar's *epāmeroi*, and the very similar statement at *Od.* 18.136–7). Many more passages could be cited. What I find noteworthy about Pindar's version here is the imbrication of so many different perspectives and layers in such a short space: general vs particular; concrete vs abstract; divine vs human; theoretical vs pragmatic; knowledge vs ignorance; hope for the future vs imprisonment in the day. Nothing could be less commonplace than the way Pindar expresses these traditional ideas; his 'dream of a shadow' is a coup of defamiliarization. For some of us, the gleam of Zeus may come: surely of all the inhabitations Pindar encourages, one instinctively feels attracted to this sunbeam of happiness amid the surrounding gloom. But we know the sweetness will not last. Hopes rise high, only to be 'shaken by an adverse judgement'. Who is judging? Is it us making a bad decision, or a god disapproving of our happiness? It could be both, for in Greek thinking gods work with and through human psychology – which makes it even harder to know where we stand. We can only pray, and (in spite of everything) hope: on such a note the poem ends, in the company of the heroes of Aegina. They at least do not change.

The whole passage is a brilliant example of the technique of juxtaposition we discussed in the first chapter. We can further observe that, in this case, the co-existence of incommensurable perspectives, emotions and forces is a manifestation of the sublime. Kant spoke of perpetual oscillation of opposites; if one side prevails, the sublimity ceases. In his ode Pindar brings the oscillation into being and holds it in equilibrium. The poem creates the illusion that, however precariously and briefly, we bask in Zeus's radiance. To do so, it must also acknowledge the darkness. Eternal day has meaning only for a god. Paradoxically, though, the poem triumphs over time in the end, for within *its* frame of reference – the lyric 'now' – the moment of balance is frozen forever, to be relived – necessarily including the sense of its precariousness – every time the poem is read.

A final, very important nuance in this immortal passage pleasingly brings the opening of the first *Pythian* into the same frame. The 'gleam of Zeus' (*aiglā diosdotos*) is in the eighth *Pythian* the splendour of the victory. But *aiglā* is also a quality of music, poetry and dance, and this association is very much in play here, for the splendour of the victory is reflected in the splendour of the festivities. Light is in Pindar a favourite metaphor of poetry and celebration.[171] In other texts Apollo himself bears the epithet Aigletes, the Shining One, and the *Homeric Hymn to Apollo* (202) tells of how *aiglē* shimmered round the god as he danced.[172] It is a general quality of gods in Greek poetry that their presence is marked by ethereal radiance and ambrosial fragrance. Aglaia is also the name of one of the Graces (O.14.13); whatever modern philology may say to the contrary, the Greeks connected her name with *aiglē* / *aiglā* (dialect forms of the same word).[173] The first *Pythian*'s dancers heed the lyre 'to start the gleaming celebration' (above, p. 59); the last two words are my rendition of *aglaïā*. In the first *Pythian*, the poet imagines the earthly celebration as a reflection of the heavenly one (and vice versa), in such a way that it becomes difficult to disentangle the two. According to Pindar (fr. 31), in a myth he very likely invented, Zeus created the Muses to fill a perceived need in the otherwise perfect life of Olympus: the need for adornment, beauty and celebration. In epic poetry, the Muses sing not only of the gods – their birth, attributes and deeds – but also of humans (Hes. *Theog.* 36–52). Unexpectedly, they even sing of human suffering and misery (*Hymn. Hom. Ap.* 189–93). In a fine discussion, Stephen Halliwell draws out the implications of this paradox that the Muses should devote their perfect singing to such a subject. By attributing a song-culture like their own to the gods, the Greeks wrote the necessity and value of reflective, aesthetic contemplation into the fabric of the cosmos. 'At the heart of this aesthetic,' writes Halliwell, '… lies a sense of the transformative power of song: the power to convert even suffering and negativity into beauty and expressive intensity, though without thereby erasing the significance of suffering itself.' The gods are both perfect performers and perfect listeners. Halliwell does not fail to cite the close of the eighth *Pythian* in this context. He concludes:

> The song-culture ascribed to the gods themselves is both an authenticating mirror of human song and yet also the projection of an ideal beauty which can never be fully possessed by humans, only aspired to. An essential intuition of Archaic Greek aesthetics lies in the problematic space between these two things.[174]

In this gap lies the sublime.

## On the razor's edge: The poet, the *kairos*, art and politics

Perhaps the most characteristic feature of the Pindaric speaker is his habit of intervening in his own progress, pretending to have lost his way, to be going on too long, to have been distracted, to have embarked on a false path and so on. Superficially it gives an impression of extemporization, as if the poet, overcome with excitement, responds on the spot to the great news. Christopher Carey usefully dubbed this practice the 'oral subterfuge'.[175] Needless to say, a true improvisation would look quite different, but it is easy to go along with the fiction as one experiences the poems. The voice is vivacious, breathless, and committed; its mood is catching. There are other benefits of this tactic. As Andrew Miller has written:

> Through this mimetic representation of a person intently engaged in the generation and formulation of his thoughts at the very moment of public utterance Pindar gains for himself great freedom in the disposition of the heterogeneous materials that make up the typical epinician ode. Not only does the carefully sustained illusion of spontaneity permit all manner of stops and

starts and changes of direction, but persuasively verisimilar motivation for those stops, starts, and changes of direction can be supplied by the speaker's supposed state of mind and feeling.[176]

Miller goes on to emphasize the danger of taking these motivations at face value, as if Pindar is speaking; his point is that, while we so easily inhabit the 'I' (as I have been putting it) and tolerate its seeming waywardness, when interpreting we must bear in mind the contrast with 'the hard-working professional poet who actually crafted [the poem] with care and skill'. We know the poem is pre-composed, and that we are witnessing a mimesis of composition-in-performance; we (at the first or at any performance) can choose to dwell on what is represented, running abandoned through the poem's career of surprises, or we can choose to stand back and follow the artful mimesis (uncritical immersion in the poem versus critical detachment). To choose the first is to experience the world as it is, in all its unpredictability, exhilaration and lethal risk. To choose the second is to see how, in the right circumstances, with the right judgement, and with divine help, we gain perspective and understanding. For a moment we are prevented from tumbling into the abyss; for a moment we balance on the razor's edge.[177]

Even while dramatizing his impulsiveness, Pindar speaks repeatedly of the need for control and judgement. The epinician song has its rules (*tethmos*); it must observe the right measure (*metron*); it must avoid surfeit (*koros, makrāgoriā*); it follows the short path (*oimos brachus*), the straight path (*orthā keleuthos*); it shoots right at its target (*skopos*). The most important of the words of this kind is *kairos*, long recognized as a key concept in Pindar's poetics.[178] Whereas in Homer the word (appearing in the form of its adjectival derivative *kairios*) has spatial application – the weapon finding the 'right spot' to inflict the wound – in Pindar it can also have a temporal sense, and sometimes carries moral overtones of what is proper and fitting. In several passages the concept is explicitly linked to the poet's management of the poem. At *O*.9.38, he chides himself for embarking on an impious story about Heracles: it is 'hateful *sophiā*' and '*para kairon*' (literally 'contrary to *kairos*'): unseemly and therefore untimely. At *O*.13.47–9, where he has told us the victor's achievements defy enumeration, he remarks 'Due measure follows in everything; the *kairos* is best able to perceive it. I am a private person with a public commission …', and moves on to celebrate Corinth's mythical heritage. The implication is that the poet has meted out just the right amount of praise for the victor, at the right time. At *P*.9.76–9, we hear that 'Great achievements are much talked of; but to embroider a few points among many is what the *sophoi* like to hear. The *kairos* [i.e. judicious selection] captures the best in all things alike.' To 'embroider' here is *poikillein*, cognate with *poikiliā*, variation; the poet's skilful recounting of the right things in the right measure achieves the purpose better than prolixity. The tenth *Pythian* opens 'Happy Lacedaemon, blessed Thessaly! The descendance of one father, Heracles, fighter supreme, reigns in both. But why do I vaunt *para kairon?*' the speaker asks, and reminds himself that his immediate task is to praise Hippocleas. His mention of the links between Sparta and Thessaly is of course anything but accidental, but he represents himself here as excitedly blurting out one overwhelming thought before reining himself in; here in the earliest lines of Pindar we possess we already find the tussle of immersion vs control. At *N*.1.18–20, the speaker says, 'I have touched upon many themes; I have not cast the *kairos* upon falsehood', that is, he has hit the mark truthfully. He continues, 'I have come to a halt in the forecourt of a hospitable man, to celebrate his fine deeds in song and dance', an emblematic pronouncement we have discussed before (above p. 76).

Elsewhere others are praised for knowing or experiencing the *kairos*: Damophilus (*P*.4.286), Theron (*O*.2.54), Thearion (*N*.7.58), Nicomachus (*I*.2.22). It is easy to see these figures as avatars of the poet, in the same way that characters in Herodotus who conduct researches (*historiē*) are avatars of the historian. Finally, the eighth *Pythian*, which closes with the 'dream of a shadow' passage we discussed above, opens remarkably with a prayer to Hesychia (Peace, Tranquillity):

| | |
|---|---|
| Kind Peace, daughter | Φιλόφρον Ἡσυχία, Δίκας |
| Of Justice, thou of the greatest cities, | ὦ μεγιστόπολι θύγατερ, |
| Who hold the exalted keys | βουλᾶν τε καὶ πολέμων |
| Of counsel and war, | ἔχοισα κλαΐδας ὑπερτάτας |
| 5   Receive from Aristomenes the honour | 5   Πυθιονίκαν τιμὰν Ἀριστομένει δέκευ. |
|      of his Pythian victory. | τὺ γὰρ τὸ μαλθακὸν ἔρξαι τε καὶ παθεῖν |
| For of gentleness both giving and | ὁμῶς |
|      receiving | ἐπίστασαι καιρῷ σὺν ἀτρεκεῖ· |
| You know the art equally well, in fitting | |
|      time and measure (*kairos*); | |
| | |
| But when someone plants implacable | τὺ δ' ὁπόταν τις ἀμείλιχον |
|      anger | καρδίᾳ κότον ἐνελάσῃ, |
| Firmly in his heart, | 10   τραχεῖα δυσμενέων |

10 Ferociously you confront
   The might of the enemy and consign
   Their arrogance to the flooded deep.
       Nor did Porphyrion realize
   That against fate he incited your wrath.
       Gain is most welcome
   If borne from the house of your willing
       giver.

ὑπαντιάξαισα κράτει τιθεῖς
ὕβριν ἐν ἄντλῳ, τὰν οὐδὲ Πορφυρίων
   μάθεν
παρ' αἶσαν ἐξερεθίζων. κέρδος δὲ
   φίλτατον
ἑκόντος εἴ τις ἐκ δόμων φέροι.

15 Force brings down even the loud
       boaster in time.
   Cilician Typhos of the hundred heads
       could not dodge it,
   Nor yet the king of the Giants
       [Porphyrion]; they were overcome
   By the thunderbolt [of Zeus] and the
       arrows of Apollo,
   Who in benevolent spirit welcomed
       Xenarces' son from Cirrha [Delphi]
20 Crowned with a Parnassian frond and
       a Dorian *kōmos*.

15 βία δὲ καὶ μεγάλαυχον ἔσφαλεν ἐν
       χρόνῳ.
   Τυφὼς Κίλιξ ἑκατόγκρανος οὔ νιν
       ἄλυξεν,
   οὐδὲ μὰν βασιλεὺς Γιγάντων· δμᾶθεν
       δὲ κεραυνῷ
   τόξοισί τ' Ἀπόλλωνος· ὃς εὐμενεῖ νόῳ
   Ξενάρκειον ἔδεκτο Κίρραθεν
       ἐστεφανωμένον
20 υἱὸν ποίᾳ Παρνασσίδι Δωριεῖ τε κώμῳ.

Here we meet our old friend Typhos, along with the equally insolent Porphyrion, who with his Giants posed the same threat to the order of Zeus (above, p. 62). The same constellation of ideas is in play in both poems; in the first *Pythian*, Pindar prays that Hieron and his son Deinomenes, ruler of Aetna, with Zeus's help will honour the people and induce a harmonious *hēsuchiā* (70). Hesychia 'loves the city' (O.4.16); to have her is to be a good citizen (P.4.296); those who seek her banish 'angry sedition (*stasis*) from their heart, giver of poverty, nursemaid of hatred' (fr. 109). Stasis – sedition or factionalism – was the curse of the Greek cities, Aegina no less than others, leading on many occasions to civil war. Hesychia is an eminently political concept, personified here and elsewhere (fr. 109) by the poet and treated as a quasi-deity.[179] She too holds the secret of the *kairos*.

*Kairos* thus has a range of meaning that is not limited to aesthetics, and when the poet flaunts his mastery of the *kairos* in a poem praising civic rulers he is at the same time speaking politically, since his choice of what to say responds to and confirms their record of achievement. But the poet's aim, I shall argue, is to place politics in the service of aesthetics, not the other way around. Closing the chapter with the poem that began it, let us see how this process works in the final triad of the first *Pythian*.

After his call for *hēsuchiā* in the city (70), the poet prays to Zeus that the Carthaginians and the Etruscans will pose no further threat, now that they have seen the power of Hiero in his victory at Cymae; he goes on to say that, just as the Athenians will earn his gratitude for their victory over the Medes at Salamis, and the Spartans for theirs at Plataea, so will the sons of Deinomenes (Hieron and his brothers) for theirs over the Carthaginians at Himera. Greek sovereignty in the entire human world, from East to West, happily mirrors the cosmic sovereignty of Zeus. Pindar then pauses for breath before closing with some truly remarkable praise of Hieron:

| | |
|---|---|
| If you speak in due measure (*kairos*), gathering many threads | καιρὸν εἰ φθέγξαιο, πολλῶν πείρατα συντανύσαις |
| In brief compass, people's censure in the wake is less; galling | ἐν βραχεῖ, μείων ἕπεται μῶμος ἀνθρώπων· ἀπὸ γὰρ κόρος |
| Excess blunts swift hopes, | ἀμβλύνει |
| And to hear it (*akoā*), above all of others' success, secretly aggrieves the hearts of citizens (*astoi*). | αἰανὴς ταχείας ἐλπίδας, ἀστῶν δ' ἀκοὰ κρύφιον θυμὸν βαρύνει μάλιστ' ἐσλοῖσιν ἐπ' ἀλλοτρίοις. |
| 85  Nevertheless, since envy (*phthonos*) is better than pity, | 85  ἀλλ' ὅμως, κρέσσον γὰρ οἰκτιρμοῦ φθόνος, |
| Do not pass over fine deeds. Steer the host with a just tiller; forge the bronze of your tongue on the anvil of truth. | μὴ παρίει καλά. νώμα δικαίῳ πηδαλίῳ στρατόν· ἀψευδεῖ δὲ πρὸς ἄκμονι χάλκευε γλῶσσαν. |
| Should even a tiny spark fly off, it is great: | εἴ τι καὶ φλαῦρον παραιθύσσει, μέγα τοι φέρεται |
| For it comes from you. You are steward of many things. Many are the honest witnesses of both virtues.[180] | πὰρ σέθεν. πολλῶν ταμίας ἐσσί· πολλοὶ μάρτυρες ἀμφοτέροις πιστοί. |
| Abide in your flourishing temperament, | εὐανθεῖ δ' ἐν ὀργᾷ παρμένων, |
| 90  Should you like always to hear fair report (*akoā*), and flag not in largesse; | εἴπερ τι φιλεῖς ἀκοὰν ἀδεῖαν αἰεὶ κλύειν, μὴ κάμνε λίαν δαπάναις· ἐξίει δ' ὥσπερ κυβερνάτας ἀνὴρ ἱστίον ἀνεμόεν. μὴ δολωθῇς, ὦ φίλε, |

| | |
|---|---|
| Like a captain loose | κέρδεσιν ἐντραπέλοις·[181] |
| The windy sail. Be not deceived, my | ὀπιθόμβροτον αὔχημα δόξας |
| friend, by shameful gain; for when | |
| men are gone, the vaunt of glory that | |
| follows | |

| | | |
|---|---|---|
| Alone can tell your way of life | | οἷον ἀποιχομένων ἀνδρῶν δίαιταν |
| To the chroniclers and the poets. The | | μανύει |
| benevolent virtue of Croesus withers | | καὶ λογίοις καὶ ἀοιδοῖς. οὐ φθίνει |
| not, | | Κροίσου φιλόφρων ἀρετά. |
| 95   But the man who roasted his victims | 95 | τὸν δὲ ταύρῳ χαλκέῳ καυτῆρα νηλέα |
| in the bronze bull, that pitiless mind, | | νόον |
| Phalaris – hateful talk (*phatis*) besets | | ἐχθρὰ Φάλαριν κατέχει παντᾷ φάτις, |
| him all round, | | οὐδέ νιν φόρμιγγες ὑπωρόφιαι |
| Nor do lyres within the halls accept him | | κοινανίαν |
| As a gentle companion to the talk of the | | μαλθακὰν παίδων ὀάροισι δέκονται. |
| young. | | τὸ δὲ παθεῖν εὖ πρῶτον ἀέθλων· εὖ δ' |
| Success is the first prize; fame the | | ἀκούειν δευτέρα μοῖρ'· ἀμφοτέροισι |
| second portion; but whoever finds | | δ' ἀνήρ |
| and seizes both | 100 | ὃς ἂν ἐγκύρσῃ καὶ ἕλῃ, στέφανον |
| 100  Has got the highest crown. | | ὕψιστον δέδεκται. |

The destructiveness of human envy (*phthonos*) is a constant theme in the odes; arrayed with things like anger, blame, censure, resentment, whispering and muttering, it is the opposite of honest praise and celebration.[182] Great deeds inevitably attract *phthonos*, but the poet has an obligation to praise. His hope is that he can make his audience renounce envy. Right-thinking folk even praise their enemies when they deserve it (*P*.9.95–6). The mention of the citizens, the *astoi*, in the present passage is highly significant. They are contrasted with the ruling oligarchy headed by Hieron (line 68; similarly *P*.3.71, 4.297), and the picture is one of a benevolent monarch mindful of the *astoi*'s best interests, while the *astoi* show their appreciation in the form of civic harmony and obedience. Jealous and deceitful *astoi* are decried (*O*.6.7, *P*.2.82); *astoi* who share the values of their good fellows are commended (*O*.13.2, *N*.8.38, *I*.2.37). Here the poet frankly acknowledges that discontent can lead to muttering and eventually to open stasis, and recognizes that his own excessive praise might even light the slow fuse. He seems to concede that his picture of a docile, happy people is far from reality, or at least that the goodwill of the people can be turned to ill will by bad rulers and worse poets. Political and poetic practice here go hand in hand. The first triad expounded the perfect consonance of music and society on heaven and earth; here dissonance and discord are at one, as if Typhos is threatening to escape from the volcano.

By stating the risk and pressing on regardless, Pindar certainly raises the stakes. The closer he ventures to the edge of the falls, the more triumphant will be the escape. The heart of the triad's aesthetics is alternation of perspective and tone, mixing viewpoints and registers in a way that skilfully reflects, as creative tension, the social and political tension that the poet addresses. There is outright flattery, most notably in the statement that even a wayward spark is great, 'for it comes from you'. 'Do not flag in largesse' implies that Hieron is already notable for generosity; he need only continue with his 'flourishing temperament', a captivating metaphor likening Hieron's sunny disposition to a blooming flower. It comes hard on the heels of another pair of metaphors comparing Hieron's government to the steering of a ship, and his steadfast truthfulness to a bronzed tongue, the latter somewhat baroque image further elaborated by the spark idea. Another nautical metaphor is differently applied in line 92. These manoeuvres of high poetic style sit alongside the punchy, straight-talking style of lines 88–9, using figures of speech (anaphora, parallelism) characteristic of popular wisdom and public pleading. The 'many witnesses' are the people who have benefited from his justice and truth; we are meant to understand that the whole city will speak up for him. Also at this end of the stylistic spectrum is the expression 'envy is better than pity'; a striking formulation, but not in fact Pindar's: it was a popular saying attributed to one of the Seven Wise Men (to Periander by Herodotus, 3.52.5, to Thales by Stobaeus, *Vors.* 10δ.17). The shrewd change of register reinforces the subtext that this is how the world works. Absolutely the wrong response would be to abandon the pursuit of excellence (or its praise).

Note the prevalence of the imperative mood. Addressed to Hieron, in part the commands serve to tone down the flattery. Had the whole passage consisted in remarks like 'for it comes from you' the popular uprising might have started at line 101. It is also possible to understand the imperatives as addressed to a generic 'you' ('do not pass over fine deeds' is straightforwardly such, addressed in the first instance by the speaker to himself, in the second to everyone). However elaborately expressed, the content of these injunctions is commonplace: be just, be honest, be generous, be not greedy, look to the future. Any listener would agree. Yet the presumption is obvious enough that Hieron already exemplifies these virtues ('abide', 'do not flag'); and the tone ('my friend') is not that of a lecturer, but of a peer, as at a symposium (evoked in line 97) where poetry traditionally traded in such exhortations, and genteel symposiasts nodded in sympathetic appreciation as would a congregation to a good sermon. We derive an image of Hieron modestly absorbing this wise advice, in spite of being – or rather, because he already is – a paragon.[183] In any case, the praise is tempered with warning, and the point of view of the subjects is not overlooked. If Hieron wants to keep hearing fair report (*akoā*) of himself among the people, counting on their acclaim (88), he must continue as he has begun. The flip side of *akoā*, what one hears, is *phatis*, what is said, and this can be deadly (line 96). The chorus of Aeschylus' *Agamemnon*, worried sick about the state of politics in Argos, uses very similar language: 'heavy [*bareia* ~ Pindar's *barūnei* in 84] is the *phatis* of the *astoi*, mixed with wrath' (456); the chorus commends a quiet life without *phthonos* and flattery. Later in the play, Agamemnon says to Clytaemnestra upon his return that 'the talk of the people is a powerful thing'; she replies that 'he who is without envy is also without admiration' (938–9), as she urges him to tread hybristically on the precious carpet. As he is about to discover, things can go very wrong for those in power.

The advice to avoid short-term gain pivots to the theme of posthumous reputation among chroniclers, poets and symposiasts; this applies only to Hieron. The young people who hear his praise will become adults and pass it on to their children (the reference deftly evokes ongoing, future tradition). Hieron is compared with pious Croesus, and contrasted with impious Phalaris. 'Withers' translates a word (*phthinei*) which inevitably recalls the ancient epic formula *kleos aphthiton*, 'undying fame', used of the great heroes. The famous lyre of the opening reappears in the plural (97), generalized now as an icon of all that poetry is and does; the 'symposium' we find ourselves at in this poem is both a specific occasion and an idealized one, bridging the gap between then and now, fidelity and farewell. When Pindar speaks of Hieron obtaining the highest crown, this is of course what he has just ensured with his poem. Yet even this crowning praise entails a warning: this is as far as one can go; you have reached the Pillars; do not think to go further. The closing flourish is rhythmically powerful, with a crescendo of clauses hammered home by a three-word apodosis, *stephanon hupsiston dedektai*. The conductor lays down his baton.

One view of Pindar's procedure would say that these tactics, however subtle, are merely designed to make his message palatable and prop up a tyrannical regime. Aesthetics in service of politics, in other words. Anyone holding such a view might wish to cite certain brutal realities. In the poem Pindar praises with some emphasis the Dorian Greek heritage and way of life (61–6), and prays that Zeus may preserve it forever amongst the citizens and rulers of Aetna. We happen to know that Hieron did not found Aetna on virgin soil; he forcibly evicted the Ionian Greek inhabitants of the existing city, and refounded it under its new name. Hieron's family had plenty of enemies and were ousted not long after his death. The original Aetnaeans returned and kicked out the interlopers. Arcesilas of Cyrene, honoured in the fourth and fifth *Pythians*, was driven from the city and murdered *c.* 440 BCE during an attempt to recover his throne. Theron of Acragas (second and third *Olympians*) died in power but his successor lasted only a year. A couple of generations later the entire clan of Diagoras of Rhodes (seventh *Olympian*) was massacred in the democratic uprising of 395 BCE. Such were the odious patrons whom obsequious Pindar served.

There are several responses to this view. One is to point out that it is rather presentist; earlier ages did not approach panegyric poetry with a predisposition to condemn it. Another response is to point out that Hieron and his ilk also had plenty of friends and supporters. For all we know, when these poems were written Pindar truly was speaking for the majority. Another is to note that 'not all Pindar's patrons were ruthless individuals and oligarchs determined to hold on to power';[184] many were individuals who, as members of the aristocratic elite, would have been part of their community's governing class, but no more than that so far as we know (Diagoras of Rhodes, for instance, or the Aeginetan victors). A fourth, more interesting response is to argue that this view simply misses the point. The politics are only the raw material (along with other poetry and much else) which undergoes a transfiguration to become the poem we have. One can of course read it as a historical document alongside other texts in searching for facts, values, beliefs and so on. But a historical situation thus reconstructed is of limited use in interpreting the poem as a poem. In the first *Pythian*, we do not need to know (and can never know) how secure Hieron's grip on power was at the time of composition. The *kairos* of Hieron's success is ultimately identical with the *kairos* of the poem. The success may have been won in the 'real' world (whatever that really means), but without the poem it might as well not exist. Furthermore, it exists on the *poem's* terms, as a perilous, exhilarating, sublime balancing act between antithetical forces. That is its essence; it has meaning only thus. In the world outside the poem the messiness of life prevents any such clarity of perception.

Hieron's *kairos* of success is interpreted within a general framework of understanding that is the same throughout the poet's oeuvre. This is an important point. The genesis and meaning of Hieron's success, as Pindar presents it, is not unique to him; it is an example of a pattern that the *sophos* Pindar sees repeating in the world amid the flux of ephemera, which he then represents in poetry (as

Hölderlin would put it, he sees the harmony underlying the change of tones). Thus, the politics serve the aesthetics. There will be variations in the schema according to the particular circumstances of each composition, but ultimately the manner of representation is the real locus of meaning.

Nevertheless, if one is out of sympathy with Pindar's 'odious beliefs', as Moses Finley called them, one might find it difficult to admire the beauty and sublimity of his verse.[185] In the first chapter I said that for any social action to be thought sublime in Kantian terms there must be occlusion, because such action always entails morality, politics and interested judgements.[186] The question is, whether ethical and aesthetic judgements can be teased apart, and the contribution of the latter to the experience of the art identified, or whether the two are inextricably linked. The political implications of many passages in Pindar – one thinks for instance of the myths – are quite oblique, and one would expect that their aesthetic properties would be evident also in overtly political passages such as the end of the first *Pythian*. In that respect it might be best to postpone discussion of this problem until after we have discussed Pindar's myths. The issue is most acute, however, when politics are in plain view, so it is best to confront it now.

Kant instances a beautiful palace, of which one might disapprove for many reasons (it is a waste of money, it was built by exploited labourers, it is the home of a tyrant, one needs no more than a simple dwelling, etc.); but these interested judgements are not ones of taste. The judgement that something is beautiful is merely about whether the representation of the building to the senses gives one satisfaction, without the least bias concerning its existence or purpose.[187] Perhaps some viewers of the palace would find this impossible, or argue that to ignore the context of the palace's existence is a dereliction of moral duty. The judgement of taste remains a different kind of judgement all the same. We have all had, or can imagine, the experience of coming across an object new to our experience, about whose origin and purpose we know nothing, and our first impression being one of the thing's beauty. If, subsequently, I learn that the object in question was made by a mass murderer, it cannot but affect my relationship to it; it may require much effort on my part to bracket my feelings of distaste and focus on the object's beauty. If among the murderer's victims were my own friends or relations, I might not even wish to make the effort, or find it impossible. But the thought experiment shows, I think, that these are different kinds of response, and we should be able to identify what is exclusively aesthetic in our experience.[188] This does not entail ignoring other kinds of response. I might agree with you that the palace should be blown up, but until it is, it remains a beautiful building. If moral considerations are thought to be integral to aesthetic judgements, they effectively negate their independence and therefore their existence. To persuade others that something is beautiful you would first need to bring them round to your moral point of view. You would need a calculus to decide how strong your attraction to or revulsion from the morality or politics must be before you can agree or disagree that the object is beautiful. This is so problematic as to be hardly worth considering.

If the object contemplated involves human suffering, further aspects of the problem come into view. These may, however, point to a way forward. It would be a monster indeed who, observing human suffering directly, found it beautiful and thought that everyone should share that judgement. Yet we can find representations of human suffering beautiful in all art forms. And there are those who have found large-scale human suffering, even directly observed (such as Stockhausen on 9/11), to be, not beautiful, but sublime in the sense that it exceeds comprehension. As we saw in the first chapter, this attitude outrages most people; surely it, too, is monstrous. Is this to admit that moral considerations are integral to at least some kinds of aesthetic judgement?

One response to this conundrum is to point out that such a judgement about 9/11 is possible only if one divorces the sublime from the beautiful. Kant subsumed both in the power of judgement, unlike Burke who drove a wedge between them. Much twentieth-century thinking about the sublime takes the Burkean line.[189] A disaster like 9/11 does indeed display many of the qualities of the Burkean sublime, but it is not beautiful. This seems a promising defence. If one can have sublime objects of which no part is beautiful, then one would have to allow even the monumentally revolting to be sublime, on some other grounds than aesthetic pleasure; but in such a case, 'sublime' is surely the wrong word, unless you feel uplifted by revulsion (which does not seem much different from taking pleasure in suffering; at any rate, it must raise questions about one's mental health, if not about ethics).

Another response is to point out that the process of artistic representation makes all the difference. Representation opens up possibilities of understanding and redemption because art represents not the object but its meaning. If an artist chooses to represent a revolting object or theme (one can think of many examples, beginning with Greek epic and tragedy), any initial feeling of disgust must always be superseded by contemplation of meaning, unless one simply refuses the work. Often such a feeling does not even arise, or at least not in the same nauseating way, because one knows going in that it *is* a representation (as Aristotle already pointed out, *Poetics* 1448b11). In the contemplation of such a creation thoughts of sublimity may obtrude themselves sooner than thoughts of beauty, but it may be argued that the pleasure of contemplation is itself a thing of beauty. That is, in a way, the secret of artistic representation, of the pleasure of the tragedy:[190] it engenders the pleasure of learning, which even at its most uncomfortable and unsettling constitutes something more than merely agreeable. It is a pleasure one can reasonably impute to everyone.

A position not unlike this was developed by Hans Robert Jauss, rehabilitating Kant (and pleasure) and reacting primarily to the 'aesthetics of negativity' of Theodor Adorno. There is a dialectical process between art object and receiving subject; the latter balances between pleasurable immersion and disinterested detachment, in a manner which (I would add) easily transmutes into a sublime experience (cf. above, pp. 105, 124). Jauss writes:

> the definition of aesthetic pleasure as enjoyment of self in the enjoyment of what is other presupposes the primary unity of understanding enjoyment and enjoying understanding and restores the meaning of participation and appropriation which originally characterized German usage. In aesthetic behavior, the subject always enjoys more than itself. It experiences itself as it appropriates an experience of the meaning of the world which both its own productive activity and the reception of the experience of others can disclose, and the assent of third parties can confirm. Aesthetic enjoyment that thus occurs in a state of balance between disinterested contemplation and testing participation is a mode of experiencing oneself in a possible being other which the aesthetic attitude opens up.[191]

Since literature deals in words and propositions, it is more difficult to separate representation from proposition than it is, say, in music, where making ethics or politics relevant to the aesthetics usually needs hard arguing. The sounds themselves cannot be translated into discursive statements, and apologetics for or diatribes against this or that kind of music (serialism, for instance, or 'popular' music) – even the most philosophically sophisticated of such disquisitions – usually have little or nothing to do with the aesthetics. Literature, conversely, may find it difficult to persuade the sceptic that what is represented is not the proposition (object, theme) as such. Yet it is so; if literature is nothing but advocacy, it has sold its soul.

The great Victorian critic Walter Pater famously posed the question, 'What is this work to *me*?'[192] If I ask what is it about Pindar that I find beautiful (and sublime), I could (and would) appeal to his majestic language, his aesthetics of surprise, his kaleidoscopic imagery, his profound mythological imagination and more, but perhaps most of all I would appeal to his way of wringing every drop of meaning out of his occasions, to his melding of the ephemeral and the transcendental, and to those breathtaking moments, like the end of the eighth

*Pythian*, when he captures the transient *kairos*, the sublime but doomed moment of human excellence and happiness. It matters not whether it is found in a hereditary king like Arcesilaus, an oligarchic clan like the Aleuads, a sole ruler like Hiero, or a leading family in a democratic city like the Alcmeonids of Athens. Aristocrats all, you may say, but thus was his world constructed; it could hardly be otherwise. All criticism is a kind of allegoresis. Few of Pindar's readers will be Olympic athletes, much less tyrants of Syracuse, yet all of us can thrill to his vision and ponder its implications for ourselves. For this dialectic to be possible, the means to activate it must already be in the text, and this is what Pindar has accomplished. It is the essence of literature.

# Exceeding Limits

## Greek myth, Greek religion

Pan, it seems, was a great admirer of Pindar. The ancient *Lives* of Pindar tell us that the god was observed in the mountains singing one of the poet's paeans, and that in appreciation Pindar composed a poem in his honour. Of this poem, unfortunately, only a few scrappy quotations survive.[1] As is the way with anecdotes about poets in the ancient world, this one was probably spun out of the poem in question; if we had more of it, we might know what Pindar said that prompted the tale. However that may be, the principal ancient sources that allude to it were well known in early modern Italy. None was better known to painters than Philostratus' *Images*, which might have been the stimulus for a remarkable painting of 1666 by Salvator Rosa (Fig. 1). From Philostratus Rosa would have learned how Pan danced when Pindar was born, how Rhea's drums resounded in the house at the happy event, how bees dripped honey into the baby's mouth, and how Pan later neglected his dancing in favour of singing Pindar's odes. Pan's pipes lying on the ground in Rosa's painting might be a nod to the last of these details; on the whole, however, the scene is his own free invention. It appears to be an example of the 'dedication of the poet', wherein a god (usually Apollo or the Muses) awakens the poet to their calling, or tells them they have been writing the wrong kind of poetry hitherto. Famous examples in ancient literature include Hesiod at the opening of the *Theogony*, Callimachus at the opening of his *Aetia*, and Virgil at the start of the sixth *Eclogue*. Pan was king of the satyrs – half-goat, half-human woodland creatures. In Rosa's day it was supposed that satyrs and satire were etymologically related; so one can infer that satire is what Pindar is being called on to compose, instead of whatever he has written on the scroll in his hand. Satire in a technical sense (it is originally a Roman genre) is not something one associates nowadays with Pindar, but Rosa wrote satires himself, and there is a very good chance that his Pindar is a self-portrait. In one of his satires he prays that he might sing like Archilochus,

Tyrtaeus and Pindar (*Sat.* 2.37–42), as if all three were fellow practitioners; Archilochus certainly could be so described, and Tyrtaeus castigated cowardly soldiers, while in the case of Pindar Rosa was perhaps thinking of passages that denounce disreputable behaviour as a foil to praise.[2]

The key point, however, is the poet's response. Pindar is a study in astonishment, fear and diffidence. Should he, can he, take up the calling? The god seems to be showing him the way: but is he beckoning upwards to nobler themes in heaven (the source of the light, which is a metaphor for artistic inspiration in Renaissance painting), or to the human world beyond the woods? Is his smile really benign? The god's cloven hoof is given a certain prominence – not an encouraging attribute (the devil's feet are cloven). And if you think that perhaps Pan *can* be trusted, what of those leering satyrs in the background? The brooding woods, the half-hidden terrors, the sudden apparition of a higher being, and the vulnerable solitude, yet at the same time the direct communion with what is, after all, a god, and the possibility of artistic greatness, all contribute to the sublimity of this scene.

Rosa has caught something here of the old pagan feeling about the divine: terrifying but inspiring, dangerously ambiguous and always to be treated with extreme caution. The conjunction of poetic mission, divinity and the sublime in this painting picks up some important strands of the themes proposed in Chapter 1 for discussion in the present chapter: myth, time and language. Each of these could be, and has been, the subject of separate books, but our focus is the Pindaric sublime; as I hope to show, under that rubric these topics cohere closely. Of the three, myth is the foundation. It underpins the world-view of the poems, and gives the praise its larger meaning. It is crucial to the poems' temporality, for Pindar strives to bring the time of myth into the time of the present, and to unite the time of humans with the time of the gods. Finally, the myths themselves are easily read as metaphors, and it is not accidental that Pindar's linguistic metaphors proliferate and cluster in passages where he speaks of his mission (often at the point where the mythical part of the ode begins or ends).

Let me begin, then, with a few general words about Greek myth and religion as they are relevant to Pindar, before turning to the considerations identified in the first chapter as a guide to further exploration of the Pindaric sublime.

Rosa depicts the epiphany of Pan; Pindar too depicts memorable epiphanies, as we shall see. In the time of the heroes, gods communicated easily with humans; the heroes, indeed, were the product of unions between gods and mortals (or descended from such unions). In historical times the gods were less sociable, but continued to make themselves manifest in many ways; alongside the spectacular, if rare, form of actual apparitions, there were indirect forms like dreams, oracles,

**Figure 1** Salvator Rosa, *Pan and Pindar* (1666).

omens and the like. Lesser divinities were more apt to communicate with mortals than the grandees of Olympus. The category includes the many heroes who were worshipped in local cults centred on their tombs, whence a protective power was thought to emanate; Pindar himself claims to have met Alcman, on the commonest if disputed reading of a passage in the eighth *Pythian* (56–60). These modes of communication illustrate a general characteristic of Greek religion, which is that the divine tends to be something that happens *to* you, rather than something you actively seek out in your spiritual life. Wilamowitz brilliantly summed this up by saying that in Greek religion 'god' is a predicate, whereas in monotheistic religions God is a subject. Nowadays we learn as children the attributes of God: God is loving, good, all-knowing, all-powerful and so on; a subject for a series of predicates, which are revealed to us by Scripture and theology. In Greek religion, when something remarkable happens – an omen, a miracle, a natural wonder, a disaster, a triumph – one senses the divine agency: 'that (subject) was a god (predicate)!'[3] An early literary example of this sort of experience comes in the first book of the *Odyssey*, in which Athena, in human disguise, converses with Telemachus; Telemachus has no inkling of who he is dealing with until she turns into a bird and vanishes through a hole in the ceiling, whereupon the penny drops (l. 323: 'he surmised it was a god').

There is a Romantic tinge to Wilamowitz's generalization, and one can point to many Greeks, including Pindar, who thought deeply about the nature of gods. Yet there is a good deal of truth in what he says. Greek religion was characterized by immanence rather than transcendence. The gods do not exist above or outside the world in some other order of reality. They were born into the cosmos, and are constituent elements of it. Human impulses and inspirations could be thought to be god-inspired, especially if unexpected or overwhelming. In such a system, instead of starting with an understanding of what God is and making the world conform to it, one starts with the world as experienced and infers from it the nature of the gods. They are a projection of how everyday reality presented itself to their worshippers. There being no central authority to regulate belief, the picture was as complex and self-contradictory as life itself. Religious belief and practice were established from the ground up by local communities according to their character, needs and priorities. There were hundreds of divinities great and small, from the major Olympians down to local guardian heroes or humble woodland spirits. Even a god like Zeus had scores of epithets (Zeus Meilichios, Xenios, Polieus, Herkeios, Ktesios and so on) denoting different spheres of activity; it is a question whether in such instances we have one Zeus or many. A god worshipped in Argos might look completely different from a god of the same name worshipped on Samos. Individuals could entertain contradictory beliefs about gods from one day to the next, depending on the situation (though in this respect, one might think not much has changed since antiquity).[4]

Chaotic though the system was, however, there were common themes and emphases. One, touched on in the last chapter, is the inconstancy of human life. Living day by day, the best that humans can hope for is a mix of blessings and woe, as the tale of Zeus's jars in the *Iliad* so memorably states (Pindar alludes to it at *P.*3.81). We live in ignorance of the future and our only solace is the dubious one of hope, which is often figured in Greek literature as a cruel deceiver (in Pindar e.g. *O.*12.6, *P.*3.23, 8.90). Famously in Hesiod's parable of Pandora's 'box' (actually a storage jar, *Works and Days* 90–105), it is the only evil that failed to escape before she got the lid back on. It is a notorious puzzle to say exactly what that means, but it surely does not mean that hope is an unequivocally good thing; neither does it mean that there is no hope in the world (because it is still trapped in the box), which is manifestly false.[5] Rather, hope, though a treacherous ally, at least remains in our possession and control, unlike the evils that run riot in the world.

Another recurrent theme is the boundary between mortal and immortal, probed in text after text including Pindar. The gods in Greek poetry are 'deathless', 'ageless', 'blessed', 'easy-living'; they are immensely powerful (though not omnipotent); they have no cares, illness or toil. Human beings are of course the opposite of all these things. The gods are simply the powers in the world – the 'stronger ones', the poets called them – and one must cope with them as best one can. They rule in their own interests, and do not answer to us. The gods of elements, such as Poseidon of the sea, are easiest to understand in this perspective: the sea does not much care what you think. It demands recognition and honour, which you give in the hope that the god will oblige you with safe passage. But there is no guarantee that your piety will be rewarded.

Gods could be benevolent, malevolent, or indifferent to humanity. Undiluted benevolence was not on offer, but the gods are also called 'givers of blessings', an epithet which is as old as Indo-European. One gets a quite jolly picture of gods from Greek comedy, where they instantiate the happy spirit of the festival. The example is enough to show that literary genre is an important factor here. In the *Iliad*, which adds to epic seriousness an uncompromisingly tragic world-view, the gods are fundamentally indifferent, even if they have their favourites. At times it seems we exist only to provide them with amusement, and to slake their thirst for honour.[6] Indifferent; but also capable of extreme malice if offended. Being anthropomorphic, they are not perfect, and behave much like most people would if endowed with such power and freed of any restraint. Homer does not find it impious to relate tales of their immoral behaviour (deception, adultery, cruelty) – or better said, of their amoral behaviour: human standards of good and evil do not apply to them. Yet even in Homer, a god may take offence at egregious human misbehaviour. Zeus guarantees the rights of suppliants and guests; Paris broke his law when, as a guest of Menelaus, he absconded with Helen. The act sealed Troy's fate.

The *Iliad*'s gods quarrel bitterly amongst themselves, with tragic consequences for the human players. The *Odyssey*, by contrast, presents a more clear-cut picture of good versus evil, with the wicked suitors getting what they deserve. The just gods of Hesiod's *Works and Days* also reflect what was probably the more prevalent view, that in spite of the evidence of experience gods *ought* to be good. Thinkers like Xenophanes raised a vigorous protest against the poets' tales of their scandalous behaviour. Most Greek tragedies show humans struggling with questions of divine justice – whether, and it what form, it existed; however one might think these questions are resolved in the plays, if they are ever resolved, the point is that they were regularly asked.

The line between mortal and immortal is absolute in the *Iliad*. Humans must die; thereafter they can look forward only to a shadowy existence in the underworld. This grim world-view, amplified by Greek tragedy, lies behind the notion of 'Greek pessimism'; the defiance of the hero in the face of certain death only increased its attraction to the Romantic imagination. In fact, the *Iliad* was not representative on this point.[7] Other early epics acknowledged the immortality (in various forms) of Heracles, Menelaus, Achilles, the Dioscuri, Eos, Tithonus, Diomedes, Iphigeneia, Ino, Semele, Ariadne and others. Hesiod even has all the heroes of Troy and Thebes go to the Isles of the Blessed (*Works and Days* 167–73). The *Iliad* itself nods at one point, and mentions the rapture of Ganymede (20.233–5). These are all heroic figures, but ordinary Greeks too could cherish such hopes. From the mid sixth century onwards teachings associated with Pythagoras and Orpheus promised reincarnation and, eventually, the eternal reward of the morally pure in the afterlife. These ideas are propagated in Pindar's second *Olympian*, and archaeological finds in the twentieth century have shown that versions of them were found throughout the Greek world in his time. If the soul is immortal, and the righteous enjoy a god-like life in the next world (easy-living, carefree), most of the essential differences between humans and gods would seem to vanish. We must still in some sense die; the gods remain infinitely more powerful and knowledgeable; but compared with the competing eschatology such differences seem negligible.

At the same time, Pindar says emphatically 'do not seek to be Zeus' (*I*.5.14; cf. *O*.5.24, *P*.3.61–2, *I*.7.44), and warns us repeatedly to remember our mortal limits. Hades is the normal destination of deceased people in his other poems. The seeming contradiction with the second *Olympian* has often been explained by saying that Pythagoreanism was strong in Theron's Acragas, and Pindar was simply responding to a direction from his patron to work this material into his poem. Certainly he was sensitive to such requirements, but when one considers that related ideas occur in at least one, probably two, additional poems (frr. 129, 131, 133), one begins to think a different explanation may be needed. One of the points I want to explore below is whether that contradiction is real or apparent, and to ask how a different assessment might affect our reading of the odes.

The variability of belief extended to the vast network of myth. It was stable in its broad outlines, comprising the births of the gods, the great events of the heroic age (the Argonauts, the Calydonian Boarhunt, the Theban Wars, the Trojan War), the post-Troy migrations. Most of the famous characters (Jason, Meleager, Oedipus, Achilles) come from one of these four cycles of epic; there were also tales of other mighty individuals like Perseus, Theseus and above all Heracles. The framework imposed a brake on totally free invention – nobody could claim that the Theban Wars postdated Troy, for instance – and stories could retain an unaltered core through many retellings. But within these general limits there was enormous latitude for the creative imagination. Minor characters, genealogies, causes of events, motivations of actors, sub-plots, divine machinations, speeches, conversations and so on were all possible subjects of invention.

It was the task of poets to transmit and interpret the myths for their contemporaries. Stories of gods and heroes supported familial, social and political institutions by explaining origins and purpose. The myths, it should never be forgotten, were history for the Greeks, albeit history from a special time. They established identity, whether of family, clan, city, ethnos (Dorian, Ionian, Aeolian and others) or nation (Greek or foreign); genealogies were the principal means of charting origins and connections, and as any student of Greek myth knows, these were bewilderingly complex.[8] Through myth too the poets also explored questions of meaning in life and death; in this respect Pindar merely continues a practice of which Homer was already a master. Lyric poetry, which typically accompanied local occasions, tended to give greater prominence to myths of importance to the local audience, but it very often drew also on the Panhellenic story-bank of epic poetry to set the proceedings in a wider context. Epinician poetry aimed at both local and international audiences, and praise was apt to be much more effective if the poet could suggest that his victor was in some way comparable to the heroes of epic. The dichotomy of local and Panhellenic was not in any case absolute, since the Panhellenic heroes all had strong connections with one or other of the ancient cities or regions. Younger colonies like Cyrene or Syracuse linked to the older world by means of their foundation legends and the myths of their mother cities. Consequently it was not very difficult for a poet to tell stories that worked on both levels. What we do not find in epinician, however, are myths that could only be understood by a local audience (or, if outsiders might need some explanation, that is provided in the poem).

Like any other poet, Pindar was called on to read the welter of conflicting signs in the record and explain their meaning. In that respect he was like a prophet, and the parallel has often been drawn. Pindar does not himself claim to be a *mantis*, to use the Greek word – one who reads omens like the flights of birds or entrails of sacrificial animals – and he certainly gives no detailed prophecies of the future like the famous seers of myth. He would agree to being a *prophētēs*, a spokesperson of the Muses (*Paean* 6.6, fr. 150). What he does instead is to suggest a comparison between himself and the legendary seers by working them into the myths of his odes (Amphiaraus in the eighth *Pythian*, Chiron in the ninth *Pythian*, Tiresias in the first *Nemean*, and others) in such a way that their readings of the events in the story resonate with the contemporary events celebrated by the poet.[9] Moreover, and more than other poets, Pindar inscribes his role in creating meaning into his poems; the *kairos*, discussed in the last chapter, is a large part of this endeavour.

## Transcendence and immanence

It is clear that to appreciate Pindar one must engage with his ideas about gods, heroes and myths. As discussed in the first chapter, this was a central concern of Hölderlin and his contemporaries looking for alternatives to received religion. The ubiquity and proximity of Greek gods spoke directly to their desire for authentic personal experience of the divine, and consorted well with Romantic enthusiasm for Nature. The deeply affecting humanity and beauty of Greek poetry lent support to ideas about art as an instrument of truth.

Perhaps the most crucial issue for Hölderlin was the relation of the transcendent to the immanent – a dichotomy, indeed, which dates to this period. 'Transcendence', however, has two distinct senses here. One refers to absolute reality, existing over and beyond the phenomena of this world; in theism, this is the realm of God. The other is narrower, and derives from Kant: it refers to *a priori* capacities in the mind without which perceptions and certain kinds of deduction and judgement would not have the form they do or even be possible. These transcend any individual human, but are not found in any reality outside the human (although in Kant's view they proved the existence of that reality). Kant's sense of the word was controversial, his insistence that we could not know reality in itself even more so. As we saw in Chapter 1, Hölderlin adopted a middle position, accepting Kant's analysis of how the world is cognized, but arguing also that 'intellectual intuition' and aesthetic feeling could give insight into the Absolute. For him, an 'idealistic' understanding of the world meant an understanding of how the totality of the cosmos revealed itself in the concrete particulars of history. Only with the help of art could individuals and societies work through the 'change in tones' to restore primal unity and abolish the subject–object distinction.

Hölderlin thought Pindar had the same ideas, even if he would not have articulated them in this manner (an objection which would not have troubled Hölderlin in the least). Pindar both read the changing tones – the confusing data of experience – and offered glimpses of the transcendent reality. 'All religion is in its essence poetic', as he put it, which is a truth one can feel with special force in the symbiotic relationship of Greek myth, religion and poetry. However, though his own sense of the world's immanent divinity was strong, what Hölderlin ultimately wanted to get at was the Absolute, the subject rather than the predicate. He was deeply immersed in contemporary arguments about Nature and God, specifically those about Spinoza's alleged pantheism. These debates sprang from dissatisfaction about theism's view of a transcendent God (the problem being how such a God could relate to the world at all); they sought to boost the immanence side of the equation, but the aim was always to establish the link with ultimate reality. Hölderlin embraced the motto *hen kai pan* (ἓν καὶ πάν, One and All), denoting the absolute unity of all things to which we and the world must return.[10] The visible world is the fragmentation of the All, but still partakes of its essence. Variations of the *hen kai pan* theme occur throughout Hölderlin's oeuvre from the mid 1790s on (for instance in the last line of *Hyperion*). Spinoza never actually used the expression, and would certainly have disowned many of its applications, but to deploy it in 1795 was to declare an allegiance to some version of his system. The twists and turns of these debates (which could be dangerous, since pantheism was heresy) do not concern us here; the point is that this alternative religion retained an unquestioned adherence to monotheism, which is alien to Pindar.

Yet Hölderlin's reading is not so anachronistic as it might seem. For one thing, there *was* a strong philosophical interest among Pindar's contemporaries in the problem of unity in multiplicity – it was, in fact, *the* central problem of pre-Socratic philosophy. Versions of *hen kai pan* are attributed to Xenophanes, Heraclitus, Empedocles and Parmenides, the original monist. In one fragment (on one translation) Xenophanes even declared that there was but one god.[11] These thinkers all held quite different positions, and it is seldom clear what exactly they understood by the identity of all things, or even if the sentiment is reliably attributed to them by our sources, but the drive to find an underlying (or overarching) principle in the phenomena – the subject as opposed to the predicates – characterizes Greek philosophy from the start. The *archē* of the cosmos which they sought, a word meaning both 'beginning' and 'cause', inevitably entailed thought about its relation to divinity.[12] Pindar was certainly familiar with these trends. Empedocles, whom he might have known personally, was much influenced by Pythagoras (Empedocles' dates are uncertain, but he was perhaps born *c.* 495 BCE); the second *Olympian* of 476, with its similar doctrines, was written for another citizen of Acragas. There may be allusions to Parmenides in the poems. Tantalisingly, according to the Christian writer Clement of Alexandria (late second/early third century CE), Pindar in a fit of Bacchic ecstasy (!) asked 'What is god?' and answered 'The all (*to pan*)'.[13] As expressed, this bears all the marks of a tendentious reading of a passage in his lost poetry, and we can hardly know what Pindar actually said or meant. We might take the report to imply, however, that Pindar had a reputation as a theological thinker, which indeed he was.

This philosophical environment means that such ideas could in theory occur in Pindar, but it must be conceded that nothing like *hen kai pan* is to be found in the poems. Hölderlin's Romantic attitude to Nature and its general deification find no parallel in Pindar. Yet Pindar's ideas about divinity have an overtly philosophical inflection, and evince a sense of the larger order of things. How might one understand this dichotomy of immanence and transcendence in relation to Pindar's poetry? Where would his transcendence reside and what force would it have?

It is obvious that it will not refer to anything outside the cosmos, but, as we saw in the last chapter, there are certainly ways in which Pindar seeks to escape the bounds of a particular moment and enter into the broader stream of time. These I will continue to explore in the present chapter. They represent a movement upward, as it were, from a time-bound perspective to something more like that of the gods. To this I want to add a movement downwards, and look at how gods interact with humans. I suggest that it could be fruitful to think of Pindar's gods in a sense akin to the Kantian transcendent, inasmuch as they are preconditions and enablers of meaning and value. For Pindar, of course, they are real, not merely aspects of cognition, but they do exist in this world, not outside of it. Moreover, the way gods operate means that the line between 'in the world' and 'in the person' can be blurred. Depending on context, one can sense one's affinity with the gods, or their ineffable difference. In approaching the boundary, one's protests that it is impassable can mask a query about or even an ambition as to that very possibility. These two movements up and down – human aspiration and divine condescension – meet on a transcendent level where meaning resides, both that which can and that which cannot be represented. In other words, these are potentially sublime moments.

## Personifications

To explain a little more what I mean by enablers, preconditions and transcendence, I draw attention to the phenomenon of divine personifications. There are a great many of them in Pindar, and the first problem is how to evaluate the nature of the abstraction. Personifications in Greek myth and poetry were anything but new in Pindar's day, to be sure.[14] Hesiod's *Theogony*, two centuries before, has scores of them, and they do heavy mythological work in explaining the world's origin and constitution. Alongside physical building-blocks like Earth, Sky, Sun, Moon and Ocean we find a host of more abstract notions like Strife, Toil, Old Age, Lies, Quarrels and Forgetfulness. Genealogy expresses conceptual relations and causality; Strife, for instance, is the mother of Lies, Quarrels and other kinds of conflict. It can be difficult to say whether these abstractions are fully anthropomorphized, even if they are figured as children and parents. Some of them (the brothers Sleep and Death, for instance) are depicted anthropomorphically on vases; others we know were worshipped in cult. Many of them, however, have no cult or other myths that we know of.

It is often difficult to say too whether a noun like, say, Peace is being used as an ordinary word in conversation to describe a state of affairs, or as a personified deity. The capital letter is of course a modern convention; ancient Greek had only one letter form. If we encounter a passage in which 'peace' is an active character, we can infer that agency implies personification, and write 'Peace'. That is a fairly straightforward case, but it still differs from modern usage in that we would not think such a move implied divinity. Then there are the myriad borderline cases, and one can have a fruitless discussion about how to distinguish one usage from the other. That is perhaps the significant point in the end, for it reflects the thorough imbrication of gods in everyday activity. They are always there; their presence usually goes unremarked, but a perspectival shift can bring their agency to light.

Overt theorizing about the concept in question can also help. This is seldom discursive in Greek poetry, but may be implied, for instance, by a list of attributes. Yet even so the divinity of a personification is not always clear. When Hesiod writes (*Works and Days* 287–92):

> Vice is easy to get, and in abundance; the path is smooth, and it ['she'?] resides close to hand. But the gods have put sweat in the way of virtue; the path to it ['to her?'] is long and steep, and rough going at first. But when it gets to the top, then it is easy, though it was hard before.

should we use the personal pronouns, and write 'Virtue'? When, adapting him, Simonides writes that 'Virtue lives in rocky hills, hard to climb, and tends a holy spot' (*PMG* 579 = fr. 257 Poltera), agency at least makes the personification clearer. Or when Solon, diagnosing the cause of civil unrest, says that 'excess begets hybris' (fr. 6.3), is the genealogical metaphor, which was live in Hesiod, now dead, or may we write 'Excess begets Hybris'? Decision is often impossible, which suggests if nothing else that the problem is more ours than the ancients'.

Just about anything can be personified in Greek poetry, and a certain amount of ad hoc invention is to be expected. Euripides even says that recognizing friends is a god (*Helen* 560). Pindar has his Hesiodic moments, for instance when he declares that Excuse is daughter of Afterthought (*P.*5.27–9) or that Warcry is daughter of War (fr. 78). If, however, we consider personifications which occur with some frequency in Pindar *and* which attract the language of agency, then an interesting result emerges: the abstractions so favoured are Potmos (Fate), Moira (Portion or Fate), Chronos (Time), Tyche (Fortune), Aion (Lifetime) and Horae (Seasons). Together, these mark out a clear thematic field: the great stream of time, the order of things, and their interaction with lived lives.

Some of these figures have agency in previous poetry or prose. Chronos is a governing principle in Anaximander of Miletus, and in Pherecydes of Syros he is one of three primeval deities in the cosmos.[15] Time is personified by Solon and Simonides.[16] Tyche and Moira 'give all things to a man' according to Archilochus.[17] The Horae, who oversee the flourishing of agriculture, in Hesiod are named Good Order, Justice and Peace and said to be daughters of Themis (Right) (*Theogony* 901–2). Aion and Potmos are new, however, and the combination and remarkable frequency of these personifications in Pindar reveal his engagement with related philosophical issues.

It would take us too far afield to offer a detailed study of all of these words, but a few points can be mentioned here in order to illustrate the essential thrust of Pindar's thinking.[18] In texts before Pindar, Potmos means 'fate' simply in the sense of 'death' (as in a warrior 'met his fate', often in Homer). In Pindar it does more work: he (it is masculine in Greek) assigns a victor's family to Zeus (that is, the family has won in the games honouring Zeus at Olympia and Nemea); 'Great Potmos' looks favourably on Hieron; he grants wealth; 'Lord Potmos' bestows Excellence; he inscribes a course for us to run.[19] Twice, Potmos is said to be 'innate' or 'inborn' (*suggenēs*): 'Inborn Potmos judges all deeds' (*N*.5.40, with reference to the victory: that is, if one rationalizes, the victor was bound to win because of his inherited ability; but really we ought to try to understand the notion that a deity Potmos, who pre-exists, is also born with one); and 'Now his innate Potmos has returned him to fair weather' (*I*.1.40; that is, he has won after a bout of misfortune). Pindar elsewhere praises inherited talent,[20] but linking it to Potmos brings out the melding of external and internal agency. The family has a Potmos which manifests itself through the generations, but not without the strenuous efforts of each individual.

In Homer, the personified Moira is most often associated with death, which is the ultimate lot of humans (most emphatically stated at *Il.* 16.433–42, where Zeus expresses the vain hope that he might avert his son Sarpedon's *moira*). Given the subject matter of the *Iliad* this preponderance is to be expected. If death is our *moira* (whose root meaning is 'share', 'portion', 'lot'), and the precise moment is determined by Moira, she is logically involved at birth too, for it leads inevitably to that result; the image of her starting to spin the thread of our life is used at *Il.* 24.209–10 (also at 20.127 and at *Od.* 7.197 of the closely related concept Aisa).[21] There are some hints of a wider purview in Homer, however. At *Il.* 24.49, the Moirai endow humans with an enduring spirit in the face of misfortune; this points to an essential aspect of our lot in life, which must always involve suffering. A pre-ordained sequence of events can be someone's *moira* (*Od.* 4.475, 5.40, 5.345); the agency of the *moira* is not stated in these passages, but the events in question must run their course. At *Od.* 20.76, Penelope says that Zeus knows what is *moira* and what is not *moira* for all of us, and at 19.592 she says that everything is allotted its *moira* by the gods.

Most interesting is a reference at *Il.* 19.87 where Agamemnon claims that Zeus, Moira and the Erinyes inflicted him with madness when he insulted Achilles. The combination has an eerily Aeschylean ring: it is divine ordinance

(Zeus) that punishment (the Erinyes) must inevitably (Moira) follow upon transgression.[22] It is Zeus's will, but it is not something he can change; even he is subject to Fate. Pindar would agree: 'sitting upon the golden clouds and peaks of Olympus, Zeus the gods' watchman did not dare undo the course of Fate [that Troy should fall]' (*Paean* 6.92–5); similarly at *I.*8.31–5a, Themis pronounces what is fated, that should anyone marry Thetis, the son will overthrow the father, even if he is Zeus. In spite of such statements, however, Fate is not some kind of cosmic puppetmaster. It is better thought of as a pattern set in the fabric of the cosmos that includes both gods and humans. Fate's enactments always require the agency and motives of individual actors. If questions of responsibility arise, as they do in the *Iliad* passage just quoted, blaming Moira or the gods can help one save face, but Agamemnon does not for a moment doubt that he also shares the blame, and sets about making amends. The problem of fate versus free will had not yet been articulated by Greek philosophy in those terms; causality simply has multiple facets in these earlier writers.

In Pindar as in Homer, Moira or the Moirai are present at births, setting the pattern of what is to come. They are found also at momentous beginnings like the founding of the Olympics or the settlement of Cyrene. The Moirai send prosperity; they also send misery, and ordain that no one has only happiness.[23] They thus ensure this basic pattern of human life. The adjective 'fated' (*morsimos*) is twice applied to *aiōn*, the general course of one's life (*O.*2.10, *I.*7.41); the poet can even suggest that his skill in cultivating 'the garden of the Graces' is his destined lot (*O.*9.25). Chiron foiled Acastus' attempt to murder Peleus, so that the 'fate allotted to him by Zeus' might be fulfilled by his marriage to Thetis (*N.*4.61).[24] It was fated that Neoptolemus should be buried at Delphi (*N.*7.44) and that Troy would only fall with Philoctetes' help (*P.*1.55). In another Aeschylean moment, Pindar makes Jason say that the Moirai stand aside when there is enmity amongst kinsmen.[25]

Even so brief a survey as this shows how much more involved with events during life, not just its end, these gods are in Pindar than in Homer. The same is true of Chronos, Time, about which Pindar has much to say. The noun *C/chronos* occurs no fewer than forty-seven times, the adjective *chronios* four times, far exceeding anything in previous literature. Chronos is, remarkably, 'father of all things' and 'the lord, surpassing all the blessed gods'. He brings to pass what is fated; with Moira he was present at the foundation of the Olympic Games, that 'primeval rite'. In the same passage he is described as 'he who alone proves the real truth'; the same notion lies behind the statement that he is 'the best saviour of the just' – that is, whatever calumny the just might endure in the short term,

Time will show their true worth.[26] But if it brings truth to light, it can also help one forget sorrows. Like Moira, Chronos brings both good and bad; one prays to him therefore to preserve one's good fortune.[27] Time comes at Pindar and shames him for his forgetfulness (*O*.10.7–8). In a remarkable concretization, it is not the baby Heracles who squeezed the life out of the two snakes in his cradle, but Time (*N*.1.46). This marks the beginning of a career which ends at line 69 with his living 'for all time (*chronos*)' in heavenly bliss, having achieved just reward for his labours, wedded to Youth and embracing the dispensation of Zeus.

I will spare the reader further catalogues of this kind and refer to a footnote for a few passages about Aion and the Horae that reinforce the general point, that the interlocking movements of human beings and these active personifications of fate and time constitute an important theme in Pindar.[28] So far our study has been lexical; I will return below to a closer consideration of the work that time (whether or not flagged lexically) is doing in the poems in relation to myth and transcendence.[29] To stay with personifications for a while longer, I draw attention to two remarkable openings and the whole of a short poem in which Pindar expatiates on the attributes and meaning of some personifications: Hesychia, 'Peace', at the start of the eighth *Pythian*; Theia, 'Divinity' itself, at the opening of the fifth *Isthmian*; and Tyche (or Tycha in Pindar's dialect), 'Fortune' or 'Chance', all of *Olympian* 12, which I give first:[30]

| | | | |
|---|---|---|---|
| | Child of Zeus the Liberator, I pray you | | Λίσσομαι, παῖ Ζηνὸς Ἐλευθερίου, |
| | Watch over a strong Himera, Saviour | | Ἱμέραν εὐρυσθενέ᾽ ἀμφιπόλει, σώτειρα |
| | Tycha! | | Τύχα. |
| | For by you at sea are guided swift | | τὶν γὰρ ἐν πόντῳ κυβερνῶνται θοαί |
| | Ships, by land rapid-shifting wars | | νᾶες, ἐν χέρσῳ τε λαιψηροὶ πόλεμοι |
| 5 | And assemblies giving counsel. | 5 | κἀγοραὶ βουλαφόροι. αἵ γε μὲν ἀνδρῶν |
| | Human hopes | 6 | πόλλ᾽ ἄνω, τὰ δ᾽ αὖ κάτω |
| | Often up and then again down | 6a | ψεύδη μεταμώνια τάμνοισαι |
| | Pitch and roll, carving a vain, | | κυλίνδοντ᾽ ἐλπίδες· |
| | mendacious path. | | |
| | | | |
| | No earthly being has yet discovered | | σύμβολον δ᾽ οὔ πώ τις ἐπιχθονίων |
| | from god | | πιστὸν ἀμφὶ πράξιος ἐσσομένας εὗρεν |
| | A trustworthy token of what will | | θεόθεν, |
| | happen, | | τῶν δὲ μελλόντων τετύφλωνται |
| | And of coming events our perceiving[31] | | φραδαί· |
| | is blind. | 10 | πολλὰ δ᾽ ἀνθρώποις παρὰ γνώμαν |

| | | | |
|---|---|---|---|
| 10 | Much befalls humans against expectation, | | ἔπεσεν, |
| | | | ἔμπαλιν μὲν τέρψιος, οἱ δ᾽ ἀνιαραῖς |
| | The opposite of delight, while others | 12 | ἀντικύρσαντες ζάλαις |
| 12 | Plunged into a maelstrom of agony | 12a | ἐσλὸν βαθὺ πήματος ἐν μικρῷ |
| 12a | Swap deep happiness for woe in an instant. | | πεδάμειψαν χρόνῳ. |

| | | | |
|---|---|---|---|
| | Son of Philanor, like a cock | | υἱὲ Φιλάνορος, ἤτοι καὶ τεά κεν |
| | Who fights only at the family hearth, the honour of your sprinting | | ἐνδομάχας ἅτ᾽ ἀλέκτωρ συγγόνῳ παρ᾽ ἑστίᾳ |
| 15 | Might ingloriously have shed its feathers | 15 | ἀκλεὴς τιμὰ κατεφυλλορόησε ποδῶν, |
| | Had not discord that divides men deprived you of your Cnossian homeland. | | εἰ μὴ στάσις ἀντιάνειρα Κνωσίας σ᾽ ἄμερσε πάτρας. |
| | Instead, Ergoteles, you have been crowned at Olympia | | νῦν δ᾽ Ὀλυμπίᾳ στεφανωσάμενος καὶ δὶς ἐκ Πυθῶνος Ἰσθμοῖ τ᾽, |
| | And twice at Pytho and at the Isthmus, | | Ἐργότελες, |
| | And abiding in fields that are yours you embrace the warm baths of the Nymphs. | | θερμὰ Νυμφᾶν λουτρὰ βαστάζεις ὁμιλέων παρ᾽ οἰκείαις ἀρούραις. |

The noun *tuchā* is from the same root as the verb *tungchanō*, to meet with; it is a word that seems very suited to Greek religion, as outlined at the outset of this chapter. Fortune or Luck does not receive much theoretical attention in our evidence before Pindar, however, in whom (once again) we find a step change in this regard (nineteen instances of the noun in the poems). Because he is celebrating success, for the most part his *tuchā* refers to good fortune, but it can also be bad luck (fr. 40). Tyche was not yet the blind goddess of chance widely attested in the Hellenistic period, but Pindar does here focus on the perspective of mortals who are on the receiving end of her unpredictable workings, to which he assigns a very broad purview. Remarkably, in another place he makes her one of the Moirai, and the strongest one at that (fr. 41). We have no context but the implication should be that there is something divine underlying 'chance' events; the concept of a purely random, impersonal process such as mathematicians or chaos theorists work with was not available and would have seemed counter-intuitive. Fate, however manifested, is only clear in retrospect; in prospect it is unpredictable. From the gods' point of view the process is not random.[32]

In the third stanza, the focus shifts abruptly to the victor, who has left civil strife behind in his native Crete and found good fortune in Sicily. The tone here suddenly becomes light-hearted, even comical: a stylistic enactment of the change of fortune. The sustained nautical metaphor and elevated diction of the first stanzas give way to a homey simile, baffling in its odd commingling of comparanda.[33] The poem ends with the image of Ergoteles luxuriating in the hot springs for which the city was famous: the implication is that he is, like Heracles, renowned for his love of hot baths (and for whom the gods created those at Himera), relaxing after his Labours (the same idea at *N*.4.4). I imagine Pindar delivering this short poem at a symposium, with the guests laughing at its outrageous wit. Though Tyche can be cruel, on this occasion she has been wonderfully good both to the city and its newest citizen. Celebrate!

Nevertheless, the opening stanzas reveal some serious thought about Tyche. The form here draws on hymns, in which a god's epithets and attributes are listed by way of compliment. Such attributes were given by tradition; the difference here is that there is almost no such tradition for Tyche, so Pindar must provide his own. Success or failure in seafaring and war are obvious places to look for her power, public assemblies perhaps less so to a modern reader; but an appeal for 'good fortune' is found in many decrees of the Greek cities (in an unknown context Pindar calls Tyche 'upholder of cities', fr. 39; in fr. 40 she is figured as a ship's pilot, perhaps in a ship-of-state metaphor). There follows a familiar reflection about the uncertainty of human life, and a compactly expressed view of human hopes: they pitch up and down on the sea of fortune, like fortune itself. The noun 'hopes' (*elpides*, 6a) is positioned far from its article (*hai*, 5); normally hope would be the one thing that keeps us going in times of trouble, and here hope holds out as long as grammatically possible, but with a hyperbatic thud we realize that its path through the sea has been nothing but empty lies.

Tyche is the underlying condition that creates the need for hope, but also brings the joy of the victory. Elsewhere Pindar goes so far as to say that 'in deeds, not strength but *tuchā* prevails' (fr. 38). Most interesting is the locution 'by the *tuchā* of god(s)', which Pindar is the first to use in our record. The god is unnamed in three cases (*O*.8.67, *P*.8.53, *N*.6.24); once he says 'by the *tuchā* of *potmos*', doubling the abstraction. Usually humans are not in a position to say which god is responsible for a stroke of luck, but when speaking of poetry Pindar is able to say the *tuchā* of the Graces will help him (*N*.4.7). Why not just the Graces, or the gods, or Potmos? Pindar reaches for the undefined quality that characterizes all of these divine interventions, a single word to denote the process. One could say, to pick up the terminology used earlier, that he is looking for the subject that these predicates presume.

The same can be said of his thoughts on Hesychia at the beginning of the eighth *Pythian*, quoted and discussed in the last chapter (p. 125). Pindar here is once again on his own; in our evidence the only previous personification of Hesychia is a brief quotation from the Sicilian comedian Epicharmus (fr. 100 K.-A.), where it seems Odysseus is hoping for a quiet life. She is rare afterwards too, in the fifth century only Aristophanes *Birds* 1321, which echoes the eighth *Pythian*. So her attributes are entirely the product of Pindar's contemplation. Remarkably, Peace is not the *result* of good counsel, concluded wars or defeated anarchy, but the agent which produces these successful outcomes. Gods combine opposites in themselves; to secure peace, Peace will react with extreme violence against threats like Typhos and Porphyrion.[34] She dispenses kindness but also receives it, in the form here of the happy *kōmos*. Gods grant favours in return for honour; what better way to honour Peace than by being peaceful? As in the first *Pythian*, praise freely given by all citizens is a synecdoche for harmonious political order; Pindar does not find it overstated when he moves in the same breath from Apollo's victory in the cosmic battle against the Giants to Apollo's crowning the victor at Delphi. What all these predicates – victory, tranquillity, absence of stasis, good order, justice – have in common is Hesychia. She exists among and between us, divine *and* in this world. Working through humans, the divinity is the enabler.

Lastly, Theia – Divinity herself (*I*.5.1–16):

| | | |
|---|---|---|
| Mother of the Sun, Divinity, O thou of<br>    many names, | | Μᾶτερ Ἀελίου, πολυώνυμε Θεία, |
| For your sake we value also mighty<br>    gold | | σέο ἕκατι καὶ μεγασθενῆ νόμισαν<br>χρυσὸν ἄνθρωποι περιώσιον ἄλλων· |
| Above other things: | | καὶ γὰρ ἐριζόμεναι |
| Ships too that compete | 5 | νᾶες ἐν πόντῳ καὶ <ὑφ'> ἅρμασιν ἵπποι |
| 5  At sea, and steeds yoked to chariots | | διὰ τεάν, ὤνασσα, τιμὰν ὠκυδινάτοις ἐν |
| Win admiration in the fast-wheeling<br>    contests, Lady, because of your<br>    esteem; | | ἀμίλλαισι θαυμασταὶ πέλονται, |
| And in the competition for prizes he<br>    secures | | ἔν τ' ἀγωνίοις ἀέθλοισι ποθεινόν |
| Coveted fame whose locks the thick<br>    wreathes | | κλέος ἔπραξεν, ὅντιν' ἀθρόοι στέφανοι<br>χερσὶ νικάσαντ' ἀνέδησαν ἔθειραν |
| Crown for victory with hands | 10 | ἦ ταχύτατι ποδῶν.<br>κρίνεται δ' ἀλκὰ διὰ δαίμονας ἀνδρῶν. |

10 Or swiftness of feet.
 Men's strength is determined by gods.
 Two things only shepherd the sweetest
  prize of life with blooming
  prosperity:

Good fortune and good repute.
Do not seek to be Zeus. You have
  everything,
15 If a portion of these blessings finds you.
 What is mortal befits mortals.

δύο δέ τοι ζωᾶς ἄωτον μοῦνα
ποιμαίνοντι τὸν ἄλπνιστον εὐανθεῖ
σὺν ὄλβῳ,

εἴ τις εὖ πάσχων λόγον ἐσλὸν ἀκούῃ.
μὴ μάτευε Ζεὺς γενέσθαι· πάντ᾽ ἔχεις,
15 εἴ σε τούτων μοῖρ᾽ ἐφίκοιτο καλῶν.
θνατὰ θνατοῖσι πρέπει.

Before Pindar Theia occurs only once, as the mother of the Sun in Hesiod's *Theogony* (135, 371): a mere filler of a name to provide Hyperion with a partner. It is sufficient to serve as a springboard for Pindar's mediation, however, who asks himself what a 'mother of the Sun' does in the world: the answer is, she is that goddess who unites the power of gold and the resplendence of victory. We may perhaps suppose that the mysterious luminescence of gold is an unspoken *tertium quid* in the collocation, but more obviously one would think of Pindar's often stated view that the purpose of wealth is to enable good things such as pious dedications, hospitality and poetry.[35] The Sun makes the gold glow, and shines brightly on the champion, but it is not of him that these things are metonyms, and therefore not for him that we value them; it is because of that which is his origin, Divinity, his mother. Ontologically she resides on the level of transcendence. As Fränkel well remarks, Divinity here has become the valued-ness of value, almost the Platonic Form of value.[36] The gnomic statements in lines 11–13 broaden the scope to 'the sweetest prize of life': whatever we find worthy, it is because of the reverence in which we hold Divinity. In this perspective, 'of many names' in the first line is pregnant with meaning. It is a most unusual application of the adjective. Common in prayers, it normally means that the god has many epithets denoting attributes and places of worship. Theia has no cult, no tradition in poetry: what, then, are her many names? We must provide them ourselves, and in effect they are infinite: whatever is valued, a transcendent source of wonder. Without her, nothing of significance happens.

Operating both within and between individuals, and enduring through time, these abstractions are fairly termed transcendental. The thinking behind them is philosophical in that it involves the articulation of concepts, yet it is rooted in poetic genealogical metaphor. As Maslov stresses, Pindar takes personification to new levels of meaning and application; at the same time, one must note that his ideas are steeped in traditional Greek religious feeling, and draw their colour from specific objects or experiences that instantiate the divine.[37]

## Probing the boundary of eternity

Similarly transcendental is the way that Pindar conceives the force of myth. If the relationship between an individual and gods is one of interdependent agency, the relationship between the lived present and the time of myth is one of mutual participation in a sphere of eternal values, which manifests itself in experiential particulars. As with Potmos and the others, one can think of the two levels as either separate or conjoined; the sense of transcendence depends on keeping both conceptions in play at once. In the third *Olympian*, for instance (see p. 73), Pindar brings together in an exhilarating mix the foundation of the Games by Heracles and his presence at this very celebration; three temporalities are in play: then, now and then-now.

Exemplarity is always operative in myths. The victors are the modern counterparts of the heroes; to what extent are they the same? Pindar clearly believes that the heroes exhibited the rarest excellence, but they are not categorically superior beings, as they are in the *Iliad* (where they do things 'no mortal of our time' can do, e.g. *Il.* 5.304). Gods help contemporaries achieve the impossible just as they did the heroes. Moreover, the ultimate measure of the heroes' stature is their immortality as established by the poets, and this is exactly what Pindar claims to be doing for his victors. The ambition is not without its risks, and approaching the place where transcendence and divinity lie is an occasion for anxiety. One alternately approaches and draws back. Humility is so emphatically and so often enjoined, I suggest, precisely because ambition is the stronger force. Moreover, poetic immortality is not the only sort thematized in the poems, as we shall see. The struggle between these opposing impulses creates another instance of the sublime.

Passages on and around the boundary as enacted in the poems themselves can be revealing. Take this one in the tenth *Pythian*:

| | |
|---|---|
| Of delights in Greece | τῶν δ' ἐν Ἑλλάδι τερπνῶν |
| 20 They have no small portion; may they not meet | 20 λαχόντες οὐκ ὀλίγαν δόσιν, μὴ φθονεραῖς ἐκ θεῶν |
| Envious reversal from the gods. A god's heart | μετατροπίαις ἐπικύρσαιεν. θεὸς εἴη ἀπήμων κέαρ· εὐδαίμων δὲ καὶ ὑμνητὸς |

Would be free of pain; but fortunate
   (*eudaimōn*) and deserving praise
   from the wise (*sophoi*) is that man
Whose excellence in deeds of hand or
   foot prevails,
Whose daring and strength seize the
   greatest of prizes,

οὗτος ἀνὴρ γίνεται σοφοῖς,
ὃς ἂν χερσὶν ἢ ποδῶν ἀρετᾷ
   κρατήσαις
τὰ μέγιστ' ἀέθλων ἕλῃ τόλμᾳ τε καὶ
   σθένει,

25 And who lives to see his young son
   Destined to win the Pythian crown.
He can never scale bronze heaven,
But in all the glories the human race
   can grasp, he attains the farthest
Voyage. Neither by ship nor on foot
   could you find
30 A miraculous path to the assembly of
   the Hyperboreans,

25 καὶ ζώων ἔτι νεαρόν
   κατ' αἶσαν υἱὸν ἴδῃ τυχόντα στεφάνων
   Πυθίων.
ὁ χάλκεος οὐρανὸς οὔ ποτ' ἀμβατὸς
   αὐτῷ·
ὅσαις δὲ βροτὸν ἔθνος ἀγλαΐαις
   ἁπτόμεσθα, περαίνει πρὸς ἔσχατον
πλόον· ναυσὶ δ' οὔτε πεζὸς ἰών <κεν>
   εὕροις
30 ἐς Ὑπερβορέων ἀγῶνα θαυμαστὰν
   ὁδόν.

With whom once Perseus, leader of
   people, feasted…

παρ' οἷς ποτε Περσεὺς ἐδαίσατο
   λαγέτας…

The myth of Perseus then follows. In line 27 we have a version of the familiar warning (the fifth *Isthmian*, above, offered another): success is owed entirely to the gods; do not presume to think more than mortal thoughts; be satisfied with what you have. The border seems closed. Yet at the same time, Pindar in this poem is celebrating the pinnacle of human achievement. As Hubbard puts it, 'the assertion that heaven cannot be scaled not only implies mortal limitations, but also human potential (to do everything short of that)'.[38] We may go even further: the warning implies a strong temptation precisely to claim more credit than is due, think more than mortal thoughts, and want more than we have. 'Do not seek to be Zeus': it is a remarkable admonition, when one thinks of it; why would it even be necessary to say such a thing? It seems that humans not only harbour a secret ambition to scale heaven, but cannot resist trying. Thus in the tenth *Pythian,* when the story of Perseus' trip to the Hyperboreans follows immediately on the statement that heaven is unattainable, the progression causes one to ponder. Perseus didn't go by ship or on foot, but go he did, with divine

help. So did Heracles, twice (*O*.3). If the only purpose of telling such stories –
again and again – is to inform us about what we cannot have, one wonders how
such a genre could ever gain traction.

It is, to be sure, perilous to think such thoughts. Commentators rightly speak
of the epinician poet's challenge of striking the balance between offering
sufficient praise and avoiding divine jealousy. That relationship, however, can
also be described as a dialectical one (so Hubbard), in which each side implies
and needs the other. Human ambition propels even as divine prerogative repels:
the dangerous boundary *exists* to be probed. Within Pindar's myths, there are
times when it is actually blurred if not removed. Diomedes (*N*.10.7) and Heracles
(*N*.1.72, 10.18, *I*.4.55) do not even die, and others dwell in the Isles of the Blessed,
their death being only a transition (Peleus, Cadmus and Achilles: *O*.2.78–9,
*N*.4.49). Ino, Semele, the Dioscuri (on alternate days), Aristaeus – all
immortalized.[39] Moreover, we know of multiple cases of historical athletes
receiving posthumous cults, and one possible fifth-century case, Euthymus of
Locri, of an athlete so honoured in his lifetime. Founders of colonies were
worshipped as heroes after their deaths (see *P*.5.95). Bruno Currie has explored
at length the implications of this prospect in Pindar's poems; it is inevitably
discreet and indirect, but it remains a real possibility.[40] There is then the
immortality offered by Pindar's own celebration of the victors, which he
anticipates and we can now confirm. None of these – Isles of the Blessed, hero-
cult, immortal praise, or even trips to the Hyperboreans – makes us equivalent
to the Olympians, but surely they represent a sublimation, as Freud would say, of
that unacceptable desire.

Perseus' trip to the Hyberboreans (invented by Pindar, so far as we know) was
a reward for his exploit of killing the Gorgon, just as Pindar's poem is a reward
for Thrasydaeus' victory. The parallel has been noted by Hubbard, Köhnken and
others, who have also pointed out that the land of the Hyperboreans is functionally
and symbolically equivalent to the Isles of the Blessed.[41] Köhnken cites
Bacchylides' tale of how Croesus of Lydia – a figure of relatively recent history –
was transported to the Hyperboreans on account of his piety, because he had
made the greatest gifts to Apollo at Delphi; Bacchylides goes on immediately to
say, in his direct manner, that no Greek has given as much gold to Apollo as
Hieron (3.63–6). It is all but a prediction of Hieron's coming immortality.

These considerations suggest that we should give the parallel the strongest
possible force and read it in both directions, from the Hyperboreans to Pindar
and vice versa. That is, the idea of visiting that distant land is more than a
comparandum for the immortality offered by poetry; the poetry also documents

the candidacy of its honorand for other kinds of immortality. The myth is a metaphor for glory and eternity, a 'schema of the supersensible' in Kant's phrase; yet like many Pindaric metaphors, vehicle (the myth) and tenor (the poet's celebration) seep into and shape each other – in fact, in the case of myth one could wonder which is which.

These considerations also suggest that the ideas about blessed immortality in the second *Olympian* can find a place in the rest of Pindar's epinician oeuvre as a possibility that is always in play. In fact, on the assumption that translation to the Isles of the Blessed nevertheless requires death, I am not sure that any passage in Pindar outright contradicts the second *Olympian*.[42] It is not really necessary, however, to (try to) combine every detail of every statement into a consistent theology that one would then claim as Pindar's. Different impulses are competing here, and one may be more prominent than another in a given poem. Nonetheless, because these ideas of immortality in various guises are evidenced in many passages, the audience or reader is authorized to ponder their applicability throughout the corpus. The possibility of true immortality may seem more or less remote but it is enough that it is there.

It is central to Pindar's strategy that it remains a possibility not a certainty. The second *Olympian* seems very assured in its doctrine about what comes after death, but everywhere else Pindar places great emphasis on the uncertainty of what comes before. Tyche is the most powerful of the Moirai. Even in the second *Olympian*, winning the Isles depends on completing three cycles of perfectly just life – a very high bar; how can one be sure it has been cleared? Pindar's constant message is not to presume; to take things one day at a time; pray that misfortune not strike, but accept the inevitability of change; credit all things to god; live modestly, and hope to avoid divine *phthonos*. Unlike human envy, the divine does not arise from malice: it is simply part of the natural order that our happiness should not be undiluted, and Pindar never evinces any resentment about this situation or suggests, as characters sometimes do in Greek tragedy, that the gods are unjust. Closely related to *phthonos* is *nemesis*, which in Pindar denotes this natural order rather than divine punishment of crime. Hence the Hyperboreans, who live without disease, war, toil or old age, are said to have 'fled Nemesis the very Just' (*P*.10.43–4); this does not mean that they have avoided wrongdoing, but that they are exempt from the ordinary human dispensation, which is just in every way.[43]

How like the heroes or even the gods are we? Whatever philosophical consistency one might wish to extract from the poems, poetically this hesitation is much more powerful than any pretence of certainty. The questions are posed but not answered; in fact they cannot be answered. Without uncertainty, sublimity is mere delusion.

I give three further examples. In the fifth *Isthmian*, after the opening discussed above with its 'do not seek to be Zeus', Pindar goes on to say, 'I have come to praise you, Phylacidas (17–22). We should not begrudge praise to those who travel the gods' pure path in recompense for their toil (22–5). For the warrior heroes have been celebrated forever by poets (26–9).' A roll call of these heroes ensues: the Oeneidae in Aetolia, Iolaus at Thebes, Perseus at Argos, Castor and Polydeuces at Sparta; but in Aegina, it is Aeacus and his progeny (the ode is for an Aeginetan). There follows the impressive list of their achievements at Troy, and then at the battle of Salamis, which took place only two years before; they are still with us. (Herodotus tells us that the Greeks arranged for Aeacus, Ajax and other Aeacids to be at the battle, in the form (apparently) of their statues; after the victory, one of the captured triremes was dedicated to Ajax: 8.64, 121.) We have now come to the border, and the speaker reveals his anxiety: 'But nevertheless, drown your vaunt in silence. Zeus dispenses now this now that, Zeus, lord of all' (51–3). But then (nevertheless) there is more praise of the victor and his grandfather Cleonicus (read 'Aeacus and Ajax'): let him who would compete emulate them. As we know from Herodotus, Simonides and many others, the warriors of the Persian wars were put on a par with their legendary counterparts. As we gaze on the form of the young victor, touched as he is by the hand of god, we may press the analogy as hard as we wish. In such a gaze, self-identification is never far away, but beware the dangerous impulse; drown your vaunt in silence.

The glorious sixth *Isthmian*, also for Phylacidas of Aegina, opens with one of Pindar's splendid images, an effervescent symposium whose metaphorical third toast for Zeus, the poet prays, will be a third victory to match the two already won. He then offers an emphatic version of the 'live long and modestly' topos: 'If a man takes pleasure in expense and labour and fashions god-grounded success, and with him the god sows a delightful reputation, already has he cast the anchor of bliss upon the furthest shores, for he is honoured by god. In such a spirit does the son of Cleonicus pray to meet Hades and welcome grey old age; and I beseech high-throned Clotho and her sisters, the Moirai, to heed the noble wishes of a man dear to me' (10–18). Yet this is followed at once by 'But, ye Aeacids of the golden chariots, I say it is my clearest duty when I set foot on this island to sprinkle you with praise' (19–21). Any self-identification of the audience with the Aeacids threatens to undercut the modesty just commended.

The Aeacids' posthumous fame (Pindar continues) spreads from the Nile to the Hyperboreans; no city is so barbarous as not to have heard of them. Everyone knows of Peleus and Ajax son of Telamon, and Telamon himself, who helped Heracles sack Troy, defeat the Meropes and the giant Alcyoneus (22–35). There follows the beautifully elaborated tableau in which Heracles, having come to fetch Telamon, finds him celebrating his wedding. Standing there in his lionskin, he takes the wine cup, raises his invincible hands to his father Zeus in heaven, and prays that Eriboea may give birth to a son: 'Let his body be unbreakable, like this skin of the beast that now envelops me, first of my labours, which I killed at Nemea; and may his heart be to match.'[44] Zeus obliges instantly by sending a mighty eagle (*aietos*), king of birds; Heracles shivers with delight, and speaks 'like a prophet: "You shall have the son you seek, Telamon. Call him after this bird's appearance Ajax (*Aias*) of broad strength, terrifying among the people in the labours of Enyalius [the war god]." So he spoke and sat down at once. But for me it were too long a task to recount all his achievements; I have come to praise Phylacidas …' Heracles' prophecy is given mimetically in direct speech, so the speaking 'I' of the poem ventriloquizes him. After delivering the heart-warming prophecy of a mighty son for Telamon, whose truth we all know very well, the speaker, crossing the boundary, proceeds immediately to praise Phylacidas, that superb Aiantian youth, son of Lampon-Telamon, while the prophecy of Pindar-Heracles still echoes round the room. By this trick of performance the two 'I's, the two times, and the personages converge; can one say they meld? The wedding-feast too, especially Heracles' prayer to Zeus, picks up the opening sympotic image, and both reflect the spirit of the event at which we may imagine the ode was performed.

　　　Finally, the third *Nemean* for Aristoclides of Aegina:

| | |
|---|---|
| If Aristophanes' son, fair of form with deeds to match, | εἰ δ' ἐὼν καλὸς ἔρδων τ' ἐοικότα μορφᾷ |
| 20 Has trodden the heights of manly achievement, to go further | 20 ἀνορέαις ὑπερτάταις ἐπέβα παῖς Ἀριστοφάνεος, οὐκέτι πρόσω |
| And traverse the unattainable sea beyond the pillars of Heracles, is not easy; | ἀβάταν ἅλα κιόνων ὕπερ Ἡρακλέος περᾶν εὐμαρές, |
| | |
| Which the hero-god placed, renowned markers | ἥρως θεὸς ἃς ἔθηκε ναυτιλίας ἐσχάτας μάρτυρας κλυτάς· δάμασε δὲ θῆρας ἐν πελάγεϊ |
| Of sailing's limit. In the sea he subdued the monstrous | ὑπερόχους, ἰδίᾳ τ' ἐρεύνασε τεναγέων |
| Beasts. Unaided he found the flowing | 25 ῥοάς, ὅπᾳ πόμπιμον κατέβαινε νόστου |

25 Shallows that marked his journey's end
    and sent him homeward;
    And he made known the earth. – My
      heart, to what foreign
    Shore do you divert my voyage?
    Bring your Muse to Aeacus and his
      clan, I say.
    The best of justice attends the saw,
      'praise the noble',

    τέλος,
    καὶ γᾶν φράδασε. θυμέ, τίνα πρὸς
    ἀλλοδαπάν
    ἄκραν ἐμὸν πλόον παραμείβεαι;
    Αἰακῷ σε φαμὶ γένει τε Μοῖσαν φέρειν.
    ἕπεται δὲ λόγῳ δίκας ἄωτος, 'ἐσλὸν
    αἰνεῖν',

30 And passion for the faraway is not
    better for a man to bear.
    Begin your search from home.

      . . . . .

    From there [Troy] is the far-shining
      light of the Aeacids set firm.
65 Zeus, yours is the blood, yours the
      Games which our hymn has pelted,
    Celebrating our country's joy with the
      voice of young men.
    Cheering befits Aristoclides in his
      victory.

30 οὐδ' ἀλλοτρίων ἔρωτες ἀνδρὶ φέρειν
    κρέσσονες·
    οἴκοθεν μάτευε.

      . . . . .

    τηλαυγὲς ἄραρε φέγγος Αἰακιδᾶν
    αὐτόθεν·
65 Ζεῦ, τεὸν γὰρ αἷμα, σέο δ' ἀγών, τὸν
    ὕμνος ἔβαλεν
    ὀπὶ νέων ἐπιχώριον χάρμα κελαδέων.
    βοᾷ δὲ νικαφόρῳ σὺν Ἀριστοκλείδᾳ
    πρέπει.

The excerpt begins with the 'seek to go no further' topos, but its mention of Heracles sets the poet off on a digression, from which he theatrically hauls himself back on track. These 'digressions', of course, always have their purpose in context. Here, the speaker comes close to breaking the very advice he has just given; he thus dramatizes the seductions of the dangerous impulse. His unique description of Heracles as a 'hero-god' may also be pertinent. Heracles joined the gods on Olympus after his death on Mount Oeta, or rather his translation, and he was worshipped as both hero and god.[45] This is someone who straddles the boundary. What follows – praise of the Aeacids – is advertised as an acceptable alternative, because closer to home. But it is actually no different in respect of crossing that ultimate boundary, because the praise of the Aeacids (in the portion omitted above) is mostly devoted to the immortal Achilles, denizen of the Isles. One could almost accuse Pindar of being disingenuous by making us think that Aeacus is somehow safer than Heracles in the point under consideration here; at any rate, we can unmask his pretence that Heracles is *not* relevant. Upon finishing the myth (where the excerpt resumes above) the progression of thought once again undercuts the modesty topos. 'Zeus's blood' refers to the Aeacids; although these were not the literal ancestors of the contemporary Aeginetans, they were very much the symbolic ones.[46] The poet then moves seamlessly to praise of the victor, as if it is all one. Both these heroes, Heracles and Achilles, exemplify the fearful thrill of the boundary, which is replicated in the ode's rhetorical structure. The question of how closely the victor, and we, might match their inspiring example is left hanging in the air.

# Divine epiphanies

That question runs through the whole epinician corpus, keeping pace with exhortations of modesty and warnings about divine jealousy. Pindar's extreme concern to credit the gods with all things can be seen in dozens of passages, for instance in the sixth *Isthmian*, quoted above, where in a single sentence the gods' contribution to Lampon's happiness is stated three times. In speaking of the collaboration of god and human, one can look on that 'and' as either conjunctive or disjunctive, depending on context. The workings of Moira and the human agent are conjunctive; they work absolutely in lockstep. The relationship of victors and heroes is disjunctive; their superiority, and anteriority in time, create a gap which one tries to bridge, in order to fashion a unity in the transcendent realm of immortal fame. When it comes to the great gods of Olympus, the gap is beyond question unbridgeable. Consequently, they rarely deign to interact with humans, and when they do it is a highly charged moment.

Epiphany can take many forms. A broad definition would include any form of divine manifestation: signs such as the eagle sent by Zeus in the sixth *Isthmian*, or the snakes sent by Zeus foretelling the breach of Troy's walls in the eighth *Olympian*, or the snakes sent by Hera to destroy the infant Heracles in the first *Nemean*; or a god assuming human form, such as Triton-Eurypylus in the fourth *Pythian* or Zeus-Amphitryon in the seventh *Isthmian*. Most spectacular, however, are direct encounters with one of the great gods, and it is Pindar's dramatizations of these that have the greatest potential for the sublime. Such meetings, though not impossible in everyday life,[47] are in Pindar confined to the myths. This displacement creates greater possibilities for imaginative engagement, and the audience's vicarious experience of the epiphany gains in power accordingly.

Ancient rhetoricians called this *enargeia*, vividness; recent studies drawing on cognitive science have stressed that successful enlivening of narrative depends much less on the accumulation of details (which can actually hinder vividness) than on choosing the salient ones.[48] Pindar, like Homer, is a master at this.

Four passages come into view: the appearance of Poseidon to Pelops (*O*.1.67–87); of Apollo (or rather his voice, *O*.6.57–66) to Iamus; of Athena in a dream to Bellerophon (*O*.13.66–72); and of Zeus to Polydeuces (*N*.10.79–88). I choose the last for fuller discussion, but first a few words about the others are appropriate.[49]

In the first *Olympian*, Pelops seeks Poseidon's help in the chariot race with Oenomaus to win his daughter Hippodamia's hand. The king had already executed thirteen losers. Pelops goes alone to the seashore and calls out to the god in the darkness (71). This solitary withdrawal to a liminal place and time is well known from Homer;[50] here the liminality is compounded by Pelops' own status as one who has recently attained manhood. Poseidon appears at once, directly before him, eye to eye. Pelops' speech is strongly reminiscent of Sarpedon's paradoxical declaration in the *Iliad* (12.309–28) that precisely because we are mortal, we must pursue glory at the possible cost of our life. If we must die, Pelops asks, why would one choose anonymous, inglorious, brooding old age (82–4)? Ambition, as we have seen, is acceptable if one gives due credit to the gods, but achieving the right balance is very tricky. Outside the myths, Pindar safely overdoes the thanking; here, Pelops' attitude to the conjunctive 'and' is almost defiant: 'Great risk finds not the man who lacks fortitude … This challenge is for me to take up; but do you grant a kindly outcome'. He had begun by reminding Poseidon that their former erotic relationship created a presumption that the favour would be granted. Poseidon obliges him with the gift of a chariot and winged horses. Pelops' forthrightness and easy familiarity with the god give voice, through myth, to inclinations that must remain suppressed in real dealings with divinity.

In the sixth *Olympian*, Iamus, having reached young manhood, wades into the Alpheus, the river that runs along the edge of Olympia, at night, and calls out to his grandfather Poseidon and father Apollo, seeking an honour suitable to his standing. The pattern of speaking is the opposite of the first *Olympian*: we are not told Iamus' words, but we do hear Apollo's response. The god does not appear in person like Poseidon, however; instead, he is heard from afar, though clearly: 'Arise, my child, and follow my voice hither to the place all will share' (62–3), that is to the future sanctuary, where the god granted 'a twofold treasure of prophecy' (65); this gift consisted first in the ability to understand the god's voice, and later, after Heracles founded the Games, an oracle on the site. If the absence of a visual epiphany is in any way disappointing, Pindar's arrangement here has considerable advantages of another kind and loses nothing in *enargeia*. With a few touches he conjures the superb image of Iamus, the victor's ancestor, moving from the edge of the sanctuary to its centre, following the awe-inducing, supernatural voice in the darkness. 'This way, this way', one hears the god calling. It is a mysterious and sublime moment, putting one in mind of encounters with the voice of God in the Old Testament, such as that of God and Abraham in the scene (*Genesis* 22) so beautifully explored by Auerbach in the first chapter of *Mimesis*, or Moses and the burning bush (*Exodus* 3), or Elijah and the 'still small voice of God' (*1 Kings* 19:13, King James Version); but it is not unknown to Greek literature either, in the equally mysterious and sublime closing of the *Oedipus at Colonus* where the voice of god summons Oedipus to eternity.[51]

The border in the thirteenth *Olympian* is between sleep and wakefulness. Bellerophon needed help to tame Pegasus, and as he 'slept in the darkness' (70–1; 'darkness' is otiose, but appropriately emphasized) Athena appeared in a dream and showed him the new invention of the bridle. 'And dream straightway became reality' (66–7): Bellerophon awakes, and there it is, a *teras* (a supernatural marvel) on the ground beside him. *Enargeia* in this passage is boosted by some clever focalization. That the dream would become reality is announced for our benefit before Athena's speech, which opens 'Do you sleep, Aeolid king?' (67); through her eyes we look down on the slumbering hero. When she finishes, the poet says, 'so much did the maiden of the dark aegis *seem* to him to say' (71–2), which is focalized through Bellerophon. We have all had the experience of a remarkably realistic dream, and the focalization induces us to share his split second of doubt, yet at the same time we look on from the outside and know the dream is real.[52] Any doubts are resolved by Bellerophon's next move. He leaps to his feet, instantly awake; the swiftness of the language mimics the shock of realization that a god has just spoken to him. Through his eyes we look down now on the *teras*, a sublime object if ever there was one. In the sequel we learn that he had slept by Athena's altar on the advice of the seer Polyidus; such incubation in sanctuaries (a liminal space) was a well-known method of soliciting messages in historical times, if not always so spectacularly efficacious.

The liminality of these encounters mirrors the border on which gods in sensible form and humans meet, a confrontation of worlds. In the magnificent tenth *Nemean*, the border is the ultimate one between life and death. The myth is introduced by the comment that an ancestor of the victor, one Pamphaes, had entertained the Dioscuri, so it was no surprise if their clan enjoyed hereditary excellence in the Games. The reference is to a theoxenia, as in the third *Olympian* (see p. 70); the feast had clearly attained legendary status, like that given by Euphorion of Paeon in Herodotus (6.127.3). In both cases, I suspect, the Dioscuri were actually seen by the guests. The Dioscuri then bestowed this hereditary gift on the family in return for the hospitality; they take care of just men, says Pindar, 'and the race of gods is truly reliable (*piston*)' (54), a truth that will be proven again by Zeus in the sequel.

The myth is told in a ring-composition pattern, stating the endpoint as a heading at the beginning: the Twins will live and die on alternate days forever, owing to the choice made by the immortal Polydeuces when his brother Castor was fatally wounded. They had the same mother Leda, but different fathers, Tyndareus and Zeus. In previous tellings of the myth, there is much variation on these points; some make both of them sons of Tyndareus and mortal, others make them both sons of Zeus and immortal. Pindar himself at the end of the eleventh *Pythian* calls them 'sons of gods', while saying in the same breath that they spend only alternate days in heaven. The *Odyssey* has the same arrangement but makes them both sons of Tyndareus (11.298–304).[53] The heading reveals which version Pindar will follow, but matters are more complicated than that. At line 55 (part of the heading) he says that they spend alternate days 'with dear father Zeus' without specifying whose father he was ('dear' makes it clear that this is more than the standard appellation 'father Zeus'). At line 38 he had already called the Twins 'sons of Tyndareus', and at line 73 he calls the immortal Polydeuces 'son of Tyndareus'. At line 76 Tyndareus in his anguish calls out to 'Father Kronion' (i.e. Zeus, son of Kronos), but that need be no more than the usual formula; until Zeus explains the situation to him, Polydeuces was unaware of the truth.[54] What is happening here is that Pindar has turned the ambivalence about their godhood to brilliant thematic advantage, as we shall see in a moment.

The poet next narrates the fight between the Tyndaridae and the sons of Aphareus over cattle. Idas wounds Castor, and Polydeuces comes to his aid. The sons take their stand at the tomb of their father, a detail which marks them as indisputably mortal, and doomed. They attempt to ward off Polydeuces' murderous onslaught by heaving the very tombstone at him, a sacrilegious and futile gesture. This 'ornament of Hades', symbol of death, bounces ineffectually off Polydeuces' chest, who launches his lethal spear at Lynceus, while Zeus flings his thunderbolt at Idas, and the Apharetidae are incinerated 'in their isolation' (72): they are utterly abandoned, unlike the Tyndaridae who are dear to the trustworthy race of gods.[55]

Then the final triad:

The son of Tyndareus rushed back to
  his mighty brother
To find him not yet dead, but
  shuddering, his breath in laboured
  gasps.
75 Shedding hot tears, with groans
He cried aloud: 'Father Kronion, what
  deliverance
From sorrow will there be? Decree
  death for me too, Lord, with him.
A man who lacks friends lacks honour.
  In hardship few mortals can be
  trusted

To share the burden.' So he spoke.
  Zeus appeared before him
80 And uttered these words: 'You are my
  son. To your mother thereafter her
  lordly spouse
Drew near and spent his mortal seed.
But come, nonetheless I offer you
This choice: if you wish yourself to
  escape death and hateful old age
To live with me on Olympus, with
  Athena and with Ares of the black
  spear,

85 This can be your lot; but if it is for your
  brother
You fight, and mean to share all things
  alike,
You may breathe half your time
  beneath the earth,
And half in the golden house of
  heaven.'
So he spoke. No doubt attended the
  decision.
90 First the eyes he freed, then the voice
  of bronze-girt Castor.

---

ταχέως δ' ἐπ' ἀδελφεοῦ βίαν πάλιν
  χώρησεν ὁ Τυνδαρίδας,
καί νιν οὔπω τεθναότ', ἄσθματι δὲ
  φρίσσοντα πνοὰς ἔκιχεν.
75 θερμὰ δὴ τέγγων δάκρυα στοναχαῖς
  ὄρθιον φώνασε· Πάτερ Κρονίων, τίς
  δὴ λύσις
ἔσσεται πενθέων; καὶ ἐμοὶ θάνατον σὺν
  τῷδ' ἐπίτειλον, ἄναξ.
οἴχεται τιμὰ φίλων τατωμένῳ φωτί·
  παῦροι δ' ἐν πόνῳ πιστοὶ βροτῶν

καμάτου μεταλαμβάνειν.' ὣς
  ἤνεπε· Ζεὺς δ' ἀντίος ἤλυθέ οἱ,
80 καὶ τόδ' ἐξαύδασ' ἔπος· Ἐσσί μοι
  υἱός· τόνδ' ἔπειτα πόσις
σπέρμα θνατὸν ματρὶ τεᾷ πελάσαις
στάξεν ἥρως. ἀλλ' ἄγε τῶνδέ τοι ἔμπαν
  αἵρεσιν
παρδίδωμ'· εἰ μὲν θάνατόν τε φυγὼν
  καὶ γῆρας ἀπεχθόμενον
αὐτὸς Οὔλυμπον θέλεις <ναίειν ἐμοὶ>
  σύν τ' Ἀθαναίᾳ κελαινεγχεῖ τ' Ἄρει,

85 ἔστι τοι τούτων λάχος· εἰ δὲ κασιγνήτου
  πέρι
μάρνασαι, πάντων δὲ νοεῖς
  ἀποδάσσασθαι ἴσον,
ἥμισυ μέν κε πνέοις γαίας ὑπένερθεν
  ἐών,
ἥμισυ δ' οὐρανοῦ ἐν χρυσέοις
  δόμοισιν.'
ὣς ἄρ' αὐδάσαντος οὐ γνώμᾳ διπλόαν
  θέτο βουλάν,
90 ἀνὰ δ' ἔλυσεν μὲν ὀθφαλμόν, ἔπειτα δὲ
  φωνὰν χαλκομίτρα Κάστορος.

This justly admired passage opens with emotional turmoil: grief for a brother, a bitter question flung at heaven, a heroic plea for death. In tone the question resembles that of Croesus burning on the pyre in Bacchylides' poem ('Where is the gods' gratitude?', 3.38), and his subsequent rescue and translation to the Hyperboreans offer further similarities to the Pindaric scene; but, as Currie writes, they 'mask quite different characterizations. Croesus is desperate, resigned, recriminatory, passive; Polydeuces makes an active, heroic choice (77, 89–90) – a variant of the *iuncta mors* or *Liebestod*, akin to Phaedrus' portrayal of Achilles as choosing to "die after" Patroclus in Plato (*Symp.* 179e–180a)'.[56] The king of gods then appears and says simply, 'You are my son': a Longinian thunderbolt, and a truly heart-stopping moment. Forthright language is typical of epiphanic gods, but the effect is heightened here by Pindar's use of the plainest of stylistic registers. Zeus's Olympian calm contrasts with Polydeuces' inner turmoil; yet his candid statement 'you are my son' betrays an emotion that any parent (or child) can identify with. He also understands Polydeuces' deep love for his twin. Zeus knew this moment would come one day, and, seeing his son's distress, he makes his unique offer. He does not have to wait long for an answer. Polydeuces' heroic decisiveness and excitement alike are conveyed by the rapidity of the language ('no doubt attended the decision', *ou gnōmāi diploān theto boulān*). He then opens the eyes and mouth of his brother, reversing the usual ritual of death, in which they are closed.[57]

The sublimity of the passage lies above all in its Longinian grandeur: a noble theme, the noblest of characters, an uplifting sense of happiness achieved. The outcome is as surprising and swift as Zeus's epiphany, the progress from the depths of despair to the heights of bliss is as extreme as it could be. Contributing further is a series of incommensurables, also characteristic of the sublime. When Zeus appears, eternity and ephemerality meet at a single point which is both in and out of time. The notion of life in a timeless heaven alternating with death under the earth – forever – is categorically baffling, if one stops to think about it. At the end of the poem we have not yet returned from the time of myth to the present; we are left, that is, forever in the temporality of then-now. To formulate that analysis, of course, one must step outside the magic circle into ordinary time – which only heightens the sense of conundrum. Strongly reinforcing that sense is the single word 'voice' instead of 'mouth' in the last line. It creates the desperate but impossible wish to know what Castor said. It was a wise decision of Pindar's not to tell us, for precisely because of this ellipsis, this closure denied, the voice reaches out of the poem across the centuries.

Pindar here strains every sinew to overcome the limits of mortality, which he elsewhere warns us in all earnestness to respect. As Young notes, the Twins' fate is an apt parallel to the quasi-immortality of the victor, which Pindar's own poem has bestowed. The parallel applies equally well to the balance of hope and doubt that all of us share about immortality; and with Polydeuces we may all ask whether we are or are not children of the gods. This ambivalence, as suggested above (p. 159), prevails throughout Pindar's oeuvre. In the remarkable opening of the sixth *Nemean*, quoted in the last chapter (p. 120), it is at its plainest. We are one with the race of gods! proclaims the poem. Yet (it continues) we are separated by an immense difference in power; one of us is nothing, the other dwells in heaven. Yet ... we have something in common with them. Yet ... we are creatures of a day. As Pindar asks elsewhere, just what are we, in the end? Or what are we not?

The oscillation between desire to surpass the limits and fear of doing so is comparable to that motivating the *kairos*, in that both involve the meeting of eternity and the present. But there is a difference. The *kairos* is an intense moment in the lyric now. The focus is all on that moment; one loses oneself in it. Pindar is supremely confident in the poetic wizardry that enables him to create it. As soon as attention strays to the transcendental level in which the immanent moment participates, doubt creeps in, since there is much about that level we simply cannot know. This uncertainty is reflected, as I have been suggesting, in the poetics, since the admonition to curb one's ambition to immortality is so easily deconstructed within the poems themselves. Another reflection is Pindar's regular practice (outside the myths) of referring to the gods anonymously, using the terms *theos* or *daimōn*. This accords with everyday Greek usage; we may feel sure *some* god is involved in an incident, but usually have no idea which one. In some circumstances one can make a reasonable guess; if one wins at Delphi, Apollo will have had a hand in it, and one can always credit Zeus, who is notionally in charge of everything.[58] But on the whole, we grope in the dark.

It is notable, however, that Pindar's thoughts on his various abstractions and personifications display a greater measure of assurance (the names alone imply it), which derives from his own pro-active theorizing – creating subjects out of predicates. Then within the myths, the case is altogether altered: the poet can write detailed scripts for named gods, and the narratives, in their displaced, metaphorical mode, offer, if not certainty, a degree of clarity about questions and possible answers. Gods in ordinary life are a diffuse omnipresence, often impossible to read, often contradictory. Myth can discern the precise point of intervention. It knows where the border is; it can observe the approach from either side, and the electrifying meeting in the middle.

## In and out of time: Pindaric temporality

The tenth *Nemean* is not the only poem that ends with its myth; so do the fourth *Olympian*, the ninth *Pythian* and the first *Nemean*. At the close of some other poems (O.10, P.3, P.11) Pindar reverts to the time of myth with a brief reference to another story or character. These tellings all have their different purposes in context,[59] but they all have in common that they bring the time of myth and the time of the present into the same space. The collocation invites comparison and reflection, but above all it invests the present with the glow of the mythical past. Doing so at the end of a poem can amplify the effect by projecting the unique temporality forward into the time of reception, but wherever the myth is placed in the poem the overriding purpose of juxtaposing past and present remains the same.[60]

Some aspects of Pindar's technique in this regard have already been noted. His favourite trick of launching a myth by pivoting unexpectedly on a relative pronoun (p. 71) reduces the boundary to almost nothing. This irruption of the heroic world into the time of the performance is itself a kind of epiphany, as if that world has been here all along, waiting for the poet to dispel the mist from our eyes. Upon concluding a myth, as discussed above, Pindar has various ways of suggesting its continuing force in the poem. His typically abrupt endings of myths do nothing to undermine his tactics – just the opposite, in fact, since they frustrate closure. At such points too we frequently find metapoetic remarks which encourage reflection on the intentions of the poet and his myths.

I noted Pindar's ventriloquism of Heracles in the sixth *Isthmian* (above, p. 161), which brings the character into the audience's space as if in a theatre. In fact, Pindar makes relatively little use of direct speech in his myths, in contrast to Homer and, among lyric poets, Stesichorus and Bacchylides. If we ask when Pindar chooses to adopt the mimetic mode, the answer is revealing: in most cases, the speech in question is a kind of prophecy. Apart from Heracles in the sixth *Isthmian*, there are the speeches of Apollo in the eighth *Olympian*, Chiron in the ninth *Pythian*, Amphiaraus in the eighth *Pythian*, Themis in the eighth *Isthmian*, and others. Zeus's speech in the tenth *Nemean* (above) is about the future, and Apollo's directive to his son in the sixth *Olympian* is followed by a prediction about the future oracle at Olympia (above, p. 164). Speeches which are not prophecies, on the other hand, are few and sometimes very short (O.1.75–85, 4.24–7, 6.16–17); the main exceptions, unsurprisingly, are in the fourth *Pythian*, but even here the longest speech is Medea's prophecy at the outset (12–56).[61]

Bacchylides, as often, provides a useful contrast: of the ten speeches in the epinicians, only one is a prophecy (13.44–57); of the sometimes lengthy speeches in the dithyrambs, none is prophetic. The content differs too. As Pavlou writes:

> [Bacchylidean] speeches aim to evoke pathos, sympathy, pity and fear, and reveal the weak and human side of the characters: their despair and distress, their pain, and anxiety, in a few words, their inner self and feelings … Pindaric speeches serve first and above all to evoke feelings of awe and amazement and to underline the power of the gods, the bliss enjoyed by their beloved ones, and the existence of providence and of a divine plan which always finds fulfilment.[62]

The prophecy of Hecate in *Paean* 2.73–5 has no introductory or closing formula; the fact that it is in direct speech is inferred from its content (then retrospectively confirmed by the identification of the speaker in line 78). In this way the melding with the speaking voice on either side is total, and time is completely collapsed. Similarly, Themis' speech switches to direct discourse without notice at *I*.8.35a. A comparable blending occurs in the seventh *Olympian*, where Apollo's oracle in indirect speech lacks a concluding formula (33–7). Teiresias' summary of Heracles' future life at *N*.1.61–72, in indirect speech, concludes the poem and thus merges with the speaker's voice. Pavlou notes further that Pindar's prophecies all have second-person addressees, even though the third person is common, for instance in Calchas' prophecy in Aeschylus, *Agamemnon* 126–55. In this way the external audience of the poem merges with the internal audience of the narrative. Unlike tragedy, which never explicitly draws attention to the circumstances of its performance, the lyric frame is full of such references, creating a 'double present', the present of the execution, and the present of the narrative (combining into 'then-now', as I have been calling it). Pindar fully exploits the potential of this situation. Not only does the content of his prophecies often have obvious relevance to the victor, his family and his city, but the future tense sets up a self-reinforcing temporal loop: the live audience looks back on the narrated audience looking forward to the live audience.[63]

Myth as exemplum was nothing new in Greek literature. Homer already represented his characters drawing on traditional tales to point a moral (Phoenix in *Iliad* 9 adapting the story of Meleager to fit Achilles' circumstances is the egregious instance).[64] In cultic poetry, some aspect of the ritual's aetiology is very apt to figure, and since the ceremony is itself a re-enactment of the primal founding, the sense of the myth coming alive in the here-and-now, such as we have been highlighting in Pindar, is strong.[65] As so often, however, Pindar takes matters to a new level of intensity. The temporal mirroring and his ventriloquism of the mythical prophecies are one part of that. Another is the complexity of the relationship between the original model and its avatar. Pindar's myths typically bring out not only more obvious points of comparison – athletic or soldierly prowess, youth, beauty and the like – they also explore underlying themes: the nature of divinity, the varied lot of humans, fate and chance, loyalty, piety, leadership, hospitality, reciprocity (*charis*), hereditary excellence and so on. In this respect his odes resemble those of Greek tragedy more than those of the earlier lyric tradition. It is not that such reflections are entirely absent, but with some exceptions (principally Sappho) the application of the exemplum is usually straightforward. Alcaeus, for instance, tells the story (fr. 298) of how the lesser Ajax mortally offended Athena during the sack of Troy by raping Cassandra in her very temple; as a result, Athena sank the Greek fleet on its way home, not caring (as is the gods' way) about who else was destroyed alongside the offender (so also Coronis' townsfolk in the third *Pythian*, 36). As Alcaeus comments, it would have been better for the Greeks had they killed Ajax before setting sail. The point is that the Mytileneans would do well to kill the oath-breaker Pittacus, or they will all be dragged down with him. The poet wrings every ounce of horror out of the tale; the poem is a masterpiece from that point of view, but one would not claim that there are further symbolic depths to be plumbed. Contrast the thematic richness of any number of Pindaric myths. Typhos in the first *Pythian* yielded cosmic, political, social and artistic implications (p. 62). The first *Olympian* not only offers multiple points of contact between Pelops and Hieron – equestrian championship at Olympia, divine favour, royalty, extensive domains – but the fate of Pelops' father Tantalus entails lessons about the rightful place of gods and human beings.[66] Pindar's renunciation of the received myth in this poem thematizes the role of myth itself, and the poet. In the ninth *Pythian*, the myth of Apollo and Cyrene does more than echo the imminent marriage of the victor Telesicrates (as also does the myth of Alexidamus at the end); it is about the wedding of the colonists of Cyrene to the land, and offers a superb meditation on the theme of nature versus culture.[67] The third *Pythian* uses the sin of both Coronis and her healer son Asclepius of loving 'what lay afar' to reflect on possibilities and limits in human life; it sets up a pensive and delicate dialogue between hope and resignation, pain and joy, and ultimately mortality and immortality, to create this most moving of consolations of a dying friend.

One final feature of time in Pindaric myth-making I mention here is his preoccupation with beginnings. In this, Pindar is a man of his age, sharing this interest with contemporary philosophy (above, pp. 145–6), Herodotus' *Histories*, the Aeschylean *Prometheus Bound* and other texts. Many of his myths concern origins: of Zeus's own rule, and of Aetna (*P*.1); the Olympic Games (*O*.1, 3, 6, 10); the victor's city (*O*.7, 9, *P*.4, 5, 9); the wedding of Peleus and Thetis, which led to the Trojan War (*N*.3, 4, 5, *I*.8); inventions such as the bridle (*O*.13) and the aulos (*P*.12). We might include also the account of how Neoptolemus came to have a shrine at Delphi (*N*.7) and the building of Troy's walls (*O*.8, and *N*.4 again). Going the other way, the eschatology of the second *Olympian* gives us the end of life – but also its beginning through reincarnation. Ritual texts can look to aetiology for their founding moments; there being no such moment for the epinician, the genre had to find an alternative.[68] In cases where the ode was performed as part of a festival, such as the fifth *Pythian* at the Carneia in Cyrene, the poet could draw on its aetiology; but this is only one of the ingredients in an ode which always has much more to say. Conceived on a grand scale and bearing his unique stamp in every case, his myths suggest that all the significant events of the past have combined to produce the present moment. It is the latest manifestation of the transcendent sphere where gods dwell, a moment in a process that will continue forever, unalterable in essence but contingent in its accidents.

Let us consider as an instance of all these characteristics of Pindaric myth-making the seventh *Olympian*, written for Diagoras of Rhodes in 464 BCE.[69] Pindar proposes to tell the story of the island 'from the beginning' (*ex archās*, 20), and he does not disappoint, tracing it all the way back to the geological origins. The narration is remarkable for its chronological nesting, working backwards from the arrival of the Thessalian colonist Tlapolemus to the establishment of Athena's cult to the emergence of the island from the sea before moving rapidly forward again to the present day. Unusually, the myth occupies the three middle stanzas precisely; the well-wrought structure gives the poem a monumental feel, and the story, perhaps apocryphal, that the poem was inscribed on stone in golden letters and placed in Athena's sanctuary on the acropolis of Lindos seems altogether appropriate, even if the dedicators' motives were not purely aesthetic.[70]

Pindar says that he will tell the story from the beginning, but first identifies this as the arrival of Tlapolemus, son of Heracles, who established the existing order on the island. As we soon discover, the story will go back to a time far before that.[71] So Tlapolemus' arrival, though the more significant, turns out to be a second beginning, in a pattern typical of Greek (and indeed modern) myths of colonization: the Hellenes supersede an indigenous population, whose traditions (as understood or constructed by the colonists) are appropriated, sometimes in the spirit of a hostile takeover, sometimes (so the colonists would have it, anyway) as a friendly merger.[72] Very often, the history both before and after the settlement had purchase on the contemporary *imaginaire*. That is very much the case in the seventh *Olympian*, where the tradition of the earlier inhabitants, children of the sun-god Helios, is used alongside Tlapolemus to support the poem's focus on Rhodes as a whole rather than on any one of its cities. (It is probable that the sense of pan-Rhodian identity was already emerging which eventually led to political unity in 408/7 BCE.)

Tlapolemus' start was not auspicious; he killed his bastard brother Licymnius in a fit of rage. The fact is hedged round with exculpatory remarks: 'human wits are beset by faults beyond count'; 'impossible to know, what is best for a man to meet with now or in the end'; 'mental disturbances knock even the wise astray' (24–6, 30–1). Apollo told him he must emigrate to Rhodes, where Zeus had once sent a storm of golden snowflakes when Athena was born. Helios had forewarned his sons to be the first to establish an altar for the goddess and sacrifice to her. But a 'cloud of forgetfulness' overcame them (the sort that 'diverts the straight path of affairs away from one's intentions', 46–7), and after they toiled up to the top of the acropolis they found they had not brought fire. So they instituted a rite of fireless sacrifice (a ritual attested in later sources; the tale in this respect is straightforwardly aetiological). Zeus sent the golden snow (a sublime moment in itself), and Athena gratefully made the Rhodians the best artisans in the world, famous particularly for sculpture (also true of the historical Rhodians). A different, hostile tradition spoke of a primeval tribe of malevolent craftsmen on Rhodes, the Telchines (crafts and sorcery go together in many stories worldwide), who were superseded by the sons of Helios; in Pindar, the Heliadae are the only indigenous people, and it is their skill, and their god, that the Rhodians inherit. When Pindar says pointedly, however, that their skill was 'honest' (53), he may be acknowledging and contradicting the vicious alternative.[73]

'Tales of old', continues Pindar (thus inscribing a tradition of story-telling, including his own, which tracks the story; reinforcing the sense that the present is the product of the past, and will send the tradition into the future), say that when Zeus and the gods were dividing up the earth, Rhodes still lay hidden beneath the waves. We have now arrived at the very beginning of time, and the third of the three triads containing the myth:

| | |
|---|---|
| Helios was not there, and nobody indicated his portion (*lachos*). | ἀπεόντος δ' οὔτις ἔνδειξεν λάχος Ἀελίου· |
| So they left him without a land allotted, | καί ῥά νιν χώρας ἀκλάρωτον λίπον, |

60 Reverend god.

He made mention of it, and Zeus was
    ready to rerun the lottery, but Helios
    would not permit it, since within the
    grey
Sea, he said, he could himself see
    growing from the floor
A land rich in food for people and
    kindly for flocks.

Straightway he bade Lachesis of the
    golden diadem
65 Raise her hands, and not gainsay
The mighty oath of the gods;
To nod agreement with the son of
    Kronos that when it was sent forth
    to the bright light above, it would
    henceforth be
An honour for himself. The sum of
    these words was accomplished,
Falling on a ground of truth. From the
    damp sea there grew

70 The island, and the father who
    engenders the sharp sunrays has
    possession,
Master of fire-breathing horses. Here of
    a time he united with Rhodos[74] and
    sired
Seven sons, heirs to the greatest
    wisdom among men of yore;
Of them, one sired Camirus,
And Ialysus the eldest, and Lindus.
    Separately
75 Throughout the ancestral land divided
    in three
Each had his allotment of the towns,
    seats named after them.

60 ἁγνὸν θεόν.

μνασθέντι δὲ Ζεὺς ἄμπαλον μέλλεν
    θέμεν. ἀλλά νιν οὐκ εἴασεν· ἐπεὶ
    πολιᾶς
εἶπέ τιν᾽ αὐτὸς ὁρᾶν ἔνδον θαλάσσας
    αὐξομέναν πεδόθεν
πολύβοσκον γαῖαν ἀνθρώποισι καὶ
    εὔφρονα μήλοις.

ἐκέλευσεν δ᾽ αὐτίκα χρυσάμπυκα μὲν
    Λάχεσιν
65 χεῖρας ἀντεῖναι, θεῶν δ᾽ ὅρκον μέγαν
    μὴ παρφάμεν,
ἀλλὰ Κρόνου σὺν παιδὶ νεῦσαι,
    φαεννὸν ἐς αἰθέρα μιν πεμφθεῖσαν
    ἑᾷ κεφαλᾷ
ἐξοπίσω γέρας ἔσσεσθαι. τελεύταθεν δὲ
    λόγων κορυφαί
ἐν ἀλαθείᾳ πετοῖσαι· βλάστε μὲν ἐξ
    ἁλὸς ὑγρᾶς

70 νᾶσος, ἔχει τέ μιν ὀξειᾶν ὁ γενέθλιος
    ἀκτίνων πατήρ,
πῦρ πνεόντων ἀρχὸς ἵππων· ἔνθα Ῥόδῳ
    ποτὲ μιχθεὶς τέκεν
ἑπτὰ σοφώτατα νοήματ᾽ ἐπὶ προτέρων
    ἀνδρῶν παραδεξαμένους
παῖδας, ὧν εἷς μὲν Κάμιρον
    πρεσβύτατόν τε Ἰάλυσον ἔτεκεν
    Λίνδον τ᾽· ἀπάτερθε δ᾽ ἔχον
75 διὰ γαῖαν τρίχα δασσάμενοι πατρωΐαν
    ἀστέων μοῖραν, κέκληνται δέ σφιν
    ἕδραι.

Helios was not commonly worshipped in the Hellenic world, and his unusual prominence in Rhodes might have encouraged Pindar to elaborate or even invent this charming mythological vignette of how the association came about. At all events, the vegetal imagery (*rhodon* being Greek for 'rose') must be his, as also the imagery of fire and light here and elsewhere in the poem. Particularly striking is the *enargeia* of the infant island's emergence from the floor of the sea, focalized from high above through the eyes of the all-seeing Sun himself; it swells and blooms out (*blaste*, 69) as the rose itself, another sublime image. As all commentators note, each of the three myths involves a successful outcome after an ill-omened beginning: Licymnius' murder leads to the Greek settlement of Rhodes; the sacrificers' forgetfulness results in a famous rite; a god nearly deprived of honour forms a unique bond with his chosen land. The cause of the first two mishaps was human weakness, a fault which Pindar can hardly impute to gods in the third, so he says only that Helios was absent (presumably driving his chariot across the sky) and no one thought to act as his proxy (not exactly faultless behaviour, one might think, but diplomatically expressed. Pindar's gods can be wonderfully down-to-earth sometimes; I think for instance of the deferential Apollo in the ninth *Pythian*. Such are the possibilities of anthropomorphism.) Then in an atmosphere of high solemnity the arrangement is set into cosmic stone as both Lachesis and Zeus swear to it. What was an accidental oversight is now Fate.

Lachesis derives her name from *lachos*, allotted share. I noted above that Pindar regarded Tyche as one of the Moirai, and suggested how one might interpret that. The drawing of lots was employed by Greeks in political procedures, and the idea always was that the gods had a hand in it; drawing lots was also common in oracles. So the same process is both random and determined. This can be said of each stage of the myth here, with an emphasis in the first two on humans stumbling in the dark and being aided by providence. In the order of the narrative, first Apollo, then Helios, then Athena guided their path; in chronological order, Helios, Athena and Apollo. Last in the narrative but first in time are Zeus, Lachesis and Helios again. Step by step we have worked our way back to a time almost before time, but the return to the present day is rapid. Time is stretched out and layered, then collapsed. The long journey into the past reinforces the sense of time's depth, whereas the zoom forward reinforces the point that the tremendous weight all of this history bears on one moment, the one before our eyes. Everything lines up on the great arcing armature that unites remotest beginning and living present.

The myth closes with a reference to the three towns of Rhodes (the 'seats' named for the grandsons of Helios), and the poet continues: 'Where a sweet recompense for pitiable misfortune stands for Tlapolemus … as if for a god: the sacrifice of flocks rich in savoury smoke and competition for prizes. With their garlands Diagoras was twice crowned ...' (there follows the amazing list of his victories). The festival for Tlapolemus, at which (we infer) this poem was performed, includes sacrifices and competitions for the hero 'as if for a god'. The idea of recompense (*lutron*) conforms to the pattern in the poem of misfortune followed by success, but it also conforms to a pattern in many other odes whereby the hardship and expense of training are rewarded by the victory, and the victory ode.[75] So all of this comes together, and the question arises whether the poem is offered to Diagoras too 'as if for a god'. It is a thought that cannot safely be put into words, but which is inescapably implied.

If you put the question to him, however, Pindar would only claim that in this moment, at least, Diagoras is touched by divinity; he would never go so far as to say that he is, or will be, a god. In Raphael's famous fresco *The School of Athens*, Plato points upwards to heaven as the source of knowledge while Aristotle gestures down towards earth. For Pindar neither of these gestures would be correct. His transcendent forces and beings are neither earth- nor heaven-bound, but operate across time and space in the sensible world. Although their essence does not change, they are not absolutes, because they function only through circumstance. Human beings must continually negotiate their way through these circumstances in a state of deep ignorance. There are signs and indications which poets help us read, but dogmatism is entirely out of place. Even in the seventh *Olympian*, where divine providence seems to warrant optimism, the last lines tell us that the winds of fortune blow now this way, now that 'in a single portion of time' (or perhaps we should write 'Time').

## 'As when': Pindaric metaphor and the limits of language

At times Pindar seems unable to say anything untroped. In the tenth *Nemean*, for instance, 'olive oil came in painted vases to Argos' (olive oil being the prize in the games at Athens) becomes 'the fruit of the olive came to the manly folk of Hera in the all-decorated fences of vessels of earth burnt by fire' (35–6). The ancient rhetoricians, Longinus at the head, would surely call this passage *psūchron*, 'frigid'. Yet Longinus also well remarks (§5) that our faults generally spring from the same source as our virtues, and if Pindar's images seem overwrought on occasion, his brilliance in their use makes up for it many times over. His distinctiveness in this respect has often been admired, and in many ways it lies at the heart of his poetics.

Much fine work has been devoted to the Pindaric metaphor, so I shall confine myself here to some features of his practice as they relate to the sublime.[76] For my purposes the difference between metaphor and simile makes no odds, as I am interested in the process of comparing and juxtaposing rather than the outward form. It is significant, though, that similes are much rarer than metaphors in Pindar.[77] Just as he avoids the untroped, he avoids the more straightforward comparison of a simile, and even when he does use one he tends to do things differently. As Maslov has discovered, 'the most striking feature of the Pindaric usage is his avoidance of the simple ὡς [*hōs*, 'as'], otherwise the default comparative construction in classical Greek and the only one used by, for example, Sappho and Alcaeus'.[78] Of the many other words Pindar uses, ὥτε and ἄτε ('just as', 'in the manner of') are the commonest, and support connections with the surrounding sentence which can be loose in both syntax and concept.

Maslov credits this state of affairs to Pindar's preference for comparing 'ideas or situations rather than objects or events'.[79] He stresses the conceptual work that Pindaric metaphors often do, combining image and idea. A cardinal passage, discussed by Maslov and many others interested in Pindar as a thinking poet, is the opening of the fifth *Isthmian* with its disquisition on Theia (above, p. 154). As he writes, 'In this passage the "divine," hypostasized as a female figure ... becomes the ultimate *raison d'être* and the driving force behind the dynamic of all human existence.' Two images underpin the conceptual innovation, first the genealogical metaphor of Theia as mother, then gold as a metonym. He continues:

> Rather than being a conventional value standard, [gold] is an image anchored in the physically perceptible object, the sun, which is linked to an abstract notion of divinity by the image of kinship. This powerful essentializing construction does not produce a mythic narrative, nor does it depend on one. It is a conceptual operation that deploys 'religious' and 'poetic' categories in ways that do not admit of easy separation.[80]

One can also think of the process in terms of juxtaposition (and melding) of tenor and vehicle. The multi-faceted metaphors are offered for examination from every point of view; questions are raised, connections are suggested, literary echoes resonate. As a method of thinking and composition, as we have discussed in previous chapters, juxtaposition pertains at every level, from the individual word to the myths to the representation of the *kairos*.[81] The world is pregnant with meaning.

The point is most easily illustrated from the myths and the metaphors, but is perhaps less obvious in the case of individual words. Lyric poets from Archilochus on had always been creative in their diction, and by the time of Pindar and Bacchylides, neologism seems to have become almost a mania, finding its way also into tragedy in the person of Aeschylus. Maehler counts some 230 words in Bacchylides that occur only once in surviving Greek literature (*hapax legomena*, in the jargon) or for the first time;[82] Cannatà Fera indexes forty-four unique words in Pindar's *Nemeans* alone.[83] The great majority of these are compound adjectives. A distinguishing feature of Bacchylides' usage is his marked liking for words from a visual semantic field, especially colour-words; another is his close relation to Homeric precedents, which are modified in interesting ways to suit the context.[84] These characteristics account in no small measure for the vividness, charm and sometimes deceptive simplicity of his style. Pindar, by contrast, is much more likely to invent words of such novelty that scholars still puzzle over their exact meaning. They bring you up short, and raise questions that can't quite be answered. An instance is *anaxiphorminges hymnoi*, 'lyre-ruling hymns' (*O*.2.1), possibly his most famous coinage.[85] In what sense does the hymn rule the lyre? Commentators will tell you that in Greek poetry of this period the music was subordinate to the words, in the sense that the poet composed his accompaniment to suit the rhythm and shape of the words rather than altering the pronunciation of words to fit pre-composed music. It is true that innovations of that kind were introduced after Pindar's time, but Pindar too was a daring reformer in music and metre,[86] and the lyre's powers, if not its dominance, are celebrated at the opening of the first *Pythian*. However, Pindar is hardly making a technical musicological point here. He continues by asking the poem: 'What god, what hero, what man shall we celebrate?' This is a partnership of text and music to deliver the commission; the apostrophe of the hymn serves to point out the presence of the third partner, the poet (p. 111). The formulation has metapoetic effect, inviting us to think throughout the poem how poet, words and music work together, in that order of hierarchy, to create meaning. This is a question which can be answered in many ways. Moreover, as Silk points out, the idea of ruling aligns with the lordship of the man being praised, Theron; together with the second line, the epithet 'proposes the problematic that underlies Pindar's poetic ideology as a whole', which is how porous, exactly, are these categories of god, hero and man.[87]

It will have been noticed that 'lyre-ruling' incorporates a metaphor. Other examples among Pindar's unique words are not difficult to find. At *Nemean* 2.7, Pindar hopes that a victor's 'straight-guiding (*euthupompos*) life' will take him along the same path as his father to further victories; life here takes the young man in hand and escorts him in the right direction. 'Life' is *aiōn*, which provides another instance of this concept's agency (above, n. 28). Victory crowns are 'woven with (or by) *themis*' (*themiplektois*, *N*.9.52), which exploits two aspects of *themis*, both what is custom ('duly woven') and what is just (he won his prize without cheating); but can we also hear an overtone of 'woven by Themis', the goddess?[88] At *Nemean* 11.18 Pindar says we should 'celebrate (Aristagoras) embellished with honey-sounding songs', *meligdoupoisi daidalthenta melisden aoidais*. The verb *melisden* (celebrate in song) is derived from *melos*, song, but *meligdoupoisi* (only here in Greek) comes from *meli*, honey, and *doupos*, sound; *meligdoupoisi ... melisden* is a pun, a quite brazen one considering that *doupos* is normally used of heavy, dull sounds: 'honey-thudding' is in itself an oxymoron. Then too the verb *daidallō* (>*daidalthenta*, 'embellished') is at home in the visual and plastic arts (Daedalus owes his name to it), which compounds the synaesthesia here (of which more below).[89]

These unique words – *anaxiphorminges, euthupompos, themiplektois, meligdoupoisi* – among many others illustrate on a small scale how Pindar puts ideas into the same space and lets them jostle against one another. Their creativity and uniqueness, as Sigelman points out, draw attention to the poet's craftsmanship and amplify the special nature of the occasion he celebrates.[90] The metapoetic aspect of his imagery is visible also in the epithets he uses to describe poetry itself, which, as Nünlist has documented, activate a range of semantic fields wider than those of any other early Greek poet.[91] It is even more obvious in the elaborate metaphors he deploys at junctures in the poems' structure (to move up now from the level of individual words). At the beginning or end of a myth, at the start or close of an ode, or other key moments the poet inserts his voice, and parades his awareness of his art; unsurprisingly, we find at these points a profusion of metaphors. Here are some examples:

1. *O*.6.82–3:

   | I have a certain impression of a shrill whetstone on my tongue. | δόξαν ἔχω τιν' ἐπὶ γλώσσᾳ λιγυρᾶς ἀκόνας, |
   |---|---|
   | It creeps upon me, willing as I am, with fair-flowing winds. | ἅ μ' ἐθέλοντα προσέρπει καλλιρόαισι πνοαῖς. |

2. *P*.10.51–4:

   | Check your oar! Quick, fix the anchor on the shore | κώπαν σχάσον, ταχὺ δ' ἄγκυραν ἔρεισον χθονί |
   |---|---|
   | From the bow, protection from the rocky reef. | πρῴραθε, χοιράδος ἄλκαρ πέτρας. |
   | The best of *kōmos*-songs | ἐγκωμίων γὰρ ἄωτος ὕμνων |
   | flits from thought to thought like a bee.[92] | ἐπ' ἄλλοτ' ἄλλον ὧτε μέλισσα θύνει λόγον. |

3. *N.7.70–9:*

| | |
|---|---|
| I swear | ἀπομνύω |
| I will not step up to the mark only to fling my swift tongue | μὴ τέρμα προβαὶς ἄκονθ᾽ ὥτε χαλκοπάραον ὄρσαι |
| Like a bronze-cheeked javelin that eliminated | θοὰν γλῶσσαν, ὃς ἐξέπεμψεν παλαισμάτων |
| neck and undampened strength from the wrestling before a limb fell in the blazing sun.[93] | αὐχένα καὶ σθένος ἀδίαντον, αἴθωνι πρὶν ἁλίῳ γυῖον ἐμπεσεῖν. |
| If toil there was, the joy is greater after. | εἰ πόνος ἦν, τὸ τερπνὸν πλέον πεδέρχεται. |
| 75 Let me proceed! If in my excitement I have shouted too much, | 75 ἔα με· νικῶντί γε χάριν, εἴ τι πέραν ἀερθεὶς |
| I am not stubborn when it comes to paying favour owed the victor. | ἀνέκραγον, οὐ τραχύς εἰμι καταθέμεν. |
| Weaving garlands is easy. Strike up the lyre! The Muse | εἴρειν στεφάνους ἐλαφρόν. ἀναβάλεο· Μοῖσά τοι |
| Welds gold and white ivory | κολλᾷ χρυσὸν ἔν τε λευκὸν ἐλέφανθ᾽ ἁμᾶ |
| And the lily-flower she has plucked from the dew of the sea.[94] | καὶ λείριον ἄνθεμον ποντίας ὑφελοῖσ᾽ ἐέρσας. |

4. *N.8.13–16:*

| | |
|---|---|
| A suppliant of Aeacus, I clasp his knees | ἱκέτας Αἰακοῦ σεμνῶν γονάτων πόλιός |
| On behalf of a nation I love and these its townsfolk | θ᾽ ὑπὲρ φίλας ἀστῶν θ᾽ ὑπὲρ τῶνδ᾽ ἅπτομαι φέρων |
| And bring a Lydian headband loudly embroidered,[95] | Λυδίαν μίτραν καναχηδὰ πεποικιλμέναν, |
| A Nemean dedication[96] for Deinias and his father Megas for their double wins in the stade-race. | Δείνιος δισσῶν σταδίων καὶ πατρὸς Μέγα Νεμεαῖον ἄγαλμα. |

The metaphors are mixed and in some cases synaesthetic. It is common to observe about metaphors that their force depends as much on what is dissimilar in the comparison as on what is similar. Cognitive theorists note that the mind instinctively looks first for the common ground between tenor and vehicle (which there must be if the comparison is to work at all); but if there is nothing but similarity, 'there is no illustration', as Johnson said about a passage in Dryden.[97] One takes pleasure in exploring the area outside the common ground, thinking of surprising ways in which, nevertheless, this or that patch of it might be brought within the pale and so illustrate the comparandum. This effort cannot be resisted but will never wholly succeed; there is always a residue of meaning that lies just out of reach. Every metaphor, in other words, has an element of the sublime about it. When the metaphor is mixed, as in the examples above, the cognitive effort is doubly challenging. Attempts to find the common ground between all the constituent images fail. Gaps multiply. Any paraphrase requires omissions and additions, and drains the life out of the metaphors.

Interpretation of Pindar's extravagant imagery (a translator's despair) is often further complicated by unique usages or variants in the manuscripts, as is the case in the first passage above.[98] Critics who reject a reading or translation because it is unparalleled or impossibly obscure could be right that Pindar would never say such a thing, but they could also be trying to tether the eagle. Regardless of these challenges, the situation prompts a larger question: why is it that we so often meet such difficulties in Pindar's metapoetic passages?

In seeking an answer, we might first look at how Pindar himself thematizes language. He says on two occasions that his victors' accomplishments are as the grains of sand, beyond counting (O.2.98, 13.46); in other places he confesses that listing all the glorious exploits of Argos or of the Aeacids is beyond him (N.10.19, N.4.71–2). These are laudatory and to an extent conventional gestures, emulating a famous passage in Homer (Il. 2.488–90: 'I could not tell or name the host [of the Greeks], not even if I had ten tongues and ten mouths, a never-failing voice and a heart of bronze'). Nevertheless, the difficulty facing the poet is genuine enough, as emerges also from the many passages where he claims to have overcome the difficulty; I mean those where he vaunts his ability to make the right choices, in the right words, from a rich array of possibilities.[99] Chief among these is the ending of the second *Olympian*, the 'arrows in my quiver' that speak to those who have understanding (the *sunetoi*) as opposed to babblers who do not know when to stop (p. 98). Interpreters are required, he says. Here we have the need for selectivity bound up with meaning which is accessible only to those who have the right qualities (*phuā*) to understand it. Making language succeed requires talent and graft, but in the right hands (mouth) it takes one into rarefied spheres.

Language is the instrument of truth in Pindar's poetics. Homer is called a liar for magnifying Odysseus more than he deserved (N.7.21–3); Pindar follows this remark with his forceful rehabilitation of another hero, Neoptolemus.[100] On the other hand, Homer is lauded for giving Ajax due praise (I.4.37–9); Pindar then adds that 'a well-spoken word is immortal'. In both passages cases he explicitly stresses the power of artful language; this is about words as much as content and the poet's character, though the three go together. Incorrect language in a poet is a culpable fault. Pindar is frequently concerned to emphasize the truth of what he himself says, with the help of the Muse (Muse and Truth are a pair at the start of the tenth *Olympian*).[101] The Muse, he says, is 'magnified by upright reporting' (*P.*4.279). This does not (of course) mean that the Muse speaks anything less than truly, but that she gains in power with the right sort of poet; this is the sense of the verb 'magnified' (*auxetai*),[102] and the adjective 'upright' (*orthā*) suggests not only accuracy but moral worth. In the passage about Ajax just mentioned, Pindar says that Homer 'set upright (Ajax's) entire excellence, and spoke by the staff of his divine words' (*pāsan orthōsais aretān kata rhabdon ephrasen / thespesiōn epeōn*). In the first instance this refers to the epic performer's staff (*rhabdos*), so that the surface meaning is 'in his epic verses'; but to my ear there is an intertext with the common epic formula *panta ... kata moiran eeipes*, 'you have said everything in the proper manner', so that *kata rhabdon* (~ *kata moiran*) evokes epic's august authority, 'you said everything by the staff'.[103] Homer has said all that epic ought to say according to the rules of its genre; the implication is that Pindar does the same for his.

Moreover, Homer's words are 'divine'. Truth for Pindar lies in the same transcendental space as the gods. For him *alātheia*, truth, goes beyond the earlier Greek etymologizing meaning of *a-lātheia*, 'not-forgetting', that is, faithfully preserving tradition. Tradition must sometimes be challenged, as in the first *Olympian*'s myth of Pelops, and truth needs the right language to drive it home. It is worth noting that in contemporary philosophy we find theorizing about language, specifically the view that words have an indirect relationship with reality; they are indicators which need careful assessment by the *sophos*. The view that words were assigned by convention only, without any natural connection to what they denote, lay not far in the future, but nonetheless postdated Pindar.[104]

Pindar, I believe, subscribes to this view of language, as his explicit remarks suggest and even more as his imagistic practice implies. Passages like those above are a large part of what makes 'Pindar' such a strong presence in the odes. Maslov has documented that the poetic ego is the commonest tenor in Pindaric similes, and Kirichenko has demonstrated how the self-referential metaphors contribute to the 'presentification' of the original victory in the odes (that is, the illusion of the presence of an absent object; compare the 'historical sublime' discussed in Chapter 2).[105] Metaphors with vehicles drawn from athletic and competitive semantic fields are common in these contexts (as in excerpt no. 3 above).[106] As he often makes clear, Pindar and his victors are on a journey together; without the commemoration the victory in effect did not happen. So there is an equivalence between his winning language and their winning discus-throw. In this regard a passage in the fourth *Nemean* seems quite significant. After running through the roster of glorious, immortal Aeacids, he dwells on the career of Peleus and his blessed wedding to the goddess Thetis. He breaks off the myth: 'One cannot travel west of Cadiz; turn the ship back to Europe's continent. I cannot recount the whole tale of Aeacus' sons' (69–72). Elsewhere it is his victors who are warned they cannot pass beyond the Pillars of Heracles, but here this limit is applied to poetry. The end of the third *Olympian* (see p. 72) is another instance; there, the warning is issued to victor and poet simultaneously. If, as I argued above, the limit exists to be probed, then everything I said there about athletes applies to the poet and his language. This is not so surprising, after all. If the fame of the Aeacids can reach the people beyond the Nile and the Hyperboreans (*I*.6.23), so must Pindar's; it is poets who spread the fame.

Language, then, takes us to the edge, and looks beyond. This assessment may sound more modern than ancient. Ancient rhetoricians from Aristotle onwards regard metaphor as an ornamental device lending vigour, vividness, elegance and so on; in essence a substitution of one word for another (Aristotle's definition, *Poetics* 1457b7). Longinus asks how many metaphors one can decently use. Caecilius, he says, allows three at most, but according to Longinus the way one uses them is more important than the number. We can forgive the orator if the metaphors are accompanied by:

> strong and timely passion and noble sublimity ... For it is the nature of the passions, in their vehement rush, to sweep and thrust everything before them, or rather to demand hazardous turns as altogether indispensable. They do not allow the hearer leisure to criticise the number of the metaphors because he is carried away by the fervour of the speaker.[107]

He would doubtless analyse our Pindaric passages in these terms, and he would have a point. It is a characteristic part of Pindar's rhetoric to suggest that he is barely hanging on for the ride. Burke had a comparable view:

> The mind is hurried out of itself, by a croud of great and confused images; which affect because they are crouded and confused. For separate them, and you lose much of the greatness, and join them, and you infallibly lose the clearness. The images raised by poetry are always of this obscure kind.[108]

More recent theory, on the other hand, to simplify massively, focuses on the process of representation, or more precisely on what cannot be represented, and on the creation of new meaning rather than the enhancement of a single meaning.[109] As often, however, the practice of ancient poets outstripped ancient theory. Pindar's concentration of metaphor at places where his role is emphasized reflects not merely enthusiasm but his awareness of the difficulty of conveying meaning. It is significant that he speaks of his craft habitually through images. It is as if the essence of poetry lies beyond the reach of untroped language. Like Homer multiplying his similes before the virtuous performance that is the *Catalogue of the Ships* (*Il.* 2.455–84), Pindar raises his game at these junctures.

The mixing of metaphors reinforces the sense of exceeding what could ever be paraphrased. Like the priamel, it places its varied wares on the table and invites comparison (p. 46). As Silk writes about a metaphor in Yeats ('bursting dawn'), 'we have an instant impression of what … the coming of the dawn *feels* like, though not exactly what it feels *like* … We *are* aware of an underlying analogy, but not of exactly what it is (if only for which reason, substitutional talk *is* clearly unhelpful), and for the efficacy of the image that inexactness may be – exactly – what we need.'[110] Mixed and synaesthetic metaphors take this even further. The images individually suggest aspects of the subject, but together partake of an ineffable sphere of meaning. Ineffability is precisely the point; it is the meaning. This or that image can point the way, but if they could do so with total transparency they would, paradoxically, fail of their purpose.

As already remarked, however, there must be some sense of analogy or the experience cannot get off the ground. Not every mixed metaphor will be sublime; they might be merely frigid, in Longinian terms. In the assortment of images Pindar offers, we typically find familiar ones which we can parallel from any number of passages, alongside others that may be partially paralleled and those that are utterly unique; we find many familiar usages that are defamiliarized by a new context or by the descriptors they are given. The familiar parts provide secure starting points for exploration further afield. It is safe to say that the situation would not change much if the rest of Greek literature survived; some of the unique usages would find parallels, but this looks very much like a deliberate strategy. It is a seductive mix that elicits the question, what *exactly* does that mean, which we feel we ought to be able to answer, but can't.

Let us look more closely at the first excerpt. 'I have a certain impression' (*doxan tin' echō*) is straightforward, but is immediately complicated by the following words.[111] In Greek as in English a tongue can be sharpened (in *P.*1.86

it is even forged), but to have an impression (idea, feeling) of the sharpening instrument upon the tongue is unusual. 'Tongue' must be a metonym for 'faculty of speech'; so we decode: some pointed words are taking shape in his mind. Still, the tongue hovers strangely here between concrete and abstract. 'Shrill' then thickens the mixture; the adjective (*ligurās*) denotes high, clear, piercing sounds, normally thought of as pleasant, whereas the whetstone has a harsh, unarticulated sound. Very well, we think; a transferred epithet, an oxymoron; let us move on. Another metaphor: the impression (or the whetstone; it is grammatically ambiguous) is creeping up on him as if to attack, but he is willing, even eager to be ambushed. A question of agency arises, which we might answer by recalling those many passages where the poet's dramatization of his impulsive behaviour serves ultimately to reinforce the sense of his mastery. But just when we were starting to think we have all this under control (if we do), we learn that the creeping impression of a whetstone is accompanied by fair-flowing winds – one presumes those of poetic inspiration. It is a faded metaphor, but revivified in this strange new context.[112] We started with the deceptively workaday word *doxan* and end by wondering exactly what kind of impression is in play here.

This passage is among the most complex in Pindar. Some scholars have resorted to emendation and many would explicate parts of it differently. My point, however, is that every reader who lingers over the passage will go through something like the process just described, and every conclusion will have an aporetic element. In such circumstances, one asks whether it is sensible even to speak of tenors and vehicles. What is the tenor in this passage? Poetic inspiration? The poet's excitement about that? His rhetorical skill? Or just 'what I will say next'? All of these things, alongside a plethora of vehicles. We should think rather of a matrix of interacting images, creating a new point or points of reference which is neither tenor nor vehicle, but somewhere in between, with each informing the other. Readers will interact with these in different ways, but within a common sphere that renders conversation mutually intelligible.

Such a profusion of images to some readers might seem beautiful, mysterious and sublime, while to others might seem grotesque (though to a modern taste grotesqueries too can be sublime).[113] The practice being characteristic of Pindar it is not surprising that comparisons have been drawn with the Symbolists. Recently, Shane Butler and Alex Purves have made the same comparison in relation to a lushly imaged poem of Sappho (fr. 2):

Come to me here from Crete to [this] holy †δευρυμμεκρητεϲιπ̣[.]ρ[    ]].† ναῦον
temple, whe[re there is] a charming grove ἄγνον ὄππ[αι  ]‖ χάριεν μὲν ἄλϲοϲ
of apple trees, and altars smoke μαλί[αν], | βῶμοι δ' ἔ<ν>ι θυμιάμε-
    with frankincense; νοι [λι]‖βανώτω<ι>·

Cold water murmurs through ἐν δ' ὔδωρ ψῦχρο⌞ν⌟ | κελάδει δι' ὔϲδων
the apple-branches; all about the roses μαλίνων, | βρόδοιϲι δὲ παῖϲ ὀ χῶροϲ
cast their shade; from shimmering leaves ἐϲκί‖αϲτ', αἰθυϲϲομένων δὲ φύλλων|
    sleep drips down. κῶμα †καταιριον·

A meadow flourishes, good fare for ἐν δὲ λείμων | ἰππόβοτοϲ τέθαλε
    horses… †τωτ … (.) ριν|νοιϲ† ἄνθεϲιν, αἰ <δ'> ἄηται
        …with flowers, and the breezes μέλλι|χα πν[έο]ιϲιν [
gently sigh; [
    [              ]              [           ]

Where, Kypris, be pleased to take ἔνθα δὴ ϲὺ †ϲυ.αν† | ἔλοιϲα Κύπρι
the nectar mixed in golden cups χρυϲίαιϲιν ἐν κυ|λίκεϲϲιν ἄβρωϲ
with festive joy and gently <ὀ>μ<με>μεί|χμενον θαλίαιϲι | νέκταρ
    pour for us. †ωνοχοαιϲα

They juxtapose her poem with Baudelaire's programmatic *Correspondances* of 1857, and comment:

> One could easily claim that Sappho's rich interweaving of the senses here simply draws on poetry's license to push the bounds of the literal and to break categories that are more rigid in ordinary speech. But something is lost when we consider Sappho's move here as simply the dense literary accumulation of imagery and metaphor. Rather, Sappho, like Baudelaire long after her, seems to be asking a question about the complex, synaesthetic nature of experience itself.[114]

Baudelaire himself proclaimed in 1859 that:

> The entire visible universe is nothing but a storehouse of images and signs to which the imagination will assign a place and a relative value; it is a kind of pasture which the imagination digests and transforms.[115]

'Nothing but' would overstate the matter for Pindar, for whom concrete experience claims its rights. Nor would one quite say that Pindar's lavish imagery raises a question about the synaesthetic nature of experience itself. Rather, in seeking to interpret experience he reaches for a multitude of imagistic comparators which, together with the experience, are mutually reinforcing predicates transcended by a larger subject, or subjects, within the flow of time. In such a vision, literal and figurative may combine to the point where it is impossible to say where one ends and the other begins. Such is the case in the moving close to the sixth *Isthmian*, where Pindar proclaims:

| | |
|---|---|
| I shall give to them to drink from the pure water of Dirka, which the deep-robed daughters<br>Of Memory, her of the golden gown, have made to rise beside the fine walls of Cadmus' gates. | πίσω σφε Δίρκας ἁγνὸν ὕδωρ, τὸ<br>    βαθύζωνοι κόραι<br>χρυσοπέπλου Μναμοσύνας ἀνέτειλαν<br>    παρ' εὐτειχέσιν Κάδμου πύλαις. |

The sacred spring of Dirka rose by the north-west gate of Thebes, Cadmus' town, and Pindar's. This is the water he brought to his beloved Aegina, to mix with the wine of the poem's opening simile.

One of Hölderlin's great Pindaric odes begins 'As when on a holiday' (*Wie wenn am Feiertage*). 'As when' is the standard way Homer introduces his similes, but the first allusion here is to three grand Pindaric openings in which the elaborate 'when' part corresponds much more closely to the situation at hand than do Homer's notoriously free-roaming similes: the sixth *Isthmian*, just mentioned (and above, p. 160); the seventh *Olympian* (p. 102); and the sixth *Olympian*, the oft-quoted comparison of the poem's preamble with a 'far-shining façade' of a great house.[116] The 'when' and the 'now' merge into a metapoetic unity, with images of celebration, poetry, sympotic *charis* and monumentality. Pindar's myths – to return at the end to them – are 'as when' writ large.[117] As I suggested above in discussing the tenth *Pythian* (p. 159), in the juxtaposition of past and present one can ask which is tenor and which is vehicle: 'as they did then, so do we now' is equivalent to 'as we do now, so did they then'. Crucially for Pindar and the epinician project the unity thus forged between past and present stretches forward into the future. Ultimately it comes to us, even those who live beyond the North Wind and the Nile, so that we too can say, 'as when'.

# Epilogue

Of Longinus' five sources of sublimity – grandeur of conception, strong passion, figures of thought and speech, noble diction and dignified composition – I suppose that the first two hold a greater instinctive appeal to most modern readers than do the other three, given their technical nature. This might be put down to lingering Romantic sensibilities, but Longinus himself regards the first as the most important, and devotes his most enraptured language to it. Moreover, the technical matters he discusses – amplification, asyndeton, hyperbaton, apostrophe and so on – are important only insofar as they help deliver the emotional and imaginative impact that is the essence of the sublime. It is this focus on the inner state of the reader or audience, both emotional and cognitive, that links Longinus most directly to the theories of the sublime that developed in the wake of Boileau's translation. Incipient Romanticism in the late eighteenth century found the connection particularly congenial. Supplemented by the cult of artistic genius, it created the perfect ambience for the veneration of the sublime Pindar.

In this book I have explored some of the issues raised by this fascinating historical nexus in an attempt to gain a better understanding of Pindar. With some exceptions I have not, for reasons given in the Preface, drawn attention to connections with twentieth-century theories of the sublime. That would be a different project (although it would not be difficult to demonstrate the many continuities; there might be a surprising amount of overlap between the two books). On the other hand, I have drawn heavily on recent discussions of the lyric as a transhistorical category, and my approach by way of reception and reader response is obviously a product of this age. Reader-response theory dovetails quite nicely with Longinus, actually. The sublime is as much a matter of the reader's (viewer's, listener's) response as it is a quality of the object; it requires investment and collaboration. A reader-oriented approach also fits very well with recent developments in Pindaric criticism whereby, after a long period of emphasis on the primary audience, scholars have been asking how secondary audiences relate to the odes. I have welcomed this change of focus, which brings new aspects of Pindar's poems to the fore and opens up new lines of inquiry. I do not see these approaches as being at all incompatible. At bottom, they simply ask different questions, and both will rightly continue. I expect there will be resistance, however, to the suggestion that the perspective of the secondary audience is as important as that of the first when it comes to the poetry's meaning. A meta-question one could pose about that is why classicists are having this argument more than students of other periods of literature (and why Hellenists more than Latinists, when it comes to that). I am not sure Pindar's cultural environment is so categorically different as to justify it. A comment I have received about the thesis of this book, in fact, is that many of its considerations could apply with equal force to Sappho or even Homer. Some of them can, but on the whole I agree with Maslov that if we are to use the term 'literature' in Greece the case is best made first with Pindar. He is duly aware of the dangers of thinking in terms of development, which is a teleological metaphor, but changes and paradigm shifts do occur and require explanation.[1]

Although I have stressed the merits of thinking about Pindar from the point of view of later audiences, a distinctive feature of Pindar's poetry is the way those audiences are so urgently invited to see the occasion through the eyes of the first audience. Knowing as we do that there was such an occasion and audience, our historicist desire to see the Greek world with Greek eyes is awakened, and we approach the text as something that enables that to happen. In fact, though, the occasion exists for us because of the text, and this is entirely the effect of Pindar's artistry: the magnetic power of his imagination, and his mesmerizing voice. Through his eyes we see through their eyes. We inhabit his 'I' – or his 'I' inhabits us. We follow him on the exhilarating career through space to the Pillars and beyond, and through time from the beginning of the cosmos to now. With him we oscillate between losing ourselves in triumph and remembering the dangers of *phthonos*. We waver between exulting in the *kairos* and recalling the fearsome, uncertain forces of which it is the precipitate. In these circumstances criticism demands that we take a step back, look inwards and examine what is going on in our own engagement with this 'I'. Negotiating the distance between the two poles is, as I have been arguing, an essential part of the Pindaric sublime.

Above all, the engagement is aesthetic. Bold and baffling images, surprising twists and turns, inventive coinages, adventurous word order and syntax: Longinus recognizes the contribution of all these to the sublime, and applauds the genius who takes such risks. He would surely applaud too Pindar's power of imagination (*phantasiā*), to which he devotes chapter 15 of his treatise. It is one of the hallmarks of the grand conception, the first engine of the sublime. At the end I want to leave the reader with Pindar's *phantasiā* in mind. There are the four great epiphanies I discussed in Chapter 3. But there is much more; this is only a partial list: the picture of eternal life on the Isles of the Blessed; Heracles lost in wonder at the sight of the olive tree, as yet unknown in Greece; the infant Iamos, abandoned in the thicket, nursed by serpents with the 'blameless poison' of bees; Helios looking down on Rhodes rising from the seabed; the eagle on the sceptre of Zeus; the monstrous body of Typhos stretched out beneath the majestic, live volcano; the spectacular intervention of Apollo to snatch his son from the womb of Coronis on the pyre; the young Jason confronting the usurper Pelias; the conversation of Apollo and Chiron watching Cyrene wrestle a lion; the feast of the Hyperboreans; Heracles ascending to heaven to be with his bride Youth for all eternity; six-year-old Achilles slaying a boar and bringing its still-panting body to Chiron in his cave; Heracles prophesying the birth of Ajax.[2] Pindar could have written tragedies had he chosen, but his preferred medium was indirect; the drama plays out inside our heads – which is nothing if not sublime.

# Notes

## Preface

1 Like most scholars I use the term 'lyric' to designate the non-epic and non-dramatic poetry of the period, although etymologically it refers to poems sung to the lyre, which was not true for all the poetry it subsumes. There are many good reasons, not only practical, for considering this body of poetry together under a single rubric, while bearing in mind classical terms and distinctions between genres. Cf. p. 68.

2 E.g. Silk (2007). Studies of Pindaric metaphor are an exception to the general trend; see the references in ch. 3 n. 76. Bundy (1986 [1962]) was until recently the dominant force; a masterpiece, without doubt, but his single-minded insistence that the poem exists only 'to enhance the glory of a particular patron' (p. 3), and his concomitant emphasis on rhetoric, inevitably sidelined aesthetics, and made the poet (the 'laudator') a mere manipulator of conventions, however skilled. See also ch. 2 p. 86.

3 Costelloe (2012), 1.

4 Overview in Konstan (2015), 188–91. Exemplary in this regard for Classics are Martindale (2005) and Martindale, Evangelista and Prettejohn (2017).

5 Porter (2016); excellent on Pindar, pp. 350–60. Porter (2010) is also relevant.

6 Hardie (2009).

7 Conte (2007).

8 Gunderson (2015); Littlewood (2018).

9 Day (2013).

10 Schrijvers (2006).

11 Lagière (2017).

12 Haselswerdt (2019). The imbalance of Latin versus Greek in this list is telling.

13 Bloom (2010), xv.

14 Hopkins (2004); Martindale (2012).

15 See pp. 7–10. Cited in this regard have been Jonson, 'To the Immortal Memory and Friendship of That Noble Pair, Sir Lucius Cary and Sir Henry Morison'; Milton, 'Lycidas'; Cowley's translations; Dryden, 'Alexander's Feast', 'Ode to the Memory of Mrs Anne Killigrew' and 'A Song for St Cecilia's Day'; Gray, 'The Progress of Poesy' and 'The Bard'; Shelley, 'Ode to the West Wind'; Keats, 'Ode on a Grecian Urn'; Wordsworth, 'Ode on Intimations of Mortality from Recollections of Early Childhood'; 'Lines Written a Few Miles above Tintern Abbey'; Tennyson, 'Ode on the

Death of the Duke of Wellington'. The list could be extended; any poem entitled 'Ode' and devoted to public ceremonies, eulogy or lamentation is apt to owe something to Pindar, or what their authors thought Pindar was about. Of the poets here mentioned, Milton knew Pindar's Greek best, but 'Lycidas' is a poem with multiple strands in its composition; Jonson (who also had Greek) in his Cary–Morison ode maintains a more direct relationship with Pindar (metrically too), imitating his stylistic bumps, enjambements, odd comparisons, condemnation as foil for praise, and moralizing.

16 See Evans (2010) for a study of the sublime in Hopkins.

17 Carne-Ross (1985), 5–6.

18 Silk (1974); references on p. 239.

# Chapter 1:  Sublime Receptions

1 Wings: *P*.8.34, *I*.1.64, 5.63; arrows: *O*.2.83, 9.11; ships: *N*.3.27, 5.2; javelins: *O*.13.93, *P*.1.44, *N*.7.71; chariots: *O*.1.110, 6.22–5, *P*.10.65, *N*.1.7, *I*.2.2, 8.61; water: *O*.10.9, *N*.7.12, 62, *I*.7.19; a torch: *O*.9.22, *P*.5.45, *I*.4.43, 7.23; honey: *O*.10.98; sunlight: *N*.8.40–2, *I*.1.64–5, fr.227. The poet as archer: *O*.1.112, 2.83, 89, 9.5; javelineer: *N*.9.55, *I*.2.35; charioteer: *O*.9.81; eagle: *O*.2.88, *N*.3.80–2, 5.21, cf. *I*.1.64.

2 On Pindar's ancient reputation and influence see Wilson (1980); Most (1985), 11–25; Richardson (1985); Phillips (2016); Agócs, Carey and Rawles (2012a); Hadjimichael (2019); Spelman (forthcoming).

3 Quint. *Inst.* 10.1.61; cf. 8.6.71 *princeps lyricorum*. Pindar as the chief of the *lyrici* was a canonical judgement in the strictest sense, that is with reference to the *canones* or lists of model writers developed by ancient critics and teachers of rhetoric. For Pindar cf. e.g. Cic. *Orat.* 4, *Fin.* 2.115, Petron. *Sat.* 2.4, Stat. *Silv.* 1.3.101, 4.7.5–8, Long. *Subl.* 33.5; on the canons, see *BNP* and *OCD*[4] s.v.; Nicolai (2014).

4 E.g. Luc. *Musc. Enc.* 5; Proclus on Pl. *Tim.* 1.64; Eust. on *Il.* 20.66 p.1196.37. The word's ordinary meaning is 'loud-voiced', often in a pejorative sense ('loudmouth').

5 Already here there is a gendering of the sublime, such as has dominated much modern writing on the subject. On Dionysius on Pindar (and Thucydides) see Hornblower (2004), 354–72.

6 So MSS P and M; ἀντίρροπός 'balanced' F and some editors, which I do not understand. The point is the same as at *Dem.* 38 τὸ μὴ χρονίζειν ἐπὶ τῶν αὐτῶν πτώσεων τὸν λόγον ἀλλὰ θαμινὰ μεταπίπτειν.

7 I borrow 'patina of antiquity' from Usher's Loeb translation. Dionysius describes this style also in his treatises on Demosthenes (38–9) and Lysias (13).

8 Demetrius also has a fourth style, δεινός ('forceful' or 'vehement', §§240–304) which has some of the characteristics of Dionysius' severe style; he gains little by this

bifurcation and was not followed by other ancient critics. For detailed discussion of both Dionysius and Demetrius see Porter (2016), 213–82; on Dionysius see also de Jonge (2012).

9 *Peri Hypsous; hypsos* denotes more simply 'elevation', which sometimes serves as a translation; but 'sublime' is justified in view of the Latin examples quoted above, and the semantic field of the English 'sublime' – conditioned historically, of course, by Boileau's translation of Longinus – overlaps extensively with Longinus' subject.

10 Heath (1999); (2012), 15–16.

11 See Aulus Gellius *Attic Nights* 17.10.8 (=Macrob. *Sat.* 5.17.8), Hermogenes *On Kinds of Style* 1.6. On Pindar as the source of his own tradition see Porter (2016), 352.

12 There are many extended accounts of Pindaric reception available, e.g. Wilson (1974); Fitzgerald (1987); Schmitz (1993); Revard (2001), (2009); Hamilton (2003); Vöhler (2005, with ample bibliography); Agócs, Carey and Rawles (2012a); overviews in Michelakis (2009) and Williamson (2009). Hamilton (2012) gives a useful overview with bibliography; other studies are cited below as occasion arises. Many good accounts of the history of the sublime are available: see e.g. Monk (1935); Weiskel (1976); Ashfield and de Bolla (1996); Lamb (1997); Battersby (2007); Costelloe (2012); Most (2012b); Day (2013), 1–71; Silk, Gildenhard and Barrow (2014), 364–74; Doran (2015); Clewis (2018). See also the essays in *Aevum Antiquum* n.s. 3 (2003).

13 In English, Gilbert West's highly influential translation of twelve odes appeared in 1749, and by 1778 all the other odes had been translated one way or another, but the first complete translation seems to be that of P. E. Laurent (1824). See Wilson (1974), 240–54, 292–322; Gerber (1969); Tissoni (2014).

14 For Ronsard and Pindar see e.g. Schmitz (1993) index s.v.; Revard (2001), 78–94, (2009), 47–53.

15 Moul (2012).

16 Text from Waller (1905), 183. 'This Ode', he says in his notes, 'is truly *Pindarical*, falling from one thing into another, after his *Enthusiastical manner*.'

17 Cf. Hor. *Od.* 4.6.44 (the last line), *Ep.* 16.66 (also the last line); Nisbet and Hubbard on *Od.* 1.1.35; Newman (1967). Whether Pindar's dithyrambs were in fact metrically freer than his other poems may be doubted. The 'New' musicians and dithyrambists of the later fifth and fourth centuries certainly had a reputation for licence and enthusiasm, but their degree of innovation should not be read back into Pindar. See e.g. Csapo and Wilson (2009), Ford (2013) and LeVen (2017) for discussion. Another, more remote source of Cowley's idea could be Plato's description of poets' enthusiasm and madness in *Phdr.* 245a, *Ion* 533d–534e, *Meno* 99c–d; this too should not be read back onto Pindar (Murray 1981). On Pindar and his Muse see further pp. 114–16.

18 Preface to the translation of Ovid's *Epistles* in Hammond and Hopkins (1995–2005), 2.234.

19  In the Preface to *Sylvae*, Hammond and Hopkins (1995–2005), 2.255–7; letter to
    John Dennis of March 1693 or 1694 in Ward (1942), 72. (I owe this reference to
    David Hopkins, who notes also these lines from *Love Triumphant* of 1694: 'Oh
    Heaven unkind / That gives us Passions, strong and unconfin'd; / And leaves us
    Reason for a vain Defence; / Too Pow'rful Rebels, and too weak a Prince', IV 1.83–6).
    The letter also suggests that, in spite of Dennis's own excellent efforts in this line,
    there was still more to do. Dryden's Pindarics *Alexander's Feast, To the Pious Memory
    of the Accomplished Young Lady Mrs Anne Killigrew*, and his translation of Horace
    *Odes* 3.29 are all in Cowley's irregular style, though less exuberant.
20  Congreve (1706) in McKenzie (2011), 2.413. Coleridge said bluntly that Cowley's
    translations were themselves mad, and offered instead a word-by-word translation of
    the opening of the second *Olympian*, claiming to show that 'in the general
    movement of the periods, in the form of the connections and transitions, and in the
    sober majesty of lofty sense' Pindar was comparable in style to the prophetic books
    of the Bible: Coleridge (1983), 86 (ch.18 *ad fin.*).
21  *The Spectator* no. 160, 3 Sept. 1711 in Bond (1965), 1.128.
22  'Life of Cowley' in Johnson (2006), 1.222 (a similar sentiment in the life of Congreve,
    3.74: the nation owed to Congreve 'the cure of our Pindarick madness. He first
    taught the English writers that Pindar's odes were regular … he has shewn us that
    enthusiasm has its rules, and that in mere confusion there is neither grace nor
    greatness.') See Lonsdale's notes in Johnson (2006), 1.344–5. In Germany similar
    sentiments were expressed, e.g. by Gottsched (1751), 341; in France by the author of
    the article 'Pindarique' in Diderot (1751–72, ed.) (available at https://fr.wikisource.
    org/wiki/L%E2%80%99Encyclop%C3%A9die/1re_%C3%A9dition/PINDARIQUE,
    accessed 10 May 2021). The entry is probably not by Diderot himself, but is
    consonant with views he expressed elsewhere: Cammagre (2007), 218.
23  Wilson (1989) 27. Congreve (1706) in McKenzie (2011), 2.417 allowed that Cowley
    had 'very often happily copy'd him in the Force of his Figures, and Sublimity of his
    Stile and Sentiments'.
24  Heath (1986).
25  Perrault (1674), (1687), (1688–96). On the Quarrel see e.g. Patey (1997). Adverse
    opinions of the ancients were hardly unknown before; 'galamatias de Pindare' seems to
    originate with François de Malherbe (ob. 1628): Vöhler (2005), 6. On Boileau I have
    found Brody (1958) particularly congenial. Most recently see Porter (2016), 36–51.
26  Perrault (1964), 108.
27  Gidel (1873), 4–6. *Clélie* (1654–60) is a ten-volume novel by Madeleine de Scudéry
    set in ancient Rome, hugely popular in its day.
28  Gidel (1873), 6.
29  Gidel (1873), 366. The words 'cet esprit … vouloit' are in Longinus applied to
    Archilochus, not Pindar, but the general point applies to Pindar (who comes in the
    next sentence). See also below p. 18.

30 Available at https://www.uni-due.de/lyriktheorie/texte/1728_young.html (accessed 10 May 2021). On the general argument see Wilson (2012).

31 Available at https://fr.wikisource.org/wiki/Page:Voltaire_-_Œuvres_complètes_ Garnier_tome8.djvu/504 (accessed 10 May 2021). In his *Dictionnaire Philosophique* article on 'Enthousiasme' (Voltaire 1769), he says that the chief risks of enthusiasm are bombast, overblown language and *galimatias* (available at https://archive.org/ details/dictionnairephil04volt/page/302, accessed 10 May 2021).

32 Above, n. 22.

33 Letter to John Hough of 29 Nov. 1700; Graham (1941), 25.

34 Boileau's Longinus was first translated into English in 1680 by John Pulteney under the title *A Treatise of the Loftiness or Elegancy of Speech*. On Boileau in England see Clark (1925); Hopkins (2010), ch.1 and (2012), 167; Martindale (2012), 73. *Contra*, Porter (2016) downplays Boileau's impact.

35 Tome V (1755); https://fr.wikisource.org/wiki/L%E2%80%99Encyclop%C3%A9die/ 1re_%C3%A9dition/ENTHOUSIASME, accessed 10 May 2021.

36 Klopstock was dubbed 'the German Pindar' by Hamann (1950), 2.215. By the time he recast the poem as 'Wingolf' (published in 1771), he had decided to declare allegiance to Celtic and Germanic traditions; Pindar was ousted by Ossian, and the 'sublime, drunken son of Zeus' (Dionysus) was replaced by Uller. But the Pindaric influence remained.

37 Pindar was compared to David and the prophets already by Zwingli in the sixteenth century: Vöhler (2005), 160. The comparison was commonplace thereafter, e.g. Cowley note 1 to *The 34. Chapter of the Prophet Isaiah* (Waller (1905) 214), or Boileau, quoted above. Wilson (1974), 122–31.

38 Herder (1990), 794.

39 Fitzgerald (1987), 217 n. 5; Hamilton (2003), 234.

40 Cf. Brody (1958), 103.

41 Incomplete and disordered excerpts from *O*.2.86–8 and *N*.3.41–3, which stress the superiority of innate talent. The first is the familiar passage 'wise is he who knows much by nature; but those who have learned caw uselessly like furious ravens, all gabbling, at Zeus's divine bird'; the second runs 'but he who teaching has is an obscure fellow, blowing this way and that, never treads with sure foot, tastes a thousand excellences with unfulfilled intention'.

42 Mandelkow (1968), 1.131–2 (vol. 4.2 pp.16–17 in the Weimar edition of 1887). The 'Good Spirit' is Biblical language for God's spirit but may also recall the Greek *Agathos Daemon*, a benevolent divinity invoked for instance at the beginning of a symposium. 'Woodpecker' was Herder's not entirely complimentary nickname for the seemingly restless and flighty Goethe.

43 Though both were anticipated in many particulars by earlier writers, their discussions were by far the most influential. See Ashfield and de Bolla (1996) for a selection of representative texts.

44 The label is attributed to Baumgarten (1735), §CXVI.

45 Burke (1759), 54 (Part I §IV). Lucretius makes a strikingly similar point at the opening of book 2 of *De rerum natura*.

46 Burke (1759), 83–4 (Part 1 §XVII).

47 Burke (1759), 85 (Part I §XVIII).

48 Ashfield and de Bolla (1996), 129.

49 Marot (2007b), 24–5.

50 Burke (1759), 117–24 (Part II §V). One could put plausible answers in his mouth, but he does not face up to the problem here. Kant spotted it and gave his explanation in Kant (2000), 144, 147 (AA 5.260–1, 263–4).

51 Text in Ashfield and de Bolla (1996), 294–9.

52 'Disinterested' vs 'uninterested': for the sake of clarity, I am following the traditional distinction whereby the former means 'having no interest' in the sense of having no personal involvement or stake, whereas the latter means that one's interest is not aroused, one is indifferent.

53 Kant (2000), 145 (AA 5.261–2).

54 Kant (2000), 138 (AA5.255).

55 Kant (2000), 145 (AA 5.262).

56 Kant (2000), 141 (AA 5.258).

57 Kant (2000), 143 (AA 5.260).

58 This has been denied, but see Merritt (2018), 32–4.

59 Explicit criticism of Burke at Kant (2000), 158–9 (AA 5.277–8); see also p.149 (AA 5.266).

60 Detailed analysis of this relationship in Guyer (1993), esp. 229–74; Clewis (2009); Merritt (2012), (2018).

61 Kant (2000), 146 (AA 5.263).

62 Kant (2000), 130–1 (AA 5.247); see also pp.152–3 (AA 5.270).

63 On this episode see e.g. Battersby (2007), 21–44; Day (2013), 66–8.

64 For the relationship between Kant's pre- and post-Revolution writings on rights, freedom and political constitutions see Maliks (2014).

65 On *Schwärmerei*, see Kant (2000), 156–7 (AA 5.275).

66 Among many works I single out Goldhill (1990), 138–41, Kurke (2013), Bulman (1992), Most (2003) and Morgan (2015).

67 Kant (2000), 190, 197 (AA 5.311, 320).

68 See Kant (2000), 129 (AA 5.245); 203 (AA 5.325); Kant (2006), 138, 140–1 (AA 7.241, 243).

69 Kant (2000), 203–4 (AA 5.326–7).

70 Kant (2000), 186–7 (AA 5.307–8). See Abrams (1953), 209.

71 Kant (2000), 154 (AA 5.272).

72 Kant (2000), 157 (AA 5.275): 'if enthusiasm [*Enthusiasm*] can be compared with the delusion of sense [*Wahnsinn*], then visionary rapture [*Schwärmerei*] is to be

compared with the delusion of mind [*Wahnwitz*], the latter of which is least of all compatible with the sublime, since it is brooding and absurd'. In everyday German 'Wahnsinn' meant 'lunacy'. In his remarks on the French Revolution in the 1798 essay 'An Old Question Revisited: Is the Human Race Continually Progressing?', he implies that enthusiasm (using the English form) must be allied to morally worthy aims (AA 7.86). The word is already contrasted with reason in Locke's *Essay Concerning Human Understanding* (1689), book 4 ch.19, and Burke uses it disparagingly many times in his *Remarks on the Revolution in France* (1790).

73 On Schiller's reading of Kant's aesthetics see Guyer (1993), 116–30; Beiser (2005). See also Billings' excellent exposition of Schiller's aesthetics in Billings (2014), 80–97.

74 Schiller (1988–2002), 8.830–1 (this and following quotations are from 'On the Sublime').

75 Schiller (1988–2002), 8.839.

76 Schiller (1988–2002), 8.830.

77 Schiller (1988–2002), 8.831.

78 Schiller (1988–2002), 8.838. 'Bestimmung' is our essential character as humans, that which we are destined to be. Note 'reine Geister', 'pure minds' or 'spirits' and compare above p.17 on Herder: a very pregnant word in context.

79 See Letters 14 and 15 (FA 8.606–15).

80 Facsimile of the manuscript and transcription available online at http://www. hs-augsburg.de/~harsch/germanica/Chronologie/18Jh/Idealismus/ide_fra0.html (accessed 10 May 2021); English translation by Diana I. Behler at https:// lastedenblog.wordpress.com/2016/07/15/the-oldest-systematic-program-of-german-idealism/ (accessed 10 May 2021) and in Hölderlin (2009), 341–2. Discussion at Billings (2014), 136–9 and Leonard (2015), 43–50. The document is misnamed; the programme is not very systematic, and it is as much Romantic as Idealistic. Moreover, Hölderlin's 'Urtheil und Seyn' and the fragments of his *Philosophical Letters*, which discuss similar themes, are probably earlier (1795–1796): see Hölderlin (1998), 2.49–50, 51–7 = (2009), 231–2, 234–9; (1998), 3.384–5, 388–9.

81 Letter of 24 November 1796 in Hölderlin (1998), 2.641.

82 Hölderlin (1998), 3.263. The archaic 'Rodottagen' would now be 'Faseleien'.

83 Guyer (2014), 2.19–23 sees his stressing this concept as Hölderlin's main contribution to idealistic aesthetics. That Hölderlin associates it with the essence of tragedy (see below) contributed to the view then emerging of tragedy as the purveyor of deep philosophical truths; cf. Billings (2014), 226.

84 Hölderlin (1998), 2.57.

85 Hölderlin (1998), 2.58.

86 Kant (2000), 92 (AA 5.206). Hölderlin is not always consistent in his terminology; in 'Grund zum Empedokles' ('The Ground of the *Empedokles*', his unfinished tragedy),

Hölderlin (1998), 1.868 = (2009), 261, the union of nature and art is not a matter of
*Erkenntniß* (knowledge) but is accessible only to *Gefühl.*

87  A succinct statement of these ideas is found in the preface to the penultimate version
of *Hyperion*, Hölderlin (1998), 1.557–9. There he says that the process of achieving
unity is never quite complete (it is a matter of 'endless approximation', *unendliche
Annäherung*), so if pressed he might concede that the Greeks' unity, while not
perfect, was as close to perfect as humanly possible.

88  Hölderlin (1998), 2.56–7 = (2009), 238–9.

89  Letter to Christian Ludwig Neuffer (1769–1839, one of Hölderlin's oldest friends) of
July 1799 criticising Friedrich Joseph Emerich (1773–1802) in Hölderlin (1998),
2.802. On the subject see also the letter to Neuffer of 12 November 1798 in Hölderlin
(1998), 2.710–12 = (2009), 108–10; 'When the poet …' Hölderlin (1998), 2.80–1,
84 = (2009), 279–81, 283, and the various fragments in Hölderlin (1998), 101–
2,108–10 = (2009), 299–301, 307–10 (some of which are utterly mysterious).

90  Hölderlin (1998), 1.44.

91  Hölderlin (2008), 62 = (1998), 1.650.

92  Hölderlin (2008), 64–5. The sentiment recalls Kant's famous remark at the close of
the *Critique of Practical Reason* that two things fill him with wonder and reverence:
'the starry sky above me and the moral law within' (*Der bestirnte Himmel über mir,
und das moralische Gesetz in mir*).

93  Hölderlin (2008), 199–200.

94  For instance: 'To Diotima' (*An Diotima*) 3–10, Hölderlin (1998), 1.183; 'To the
Sun-God' (*Dem Sonnengott*) 12, (1998), 1.194 = (2004), 101; 'The Poet's Vocation'
(*Dichterberuf*), both versions line 33, (1998), 1.270, 1.330 = (2004), 235; 'The Blind
Singer' (*Der blinde Sänger*) 33, (1998), 1.282; 'The Journey' (*Die Wanderung*) 77,
(1998), 1.338 = (2004), 487; 'Homecoming' (*Heimkunft*), both versions line 103,
(1998), 1.322, 1.371 = (2004), 337; and in another passage of *Hyperion*, in 'Hyperion's
Song of Fate' (*Hyperions Schiksaalslied*), (1998), 1.744 = (2008), 192.

95  Hölderlin (1998), 2.690 = (2009), 99–100.

96  The literature on them is large. I have profited particularly from Schadewaldt (1970);
Steiner (1975), 322–3; Louth (1998), (2000); Hamilton (2003), 290–308; Billings
(2014), 189–221. As is well known, the Pindar translations were the stimulus for
Benjamin's translation theory. On Hölderlin and Pindar see also Dimoula (2012).

97  Cf. Benn (1962) 121.

98  See especially Seifert (1982), (1982–83).

99  Hölderlin (1998), 2.222.

100  The reading εὐτράπελον (one late MS) which Heyne reluctantly printed is not
generally accepted now; I have given it a meaning that it might just about bear and
that gives some kind of sense to the passage, but the basic meaning is 'ready', 'facile',
'witty', hardly what is wanted. All other MSS have ἐντράπελον 'shameful', and

ἐκτράπελον 'devious' is also attested as an ancient reading in the scholia, but as the *lectio difficilior* ἐντράπελον is more likely to be right. Hölderlin's 'after' suggests that, like Heyne, he took the Greek to mean that Jason slipped away without giving notice of his departure.

101  Knaupp in Hölderlin (1998), 3.432–5 collects contemporary receptions.

102  Letter to Casimir Ulrich Böhlendorff of 4 December 1801: Hölderlin (1998), 2.912 = (2009), 207 (on which see, as well as Billings, Leonard (2015), 91–7). Not Dionysian and Apollonian, though the contrast was in the air from the late 1790s (Vogel (1966), 95–6); for Hölderlin Apollo was god of the sun and a symbol of passionate inspiration (contrasted, in fact, with 'Junonian' in the letter).

103  See e.g. Jenkyns (1980), 39–52, 163–74.

104  Hölderlin (1998), 2.96–100 = (2009), 294–8.

105  This misreading was part of the Nazis' appropriation of Hölderlin. Adorno (1970) regarded Heidegger's essays on the poet as guilty of this distortion, which accounts for his unconcealed rage and contempt.

106  Letter to Friedrich Wilmans of 28 September 1803: Hölderlin (1998), 2.924–5 = (2009), 215.

107  *On the Composition of Words* 22 (above, p.3); Hellingrath (1911), 1.

108  Hölderlin (1998), 2.15.

109  Hölderlin (1998), 2.57–8.

110  Discussed in Fowler (1982), Steinrück (2004).

111  Hölderlin (2004), 325. Hamburger translates 'Oder er kam auch selbst' in the penultimate line as 'Else he would come himself'; literally it is 'Or (*oder*) he came too himself'. 'He' is Christ.

112  Hölderlin (1998), 1.378.

113  Adorno (1991–92), 2.132. Further on parataxis in Pindar and Hölderlin see Seifert (1982), 686–700. On Pindar, Hölderlin and parataxis see also Fitzgerald (1987), 176–87.

114  This school of thought was inaugurated by Hermann Fränkel in a classic article (Fränkel 1924); the best-known representative is Bruno Snell's *The Discovery of the Mind* (Snell 1980). Other examples and criticism in Fowler (1987a), ch. 2.

115  Schadewaldt (1966), 49.

116  For orientation on text, criticism and bibliography see Budelmann (2018a), 127–32.

117  Fraenkel (1950), 2.407–8; Bundy (1986), 4–10; Race (1990), 9–16.

118  Brown (1989).

119  Salient items in Budelmann (2018a), 128–9.

120  For the new papyrus witness see Bierl and Lardinois (2016).

121  Ewen Bowie has suggested that even Sappho's *first* performance could have been at a male symposium: Bowie (2016).

122 ἄκαν μὲν γλῶσσα πέπαγε (for the text here see Fowler (1987b), λέπτον / δ᾽ αὔτικα χρῶι πῦρ ὑπαδεδρόμακεν, / ὀππάτεσσι δ᾽ οὐδὲν ὄρημμ᾽, ἐπιρρόμβεισι δ᾽ ἄκουαι, // ἀ δέ μ᾽ ἴδρως κακχέεται (text uncertain), τρόμος δὲ / παῖσαν ἄγρει, χλωροτέρα δὲ ποίας / ἔμμι, τεθνάκην δ᾽ ὀλίγω ᾽πιδεύσην (for the form see Budelmann (2018a), 137) φαίνομ᾽ ἔμ᾽ αὔται. Longinus᾽ text seems to have had the word ψῦχρος ᾽cold᾽ modifying ᾽sweat᾽.

123 Culler (2015), 63.

124 For the Greek see ch. 2, p. 107.

125 All commentaries offer a note on this stylistic trait; e.g. Gerber (1982), 53. Des Places (1947), 48–50 gives a list; see further Carey (1981), 67 and Sigelman (2016), 24.

126 Schadewaldt (1966); cf. Stoneman (2014), 103–34.

127 See ch. 2, pp. 123–35.

128 Porter (2016), 7–17.

129 See Halliwell (2011), 327–67 for a subtle discussion.

130 Halliwell (2011), 342. Weiskel (1976), 21 makes a similar point (the Longinian sublime connects us with divinity, whereas Kant stresses discontinuity).

131 Mellor (1993); Battersby (2007), 45–67; Potkay (2012), 211. To interpret *Subl.* 7.2 as an Oedipal struggle to overcome the anxiety of influence (see Day (2013), 55–63) retains a strongly masculine gendering in a different guise.

132 Walsh (1984) and Peponi (2012) *passim.* Homer: e.g. *Od.* 1.336, 8.86, 521–31 (weeping); *Il.* 9.186, *Od.* 1.347, 8.45, 9.1–11, 17.385, 17.519 (delight); *Od.* 1.337, 11.334=13.2, 12.40, 12.44, 17.514–21 (enchantment); Halliwell (2011), ch.2.

133 Long. 9.10, tr. Roberts (1899).

134 Burke (1759), 274 (Part IV §XIV).

135 Payne (2018), 260–1 is eloquent on the suspension of ethical judgement necessary to enter into the enchanted time of a lyric poem.

136 In England Burke was by no means the first to speak in such terms; see Addison's well-known essay in *The Spectator* no. 412, 23 June 1712 in Bond (1965), 3.540–4 (though he speaks there of the beautiful not the sublime).

137 1.4, 2.2, 3.5, 10.1, 12.5, 16.3, 18.2, 22.4, 29.1, 32.1, 32.4, 42.1, 43.3; Porter (2016), 141–7.

138 The title character in *Max Havelaar* declares: ᾽Personally, I've felt little or nothing at Tondano, Maros, Schaffhausen, Niagara. You have to consult your guidebook to get the right measure of admiration, for "so many feet high" and "so many cubic feet of water a minute", and if the figures are big, you have to say: "Ooh!"᾽ Eduard Dekker, aka Multatuli (1987), 151–2.

139 Wollstonecraft (1989), 4.21 (from *Thoughts on the Education of Daughters*, though objecting to the uninformed repetition of received opinion without necessarily rejecting the judgement).

# Chapter 2: Shared Experience

1 Maslov (2015), 221 persuades me that the same juridical meaning ('supporting advocate') should pertain here as at *O*.9.98. The auloi are 'supporters' (μάρτυρες) of the dancers at *P*.12.27.

2 Echoed at Aesch. *PV* 366–72; Lucr. 6.639–702; Ov. Met. 5.346–56; Verg. *Aen*. 3.570–82 (this passage is compared with Pindar's in Aul. Gell. *NA* 17.10.8–19); cf. Seneca *Ep*. 79 (79.7 on Etna as subject of a 'grand' composition, a standard epithet of the sublime).

3 E.g. Pl. *Resp*. 398c–99e; *Leg*. 652a–660a, 700a–701c. See Csapo (2004); Phillips (2017), 147.

4 In Homer e.g. *Od*. 1.337; in early oratory, Gorgias *Vors*. 82 B11 (D24 Laks-Most) 10. Elsewhere in Pindar, *N*.4.3. Pratt (1993), 73–81; Halliwell (2011), 47–53, 266–84; Peponi (2012), ch.4.

5 Of the gods: Pindar *O*.2.13, Bacchyl. 17.130–1; at the symposium, Thgn. 531–5. For the symposium in Greek life and culture see Hobden (2013), Cazzato, Obbink and Prodi (2014, eds), Murray (2018) and Węcowski (2018).

6 *Theog*. 820–80; see Fowler (2013), 27–30.

7 On the theme of harmony in the ode see e.g. Schadewaldt (1966), 78-9; Slater (1981), (1984), 248–9 citing earlier discussions; Segal (1985), 228–31; Morgan (2015), ch.8; Athanassaki (2016).

8 Spelman (2018a). Aspects of Spelman's thesis are anticipated in earlier work on reperformance; see Currie (2004), (2017), Morrison (2007a), (2012), Carey (2007), Athanassaki (2012), Budelmann (2017). Herington (1985), 60 already flagged up the significance of the topic.

9 Spelman (2018a), 33.

10 Slater (1984), 246.

11 Spelman (2018a), 21 n. 25. He cites also *O*.8.9–10, *N*.3.3–5, 9.1–5, 10.21–2, *I*.8.1–4.

12 Spelman (2018a), 129.

13 Havelock (1963) is commonly thought to have started the trend, in the wake of Lord (1960).

14 West (2011); quotation p. 429. Theagenes: *Vors*. 8 for the few testimonia.

15 See Ford's excellent study, Ford (2002), 115–27.

16 Orpheus: *P*.4.177, fr. 128c; Olympus: fr. 157; Homer: *P*.4.277, *N*.7.21, *I*.4.37, frr. 52h.11, 264, 265, 347; Homeridai: *N*.2.1; Hesiod: *I*.6.67; Archilochus: *O*.9.1, *P*.2.55; Terpander: fr. 125; Aristeas: fr. 271; Polymnestus: fr. 188; Sacadas: fr. 269. Unnamed poets: *O*.9.49, 13.18–19, *P*.3.80, *N*.3.52, *N*.6.53, *I*.2.1, fr. 140b (on which see Steiner (2016)). D'Alessio (1995) argues that *O*.6.22–7 and *Paean* 7b.10–20 draw on Parmenides. Pindar thematizes the history of the dithyramb in frr. 71, 85, 115; fr. 128c is a remarkable survey of genres and their history. For discussion see West (2013); Spelman (2018a), 177–278.

17 Maslov (2015); Phillips (2016); Sigelman (2016); Spelman (2018a); Budelmann and Phillips (2018). West (2013) argues persuasively that Pindar's engagement with older poetry was very often in the form of written texts. Kurke (2013), 225, speaking more widely of cultural practices and values which Pindar embeds in his poetry, writes: 'Paradoxically, Pindar's greatest innovation is his self-conscious traditionality.'

18 Maslov (2015), 54, 235.

19 This is the new poem that surfaced in *PKöln* XI 429; for an overview see West (2011–13) 2.54–7.

20 *P*.3.68–77 and *I*.2.47; probably also *O*.6.90–2, *P*.4.298–9.

21 For different perspectives on the problem see Silk (2009); Jackson and Prins (2014), 11–16, 568–75; Budelmann (2018a), 2–7; Calame (2019).

22 Culler (2015), 222.

23 Culler (2015), 16.

24 Culler (2015), 16; cf. p. 226. On Greek lyric and the event, see Budelmann and Phillips (2018).

25 Booth (1998), 5–6 in Culler (2015), 185. Cf. also Fearn (2019).

26 On the triangular nature of the apostrophe see Culler (2015), 186–243.

27 Culler (2015), 294–5, referencing Pindar; Payne (2018), 258–60.

28 Ankersmit (2005), 9. Dubois (1995), 29–30 writes eloquently of her experience of reading Sappho as one of *pothos* (longing for what is absent); quoted by Fearn (2020), 17–18 who speaks (p. 66) of 'the paradoxical nature of our desire to be there, be like that, or feel like that, in the full knowledge that access to those things is endlessly deferred and thus always desired'.

29 An exception is Robbins (2013).

30 For the ritual see Petridou (2016), 289–311.

31 See p. 49.

32 See Cannatà Fera (2020), 558.

33 Some scholars, including Gentili et al. (2013), have taken 'this festival' to be the Olympics and not the theoxenia (or somehow to refer to both), thus missing the point. Apart from the reasons for rejecting this reading given by Robbins (2013) 159–60, 'this festival' here meaning 'the one I mentioned a moment ago' is flat and prosaic (one would prefer κείναν at least). The explanatory γάρ-clause gives an excellent reason why Heracles would attend a festival of the Dioscuri; he needs no reason to visit the Olympics, which he founded. *Pace* Krummen (2014), 272–3, the ring-composition starting with κόσμον ἐλαίας in 13 ends very satisfactorily with φυτεῦσαι in 34.

34 Neumann-Hartmann (2009) is a thorough study of these possibilities. See also Currie (2011), 270 on *Nemean* 10 (suggesting also the Tlapolemeia for *O*.7 and the Heraclea for *I*.4), and now Cannatà Fera (2020), 219–20.

35 Athanassaki (2009), 242 writes: 'Through different lines of enquiry these essays [Felson, 2004] have reached a common conclusion, namely the difficulty of

reconstructing the original performance context with any degree of certainty on the basis of the textual pointers.'

36 Payne (2006) 182: 'The idea that the poem's meaning is exhausted in its immediate historical context is alien to the atemporal rhetoric of the poem itself.'

37 See *O*.2.47, 10.77, 13.29, *P*.10.6, 10.53, *N*.1.7, 6.32, 8.50; on *N*.4.11, below p. 78. On the *kōmos* see Slater (1984), Heath (1988), Morgan (1993), Eckerman (2010), Agócs (2012), Budelmann (2012), Lattmann (2012) and Currie (2017), 205–7.

38 E.g. Ar. *Ach.* 980, *Nub.* 1205, fr. 505, Antiph. fr. 197, Eub. fr. 93.8, Alex. fr. 112.1, 246.5; in the satyr-play, Eur. *Cycl.* 39, 445, 507, 537; perhaps also Pratinas *TrGR* 4 F 3.7 (if a satyr-play). Cf. also the comic scene in Eur. *Alc.* 747–804. See Headlam on Herodas 2.34–7; Seaford on Eur. *Cycl.* 39, 445; Macleod (1983), 49–51; Slater (1984); Heath (1988).

39 *O*.9.1–4, 10.73–7, *N*.6. 37–8, 10.33–5, Bacch. 3.9, 4.4–10, 11.17–21, 12.37, fr. 20C.15.

40 Some of the shorter odes might have been composed for the *kōmos* on the site: *O*.11 is commonly accepted as an example. See Willcock (1995), 55. Bacch. 2 presents itself as such a poem; probably 4 and 8, and either 6 or 7 (see Maehler (2004), 129–30) are others.

41 Spelman (2018a), 19.

42 Ferrari (2012), 171. See also Neer and Kurke (2019), 203–17.

43 Slater (1984); see also Heath (1988).

44 Compare *O*.9.82, *P*.10.64, *N*.7.65, Bacch. 13.224.

45 Similar expressions at *O*.1.10, 1.111, 4.2, 5.19, 9.83, 13.97, *P*.2.4, 3.68, 3.73, 3.76, *N*.4.74, 6.57b, 7.34 (reading μόλον as 1st pers. sing.), 7.69, *I*.5.21, 6.21, 6.57, *Paean* 6.9, *Parth.* 2.39. For the 'arrival' motif see e.g. Bundy (1986), 27, Spelman (2018a), 23–4 (with particular reference to *N*.1).

46 Neer and Kurke (2019), 239, raise the possibility of performance also at Olympia. See also 255–76 for a discussion of the poem's manipulation of space, stressing its hodological perspective (but I do not agree that it is *only* hodological; it is also synoptic).

47 Quoted above p. 64.

48 Agócs (2012), 198.

49 Archil. frr. 120, 121; see Swift (2019), 306.

50 'Performative' is to be preferred, since it is found in many literary contexts besides epinicia, and in magical incantations: see Faraone (1995). On these futures, see further below pp. 111–13.

51 *P*.5.100, *N*.3.5, *I*.6.58, 8.4. Differentiated, if closely associated, at e.g. *P*.4.2–3, *N*.9.1–3, *I*.3.8, 7.20. Where the verb means simply 'celebrate' (which means, in context, with a song) the link to the other aspects of the *kōmos* is also attenuated (*P*.9.89, *N*.2.24 (I read the two verbs as a hendiadys), *N*.10.35, *I*.4.72).

52 *Pace* Bundy (1986), 2, who says *euphrosunā* and songs are contrasted here. The medical metaphor is continuous from the first line on and describes one and the

same healing process, not two different ones. Bundy cites Bacch. 11.12–13 (he could
have cited also 9.103–4 and 10.52–6, where I suppose a reference to poetry in the
lacuna at the end; cf. also 13.74) where *euphrosunā* is indeed equated with the *kōmos*
and distinguished from *humnoi*; but the point here is precisely the way Pindar
effaces this difference. At *P.* 1.99, fame does not take second place to the victory
(Bundy n. 9)! 'Second' is temporal: obviously you must win your victory first;
then you must get the fame; if you get both, then *ne plus ultra*. The same point at
*I.*5.12–15, 6.10–13. At *I.*2.30–2 *kōmos* and songs can be read as a hendiadys.

53 Maslov (2015), ch.4. Cf. also Budelmann (2012), 189 ('this omnivorous poetics is
highly self-conscious').

54 See 9.103, 11.12, 13.74; fr. 4.68 (a paean) is not relevant here. At 12.37 (in verbal form)
and fr. 20C.15 the *kōmoi* are those held at the site of the games (cf. above n. 39).

55 *O.*4.9, 6.98, 8.10, *P.*5.22, *N.*4.11. See also *O.*13.29: Zeus is asked to receive the
ἐγκώμιον τεθμόν, (the 'institution of the *kōmos*'); *P.*8.5, where Hesychia is asked to
receive the 'honour of a Pythian victor', on which Gildersleeve (1885), 328 already
commented 'Πυθιόνικον τιμάν = κῶμον'; *P.*8.20, where Apollo is said to have
received Aristomenes' *kōmos* upon his homecoming; *P.*12.5, where Persephone
(goddess of the city) is asked to receive 'this crown' of the victor
(= crown, poem and *kōmos* all together). Compare further *O.* 14.16, *N.* 11.3.

56 Such feasts are technically different from the symposium (drinking party) and
are denoted by words like δαίς, δεῖπνον, θαλίαι, but these too are associated with
the κῶμος (δαίς: *O.*14.9, 16; *I.*4.61, 74; δεῖπνον: *N.*1.7, 22; θαλίαι: *O.*10.76–7). On
the terminology and poetic usages see Budelmann (2012), Athanassaki (2016).

57 Carey (2007), 205.

58 Athanassaki (2016), 103–4. Pindar's 'often' militates against a mimetic reading.

59 The opening lines have been read as indicating the site of first performance, but they
work equally well metaphorically (cf. Phintis' trip to Pitana in *O.*6).

60 See Currie (2011), 283–5.

61 Fraenkel (1957), 278 saw this; cf. Carey (1991), 200. Morrison (2012), 129 also
points out the multiple possibilities of the opening lines, and notes the generalizing
'whenever'.

62 Dance uniting humans and gods: *Hom. Hymn Ap.* 149–52; Pindar fr. 31; Mullen
(1982), 212; Pavlou (2007), 169–70; Halliwell (2014).

63 For the affinities see Clay (1999); Budelmann (2012). *P.*5, *N.*11 and *I.*2 have also been
suggested as 'encomia': Budelmann (2012), 179 n. 20.

64 E.g. *O.*6.87–92, *P.*5.22, 5.103–4, 10.4–6, 10.55–8, *N.*3.1–12, *I.*1.1–10, Bacch. 13.190–202.
See Carey (1991) and Cairns (2010), 31–2, with references. Fr.122, from the book of
encomia, looks choral: see Currie (2011), 290 n. 83.

65 *I.*1.7 probably refers to both the Delian hymn and the epinician, but the fact that the
Delian hymn would certainly and correctly be performed by a *choros* may account

for the use of the cognate verb here. Some instances may have general reference only (*P.*12.27, *O.*14.9); some occur in narrative contexts (*P.*10.38, *N.*5.23), though these have been read as reflexes of the actual performance. Note that in *O.*14 the *kōmos* at 17, clearly the counterpart of the generalized chorus in line 9, is said to be 'treading lightly' (κοῦφα βιβῶντα), i.e. dancing; cf. *O.*13.114, *N.*8.19. But it is a *kōmos*, not a *choros*. See also Bremer (1990), 52–5.

66 Though the ancient scholia often describe the Pindaric singers as a chorus (e.g. *O.*4.7h, *P.*8.99a), it means only that they think a group is singing.

67 See Romney (2020) for a thorough study of this rhetoric. Agócs (2012) amply demonstrates the essential link between the rhetoric of Pindar's *kōmos* and his poetics. My point is that the rhetoric is as much reception-focused as occasion-specific.

68 Out of the huge bibliography I cite Goldhill (1990), 142–5, Carey (1991), D'Alessio (1994) and (2020), Schmid (1998), Felson (1999), 1–12, Calame (2004) and (2011), Morrison (2007b), 57–67, Cairns (2010), 29–37, Currie (2013), Maslov (2015), 105–14, and Lattmann (2017) (a quite different view from that taken here). Kuhn-Treichel (2020a) came into my hands too late to take full advantage of, but there are some interesting points of contact as well as differences between his general thesis and mine. The debate was instigated by Mary Lefkowitz (1988, 1991) and Malcolm Heath (1988). On Sappho's 'I' see Purves (2021) and Lardinois (2021).

69 D'Alessio (1994), 127.

70 Hamburger (1973); further elaborated by Culler (2015). See also Payne (2006).

71 Austin (1975).

72 Overview of performativity in Loxley (2007), Schechner (2013) and Shepherd (2016); see also Schechner (1985). Richard Schechner, producer and director of *Dionysus in 69*, is one of the founding figures of performance studies. Wilshire (1982) may also be consulted.

73 Wilamowitz-Moellendorff (1922); Bundy (1986 [1962]).

74 Culler (2015), 287–95, with a glancing reference to performativity on p. 290; Pindar on p. 294. See also Wright (1974).

75 See Purves (forthcoming) for an interesting discussion of this fragment in this perspective, and Budelmann (forthcoming) on the lyric present. For text, translation and problems of authenticity see Rainer and Kovacs (1993); Davies (2021) 319–22. If Sappho herself is not speaking, she could be representing another woman's imagined monologue (a dramatization, therefore, inviting the audience to inhabit the represented 'I'), or we are dealing with a folk-song (which would also be performative).

76 See further below pp. 113–14.

77 I adopt the term 'exemplary' for this recognized phenomenon from D'Alessio (1994), 128; cf. Young (1968), 58, with references to earlier discussions.

78  Here I refer to Morrison (2007b), 57–67 and Budelmann (2018b).

79  Booth (1983), (2005).

80  For detailed discussions of the concept of the implied author see *Style* 45.1 (2011); Shen (2011) therein offers a cogent defence of Booth's approach.

81  Similarly Spelman (2018a), 228.

82  See Lefkowitz (2012).

83  Rotstein (2010), 307–17; see also Swift (2019), 415–16.

84  See also *Ach.* 410–13, *Thesm.* 148–70, fr. 694; Wright (2012), 123–5.

85  Foucault (1979). For context and criticism see Wilson (2004); for the emergence of the author in archaic Greece see Beecroft (2010); Maslov (2015), 36–116; Bakker (2017, ed.).

86  Blame: Sappho fr. 55; Solon fr. 20; Stesichorus fr. 91a Davies-Finglass; Simonides fr. 262 Poltera (cf. fr. 260); Xenophanes *Vors.* 21 B 10–12 and Heraclitus *Vors.* A22, B 42, 56, 57, 104. Bragging: Hesiod *Op.* 654–9; Alcman *PMGF* 39; Sappho fr. 65.9 (probably); Ibycus fr. S151.48; Hipponax fr. 117.4 (Hipponax names himself rather frequently: frr. 32.4, 36.2, 37, 79.9); *Hymn. Hom. Ap.* 166–73.

87  On this personality see Griffith (1983).

88  Κύρνε, σοφιζομένῳ μὲν ἐμοὶ σφρηγὶς ἐπικείσθω / τοῖσδ' ἔπεσιν–λήσει δ'οὔποτε κλεπτόμενα, / οὐδέ τις ἀλλάξει κάκιον τοὐσθλοῦ παρεόντος, / ὧδε δὲ πᾶς τις ἐρεῖ· "Θεύγνιδός ἐστιν ἔπη / τοῦ Μεγαρέως· πάντας δὲ κατ' ἀνθρώπους ὀνομαστός." (West ends the internal quotation after Μεγαρέως, but see Spelman (2018a), 122.)

89  Bakker (2017), 109–10 (who also discusses Foucault's author-function in connection with Theognis). σοφιζομένῳ refers in the first instance to prowess as a poet, consisting in both technical skill and wisdom; in the present context it could highlight also the cleverness of his linguistic trick (so Bakker).

90  List in Herington (1985), 198–200.

91  On these matters see especially West (2011). The first secure attestation of this practice is Alcman's mention of Polymnestus (*PMGF* 145) (early sixth century).

92  On the origins of the genre see Spelman (2018a), 184–91; Thomas (2007).

93  An example in Classics is Oliensis (1998), whose discussion of self and mask (Horace vs 'Horace') has several points of contact with mine. McCarthy (2019) is not concerned with the actual poet beyond the text, but her discussion of the text's representation of its 'story-world' as opposed to its 'discourse world' raises some similar issues.

94  Maslov (2015), 61. See also p. 48 for antecedents in 1980s New Historicism of the rehabilitation of the author, though interestingly anxious to avoid any notion of creative genius.

95  Foucault (1979) 145 (emphasis original).

96  Budelmann (2018b). This phenomenon is also a reason, as he points out, for thinking that the projection of an implied author from poetic texts may be assumed for antiquity.

97  Greene (1991), 9–10; Hamburger (1973), 271–2, 286.

98  *O*.6.86, 6.90 (not Theban, but Boeotian is equivalent), 10.85, *P*.2.3, *I*.1.1 (the sequel show it's the poet who speaks, not a Theban chorus), 6.74, 8.16, plus two indirect indications: at *P*.3.78 the poet refers to the shrine of the Mother and Pan near his home (on which see D'Alessio (1994), 139), and at *P*.4.299 he reports that Damophilus, for whom he is here pleading, has been in Thebes during his exile, and commissioned the present ode (Θήβᾳ ξενωθείς are the last two words of the poem).

99  *P*.10.56, *N*.3.11, *I*.8.6.

100  *O*.1.103, 4.4, 9.83, *P*.3.69, 10.64, *N*.7.61, 7.65, *I*.2.48. *N*.4.74–5 κάρυξ ἑτοῖμος ἔβαν … συνθέμενος refers to the poet's commission and can be included here. Where the speaker addresses the honorand as a friend (φίλος), we might consider the poet to be speaking (esp. *P*.1.92 and *N*.3.76, the latter followed by the sending-motif; at *Parth.* 1.11 Pindar could be speaking but there is no context to help). But passages like *P*.1.51 and 11.38 show the flexibility of this word, and a chorus might well be composed of φίλοι of the honorand.

101  *P*.2.68, *N*.3.77; cf. fr. 124a–b.2. In these passages the poet is identified (in *N*.3 note φίλος in 76 and ὀψέ περ in 80), while in *O*.7.8, 9.25 and *I*.5.63 the action of sending/escorting includes or could include the chorus as far as the wording is concerned (though the accompanying metapoetic language inclines one to think first of the poet). Some critics deny that *I*.2.47 is meant literally.

102  Full list above, n. 45; the poet is specified at *O*.4.2–5 (note ξείνων), 9.82, *P*.2.4, *I*.5.21, 6.21 (in the last two, the speaker has come 'to this polis' and 'to this island' respectively; this is the language of a foreign guest).

103  The most detailed discussion is Gianotti (1975), 85–127.

104  Hes. fr. 306; Alcm. *PMGF* 13(a).9 (actually a fragment of Pindar citing Alcman? Spelman (2018a), 259); Alcm. *PMGF* 16.2; Sappho fr. 56.2 (probably); Solon fr. 13.52; Ibyc. S151.23; Thgn. 19, 770 (the quatrain is probably from the fifth century, however), 790, 995; *Hom. Hymn. Herm.* 483 (also fifth century).

105  See *I*.4.2, *P*.2.54, 9.92 and note the metapoetic use of μαχανά at *P*.1.41, 3.109, 8.34, *N*.7.22.

106  'Secret' translates ἄρρητα which is especially associated with the teaching of mystery rites such as the Eleusinia (*LSJ* s.v. III; e.g. Hdt. 5.83.3, 6.135.2, Ar. *Nub.* 302, Eur. *Bacch.* 472). As for 'gateway' (πύλαι), the first line of the Orphic theogony (*Orph.* 1) advises the profane to 'close the doors' (θύραι), i.e. of their ears. This part of the verse is quoted in the Derveni papyrus col. 47.9 §21 Janko / Kotwick; the first part is handed down in two versions by other sources, in one of which Orpheus proclaims that he shall 'sing to the ξυνετοί', Pindar's word in *O*.2.85 and Bacchylides' in 3.85 (see below). Pindar's passage follows on the heels of his exposition of mystical teachings generally taken to be Orphic; cf. Currie (2005), 390, who notes also Heraclitus *Vors.* 22 B31, B34. There is a close parallel in Pl. *Symp.* 218b where

the profane (βέβηλοι, as in the Orphic fragment) are told to close the doors (πύλαι this time) of their ears. See further Fearn (2007), 2–20; Kotwick (2017), 159–62.

107  On the meaning of the much-discussed phrase ἐς δὲ τὸ πᾶν see Race (1979), Willcock (1995) and Gentili et al. (2013) *ad loc.*, and Spelman (2018a), 42. I take the sense to be that, to really grasp τὸ πᾶν, you need instinctive wisdom, part of which is the realization that too much praise is counterproductive. Pindar goes on immediately to state τὸ πᾶν in the magnificent lines 91–5, and contrasts his practice with the excess (κόρος) of intemperate flatterers (their φυά is base). Theron's fine deeds are as many as the grains of sand, but only a fool would attempt to count them.

108  Keeping the reading of the MSS.

109  Cf. Simonides *PMG* 541.3–5 = 256.3–5 Poltera. That the passage also echoes O.1.1–7 and 3.42 seems to me to clinch the case for Bacchylides copying Pindar, if perhaps in a spirit of one-upmanship. The common expression εἰδότι τοι ἐρέω and the like (*Il.* 23.787 etc.; see Friis Johansen and Whittle (1980) on Aesch. *Suppl.* 742) connotes superfluous speech and is not the common model.

110  On this passage see Ford (2020), 14–15. Bacchylides 5.3–6 praises Hieron as a good judge of poetry.

111  Cf. above p. 83 for a similar point. That poets can speak in riddles and need exegesis is a well-established theme in Greek culture; see Ford (2002), 67–89. This does not require us to revert to the old idea that the two crows are Simonides and Bacchylides, for the passage achieves its full effect without specific names.

112  O.11.10, P.4.248 (the speaker bluntly claims to 'lead the way for many others in *sophiā*'), I.1.45 (what provides a theme for the *sophos*; compare the language here with P.3.2), *Paean* 18.3 (again what provides a theme for the *sophos*). At P.1.42 (σοφοί) the sequel indicates that he has poets specifically in mind; the same is true at O.11.10 (where the chorus's πραπίδες are hardly in question) and 14.7.

113  10.39 (two types of σοφός, the poet and the prophet); 12.1 (note ξείνοισι in 5, which marks the poet as speaker); 15.24 (no context; the σοφία here could be that of a character in a speech, like Jason's in Pindar P.4.138: see Maehler (1997), 140); outside the epinicians, fr. 5.1, cited above and fr. 14.3 (σοφία, i.e. poetry, and 'the all-powerful truth of Olympian Zeus' confirm the victor's ἀρετά; cf. 13.204, which leads, albeit with a lacuna of uncertain content, to the poet's closing self-advertisement, and Pind. O.10.4). The σοφία at 13.201 is that of the expert trainer Menander; at 26.6, of the craftsman Daedalus.

114  Henrichs (1994–95), (1996), followed by many; *contra* Slater (2000), 117–21; Scullion (2002).

115  The chorus in the parabases quite often appeals to the *sophoi* among the audience in the sense of 'discerning (of good poetry)', e.g. *Nub.* 526, 535, *Vesp.* 1049, *Ran.* 674, Pl. Com. fr. 96 K.-A.; cf. above on the same move in Pindar.

116 *Contra* e.g. Currie (2005), 323 with references either way. Cf. fr. 150, Bacch. 9.3.
      Recent discussion in Marinis (2018).

117 See above n. 16.

118 3.85–98; 5.1–16; 13.221–31. The continuation at 5.17–30 describes the superiority
      of Zeus's eagle over other birds, and the unlimited range of its flight; he then says at
      31, 'So too do I have boundless ways to sing your excellence'. There are similar
      comparisons at 3.98 (where he is a nightingale), at 4.8 (a cockerel), and at 10.10
      (a bee). His penchant for third-person self-reference occurs unmetaphorically at
      5.11 where he is the foreign guest and 'famous servant of gold-veiled Ourania', and
      at 9.3 where he is the 'divine spokesman of the Muses'. On Pindar vs Bacchylides in
      this respect cf. Most (2012a), Currie (2018), 313–14.

119 Carey (2017), 42: 'It is left unclear whether this is the poet who has composed for
      the island for forty years or the chorus which is more profoundly implicated in the
      prayer for liberation and can more literally claim the island as mother.'

120 D'Alessio (1994), 122.

121 On this kind of ventriloquism in Greek lyric see especially Currie (2013). In 72
      read τὸ δ' ἐμὸν γαρύεν with Bergk.

122 Carne-Ross (1985), 150.

123 On the proem see Young (1968), 69–75; Braswell (1976); Brown (1984); Kurke
      (2013), 104–9; Gentili et al. (2013), 475–8. With some hesitation I construe ἀπό
      with δωρήσεται. Taking τις and the owner of the rich hand to be different people
      solves the grammatical problem, but it does not strike me as Pindar's manner to be
      so vague, especially in so carefully wrought a simile. At least four guesses have been
      made about the mysterious third party's identity. Although there are matters the
      secondary audience would have known and we do not (in this case, about betrothal
      ceremonies; but were they the same throughout Greece?), here I would sooner
      suspect the text. I am tempted to write ἐπὶ for ἀπὸ: the father-in-law took the cup
      '(standing) by his wealthy hand', ἐπί locative (LSJ s.v. A I 1); πρόχειρος in prose,
      Latin *ad manum*. For a highly suggestive sympotic parallel cf. Thgn. 490 τὴν δ'
      [sc. φιάλην] ἐπὶ χειρὸς ἔχεις; unclear, unfortunately, but I take it to mean that the
      drunkard's excuse for downing yet another cup is simply that it lies to hand. The
      corruption in Pindar was easy with ἑλών.

124 On *charis* see especially MacLachlan (1993); on personifications, below pp. 147–56.

125 Above p. 70.

126 Payne (2018).

127 Retaining with some hesitation the MSS reading here. See Gentili et al. (2013), 575.

128 Barrett (2007), 72; the paper was written for oral delivery in 1964.

129 Lloyd-Jones (1990), 424.

130 Two together: *O*.3.8, 7.11–13, *P*.10.39, *N*.3.12 with 3.79, *N*.9.8, and *I*.5.27; the
      second and fourth of these refer to typical practice (and in *P*.10, to non-epinician:

the context is the constant festivity in the land of the Hyperboreans). Lyre only: e.g. *O*.1.17, 9.13, *P*.1.1, 2.71, 8.31, *N*.4.44, 10.21; aulos only: *O*.5.19, *P*.12.19; the second of these poems is for a victor in the aulos-competition at Delphi.

131 On the subject of accompaniment see Henry (2007). 'Lyre' encompasses both φόρμιγξ and λύρα, which Pindar seems to use interchangeably.

132 *O*.10.12, *P*.3.65, *N*.3.9, perhaps 4.77; Bacch. 12.3. Several characters in narratives use the plural for singular: Apollo (*P*.3.40–1), Medea (*P*.4.27), Jason (*P*.4.110, 150), Heracles (*I*.6.46).

133 Contrast and compare (also with the general argument of the chapter) Stehle (2017), who considers that in a choral performance the 'I' can only be the chorus (15). But Benveniste's view of the pronoun in ordinary communication, which she evokes, does not apply without modification to the context of utterance by a poetic chorus. On the flexibility of the voice see also the analysis of Carey (2017).

134 Wackernagel (2009), 136. Similarly *Il.* 2.484–6.

135 See Kaimio (1970).

136 In Pindar only *Hymn* 1.7, *Paean* 6.128, fr. 89.1; fr. 122.16 is an enkomion (so not ritualistic; the 'we' is 'people in general' as in the passages in n. 139). In Bacchylides only 16.13.

137 1. 51, 1.53, 2.9, 12.3.

138 *O*.1.16, *P*.3.114, 5.80, *I*.4.62, 7.49 (the whole city shares in the victory), 8.8, 8.10.

139 *O*.2.33, 11.8, *P*.3.60, *N*.3.73, 4.37, 6.1, 6.4, 6.6b, 7.4, 7.5, 7.14, 7.54, 7.87, 11.44, *I*.7.42. On the translation of *O*.2.31 see Currie (2005), 32.

140 On the referent of *O*.10.1 see Gentili et al. (2013), 555. The real difficulty (for us) is the apparent disjunction of self and the φρήν, here elaborately developed; as recent work has been arguing, however (see below n. 153), such expressions are at bottom metaphorical, a way of saying 'help me' that would be otherwise imaged now (and causes no difficulty at all in performance). Such disjunctions are especially deployed when fault is being acknowledged. Second-person plurals also at *O*.11.16, *P*.11.38, *I*.3.15, 4.35, 8.62; cf. *I*.8.1 (indefinite third person 'let someone rouse the *kōmos*', followed by 'o young men'). In theory such plurals could be addressed to the chorus (implying in *O*.10 and perhaps elsewhere a distinction between poet and chorus such as we find at *P*.10.55–7, although there with reference to future performances) but even on first performance the command can hardly be *limited* to the chorus. A chorus addressing commands to itself can do so in the plural (e.g. *Paean* 6.122) but the singular is more normal (e.g. Pind. fr. 107a.3, Aesch. *Pers.* 571–4). Bacchylides has one indefinite third person (13.201) and otherwise only three second-person plurals. Two of them come at the end of odes (9.104, 10.55), inviting the celebration to continue; the third commands 'ye young men' to celebrate the victory (13.190), followed not long after by the conclusion which clearly refers to the poet, so that we do have here a distinction between poet and

chorus, with reference to the present performance. We can imagine either the chorus dancing while the poet sings, or the chorus singing and ventriloquizing the poet. I see no way of choosing nor any need to choose.

141 Longinus *Subl.* 26; cf. Wackernagel (2009) 146–9. Excellent brief remarks on Pindaric apostrophe, deixis, faux-spontanteity and the notional *kōmos* in Pelliccia (2009), 254–5.

142 *O.*1.18, 1.114, 5.24, 9. 6, 9.11, 9.14, 9. 111, 13.114, *P.*10.51, *N.*1.13, 4.37, 4.69, 5.50 (bis), 5.51, 5.52, 5.54, 7.34 (if one reads μόλε with Bundy), 7.75, 7.77, 7.81, 10.21, 10.22, *I.*4.13, 5.24, 5.38, 5.39, 5.51, 5.62 (bis), 5.63, 7.20. Functionally equivalent are two commands in the indefinite third person (*N.*9.50, *I.*5.54).

143 More on self-address below p. 113.

144 Respectively *O.*9.6, *P.*10.51, *N.*1.13, 5.51, 7.81, *I.*5.51, *O.*13.114.

145 Other examples: *P.*1.1, *N.*4.44 (lyre); *N.*5.3 (my song); Bacch. fr. 20B 1 (the lyre); Sappho fr. 118.1 (lyre); cf. *Hymn. Hom. Herm.* 31 (tortoise, about to become a lyre).

146 Above, n. 50; Bundy (1986), 21–2; Slater (1969b); Pelliccia (1995), 317–32; Pfeijffer (1999); D'Alessio (2004).

147 Pelliccia (1995), 327.

148 D'Alessio (2004).

149 Above, p. 78. Other openings: *N.*9.1–10, *I.*8.1–8, *Parth.* 2.6–16.

150 See *O.*6.85–92, 10.78–85, *P.*9.73–5, *P.*10.55–9 with Hubbard (1995).

151 *O.*11, *N.*2, 5, 9, *I.*2, 4, 5, 6. Bacchylides also deploys this device at the close of 9, 13 and probably 10.

152 Debt-motif: e.g. *O.*3.7, *P.*8.33; the victory creates a debt, an obligation to praise, which is discharged by the poet's ode. Schadewaldt (1966), 20. n. 1. In *O.*10 Pindar exploits the motif very shrewdly, and turns his lateness to advantage; τόκος 'interest' is picked up again by the late-arriving son simile (the word also means 'offspring'). The wait has been worth it! For the text of line 9 see Barrett (2007), 61, defending Fennell's ὁράτω.

153 *ētor*: *O.*1.5; *thūmos*: *O.*2.89, *N.*3.26–31, frr. 123.2, 127.4; *psūchā*: *P.*3.61; *stoma*: *O.*9.36. In *Paean* 4.50, a speaking character addresses his *phrēn* (mind / wits / soul). There is one instance in Bacchylides (19.8–11, a dithyramb; his *merimnā*, thought, is told to 'weave something new'). For illuminating studies of words relevant to ratiocination and speech see Pelliccia (1995) and numerous works by Sullivan, e.g. Sullivan (1995); on Pindar, e.g. Sullivan (2002). Recent work on Homer, drawing on cognitive metaphor theory, throws much new light to the phenomenon; see e.g. Cairns (2014), Zanker (2019), 165–200.

154 Compare *O.*3.7, 3.38, 3.45, 4.17, 6.82, 7.16, 9.81, 13.11–12, 13.91–5, *P.*8.29–33, 9.103–4, 10.4, 11.38–42, *N.*4.33–5, 4.69–72, 5.14–21, 6.53–7, 9.6–10, 9.33, 10.18–22, *I.*1.1–6, 1.52–7, 1.62–3, 6.19–21, 6.58–9, 8.5–5a, 8.16–16a. I find three instances of personal expressions of this sort in Bacchylides' epinicians (5.195, 8.20–1,

10.51–2: lit., 'why do I steer my tongue so far and drive off course?', which sounds Pindaric); and two impersonal ones (5.187–90, 14.20). For impersonal expressions in Pindar see Slater (1969a) s.vv. δεῖ, πρέπει, χρεών, χρή. The various forms of the 'debt-motif' also imply obligation (above, n. 152).

155 D'Alessio (1994), 120.

156 Maslov (2016), 240–1 argues that the singular Muse is strongly favoured in the epinicians; I am not sure the data bear him out, though I agree with his broader thesis about Pindar's ego (n. 158 below).

157 Homeric antecedents e.g. *Il* 1.8 ('(Muse), which of the gods first set them to fighting? The son of Zeus and Leto it was'), 2.484, 2.761–2, 11.218, 14.508. Bacch. 15.47 has 'Muse, who first made a start of just argument? Menelaus the Pleisthenid …'

158 Respectively *O*.1.112, 3.4, 6.21, 11.17, *I*.8.6, *P*.1.58, 4.3, *N*.6.28, *I*.4.43, *Dith.* 1.14, *O*.13.96, *P*.4.279, *Dith.* 2.25, *O*.6.91, *N*.9.55, *I*.6.74, *N*.7.77, *O*.9.5, 7.7, *N*.6.32, cf. 10.26. Bacchylides, by contrast, does not evince the same intimacy, and speaks more like Homer: Fearn (2005), 20; Morrison (2007b), 89–90. Pavlou (2007), 95 notes that the range of Pindaric metaphors for the Muses reflects his conception of them as much more than purveyors of information: 'the Pindaric Muse does not merely report, but creates, alters and transforms'. Maslov (2016) notes that there is a sense of 'partnership' with the Muse in Bacchylides, unlike Homer, but recognizes the much stronger collaboration in Pindar; he well stresses the work the poetic ego must do in the new genre of epinician. On Pindar's Muses see also Kuhn-Treichel (2020b).

159 I take ἐπάμεροι as a nominative (understand εἰσίν), referring back to βροτῶν, and the model to be expressions in epic like νήπιοι (sc. εἰσίν), οὐδὲ ἴσασιν … (Hes. *Op*. 40, 456, *Theog.* 488, *Il*. 2.38 etc.). The antecedent is not always nominative (*Il*. 5.406, *Hom. Hymn. Aphr.* 223), i.e. it is not a simple apposition but more like an exclamation. Simonides eleg. fr. 20 νήπιοι … οὐδὲ ἴσασιν occurs in a thematic context similar to Pindar's. An explanatory sentence connected by δέ typically follows the nominative; Pindar varies this by substituting his questions, which is another aspect of his creativity. (For questions with explanatory force Spelman *per litt.* cites *O*.2.98, 9.29, *P*.7.5.) Empedocles *Vors.* 31 B 11 has the variation νήπιοι· οὐ γάρ σφιν δολιχόφρονές εἰσι μέριμναι; unfortunately we do not know what preceded. I also prefer, as do most editors, the singular ἄνθρωπος as opposed to the plural of most witnesses. The scholia do not, as commonly asserted, support the plural; they could easily substitute plural for singular in glossing, precisely because the subject is humanity in general. This would also explain the corruption. The plural also presents a metrical irregularity (correption between two long vowels).

160 Literally 'what is one? what is one not?', or '… what is no one?', then 'the human being (*anthrōpos*) is a dream of a shadow', which has most often been rendered 'man is …': but it is time to lose 'man', and the whole argument of this chapter authorizes 'we'.

161 Silk (2001), 33–6; Silk (2010), 439; Silk (forthcoming) on some close, but still not exact parallels.

162 Cf. Aesch. *Agam.* 82, 839, Soph. *Ajax* 126, *Ant.* 1170, *Phil.* 946–7, *OC* 110, frr. 13, 945.2, Eur. *Andr.* 745, *HF* 112–13, *Phoen.* 1543–5, 1722, frr. 25.3, 509; Silk (2001), 34 n. 11. Sophocles' 'seeming-dreams' (Soph. fr. 945.2) and Euridipes' 'impressions of dreams' (Eur. *HF* 112–13) and 'imitations of dreams' (fr. 25.3) come closest to Pindar's expression, perhaps under his influence; Aesch. *Agam.* 839 has εἴδωλον σκιᾶς which seems even closer, but the image there is a literal reflection in a mirror, cf. Soph. fr. 659.6.

163 Gentili et al. (1995), 229 with comm. pp. 585–6. The normal Greek for this would be οὐδείς but, again, Pindar is pushing the limits, and he has Homer's famous Nobody to draw on (below); the scholia thought it possible. In his recent translation, Miller (2019), 167 still prefers 'What is a man? What is he not?'

164 Fränkel (1946) ~ (1968), 23–39; Dickie (1976).

165 Schol. Soph. *Ajax* 125a (ἀσυστάτοις: incoherent, non-solid, insubstantial; see *LSJ*). See also Soph. fr. 13 ἄνθρωπός ἐστι πνεῦμα καὶ σκιὰ μόνον; Aesch. fr. 154a 9; Eur. *Med.* 1224. 'Shadow of smoke' also at Soph. *Phil.* 946, *Antig.* 1170.

166 *Vors.* 22 B 49a = D 65 Laks-Most; *Vors.* 22 B 88 = D 68 Laks-Most.

167 See Robinson (1987), 113: 'The more straightforward interpretation is surely existential: "we exist and we do not exist"'.

168 See Aguirre and Buxton (2020) 203–5.

169 Gendered in Greek; see Slater's *Lexicon* s.v. ἀνήρ 2 for many other cases of ἀνήρ = ἄνθρωπος in Pindar.

170 The lines are spurious, but that does not matter here. The commentators list ample parallels.

171 See Steiner (1986), 46–8; e.g. *O*.9.21–2, *P*.5.45, 9.90, *N*.3.64, 6.38, *I*.4.43, 7.23. On light imagery generally see Neer and Kurke (2019), 92–122 and their references at 320 n. 28, adding Briand (2016). Spelman points out *per litt.* the difference between a short-lived, ephemeral brilliance (αἴγλα) and the less blinding φέγγος which lasts a lifetime (note μείλιχος αἰών and compare *O*.1.97–100): 'we are asked to hold two different views of time in a very delicate balance'. The final prayer puts the athletic victory into a larger, very uncertain context.

172 Apollo Aigletes: Ap. Rhod. 4.1730 and inscriptions in Thera, Anaphe and the Peloponnese as early as the sixth century; Bremmer (2008), 255.

173 ἀγλαΐα· παρὰ τὸ ἀγλαός· τὸ δὲ ἀγλαὸς παρὰ τὴν αἴγλην. *Etym. Magn.* p. 11.32 Gaisford.

174 Halliwell (2014), 125, 127. See also Spelman (2020).

175 Carey (1981), 5. See further Carey (1989), 552, and (2011); Morrison (2007b), 67–73; Sigelman (2016), 84; Budelmann (2017), 47.

176 Miller (1993), 21.

177 Compare Sigelman (2016), 181.

178 See most recently Trédé-Boulmer (2015); 105–48 on Pindar. See also Carey (1981), 89–91. For the other words above see e.g. *O*.11.39, 13.48, *P*.1.82, 4.248, 4.286, 8.29–32, *N*.4.33, 6.27, 10.20, *I*.1.62.

179 On *hēsuchiā* see especially Hornblower (2004), 60–4; on personifications, ch.3 p. 147.

180 Not easy; already the scholia were doubtful of the meaning. The two virtues would be justice and truthfulness. ἀμφοτέροις is commonly translated as 'both good and bad' or 'true and false', but I cannot see how that is an appropriate idea here. Cf. Maslov (2015), 219.

181 Gentili et al. (1995) prefer εὐτραπέλοις; see ch.1 n. 100.

182 See the references in ch.1 n. 66.

183 The much-discussed 'learn and become who you are' (γένοι' οἷος ἐσσὶ μαθών) in *P*.2.72 adopts a similar stance; cf. Currie (2018), 306.

184 Hornblower (2004), 372.

185 Finley (1972), 45.

186 Page 24.

187 Kant (2000), 90–1 (AA 5.205).

188 Martindale (2005), ch. 3 is a brilliant discussion of politics and art, and demonstrates that not all aesthetic judgements are occluded judgements of other kinds; see also Martindale (2010), citing Coleridge's genial imagining of a conversation about the beauty of York Minster.

189 I owe this point to Charles Martindale in conversation. See also Shaw (2006), 148–52 (who, however, distorts Kant's position).

190 On this much-discussed topic I refer to Eagleton (2003) and Nuttall (1996).

191 Jauss (1982), 32.

192 Pater (1873), viii.

# Chapter 3: Exceeding Limits

1 Pindar frr. 95–100. *Vita* 1.2.2, 1.5.10, 1.9.9 Drachmann; cf. schol. *P*.3.139a, Plut. *Numa* 4.8, *Mor*. 1103A, Aristid. *Or*. 3.191, 42.12, Philostr. *Imag*. 2.12, Liban. *Or*. 64.13, Chor. *Or*. 29.48, Eust. *Proem* 3.298.9 Drachmann. Pindar mentions a shrine of the Mother and Pan near his home (*P*.3.78), which will also have influenced the legend. Thorough discussion of the hymn in Lehnus (1979). On ancient lives see Lefkowitz (2012).

2 Pindar figures again in Rosa at *Sat*. 5.550; he had considerable classical learning. On the painting see Langdon (2012), 182–4; on the self-portrait cf. Tomory (1971), Roworth (1988), and Hoare (2013). I have supposed on general grounds that Rosa

knew Philostratus' *Images*; his letters reveal that he read Philostratus' *Life of Apollonius* in 1662, and that he knew the story in Plutarch: Hoare (2013), 959; Zellmann-Rohrer (2014), 190–1 nn. 20, 23.

3  Wilamowitz-Moellendorff (1931–32), 1.18–21; Fowler (2010), 322.

4  On the last point see Veyne (1988); Versnel (1990), (1993). For overviews of Greek myth, gods and religion see Ogden (2007), Parker (2011), Bremmer and Erskine (2010), Bremmer (2021), Fowler (2021).

5  Bremmer (2008), 28 reviews some of the many interpretations. See also Cairns (2016), 28.

6  Griffin (1980), 179–204.

7  See Currie (2005), 42–4; see also Bremmer (2002), 4–26.

8  Fowler (1998); (2013), index s.v. genealogy.

9  On Pindar and prophecy see Maslov (2015), 188–201, 243–4; somewhat differently Sigelman (2016). See further below pp. 170–1.

10  See Baeumer (1967) for a useful discussion.

11  Xenophanes *Vors.* 21 A29, 30, 31, 32, 33, 34, 35, 36; 'one god is greatest' 21 B23 (the meaning is more probably that one god among the many is greatest); Heraclitus 22 A10, B10, B50; Empedocles 31 A29; Parmenides 28 B8.5–6. Thales is supposed to have said that 'everything is full of gods' (11 A22).

12  See Broadie (1999).

13  Pind. fr. 140d apud Clem. Alex. *Strom.* 5.14.129. Ferrari (2004) argues that the meaning would have been that everything comes from god, as in *P.*5.25, *I.*5.53, *Paean* 6.132, fr. 141. Pindar and Empedocles: Griffith (1991); and Parmenides: ch. 2, n. 16.

14  For an overview of the phenomenon see Stafford (2007) and Rutherford (2012), 149–62 with earlier references.

15  Anaximander *Vors.* 12 B1; Pherecydes 7 B1, on whose conception of Chronos see Schibli (1990) 14–18, 27–38.

16  Solon fr. 36.3; Simonides fr. 88.1, on which see Sider (2020) 346; see also Simon. fr. 20.15 *IEG²* (supp.), *PMG* 531.5 = 261 Poltera, Simon. T 71a Poltera.

17  Fr. 16. Tyche is a daughter of Foresight and sister of Good Order and Persuasion in the curious genealogy of Alcman *PMGF* 64; see Wilamowitz-Moellendorff (1962), 505. In Hesiod she is one of the Oceanids (*Theog.* 360).

18  Excellent overview in Eidinow (2011), 25–52.

19  Respectively *O.*8.15, *P.*3.86, 5.3, *N.*4.42, 6.6.

20  *O.*2.11, *P.*8.44–5, *N.*1.28, 3.40–2, 6.8–11, 11.37–8, *I.*3.13–14.

21  Hesiod, *Theog.* 905, has the three familiar names Clotho (Spinner, who sets the pattern), Lachesis (Allotter, who determines the length), and Atropos (the Inexorable, who cuts the thread).

22  See Fraenkel (1950), 3.728–30 on *Agam.* 1535–6, who cites *Sept.* 975–7, *Cho.* 306–12, 909–11, *Eum.* 1045–6, *PV* 516 for the association of Moira, the Erinyes and Justice.

See also *Eum.* 956–67, Eur. fr. 494.18, Paus. 2.11.4, *SEG* 30.326; Henrichs (2019a), 418.

23  Births: of Artemis and Apollo, *Paean* 12.17; of Iamus, *O.*6.42; at Pelops' re-birth, *O.*1.26; the birth goddess Eileithyia is their companion, *Paean* 12.17, *O.*6.42, *N.*7.1. Beginnings: the founding of the Olympics, with Chronos, *O.*10.52; the wedding of Zeus, fr. 30; Lachesis administers the oath assigning the emergent island of Rhodes to Helios, *O.*7.64. Cyrene: *P.*5.76. Prosperity, misery and the vicissitudes of life: *O.*2.21, 2.35, *N.*7.57, *I.*6.18. On the Moirai see also Graf (1985), 29–31.

24  τὸ μόρσιμον Διόθεν πεπρωμένον. At *P.*1.55 the word is μοιρίδιον.

25  *P.*4.145, reading ἀφίσταντ(αι). See Braswell (1988), 230 and note Aesch. *Eum.* 956–67. But Chaeris' ἀφίσταιντ(ο) is not impossible, *pace* Braswell: Jason would be praying that the Moirai keep their distance (i.e. that there should be no bloodshed) if there is any enmity. He could as well have said the Erinyes (above, n. 22).

26  Respectively *O.*2.17; fr. 33; *N.*4.43; *O.*10.55 ('primeval rite' and '... real truth'); fr. 159; cf. *O.*1.33–4. Time as 'father of all things' could well reflect Orphic doctrine: West (1983), 83.

27  Forgetting in time: *O.*2.18–22, *P.*1.46; brings good and bad: *O.*12.10–12, *P.*12.30–2; prayers: *O.*6.97, 8.28–9, *P.*1.46, *N.*7.67–8, *Paean* 2.27.

28  Although Chronos affects human life in myriad ways, *aiōn* is the experience viewed from a subjective standpoint, as our lived lifetime; thus it can be 'fated' (*O.*2.10, *I.*7.41), 'sweet' (*P.*8.97), 'mortal' (*N.*3.75), 'treacherous' (*I.*8.14), 'delightful' (fr. 126.2) and much else (see Slater's *Lexicon*). Like Chronos it is relatively rare in texts before Pindar. As an active agent, it can bring wealth (*O.*2.10), destroy (*O.*9.60), bid us attend to what lies at hand (*N.*3.75), guide us on a straight path (*N.*2.8), change the course of affairs this way and that (*I.*3.18), hang threateningly over our heads and bowl us along life's path (*I.*8.14–15). In fr. 131b, unusually, it has its Homeric meaning 'life-force', similar to ψυχή; see Pavlou (2007) 21–2, to whose clear-eyed discussion I owe much in this section. The Horae are especially associated with youth; Hora (singular) is the 'messenger of Aphrodite' at the opening of the eighth *Nemean*. This association is traditional; more innovative is the idea that, as they spin round (i.e. the time of the festival arrives once more; cf. *Paean* 1.6), they have 'sent' Pindar (and/or his chorus) to Olympia (the Horae were represented in the statuary of Zeus's temple there). At *O.*13.16–17 (for a Corinthian victor) the Horae are said to have planted in men's hearts many 'ancient devices' and that 'every deed has its inventor': the poet instances the dithyramb, horses' bits and temple pediments, all from Corinth (the myth is about Athena's gift of the bridle to Bellerophon). Pindar's lapidary statement means that, as discoveries are made (theories about the development of culture were circulating in his time), it is the Horae, that is time in due season, who inspired their inventors: again the close collaboration of human and divine. On the Horae see Bremmer (2019), 497–509.

29 See pp. 170-7.

30 Excellent analysis in Silk (2007). See also Race (2004); Maslov (2015), 152-3.

31 Silk (2007), 187 argues strongly that the meaning is 'the indications [from the gods] have been blinded' (the blindness transferred metonymically from recipient to the message); as he notes, 'perceiving' or the like for φραδαί is unparalleled. But if a native speaker (the scholiast) says it means γνώσεις, it gives one pause, and the verb φράζομαι can mean 'notice', 'mark', 'see' (e.g. Aesch. *Eum.* 130; *LSJ* II 4, who wrongly put *Eum.*130 in another category. See Sommerstein *ad loc.*). Putting the stress on the gods does come close, *pace* Silk, to saying that they send untrustworthy signs (πιστόν, line 8).

32 ἀεὶ γὰρ εὖ πίπτουσιν οἱ Διὸς κύβοι, says Sophocles (fr. 895): when Zeus plays dice every throw is perfect.

33 See Silk (2007), 190-1. For mixed metaphors in Pindar see below pp. 182, 185-6. The cock and baths featured on the coins of Himera, which enhances the wit here for those who know it. 'Zeus the Liberator' and 'Saviour Fortune' are usually taken to refer to two liberations, first from the Persian threat in 480/79 then from the rule of Theron (also subsequently of Hieron, depending on whether the date of the poem is 470 or 466. Nicholson (2016), 237-53, argues now for the earlier date, but it remains uncertain.)

34 Hubbard (1985), 84. On Hesychia in Pindar see Slater (1981); Dickie (1984).

35 E.g. *P.*1.90, 6.46-9, *N.*1.31-2, *I.*1.67-8; Bacch. 3.13-21.

36 Fränkel (1975), 487. Maslov (2015), 126-9 singles out this passage as a prime example of the philosophical work metaphor and genealogy do in Pindar's poetry.

37 Maslov (2015), 126-9. The Graces are another fine example of divine immanence; see the discussion of *O.*7 in the last chapter (p. 103). They are closely associated with the Muses, another set of gods who raise questions of agency (pp. 114-16).

38 Hubbard (1985), 30. On the 'ascent to heaven' and aspirations to divinity, see Currie (2020) 10-11.

39 *O.*2.25-30, *N.*10.83-90, *P.*9.62-5; Currie (2005), 41-2.

40 Currie (2005). With the arguments advanced here compare and contrast Meister (2020), ch. 3.

41 Hubbard (1985), 19-20; Köhnken (1971), 154-87. A reward in advance, we shall have to say, or at least a mark of special favour; on the sequence of events here, see Slater (1983).

42 At *P.*3.61-2 Pindar advises his 'dear soul (ψυχά)' not to 'be eager for immortal life'. I take this to mean 'life this side of death', in which suffering is unavoidable. Even Peleus and Cadmus, those proverbially blessed heroes, did not lack woe (87-8). Pindar does not need to tell us where they went after death. In life we must concentrate on what lies near, and make the best of our human lot (60, 80-3).

43 *P.*10.41-4; cf. *O.*8.86 and Brown (1992). Divine *phthonos*: *O.*13.25, *P.*8.71, 10.20, *I.*7.39; Eidinow (2016), Lanzillotta (2010). Long, modest or virtuous life: *P.*11.50-8,

N.8.35–42, 9.44–7, I.6.10–16, 7.39–42. Limit your ambition to what lies close by: P.3.59–60, 3.109, 8.32, 10.62, 11.51, N.3.75, 6.55, I.7.40, 8.12, *Paean* 4.32–5. Summit of happiness / know human limits / look no further: O.1.114, P.1.99–100, 10.27–9, N.9.46–7, 11.13–16, I.5.12–16, 6.10–16. The limits figured as the Pillars of Heracles: O.3.43–5, N.3.19–21, 4.69, I.4.11–13. Do not seek to be a god: O.5.24, P.3.61–2, I.5.14, 7.44. Uncertainty of fortune: O.2.30–7, 7.94–5, 12.5–12, P.3.104–6, N.7.55–8, I.3.18, 4.5–6.

44 The skin of the Nemean Lion could not be penetrated; Heracles had to strangle the beast. Ajax also was invulnerable except in one spot, his armpit.

45 Cf. Cannatà Fera (2020), 318; Bremmer (2019), 89, suggests however that ἥρως here could mean 'Lord', as in *PMG* 871.1 (possibly, but *contra* see Brown (1982) and Davies (2021), 194–5) and I think N.10.82, translated below p. 167.

46 Genealogically the aristocracy was Dorian (Paus. 2.29); the sons of Aeacus all emigrated or died. But we know little of native Aeginetan mythology and it would be no surprise to discover that a woman descended from Aeacus wedded an incoming Dorian to become the grandmother of the historical aristocracy. O.8.30 (Αἴγιναν) Δωριεῖ λαῷ ταμιευομέναν ἐξ Αἰακοῦ nicely fudges the matter. Cf. Burnett (2005), 13–28.

47 Later literature has many stories of divine epiphanies set in the fifth century, but contemporary reports are not common (epiphanies of heroes is another matter). Several are reported by Herodotus; best known is that of Pan to Phidippides (6.105–6), and it is revealing that Pisistratus' faked epiphany of Athena found ready believers (1.60). On epiphanies, apart from Henrichs (2019b) and the literature he cites see the special issue of *ICS* 29 (2004) and Petridou (2015).

48 See Grethlein and Huitink (2017). Focalization and the pacing of the narrative are also important; cf below on O.13.

49 The epiphany of Alcman in P.8.58–60 is a heroic epiphany offering many points of interest but is less pertinent to my concerns here; similarly the epiphany of the *daimōn* Triton in P.4.28.

50 *Il.* 1.34 (Chryses prays to Apollo), 1.349–50 (prelude to Thetis' epiphany), 23.59–61 (prelude to Patroclus' epiphany in a dream), *Od.* 2.260–1 (Telemachus prays to Athena, who appears at once, though disguised as Mentor).

51 See Haselswerdt (2019) for a discussion of sublime sound in this play, drawing especially on Lyotard.

52 The opening 'do you sleep?' (εὕδεις;) draws on epic (*Il.* 2.23, 23.69, *Od.* 4.804); the first of these is the false dream sent by Zeus to Agamemnon.

53 See Fowler (2013), 423–4.

54 Though one might ask why Polydeuces prays to Zeus at this moment if he does not know he is his father, the explanation of 80–1 is otiose and flat if he does know. His request to be allowed to die with his brother does not mean he expected to live

forever. Cf. Currie (2018), 294–7, who well explores the characterization of
Polydeuces here, though I resist his inference that Zeus too does not know until now.

55 On the tombstone see also Kurke (2016), 10–13.

56 Currie (2018), 296.

57 Young (1993), 131 citing Hom. *Il.* 11.453, *Od.* 11.426, 24.296, Pl. *Phd.* 118.

58 Apollo: *P.*4.66, *I.*2.18; Zeus: e.g. *P.*5.122–3, *N.*10.29–30, *I.*3.4–5, *I.*5.53.

59 The ending of *O.*10 was discussed in ch. 2, pp. 105–7.

60 There are many other aspects of Pindaric temporality, of course, some of which have
been touched on already in this study; the incorporation of a future perfect
perspective, in which secondary audiences clinch the poem's immortality, is of
particular importance (pp. 83, 104). Of various studies of Pindaric time, including
from a narratological perspective, I cite Griffith (1993); Pavlou (2007), (2011),
(2012); Nünlist (2007); Grethlein (2009), 19–46, (2011); Maslov (2012); Sigelman
(2016); Agócs (2020). On time more generally see especially Kennedy (2013); also
Calame (2009), Kahane (forthcoming).

61 At 87–92 direct speech reports the comments of anonymous onlookers; the dialogue
of Jason and Pelias encompasses 102–19 and 138–67; Aietes speaks at 229–31.
Athena's short speech in *O.*13 is in response to an oracular consultation. In the
fragments, two speeches (*Paean* 2.73–5, 8a 14–23) are prophecies and one (*Paean*
4.40–53) is not (but has a mantic tinge). The credit for this important observation
belongs to Pavlou (2007), 175–202. On speeches in the myths see also Currie
(forthcoming).

62 Pavlou (2007), 178.

63 See also de Jong (2013).

64 Willcock (1964).

65 Kowalzig (2007) for a detailed study.

66 Gentili et al. (2013), 16–17; Sigelman (2016), 177–81.

67 Robbins (1978).

68 When Pindar says that the ἐπικώμιος ὕμνος existed even before the Nemean Games
(*N.*8.50–1), he seeks to make up for this deficit in ancient origins; see also *O.*10.76–85.
Against that, *O.*9.1–5 contrasts the simple ancient celebrations with sophisticated
present-day productions.

69 The proem of this poem was discussed in ch. 2, pp. 102–5. 464 may be a *terminus
post quem*: Currie (2011), 271 n. 9, 287 n. 75.

70 Kurke (2016) argues (adventurously, I think) that the many references in the poem
to artefacts are due to Pindar's knowledge that this is what Diagoras planned to do
with it. But she shrewdly draws attention to διορθῶσαι λόγον in 21, as in erecting a
monument.

71 Compare Herodotus' description of Croesus as 'he who first harmed the Greeks'
(1.5); in the sequel we learn that there were others before him. As Croesus is the

beginning that counts for his story, so Tlapolemus is the founder of the current Rhodian order, for whom previous history was a preparation.

72 See Fowler (2013), 569–602 for a study of several such myths; for Rhodes (including the poem's pan-Rhodian perspective), see also Kowalzig (2007), 224–66.

73 *Pace* Young (1987); the reference to crafts here is highly suggestive. On the Telchines, Fowler (2013), 45–9.

74 The nymph of the island, daughter of Poseidon and Aphrodite.

75 See *I*.8.1 (λύτρον … καμάτων), *P*.5.106 (λυτήριον δαπανᾶν); the same or similar idea at e.g. *O*.11.4, *P*.5.47, *N*.4.1, 8.50, 10.24, *I*.1.42, 5.25, 6.10–12. Heracles is the great exemplar for all this (*N*.1.70).

76 On metaphor in Pindar see Dornseiff (1921); Bowra (1964), 239–77; Silk (1974), (2003); Stoneman (1981); Steiner (1986); Patten (2009); Lattmann (2010); Maslov (2015), 117–77; Matzner (2016); Sigelman (2016), 78–81, 173–5. In Homer, see Zanker (2019); in Bacchylides, Cairns (2010), 60–1; in general, Stanford (1936); Punter (2007).

77 Listed in Schmid (1929) 597 n. 3.

78 Maslov (2015), 157.

79 Maslov (2015), 159.

80 Maslov (2015), 126–7. Note already Dornseiff (1921) 56–7 on Pindar's way of combining image and concept.

81 Ch. 1, pp. 41–50; ch. 2, p. 122.

82 Maehler (2004), 19.

83 Cannatà Fera (2020), 599.

84 Cairns (2010), 38–41 with references to earlier discussions.

85 As I take it to be. Bacchylides uses it at 4.7–8 (restored), but his liking for words beginning *anaxi*- (five others, all of them *hapax legomena*) may argue against his being the debtor. The meanings are simpler: in 4.7, ἀναξιφόρμιγξ is applied to the Muse who governs the lyre; in 6.10, the Muse is ἀναξίμολπος, she who governs the song and dance; sim. 29a 1 of the chorus; in 20.8 Poseidon is ἀναξίαλος, lord of the sea; in 17.66 Zeus is ἀναξιβρέντας, lord of thunder; in 14B 10 Larisa is ἀνάξιππος, lord of horses. With regard to the second part of the compound, Simonides has χρυσοφόρμιγξ fr. 7a. 3 Poltera, Aesch. *Supp.* 697 has φιλοφόρμιγξ, and Bacchylides 1.1 has κλυτοφόρμιγξ, all unique. The formation was apparently in vogue; we find it at no other time in Greek literature.

86 Prauscello (2012); Steiner (2016).

87 Silk (2003), 130–1; he speaks of 'an explosion of suggestions and connections', citing also Finley (1955), 40.

88 Braswell (1998), 144 points out that Pindar's four other compounds in *themi(s)*- are also *hapax legomena*. Typically, however, he wants only one meaning to be operative (there was no cheating); Themis is declared to be irrelevant because she was at home in Delphi, and this victory was in Sicyon.

89 P. 187. Pindar used δαιδάλλω metaphorically also at *O.*1.29, 2.53, 5.21, *Parth.* 2.31. μελίκομπος (*I.*2.32) and μελίρροθος (fr. 246a) are also *hapax legomena*, and μελίφθογγος, which Pindar uses three times, is found nowhere else before the second century BCE: Henry (2005), 127.

90 Sigelman (2016), 20.

91 Nünlist (1998), 349. That poetological imagery should be delivered in adjectives is unusual in itself.

92 Paraphrased: Stop talking about that, move on to something else. *aōtos* is a favourite word (twenty times in Pindar), denoting the best of something; only once in Bacchylides (23.1).

93 The wrestling was the last and deciding event in the pentathlon. Although it is not clear in our sources how overall victory was decided, only those with a chance of winning were allowed to proceed to the wrestling. Paraphrased: My praise will be perfect, and I shall proceed to the winning stage like you. The victor in this poem was a pentathlete. On the many interpretations of this passage see Almazova (2017); I have followed Carey (1981), 165–72.

94 Coral.

95 'Lydian' will refer to the musical mode of the poem, but also to that country's reputation for luxurious clothing and ornaments; 'headband', such as is worn by victors; 'loudly', *kanachēda*, of the sound of the auloi.

96 The word is *agalma*, an ornament or decoration, aesthetically pleasing, often used of votive statues; the poem is a monument to be admired from all sides like precious objects dedicated to the gods. On this passage see Fearn (2020), 77–80 and Kurke (2016), 4–5, with references.

97 Johnson (2006) 2.282; quoted by Silk (1974), 5.

98 See Hutchinson (2001) 410–12 who daggers line 82 as corrupt.

99 E.g. *O.*13.47–9; *P.*8.29–32, 9.76–9; *N.*4.33–5, 7.50–3; *I.*1.60–3, 6.56–9; cf. ch. 2, pp. 123–32 on the *kairos*.

100 The rhetoric of the poem is that of one setting the record straight; we do not, however, need to invent a back-story about Pindar apologizing for the sixth *Paean*. On the endless controversy see most recently Spelman (2018a), 119–30.

101 E.g. *O.*1.28–34, 2.92, 4.17–18, 6. 20–1; *P.*1.44; *N.*6.26–8, 7.61–9. Braswell (1988), 379.

102 The noun *auxēsis* means 'amplification' in the later rhetorical tradition; as such, it is an instrument of the sublime in Longinus (11–12).

103 Homer e.g. *Il.* 1.286, *Od.* 4.266; nine times in total, and five more times without πάντα. κατὰ ῥάβδον ἔφρασεν in Pindar's line (which is basically dactylic) occupies the same end position as κατὰ μοῖραν ἔειπες. With πᾶσαν ἀρετάν compare Homer's πᾶσαν ἀληθείην (*Il.* 24.407, *Od.* 11.507; sim. *Od.* 3.254 = 16.61); echoed also by Simon. fr. 11.17, with similar metapoetic force.

104 E.g. Heraclitus *Vors.* 22 B32, B48, B62, B65, B67 on words and names; Parmenides *Vors.* 28 B8.38–41, 53–4 (admittedly exceedingly difficult to interpret). Words a matter of convention: Democritus 68 B26. Overview in Novokhatko (2015), 29–34; detailed study in Kraus (1987).

105 P. 70. Maslov (2015), 164–6; Kirichenko (2016).

106 Kirichenko (2016); Kuhn-Treichel (2020b).

107 Longinus §32, tr. Roberts.

108 Burke (1759), 106 (Part II §IV) on Milton, *Paradise Lost* 1.589–99 (the description of Satan).

109 Cf. Steiner (1986), 1–17.

110 Silk (2003), 127.

111 On this passage as a whole I continue to find Woodbury (1955) persuasive.

112 On the problem of assessing dead metaphors in Greek see Silk (1974), 27–56. Wind: Steiner (1986) 73.

113 Miernowski (2014).

114 Butler and Purves (2013), 5.

115 'Tout l'univers visible n'est qu'un magasin d'images et de signes auxquels l'imagination donnera une place et une valeur relative; c'est une espèce de pâture que l'imagination doit digérer et transformer.' Baudelaire (1868), 274; first published in the *Salon de 1859*.

116 Sigelman (2016), 78–81.

117 See Steiner (1986), 136–48 for eloquent remarks on Pindaric myth as metaphor.

# Epilogue

1 Maslov (2015), 59–60, 128–9 and *passim*.

2 Respectively *O*.2.68–83; 3.32 (p. 73); 6.46–7; 7.61–70 (p. 176); *P*.1.6–10 (p. 62); 1.15–28 (p. 60); 3.38–44; 4.102–19 (p. 38); 9.26–65; 10.31–40; *N*.1.69–72 (the poem ends with this scene: Heracles is still there); 3.47–9; *I*.6.52–4 (p. 161).

# Bibliography

## Abbreviations and editions

Abbreviations of journals, reference works, collections of texts and ancient authors follow standard authorities such as the *Oxford Classical Dictionary* or the Liddell–Scott–Jones *Greek–English Lexicon*. Note *EGM* = Fowler (2000–2013). My base texts for Homer, Pindar and Bacchylides are the Teubner editions; for Sappho and Alcaeus, Voigt (1971); for the melic poets except Stesichorus, *PMG* and *PMGF*; for Stesichorus, Davies and Finglass (2014); for the elegists and iambists, *IEG*²; for Hesiod, the *OCT*; for the Epic Cycle, M. L. West's *Greek Epic Fragments* (Loeb).

Abrams, M. H. (1953), *The Mirror and the Lamp. Romantic Theory and the Critical Tradition*. New York: Oxford University Press.

Adorno, Theodor (1970), 'Parataxis. Zur späten Lyrik Hölderlins', in Schmidt (1970) 339–78 = Adorno (1991–92) 2.109–49.

Adorno, Theodor (1991–92), *Notes to Literature*. Ed. Rolf Tiedemann, tr. Shierry Weber Nicholsen. 2 vols. New York: Columbia University Press.

Agócs, Peter (2012), 'Performance and Genre: Reading Pindar's κῶμοι', in Agócs, Carey and Rawles (2012b, eds), 191–223.

Agócs, Peter (2020), 'Pindar's *Pythian* 4: Interpreting History in Song', *Histos* Suppl. 11: 87–154.

Agócs, Peter, Chris Carey and Richard Rawles (2012a, eds), *Receiving the Komos. Ancient and Modern Perceptions of the Victory Ode*. London: Institute of Classical Studies.

Agócs, Peter, Chris Carey and Richard Rawles (2012b, eds), *Reading the Victory Ode*. Cambridge: Cambridge University Press.

Aguirre, Mercedes and Richard Buxton (2020), *Cyclops. The Myth and Its Cultural History*. Oxford: Oxford University Press.

Almazova, Nina (2017), 'On the Javelin Simile in Pindar *Nemean* 7.70–73', *GRBS* 57: 1–15.

Ankersmit, F. R. (2005), *Sublime Historical Experience*. Stanford: Stanford University Press.

Ashfield, Andrew and Peter de Bolla (1996, eds), *The Sublime. A Reader in Eighteenth-Century Aesthetic Theory*. Cambridge: Cambridge University Press.

Athanassaki, Lucia (2009), 'Narratology, Deixis, and the Performance of Choral Lyric. On Pindar's *First Pythian Ode*', in Grethlein and Rengakos (2009, eds), 241–73.

Athanassaki, Lucia (2012), 'Performance and Reperformance: The Siphnian Treasury Evoked (Pindar's *Pythian 6, Olympian 2 and Isthmian 2*)', in Agócs, Carey and Rawles (2012b, eds), 134–57.

Athanassaki, Lucia (2016), 'The Symposion as Theme and Performance Context in Pindar's Epinicians', in Cazzato, Obbink and Prodi (2016, eds), 85–112.

Athanassaki, Lucia, and Ewen Bowie (2011, eds), *Archaic and Classical Choral Song. Performance, Politics and Dissemination.* Berlin and Boston: de Gruyter.

Austin, J. L. (1975), *How to Do Things with Words.* 2nd edn ed. J. O. Urmson and Marina Sbisà. Oxford: Oxford University Press.

Baeumer, Max (1967), 'Hölderlin und das Hen kai pan', *Monatshefte* 59: 131–47.

Bakker, Egbert J. (2017), 'Trust and Fame: The Seal of Theognis', in Bakker (2017, ed.), 99–121.

Bakker, Egbert J. (2010, ed.), *A Companion to the Ancient Greek Language.* Chichester: Wiley-Blackwell.

Bakker, Egbert J. (2017, ed.), *Authorship and Greek Song. Authority, Authenticity, and Performance.* Leiden and Boston: Brill.

Barrett, W. S. (2007), *Greek Lyric, Tragedy, and Textual Criticism.* Ed. M. L. West. Oxford: Oxford University Press.

Battersby, Christine (2007), *The Sublime, Terror and Human Difference.* Abingdon and New York: Routledge.

Baudelaire, Charles (1868), *Curiosités esthétiques.* Paris: Michel Lévy frères.

Baumgarten, Alexander Gottlieb (1735), *Meditationes philosophicae de nonnullis ad poema pertinentibus.* Halle. Tr. Karl Aschenbrenner and William B. Holther (1954), *Reflections on Poetry: Alexander Gottlieb Baumgarten's Meditationes philosophicae de nonnullis ad poema pertinentibus.* Berkeley and Los Angeles: University of California Press.

Beecroft, Alexander (2010), *Authorship and Cultural Identity in Early Greece and China. Patterns of Literary Circulation.* Cambridge: Cambridge University Press.

Beiser, Frederick (2005), *Schiller as Philosopher: A Re-Examination.* Oxford: Oxford University Press.

Benn, M. B. (1962), *Hölderlin and Pindar.* The Hague: Mouton & Co..

Benveniste, Émile (1966–1974), *Problèmes de linguistique générale.* 2 vols. Paris: Gallimard. Vol. 1 tr. Mary Elizabeth Meek (1971), *Problems in General Linguistics.* Coral Gables: University of Miami Press.

Bierl, Anton and André Lardinois (2016, eds), *The Newest Sappho. P. Sapph. Obbink and P. GC inv. 105, frs. 1–4.* Leiden and Boston: Brill.

Billings, Joshua (2014). *Genealogy of the Tragic. Greek Tragedy and German Philosophy.* Princeton and Oxford: Princeton University Press.

Bloom, Harold (2010, ed.), *The Sublime.* New York: Infobase Publishing.

Bond, Donald F. (1965, ed.), *The Spectator.* 5 vols. Oxford: Clarendon Press.

Booth, Stephen (1998), *Precious Nonsense. The Gettysburg Address, Ben Jonson's Epitaphs and Twelfth Night.* Berkeley: University of California Press.

Booth, Wayne C. (1983), *The Rhetoric of Fiction*. 2nd edn. Chicago and London: University of Chicago Press.

Booth, Wayne C. (2005), 'Resurrection of the Implied Author: Why Bother?', in Phelan and Rabinowitz (2005, eds), 75–88.

Bowie, Ewen (2016), 'How Did Sappho's Songs Get into the Male Sympotic Repertoire?', in Bierl and Lardinois (2016, eds), 148–64.

Bowra, C. M. (1964), *Pindar*. Oxford: Clarendon Press.

Boys-Stones, George R. (2003, ed.), *Metaphor, Allegory and the Classical Tradition: Ancient Thought and Modern Revisions*. Oxford: Oxford University Press.

Braswell, Bruce Karl (1976), 'Notes on the Prooemium to Pindar's Seventh Olympian Ode', *Mnem.* 29: 233–42.

Braswell, Bruce Karl (1988), *A Commentary on the Fourth Pythian Ode of Pindar*. Berlin and New York: de Gruyter.

Braswell, Bruce Karl (1998), *A Commentary on Pindar Nemean Nine*. Berlin and New York: de Gruyter.

Bremer, J. M. (1990), 'Pindar's Paradoxical ἐγώ', in Slings (1990, ed.), 41–58.

Bremmer, J. N. (2002), *The Rise and Fall of the Afterlife*. London and New York: Routledge.

Bremmer, J. N. (2008), *Greek Religion and Culture, the Bible and the Ancient Near East*. Leiden and Boston: Brill.

Bremmer, J. N. (2019), *The World of Greek Religion and Mythology*. Tübingen: Mohr Siebeck.

Bremmer, J. N. (2021), *Greek Religion*. 2nd edn. Cambridge: Cambridge University Press.

Bremmer, J. N. and E. Begemann (2021, eds) *Religion in Context*. Leiden: Brill.

Bremmer, J. N. and A. Erskine (2010, eds), *The Gods of Ancient Greece. Identities and Transformations*. Edinburgh: Edinburgh University Press.

Briand, Michel (2016), 'Light and Vision in Pindar's *Olympian Odes*: Interplays of Imagination and Performance', in Cazzato and Lardinois (2016, eds), 238–54.

Broadie, Sarah (1999), 'Rational Theology', in Long (1999, ed.), 205–24.

Brody, Jules (1958), *Boileau and Longinus*. Geneva: Librairie E. Droz.

Brown, Christopher (1982), 'Dionysus and the Women of Elis: *PMG* 871', *GRBS* 23: 304–14.

Brown, Christopher (1984), 'The Bridegroom and the Athlete: The Proem to Pindar's Seventh Olympian', in Gerber (1984, ed.), 37–50.

Brown, Christopher (1989), 'Anactoria and the Χαρίτων ἀμαρύγματα: Sappho fr. 16,18 Voigt', *QUCC* n.s. 32, 7–15.

Brown, Christopher (1992), 'The Hyperboreans and Nemesis in Pindar's *Tenth Pythian*', *Phoenix* 46: 95–107.

Budelmann, Felix (2009, ed.), *The Cambridge Companion to Greek Lyric*. Cambridge: Cambridge University Press.

Budelmann, Felix (2012), 'Epinician and the *symposion*. A Comparison with the *enkomia*', in Agócs et al. (2012b, eds), 173–90.

Budelmann, Felix (2017), 'Performance, Reperformance, Preperformance: The Paradox of Repeating the Unique in Pindaric Epinician and Beyond', in Hunter and Uhlig (2017, eds), 42–62.

Budelmann, Felix (2018a), *Greek Lyric. A Selection*. Cambridge: Cambridge University Press.

Budelmann, Felix (2018b), 'Lyric Minds', in Budelmann and Phillips (2018, eds), 235–56.

Budelmann, Felix (forthcoming), 'Lyric Visuality and the Mingling of Perception and Imagination', in F. Budelmann and K. Earnshaw (forthcoming, eds), *Cognitive Visions: Image-Making and the Mind*.

Budelmann, Felix and Tom Phillips (2018, eds), *Textual Events. Performance and the Lyric in Early Greece*. Oxford: Oxford University Press.

Bulman, Patricia (1992), Phthonos *in Pindar*. Berkeley, Los Angeles and Oxford: University of California Press.

Bundy, Elroy L. (1986 [orig. 1962]), *Studia Pindarica*. Berkeley and Los Angeles: University of California Press.

Burke, Edmund (1759), *A Philosophical Enquiry into the Origin of our Ideas of the Sublime and Beautiful*. 2nd edn. London. https://archive.org/details/philosophicalenq00burkrich/page/n1 (accessed 10 May 2021).

Burnett, Anne Pippin (2005), *Pindar's Songs for Young Athletes of Aigina*. Oxford: Oxford University Press.

Butler, Shane and Alex Purves (2013, eds), *Synaesthesia and the Ancient Senses*. London and New York: Routledge.

Cairns, D. L. (2010), *Bacchylides: Five Epinician Odes (3, 5, 9, 11, 13)*. Cambridge: Francis Cairns.

Cairns, D. L. (2014), 'Ψυχή, θυμός, and Metaphor in Homer and Plato', *Etudes platoniciennes* 11. https://doi.org/10.4000/etudesplatoniciennes.566 (accessed 10 May 2021).

Cairns, D. L. (2016), 'Metaphors for Hope in Archaic and Classical Greek Poetry', in Caston and Kaster (2016, eds), 13–44.

Calame, Claude (2004), 'Deictic Ambiguity and Auto-Referentiality: Some Examples from Greek Poetics', in Felson (2004, ed.), 415–43.

Calame, Claude (2009), *Poetic and Performative Memory in Ancient Greece: Heroic Reference and Ritual Gestures in Time and Space*. Tr. H. Patton. Washington, DC: Center for Hellenic Studies. http://nrs.harvard.edu/urn-3:hul.ebook:CHS_CalameC. Poetic_and_Performative_Memory_in_Ancient_Greece.2009 (accessed 10 May 2021).

Calame, Claude (2011), 'Enunciative Fiction and Poetic Performance. Choral Voices in Bacchylides' *Epinicians*', in Athanassaki and Bowie (2011, eds), 115–38.

Calame, Claude (2019), 'Greek Lyric Poetry, A Non-Existent Genre?', in Rutherford (2019, ed.), 33–60.

Cammagre, Geneviève (2007), 'Diderot et le sublime pindarique', in Marot (2007, ed.), 205–24.

Cannatà Fera, Maria (1990), *Pindarus. Threnorum fragmenta*. Rome: Edizioni dell' Ateneo.

Cannatà Fera, Maria (2020), *Pindaro. Le Nemee*. n.p.: Fondazione Lorenzo Valla / Mondadori.

Carey, Christopher (1981), *A Commentary on Five Odes of Pindar:* Pythian *2,* Pythian *9,* Nemean *1,* Nemean *7,* Isthmian *8*. New York: Arno Press.

Carey, Christopher (1989), 'The Performance of the Victory Ode', *AJP* 110: 545–65.

Carey, Christopher (1991), 'The Victory Ode in Performance: The Case for the Chorus', *CP* 86: 192–200.

Carey, Christopher (2007), 'Pindar, Place, and Performance', in Hornblower and Morgan (2007, eds), 199–210.

Carey, Christopher (2011), 'Pindaric Metapoetics Revisited', in Martinho dos Santos et al. (2011, eds), 25–50.

Carey, Christopher (2017), 'Voice and Worship', in Bakker (2017, ed.), 34–60.

Carne-Ross, David (1985), *Pindar*. New Haven: Yale University Press.

Caston, Ruth R. and Robert A. Kaster (2016, eds), *Hope, Joy, and Affection in the Classical World*. Oxford: Oxford University Press.

Cazzato, Vanessa and André Lardinois (2016, eds), *The Look of Lyric: Greek Song and the Visual*. Leiden and Boston: Brill.

Cazzato, Vanessa, Dirk Obbink, and Enrico Emmanuele Prodi (2016, eds), *The Cup of Song. Studies on Poetry and the Symposium*. Oxford: Oxford University Press.

Christen, Felix (2007), *Eine andere Sprache: Friedrich Hölderlins grosse Pindar-Übertragung*. Basel: Engeler.

Clark, A. F. B. (1925), *Boileau and the French Classical Critics in England (1660–1830)*. Paris: Librairie Ancienne Édouard Champion.

Clarke, G. W. (1989, ed.), *Rediscovering Hellenism. The Hellenic Inheritance and the English Imagination*. Cambridge: Cambridge University Press.

Clay, Jenny Strauss (1999), 'Pindar's Sympotic "Epinicia"', *QUCC* 62: 25–34.

Clewis, Robert R. (2009), *The Kantian Sublime and the Revelation of Freedom*. Cambridge: Cambridge University Press.

Clewis, Robert R. (2018, ed.), *The Sublime Reader*. London: Bloomsbury.

Coleridge, Samuel Taylor (1983), *The Collected Works of Samuel Taylor Coleridge. Volume 7: Biographia Literaria, or, Biographical Sketches of my Literary Life and Opinions*. Ed. James Engell and W. Jackson Bate. Princeton: Princeton University Press.

Colesanti, Giulio and Manuela Giordano (2014, eds), *Submerged Literature in Ancient Greece. An Introduction*. Berlin and Boston: de Gruyter.

Congreve, William (1706), *A Pindarique ode, humbly offer'd to the Queen, on the victorious progress of Her Majesty's arms, under the conduct of the Duke of Marlborough. To which is prefix'd, a discourse on the Pindarique ode*, in McKenzie (2011, ed.) 2.411–24.

Conte, Gian Biagio (2007), 'Anatomy of a Style: Enallage and the New Sublime', in G. B. Conte, *The Poetry of Pathos: Studies in Virgilian Epic*. Ed. Stephen Harrison. Oxford: Oxford University Press, 58–122.

Costelloe, Timothy M. (2012, ed.), *The Sublime. From Antiquity to the Present*.
    Cambridge: Cambridge University Press.

Crotty, Kevin (1982), *Song and Action: The Victory Odes of Pindar*. Baltimore: Johns
    Hopkins University Press.

Csapo, Eric (2004), 'The Politics of the New Music', in Murray and Wilson (2004, eds),
    207–48.

Csapo, Eric, and Peter Wilson (2009), 'Timotheus the New Musician', in Budelmann
    (2009, ed.), 277–93.

Culler, Jonathan (2015), *Theory of the Lyric*. Cambridge, MA and London: Harvard
    University Press.

Currie, Bruno (2004), 'Reperformance Scenarios for Pindar's Odes', in Mackie (2004,
    ed.), 49–69.

Currie, Bruno (2005), *Pindar and the Cult of Heroes*. Oxford: Oxford University Press.

Currie, Bruno (2011), 'Epinician *choregia*: Funding a Pindaric Chorus', in Athanassaki
    and Bowie (2011, eds), 269–310.

Currie, Bruno (2013), 'The Pindaric First Person in Flux', *ClAnt* 32: 243–82.

Currie, Bruno (2017), 'Festival, Symposium, and Epinician (Re)performance: The Case
    of *Nemean 4* and Others', in Hunter and Uhlig (2017, eds), 187–208.

Currie, Bruno (2018), 'Pindar and Bacchylides', in De Temmerman and van Emde Boas
    (2018, eds), 293–314.

Currie, Bruno (2020), 'Aristophanes and the Cult of the Saviour', *Mythos* 14: 1–30. http://
    journals.openedition.org/mythos/2088 (accessed 10 May 2021).

Currie, Bruno (forthcoming), 'Pindar and Bacchylides', in M. de Bakker and I. J. F. de
    Jong (eds), *Speech in Ancient Greek Literature*. Leiden and Boston: Brill.

D'Alessio, Giovan Battista (1994), 'First-Person Problems in Pindar', *BICS* 39: 117–39.

D'Alessio, Giovan Battista (1995), 'Una via lontana dal cammino degli uomini (Parm.
    frr. 1+6 D.-K.; Pind. *Ol.* VI 22–27; *pae.* VIIb 10–20)', *SIFC* 88: 143–81.

D'Alessio, Giovan Battista (2004), 'Past Future and Present Past: Temporal Deixis in
    Greek Archaic Lyric', in Felson (2004, ed.), 267–94.

D'Alessio, Giovan Battista (2020), 'The Problem of the Absent I. Lyric Poetry and Deixis
    in "Mediated" Communication', *AION* 42: 1–30.

Davies, Malcolm (2021), *Lesser and Anonymous Fragments of Greek Lyric Poetry*.
    Oxford: Oxford University Press.

Davies, M. and P. J. Finglass (2014), *Stesichoros: The Poems*. Cambridge: Cambridge
    University Press.

Day, Henry J. M. (2013), *Lucan and the Sublime*. Cambridge: Cambridge University Press.

De Temmerman, Koen and Evert van Emde Boas (2018, eds), *Characterization in
    Ancient Greek Literature*. Leiden and Boston: Brill.

Des Places, Édouard (1947), *Le pronom chez Pindare*. Paris: Librairie C. Klincksieck.

Dickie, Matthew W. (1976), 'On the Meaning of ἐφήμερος', *ICS* 1: 7–14.

Dickie, Matthew W. (1984), '*Hêsychia* and *Hybris* in Pindar', in Gerber (1984, ed.),
    83–109.

Diderot, Denis (1751–72, ed.) *Encyclopédie, ou Dictionnaire raisonné des sciences, des arts et des métiers*. Paris and Neuchâtel.

Dijkstra, Jitse, Justin Kroesen and Yme Kuiper (2010, eds), *Myths, Martyrs, and Modernity: Studies in the History of Religions in Honour of Jan N. Bremmer*. Leiden: Brill.

Dimoula, Vassiliki (2012), 'Pindar and Nineteenth-Century "Poetic Religion": Hölderlin and Kalvos', in Agócs, Carey and Rawles (2012a, eds), 169–91.

Dinkova-Bruun, Greti, James Hankins and Robert A. Kaster (2014, eds), *Catalogus Translationum et Commentariorum. Volume X. Pindarus, Aelianus Tacticus, Musaeus, Agathias, Aulus Gellius*. Toronto: Pontifical Institute of Mediaeval Studies.

Doran, Robert (2015), *The Theory of the Sublime from Longinus to Kant*. Cambridge: Cambridge University Press.

Dornseiff, Franz (1921), *Pindars Stil*. Berlin: Weidmann.

DuBois, Page (1995), *Sappho is Burning*. Chicago: University of Chicago Press.

Eagleton, Terry (2003), *Sweet Violence. The Idea of the Tragic*. Malden, MA: Blackwell.

Easterling, P. E. and B. M. W. Knox (1985, eds), *The Cambridge History of Classical Literature I. Greek Literature*. Cambridge: Cambridge University Press.

van Eck, Caroline, Stijn Bussels, Maarten Delbreke and Jürgen Pieters (2012, eds), *Translations of the Sublime. The Early Modern Reception and Dissemination of Longinus' Peri Hupsous in Rhetoric, the Visual Arts, Architecture and the Theatre*. Leiden and Boston: Brill.

Eckerman, Chris (2010), 'The ΚΩΜΟΣ of Pindar and Bacchylides and the Semantics of Celebration', *CQ* 60: 302–12.

Eckerman, Chris (2018), 'The Dioscuri and the ἀγών at Pindar's *Olympian* 3.36', *RhM* 161: 109–11.

Eidinow, Esther (2011), *Luck, Fate and Fortune. Antiquity and its Legacy*. London and New York: I.B. Tauris.

Eidinow, Esther (2016), 'Popular Theologies. The Gift of Divine Envy', in Eidinow, Kindt and Osborne (2016, eds), 205–32.

Eidinow, Esther, Julia Kindt and Robin Osborne (2016, eds), *Theologies of Ancient Greek Religion*. Cambridge: Cambridge University Press.

van den Eijnde, Floris, Josine H. Blok and Rolf Strootman (2018, eds), *Feasting and Polis Institutions*. Leiden and Boston: Brill.

Eisen, Ute E. and Peter von Möllendorff (2013, eds), *Über die Grenze. Metalepsis in Texts and Artifacts of Antiquity*. Berlin and Boston: de Gruyter.

Emilsson, Eyjólfur K., Anastasia Masravela and Mathilde Skoie (2014, eds), *Paradeigmata. Studies in Honour of Øivind Andersen*. Norwegian Institute at Athens.

Evans, Robert C. (2010), '"God's Grandeur" (Gerard Manley Hopkins)', in Bloom (2010, ed.), 89–98.

Faraone, Christopher A. (1995), 'The "Performative Future" in Three Hellenistic Incantations and Theocritus' Second *Idyll*', *CP* 90: 1–15.

Fearn, David (2005), *Bacchylides: Politics, Performance, Poetic Tradition*. Oxford: Oxford University Press.

Fearn, David (2007), *Bacchylides: Politics, Performance, Poetic Tradition*. Oxford: Oxford University Press.

Fearn, David (2019), 'The Allure of Narrative in Greek Lyric Poetry', in Grethlein, Huitink and Tagliabue (2019, eds), 36–59.

Fearn, David (2020), *Greek Lyric of the Archaic and Classical Periods. From the Past to the Future of the Lyric Subject*. Leiden and Boston: Brill.

Felson, Nancy (1999), 'Vicarious Transport: Fictive Deixis in Pindar's *Pythian Four*', *HSCP* 99: 1–31.

Felson, Nancy (2004, ed.), *The Poetics of Deixis in Alcman, Pindar, and Other Lyric*. *Arethusa* 37 no. 3.

Ferrari, Franco (2004), 'La sapienza acerba e il dio-tutto: Pindaro e Senofane', *Prometheus* 30: 139–47.

Ferrari, Franco (2012), 'Representations of Cult in Epinician Poetry', in Agócs, Carey and Rawles (2012b, eds), 158–72.

Finglass, P. J. and Adrian Kelly (2021, eds), *The Cambridge Companion to Sappho*. Cambridge: Cambridge University Press.

Finglass, P. J., C. Collard and N. J. Richardson (2007, eds), *Hesperos. Studies in Ancient Greek Poetry Presented to M. L. West on his Seventieth Birthday*. Oxford: Oxford University Press.

Finley, John H. Jr. (1955), *Pindar and Aeschylus*. Cambridge, MA: Harvard University Press.

Finley, Moses I. (1972), *Aspects of Antiquity*. 2nd edn. Aylesbury: Pelican Books.

Fitzgerald, William (1987), *Agonistic Poetry. The Pindaric Mode in Pindar, Horace, Hölderlin and the English Ode*. Berkeley, London and Los Angeles: University of California Press.

Ford, Andrew (2002), *The Origins of Criticism. Literary Culture and Poetic Theory in Classical Greece*. Princeton: Princeton University Press.

Ford, Andrew (2013), 'The Poetics of Dithyramb', in Kowalzig and Wilson (2013, eds), 313–31.

Ford, Andrew (2020), 'Mythographic Discourse among Non-Mythographers: Pindar, Plato and Callimachus', in Romano and Marincola (2020, eds), 5–27.

Foucault, Michel (1979), 'What is an Author?', in Harari (1979, ed.), 141–60. French original 1969.

Fowler, Robert L. (1982), 'Aristotle on the Period (*Rhet*. 3.9)', *CQ* n.s. 32: 89–99.

Fowler, Robert L. (1987a), *The Nature of Early Greek Lyric: Three Preliminary Studies*. Toronto: University of Toronto Press.

Fowler, Robert L. (1987b), 'Sappho fr. 31.9', *GRBS* 28: 433–9.

Fowler, Robert L. (1998), 'Genealogical Thinking, Hesiod's *Catalogue*, and the Creation of the Hellenes', *PCPS* 44: 1–19.

Fowler, Robert L. (2000–2013), *Early Greek Mythography*. 2 vols. Oxford: Oxford University Press.

Fowler, Robert L. (2010), 'Gods in Early Greek Historiography', in Bremmer and Erskine (2010, eds), 318–34.

Fowler, Robert L. (2021), 'Story-Telling', in Bremmer and Begemann (2021, eds).

Fraenkel, Eduard (1950), *Aeschylus: Agamemnon.* 3 vols. Oxford: Clarendon Press.

Fraenkel, Eduard (1957), *Horace.* Oxford: Clarendon Press.

Fränkel, Hermann (1924), 'Eine Stileigenheit der frühgriechischen Literature', *Gött. Nachr.* 1924: 63–127. Repr. in Fränkel (1968) 40–96.

Fränkel, Hermann (1946), 'Man's "Ephemeros" Nature according to Pindar and Others', *TAPA* 77: 131–45.

Fränkel, Hermann (1968), *Wege und Formen frühgriechischen Denkens.* 3rd edn. Munich: C. H. Beck.

Fränkel, Hermann (1975), *Early Greek Poetry and Philosophy.* Tr. Moses Hadas and James Willis. Oxford: Blackwell.

Friis Johansen, H. and Edward W. Whittle (1980, eds), *Aeschylus: The Suppliants.* 3 vols. Copenhagen: Gyldendal.

Gentili, Bruno, Paola Angeli Bernardini, Ettore Cingano, and Pietro Giannini (1995, eds), *Pindaro: Le Pitiche,* n.p.: Fondazione Lorenzo Valla / Mondadori.

Gentili, Bruno, Carmine Catenacci, Pietro Giannini and Liana Lomiento (2013, eds), *Pindaro: Le Olimpiche.* n.p.: Fondazione Lorenzo Valla / Mondadori.

Gerber, Douglas E. (1969), *A Bibliography of Pindar 1513–1966.* n.p.: Case Western Reserve University Press.

Gerber, Douglas E. (1982), *Pindar's* Olympian One: *A Commentary.* Toronto: University of Toronto Press.

Gerber, Douglas E. (1984, ed.), *Greek Poetry and Philosophy. Studies in Honour of Leonard Woodbury.* Chico: Scholars Press.

Gianotti, Gian Franco (1975), *Per una poetica pindarica.* Turin: Paravia.

Gidel, A. Ch. (1873, ed.), *Oeuvres complètes de Boileau.* Vol. 3. Paris: Garnier Frères.

Gildersleeve, Basil L. (1885), *Pindar: Olympian and Pythian Odes.* London: MacMillan. Repr. (2010): Cambridge, Cambridge University Press.

Goldhill, Simon (1990), *The Poet's Voice.* Cambridge: Cambridge University Press.

Gottsched, Johann Christoph (1751), *Versuch einer critischen Dichtung,* 4th edn. Leipzig. 1st edn 1730. https://archive.org/details/bub_gb_pP9YAAAAcAAJ/page/n5 (accessed 10 May 2021).

Graf, Fritz (1985), *Nordionische Kulte.* Rome: Schweizerisches Institut.

Graham, Walter (1941, ed.), *The Letters of Joseph Addison.* Oxford: Oxford University Press.

Greene, Roland (1991), *Post-Petrarchism: Origins and Innovations of the Western Lyric Sequence.* Princeton: Princeton University Press.

Grethlein, Jonas (2009), *The Greeks and their Past. Poetry, Oratory and History in the Fifth Century BCE.* Cambridge: Cambridge University Press.

Grethlein, Jonas (2011), 'Divine, Human and Poetic Time in Pindar, *Pythian* 9', *Mnem.* 64: 383–409.

Grethlein, Jonas and Antonios Rengakos (2009, eds), _Narratology and Interpretation. The Content of Narrative Form in Ancient Literature_. Berlin: de Gruyter.

Grethlein, Jonas and Luuk Huitink (2017), 'Homer's Vividness: An Enactive Approach', _JHS_ 137: 67–91.

Grethlein, Jonas, Luuk Huitink and Aldo Tagliabue (2019, eds), _Experience, Narrative and Criticism in Ancient Greece: Under the Spell of Stories_. Oxford: Oxford University Press.

Griffin, Jasper (1980), _Homer on Life and Death_. Oxford: Clarendon Press.

Griffith, Mark (1983), 'Personality in Hesiod', _ClAnt_ 2: 37–65.

Griffith, R. Drew (1991), 'Oedipus's Bloodthirsty Sons: Love and Strife in Pindar's Second _Olympian Ode_', _ClAnt_ 10: 46–58.

Griffith, R. Drew (1993), 'In the Dark Backward: Time in Pindaric Narrative', _Poetics Today_ 14: 607–23.

Gunderson, Eric (2015), _The Sublime Seneca: Ethics, Literature, Metaphysics_. Cambridge: Cambridge University Press.

Guyer, Paul (1993), _Kant and the Experience of Freedom: Essays on Aesthetics and Morality_. Cambridge: Cambridge University Press.

Guyer, Paul (2014), _A History of Modern Aesthetics_. 3 vols. New York: Cambridge University Press.

Hadjimichael, Theodora A. (2019), _The Emergence of the Lyric Canon_. Oxford: Oxford University Press.

Hall, Edith and Stephe Harrop (2010, eds), _Theorising Performance. Greek Drama, Cultural History and Critical Practice_. London: Gerald Duckworth & Co. Ltd.

Halliwell, Stephen (2011), _Between Ecstasy and Truth. Interpretations of Greek Poetics from Homer to Longinus_. Oxford: Oxford University Press.

Halliwell, Stephen (2014), 'Greek Gods and the Archaic Aesthetics of Life', in Emilsson, Maravela and Skoie (2014, eds), 121–7.

Hamann, Johann Georg (1950), _Sämtliche Werke_. 6 vols. Edited by Josef Nadler. Vienna: Herder.

Hamburger, Käte (1973), _The Logic of Literature_. Tr. Marilynn J. Rose. 2nd edn. Bloomington: Indiana University Press. German original 1957, 2nd edn 1968.

Hamilton, John T. (2003), _Soliciting Darkness. Pindar, Obscurity and the Classical Tradition_. Cambridge, MA and London: Harvard University Press.

Hamilton, John T. (2012), 'Pindar', in Walde and Egger (2012), 306–11.

Hammond, Paul and David Hopkins (1995–2005, eds), _The Poems of John Dryden_. 5 vols. Vols 1–2 ed. Paul Hammond, vols 3–5 ed. Paul Hammond and David Hopkins. London and New York: Longman.

Harari, Josué V. (1979, ed.), _Textual Strategies: Perspectives in Post-Structuralist Criticism_. Ithaca: Cornell University Press.

Hardie, Philip (2009), _Lucretian Receptions: History, The Sublime, Knowledge_. Cambridge: Cambridge University Press.

Harrison, S. J. (2001, ed.), _Texts, Ideas, and the Classics_. Oxford: Oxford University Press.

Haselswerdt, Ella (2019), 'Sound and the Sublime in Sophocles' *Oedipus at Colonus*: The Limits of Representation', *AJP* 140: 613–42.

Havelock, Eric A. (1963), *Preface to Plato.* Oxford: Blackwell.

Headlam, Walter (1922), *Herodas: The Mimes and Fragments.* Cambridge: Cambridge University Press.

Heath, Malcolm (1986), 'The Origins of Modern Pindaric Criticism', *JHS* 106: 85–98.

Heath, Malcolm (1988), 'Receiving the κῶμος: The Context and Performance of Epinician', *AJP* 109: 180–95.

Heath, Malcolm (1999), 'Longinus, *On Sublimity*', *PCPS* 45: 43–74.

Heath, Malcolm (2012), 'Longinus and the Ancient Sublime', in Costelloe (2012), 11–23.

Hegel, Georg Friedrich Wilhelm (1970), *Werke in zwanzig Bänden.* Frankfurt: Suhrkamp.

Hellingrath, Norbert von (1911), *Pindarübertragungen von Hölderlin. Prolegomena zu einer Erstausgabe.* Jena: Eugen Diederichs.

Henrichs, Albert (1994–95), '"Why Should I Dance?" Choral Self-Referentiality in Greek Tragedy', *Arion* 3: 56–111.

Henrichs, Albert (1996), 'Dancing in Athens, Dancing on Delos: Some Patterns of Choral Projection in Euripides', *Philologus* 140: 48–62.

Henrichs, Albert (2019), *Greek Myth and Religion.* Collected Papers II. Ed. Harvey Yunis. Berlin and Boston: de Gruyter.

Henrichs, Albert (2019a), 'Moira', in Henrichs (2019), 415–19.

Henrichs, Albert (2019b), 'The Epiphanic Moment: Sight and Insight Ancient Greek Encounters with the Divine', in Henrichs (2019), 429–49.

Henry, W. B. (2005), *Pindar's Nemeans. A Selection.* Leipzig: K.G. Saur.

Henry, W. B. (2007), 'Pindaric Accompaniments', in Finglass, Collard and Richardson (2007, eds), 126–31.

Herder, Johann Gottfried (1990), *Volkslieder. Übertragungen. Dichtungen.* Ed. Ulrich Gaier. Frankfurt a.M.: Deutscher Klassiker Verlag.

Herington, John (1985), *Poetry into Drama. Early Tragedy and the Greek Tradition.* Berkeley, Los Angeles and London: University of California Press.

Hoare, Alexandra (2013), 'Salvator Rosa's Allegory of *Philosophy* as *Ut Pictura Rhetorica*: Eloquent Gesture and the Pursuit of Artistic Decorum', *Art History* 36: 944–67.

Hobden, Fiona (2013), *The Symposion in Ancient Greek Society and Thought.* Cambridge: Cambridge University Press.

Hölderlin, Friedrich (1998), *Sämtliche Werke und Briefe.* 3 vols. Ed. Michael Knaupp et al. Darmstadt: Wissenschaftliche Buchgesellschaft.

Hölderlin, Friedrich (2004), *Poems and Fragments.* Tr. Michael Hamburger. 4th edn. London: Anvil Press Poetry Ltd.

Hölderlin, Friedrich (2008), *Hyperion, or The Hermit in Greece.* Tr. Ross Benjamin. Brooklyn, NY: Archipelago Books.

Hölderlin, Friedrich (2009), *Essays and Letters.* Ed. and tr. Jeremy Adler and Charlie Louth. London: Penguin Books.

Holmes, Brooke and W. H. Shearin (2012, eds), *Dynamic Reading: Studies in the Reception of Epicureanism*. Oxford: Oxford University Press.

Hopkins, David (2004), '"The English Homer": Shakespeare, Longinus, and English "Neo-Classicism"', in Martindale and Tylor (2004, eds), 261–76.

Hopkins, David (2010), *Conversing with Antiquity; English Poets and the Classics, from Shakespeare to Pope*. Oxford: Oxford University Press.

Hopkins, David (2012), 'Homer', in Hopkins and Martindale (2012, eds), 165–95.

Hopkins, David and Charles Martindale (2012, eds), *The Oxford History of Classical Reception in English Literature. Volume 3 (1660–1790)*. Oxford: Oxford University Press.

Hornblower, Simon (2004), *Thucydides and Pindar*. Oxford: Oxford University Press.

Hornblower, Simon and Catherine Morgan (2007, eds), *Pindar's Poetry, Patrons and Festivals*. Oxford: Oxford University Press.

Hubbard, Thomas K. (1985), *The Pindaric Mind*. Leiden: Brill.

Hubbard, Thomas K. (1995), 'On Implied Wishes for Olympic Victory in Pindar', *ICS* 20: 35–56.

Hunter, Richard, and Ann Uhlig (2017, eds), *Imagining Reperformance in Ancient Culture*. Cambridge: Cambridge University Press.

Hutchinson, G. O. (2001), *Greek Lyric Poetry. A Commentary on Selected Larger Pieces*. Oxford: Oxford University Press.

Huxley, George (1969), 'Choirilos of Samos'. *GRBS* 10: 12–29.

Jackson, Virginia and Yopie Prins (2014), *The Lyric Theory Reader*. Baltimore: Johns Hopkins University Press.

Jauss, Hans Robert (1982), *Aesthetic Experience and Literary Hermeneutics*. Tr. Michael Shaw. Minneapolis: University of Minnesota Press. German original 1977.

Jenkyns, Richard (1980), *The Victorians and Ancient Greece*. Cambridge, MA: Harvard University Press.

Johnson, Samuel (2006), *The Lives of the Most Eminent English Poets; With Critical Observations on their Works*. Ed. Roger Lonsdale. 4 vols. Oxford: Clarendon Press.

de Jong, Irene J. F. (2013), 'Metalepsis and Embedded Speech in Pindaric and Bacchylidean Myth', in Eisen and von Möllendorff (2013, eds), 97–118.

de Jong, Irene J. F. and René Nünlist (2007, eds), *Time in Ancient Greek Literature*. Leiden: Brill.

de Jonge, Casper C. (2012), 'Dionysius and Longinus on the Sublime: Rhetoric and Religious Language', *AJP* 133: 271–300.

Kahane, Ahuvia (forthcoming 2021), 'Homer and Ancient Narrative Time'. *ClAnt* 40.

Kaimio, Maarit (1970), *The Chorus of Greek Drama within the Light of the Person and Number Used*. Helsinki-Helsingfors: Societas scientiarum fennica.

Kant, Immanuel (2000), *Critique of the Power of Judgment*. Ed. Paul Guyer. Tr. Paul Guyer and Eric Matthews. Cambridge: Cambridge University Press. Cited by page number of this translation (which is based on Kant's second edition of 1793; first edition 1790) and by volume and page number of the Akademie-Ausgabe (AA) of Kant's *Gesammelte Schriften*, Berlin 1900–.

Kant, Immanuel (2006), *Anthropology from a Pragmatic Point of View*. Ed. and tr. Robert B. Louden. Cambridge: Cambridge University Press. Cited by page number of this translation (which is based on Kant's second edition of 1800; first edition 1798) and by volume and page number of the Akademie-Ausgabe (AA) of Kant's *Gesammelte Schriften*, Berlin 1900–.

Kavoulaki, Athena (2018, ed.), *Πλειών. Papers in Memory of Christiane Sourvinou-Inwood*. Rethymnon: University of Crete.

Kennedy, Duncan F. (2013), *Antiquity and the Meanings of Time. A Philosophy of Ancient and Modern Literature*. London and New York: I.B. Tauris.

Kirichenko, Alexander (2016), 'Metaphor and Iconicity in Pindar's *Olympian* 6 and *Nemean* 5', *Mnem.* 69: 1–28.

Köhnken, Adolf (1971), *Die Funktion des Mythos bei Pindar*. Berlin and New York: de Gruyter.

Konstan, David (2015), *Beauty: The Fortunes of an Ancient Greek Idea*. Oxford: Oxford University Press.

Konstan, David and N. Keith Rutter (2003, eds), *Envy, Spite, and Jealousy: The Rivalrous Emotions in Ancient Greece*. Edinburgh: Edinburgh University Press.

Kotwick, Mirjam E. (2017), *Der Papyrus von Derveni*. Berlin and Boston: de Gruyter.

Kowalzig, Barbara (2007), *Singing for the Gods. Performance of Myth and Ritual in Archaic and Classical Greece*. Oxford: Oxford University Press.

Kowalzig, Barbara, and Peter Wilson (2013, eds), *Dithyamb in Context*. Oxford: Oxford University Press.

Kraus, Manfred (1987), *Name und Sachen, ein Problem im frühgriechischen Denken*. Amsterdam: Grüner.

Krummen, Eveline (2014), *Cult, Myth, and Occasion in Pindar's Victory Odes. A Study of Isthmian 4, Pythian 5, Olympian 1, and Olympian 3*. Tr. J. G. Howie. Preston: Francis Cairns. German original 1990.

Kuhn-Treichel, Thomas (2020a), *Rollen in Relation. Das poetische Ich in verschiedenen Gattungen bei Pindar*. Munich: C. H. Beck.

Kuhn-Treichel, Thomas (2020b), 'Pindar's Poetic "I" and the Muses: Metaphorical Role Characterization in Different Genres', *CJ* 116: 152–71.

Kurke, Leslie (2013), *The Traffic of Praise*. 2nd edn. Berkeley: California Classical Studies. http://escholarship.org/uc/item/29r3j0gm (accessed 10 May 2021).

Kurke, Leslie (2016), 'Pindar's Material Imaginary: Dedication and Politics in *Olympian* 7'. UCL Housman Lecture 2015: https://www.ucl.ac.uk/classics/sites/classics/files/housman_kurke_2016.pdf (accessed 10 May 2021).

Lagière, Anne (2017), *La «Thébaide» de Stace et le sublime*. Brussels: Latomus.

Laird, Andrew (2006, ed.), *Ancient Literary Criticism*. Oxford: Oxford University Press.

Lamb, Jonathan (1997), 'The Sublime', in Nisbet and Rawson (1997, eds), 394–416.

Langdon, Helen (2012), 'The Demosthenes of Painting. Salvator Rosa and the 17th Century Sublime', in van Eck et al. (2012, eds), 163–85.

Lanzillotta, Lautaro Roig (2010), 'The so-called envy of the gods: revisiting a dogma of ancient Greek religion', in Dijkstra, Kroesen and Kuiper (2010, eds), 75–93.

Lardinois, André (2021), 'Sappho's Personal Poetry', in Finglass and Kelly (2021, eds), 163–74.

Lardinois, André, M. H. Pierre, Josine H. Blok, and Marc G. M. Van der Poel (2011, eds), *Sacred Words: Orality, Literacy, and Religion*. Leiden: Brill.

Lattmann, Claas (2010), *Das Gleiche im Verschiedenen: Metapher des Sports und Lob des Siegers in Pindars Epinikien*. Berlin: de Gruyter.

Lattmann, Claas (2012), 'Ritualisierter Siegpreis. Anmerkungen zur pragmatischen Dimension von Epinikien', *Nikephoros* 25: 19–78.

Lattmann, Claas (2017), 'Pindar's Voice(s): The Epinician *Persona* Reconsidered', in Slater (2017, ed.) 123–48.

Lefkowitz, Mary R. (1988), 'Who Sang Pindar's Victory Odes?', *AJP* 109: 1–11 = Lefkowitz (1991), 191–201.

Lefkowitz, Mary R. (1991), *First Person Fictions: Pindar's Poetic 'I'*. Oxford: Clarendon Press.

Lefkowitz, Mary R. (2012), *Lives of the Greek Poets*. 2nd edn. London: Bristol Classical Press.

Lehnus, Luigi (1979), *L'inno a Pan di Pindaro*. Milan: Istituto Editoriale Cisalpino–La Goliardica.

Leonard, Miriam (2015), *Tragic Modernities*. Cambridge, MA and London: Harvard University Press.

Littlewood, Cedric A. J. (2018), '*Hercules Furens* and the Senecan Sublime', *Ramus* 46: 153–74.

Lloyd-Jones, Hugh (1990), *Greek Epic, Lyric, and Tragedy*. Oxford: Clarendon Press.

Loxley, James (2007), *Performativity*. Abingdon and New York: Routledge.

LeVen, Pauline A. (2017), *The Many-Headed Muse. Tradition and Innovation in Late Classical Greek Lyric Poetry*. Cambridge: Cambridge University Press.

Long, A. A. (1999, ed.), *The Cambridge Companion to Early Greek Philosophy*. Cambridge: Cambridge University Press.

Lord, Albert B. (1960), *The Singer of Tales*. 2nd edn 2000. Cambridge, MA: Harvard University Press.

Louth, Charlie (1998), *Hölderlin and the Dynamics of Translation*. Oxford: Legenda.

Louth, Charlie (2000), 'The Question of Influence: Hölderlin's Dealings with Schiller and Pindar', *MLR* 95.4: 1038–52.

MacFarlane, Kelly A. (2009), 'Choerilus of Samos' Lament (*SH* 317) and the Revitalization of Epic', *AJP* 130: 219–34.

Mackie, C. J. (2004, ed.), *Oral Performance and its Contexts*. Leiden and Boston: Brill.

MacLachlan, Bonnie (1993), *The Age of Grace. Charis in Early Greek Poetry*. Princeton: Princeton University Press.

Macleod, Colin (1983), *Collected Essays*. Oxford: Clarendon Press.

Maehler, Herwig (1997), *Die Lieder des Bakchylides. Zweiter Teil: Die Dithyramben und Fragmente.* Leiden, New York and Cologne: Brill.

Maehler, Herwig (2004), *Bacchylides: A Selection.* Cambridge: Cambridge University Press.

Maliks, Reidar (2014), *Kant's Politics in Context.* Oxford: Oxford University Press.

Mandelkow, Karl Robert (1968, ed.), *Goethes Briefe.* 2nd edn. 4 vols. Hamburg: Christian Wegner.

Marincola, John, Lloyd Llewellyn-Jones, and Calum Maciver (2012, eds), *Greek Notions of the Past in the Archaic and Classical Periods: History without Historians.* Edinburgh: Edinburgh University Press.

Marinis, Agis (2018), 'Pindar's *Sixth Paean*: Conceptualizing Religious Panhellenism', in Kavoulaki (2018, ed.), 145–77.

Marot, Patrick (2007a, ed.), *La littérature et le sublime.* Paris: Presses universitaires du Mirail.

Marot, Patrick (2007b), 'L'Écriture du sublime ou l'éclat du manque', in Marot (2007a, ed.), 15–51.

Martindale, Charles (1993), *Redeeming the Text: Latin Poetry and the Hermeneutics of Reception.* Cambridge: Cambridge University Press.

Martindale, Charles (2005), *Latin Poetry and the Judgement of Taste.* Oxford: Oxford University Press.

Martindale, Charles (2010), 'Performance, Reception, Aesthetics: Or Why Reception Studies Need Kant', in Hall and Harrop (2010, eds), 71–83.

Martindale, Charles (2012), 'Milton's Classicism', in Hopkins and Martindale (2012, eds), 53–90.

Martindale, Charles, Stefano-Maria Evangelista and Elizabeth Prettejohn (2017, eds), *Pater the Classicist: Classical Scholarship, Reception, and Aestheticism.* Oxford: Oxford University Press.

Martindale, Charles, and Richard F. Thomas (2006, eds), *Classics and the Uses of Reception.* Malden: Blackwell.

Martindale, Charles and A. B. Tylor (2004, eds), *Shakespeare and the Classics.* Cambridge: Cambridge University Press.

Martinho dos Santos, Marcos, Paula da Cunha Corrêa, Alexandre Pinheiro Hasegawa and José Marcos Macedo (2011, eds), *Hyperboreans.* São Paulo: Humanitas.

Maslov, Boris (2012), 'Pindaric Temporality, Goethe's "Augenblick," and the Invariant Plot of Tiutchev's Lyric', *Comparative Literature* 64: 356–81.

Maslov, Boris (2015), *Pindar and the Emergence of Literature.* Cambridge: Cambridge University Press.

Maslov, Boris (2016), 'The Children of Mnemosyne: A Contrastive Metapoetics of Pindar and Bacchylides', *Philologia Classica* 11: 223–43.

Matzner, Sebastian (2016), *Rethinking Metonymy: Literary Theory and Poetic Practice from Pindar to Jakobson.* Oxford: Oxford University Press.

McCarthy, Kathleen (2019), *I, the Poet: First-person Form in Horace, Catullus and Propertius.* Ithaca: Cornell University Press.

McKenzie, D. F. (2011, ed.), *The Works of William Congreve*. 3 vols. Oxford and New York: Oxford University Press.

Meister, Felix J. (2020), *Greek Praise Poetry and the Rhetoric of Divinity*. Oxford: Oxford University Press.

Mellor, Anne K. (1993), *Romanticism and Gender*. New York: Routledge.

Merritt, Melissa M. (2012), 'The Moral Source of the Kantian Sublime', in Costelloe (2012, ed.), 37–49.

Merritt, Melissa M. (2018), *The Sublime*. Cambridge: Cambridge University Press.

Michelakis, Pantelis (2009), 'Greek Lyric from the Renaissance to the Eighteenth Century', in Budelmann (2009, ed.), 336–51.

Miernowski, Jan (2014, ed.), *Le Sublime et le grotesque*. Geneva: Droz.

Miller, Andrew M. (1991), 'A Wish for Oympian Victory in Pindar's Tenth *Pythian*', *AJP* 112: 161–72.

Miller, Andrew M. (1993), 'Pindaric Mimesis: The Associative Mode', *CJ* 89: 21–53.

Miller, Andrew M. (2019), *Pindar: The Odes*. Oakland: University of California Press.

Monk, Samuel H. (1935), *The Sublime. A Study in Critical Theories in XVIII-Century England*. New York: Modern Language Association of America.

Montanari, Franco, Stephanos Matthaios and Antonios Rengakos (2015, eds), *Brill's Companion to Ancient Greek Scholarship*. 2 vols. Leiden: Brill.

Morgan, Kathryn A. (1993), 'Pindar the Professional and the Rhetoric of the ΚΩΜΟΣ', *CP* 88: 1–15.

Morgan, Kathryn A. (2015), *Pindar and the Construction of Syracusan Monarchy in the Fifth Century B.C.* Oxford and New York: Oxford University Press.

Morrison, A. D. (2007a), *Performances and Audiences in Pindar's Sicilian Victory Odes*. London: Institute of Classical Studies.

Morrison, A. D. (2007b), *The Narrator in Archaic Greek and Hellenistic Poetry*. Cambridge: Cambridge University Press.

Morrison, A. D. (2012), 'Performance, Reperformance and Pindar's Audiences', in Agócs, Carey and Rawles (2012b, eds), 111–33.

Most, Glenn W. (1985), *The Measures of Praise. Structure and Function in Pindar's Second Pythian and Seventh Nemean Odes*. Göttingen: Vandenhoeck & Ruprecht.

Most, Glenn W. (2003), 'Epinician Envies', in Konstan and Rutter (2003, eds), 123–42.

Most, Glenn W. (2012a), 'Poet and Public: Communicative Strategies in Pindar and Bacchylides', in Agócs, Carey and Rawles (2012b, eds), 249–76.

Most, Glenn W. (2012b), 'The Sublime, Today?', in Holmes and Shearin (2012, eds), 239–66.

Moul, Victoria (2012), '*A Mirror for Noble Deeds*: Pindaric Form in Jonson's Odes and Masques', in Agócs, Carey and Rawles (2012a, eds), 141–56.

Mullen, William (1982), *Choreia. Pindar and Dance*. Princeton: Princeton University Press.

Multatuli (1987 [orig. 1860]), *Max Havelaar*. Tr. Roy Edwards. London: Penguin Books.

Murray, Oswyn (2018), *The Symposion: Drinking Greek Style. Essays on Greek Pleasure 1983–2017*. Oxford: Oxford University Press.

Murray, Penelope (1981), 'Poetic Inspiration in Archaic Greece', *JHS* 101: 87–100. Repr. in Laird (2006), 37–61.

Murray, Penelope and Peter Wilson (2004, eds), *Music and the Muses. The Culture of 'Mousikē' in the Classical Athenian City*. Oxford: Oxford University Press.

Nauta, R. R., H.-J. van Dam and J. L. J. Smolenaars (2006, eds), *Flavian Poetry*. Leiden: Brill.

Neer, Richard and Leslie Kurke (2019), *Pindar, Song, and Space: Towards a Lyric Archaeology*. Baltimore: Johns Hopkins University Press.

Neumann-Hartmann, Arlette (2009), *Epinikien und ihr Aufführungsrahmen*. Hildesheim: Weidmann.

Newman, J. K. (1967), *The Concept of Vates in Augustan Poetry*. Brussels: Latomus.

Nicholson, Nigel (2016), *The Poetics of Victory in the Greek West: Epinician, Oral Tradition, and the Deinomenid Empire*. Oxford: Oxford University Press.

Nicolai, Roberto (2014), 'The Canon and its Boundaries', in Colesanti and Giordano (2014, eds), 33–45.

Nisbet, H. B. and Claude Rawson (1997, eds), *The Cambridge History of Literary Criticism. Volume 4: The Eighteenth Century*. Cambridge: Cambridge University Press.

Novokhtako, Anna (2015), 'Greek Scholarship from its Beginnings to Alexandria', in Montanari, Matthaios and Rengakos (2015, eds), 3–59.

Nünlist, René (1998), *Poetologische Bildersprache in der frühgriechischen Dichtung*. Stuttgart and Leipzig: Teubner.

Nünlist, René (2007), 'Pindar and Bacchylides', in de Jong and Nünlist (2007, eds), 233–51.

Nuttall, A. D. (1996), *Why Does Tragedy Give Pleasure?* Oxford: Clarendon Press.

Ogden, Daniel (2007, ed.), *A Companion to Greek Religion*. Malden: Blackwell.

Oliensis, Ellen (1998), *Horace and the Rhetoric of Authority*. Cambridge: Cambridge University Press.

Parker, Robert (2011), *On Greek Religion*. Ithaca: Cornell University Press.

Pater, Walter (1873), *Studies in the History of the Renaissance*. London: Macmillan and Co.

Patey, Douglas Lane (1997), 'Ancients and Moderns', in Nisbet and Rawson (1997, eds), 32–71.

Patten, Glenn (2009), *Pindar's Metaphors. A Study in Rhetoric and Meaning*. Heidelberg: Winter.

Pavlou, Maria (2007), *Time in Pindar*. Diss. Bristol.

Pavlou, Maria (2011), 'Past and Present in Pindar's Religious Poetry', in Lardinois et al. (2011, eds), 59–78.

Pavlou, Maria (2012), 'Pindar and the Reconstruction of the Past', in Marincola, Llewellyn-Jones and Maciver (2012, eds), 95–112.

Payne, Mark (2006), 'On Being Vatic: Pindar, Pragmatism, and Historicism', *AJP* 127: 159–84.

Payne, Mark (2018), 'Fidelity and Farewell. Pindar's Ethics as Textual Events', in Budelmann and Phillips (2018, eds), 257–74.

Pelliccia, Hayden (1995), *Mind, Body, and Speech in Homer and Pindar*. Göttingen: Vandenhoeck & Ruprecht.

Payne, Mark (2009), 'Simonides, Pindar and Bacchylides', in Budelmann (2009, ed.), 240–62.

Peponi, Anastasia-Erasmia (2012), *Frontiers of Pleasure. Models of Aesthetic Response in Archaic and Classical Greek Thought*. Oxford: Oxford University Press.

Perrault, Charles (1674), *Critique de l'Opéra ou, Examen de la tragédie intitulée Alceste, ou le triomphe d'Alcide*. Paris.

Perrault, Charles (1687), *Le Siècle de Louis le Grand. Poème*. Paris.

Perrault, Charles (1688–96), *Paralèlle des Anciens et des Modernes en ce qui regarde les arts et les sciences*. 4 vols. Paris.

Perrault, Charles (1964), *Parallèle des Anciens et des Modernes en ce qui regarde les arts et les sciences*. Mit einer einleitenden Abhandlung von H.R. Jauss und kunstgeschichtlichen Exkursen von M. Indahl. Munich: Eidos.

Petridou, Georgia (2016), *Divine Epiphany in Greek Literature and Culture*. Oxford: Oxford University Press.

Pfeijffer, Ilja Leonard (1999), *First Person Futures in Pindar*. Stuttgart: Steiner.

Phelan, James, and Peter J. Rabinowitz (2005, eds), *A Companion to Narrative Theory*. Oxford: Blackwell.

Phillips, Tom (2016), *Pindar's Library. Performance Poetry and Material Texts*. Oxford: Oxford University Press.

Phillips, Tom (2017), 'Pindar's Voices: Music, Ethics and Reperformance', *JHS* 137:142–62.

Poltera, Orlando (2008), *Simonides lyricus. Testimonia und Fragmente*. Basel: Schwabe.

Porter, James I. (2010), *The Origins of Aesthetic Thought in Ancient Greece*. Cambridge: Cambridge University Press.

Porter, James I. (2016), *The Sublime in Antiquity*. Cambridge: Cambridge University Press.

Potkay, Adam (2012), 'The British Romantic Sublime', in Costelloe (2012, ed.), 203–16.

Pratt, Louise H. (1993), *Lying and Poetry from Homer to Pindar*. Ann Arbor: University of Michigan Press.

Prauscello, Lucia (2012), 'Pindar and Musical Innovation', in Agócs, Carey and Rawles (2012b, eds), 58–82.

Punter, David (2007), *Metaphor*. London and New Yok: Routledge.

Purves, Alex (2021), 'Sappho's Lyric Sensibility', in Finglass and Kelly (2021, eds), 175–89.

Purves, Alex (forthcoming), 'Alcman, Sappho, and the "Lyric Present"' in C. Bloomfield & E. Hall, eds., *Time, Tense and Genre in Ancient Greek Literature*.

Race, William H. (1979), 'The End of *Olympia* 2: Pindar and the *Vulgus*', *CSCA* 12: 251–67.

Race, William H. (1990), *Style and Rhetoric in Pindar's Odes*. Atlanta: Scholars Press.

Race, William H. (2004), 'Elements of Plot and the Formal Presentation in Pindar's *Olympian* 12', *CJ* 99: 373–94.

Rainer, Paula and David Kovacs (1993), 'Δέδυκε μὲν ἀ σελάννα: The Pleiades in Mid-Heaven (*PMG* Frag. Adesp. 976 = Sappho, Fr. 168B Voigt)', *Mnem.* 46: 145–59.

Revard, Stella P. (2001), *Pindar and the Renaissance Hymn-Ode 1450–1700*. Tempe: Arizona Center for Medieval and Renaissance Studies.

Revard, Stella P. (2009), *Politics, Poetics, and the Pindaric Ode: 1450–1700*. Tempe: Arizona Center for Medieval and Renaissance Studies.

Richardson, Nicholas J. (1985), 'Pindar and Later Literary Criticism in Antiquity', *PLPS* 5: 383–401.

Robbins, Emmet I. (1978), 'Cyrene and Cheiron: The Myth of Pindar's Ninth *Pythian*', *Phoenix* 32: 91–104. Reprinted in Robbins (2013), 202–16.

Robbins, Emmet I. (1984), 'Intimations of Immortality: Pindar, *Ol.* 3.34–5', in Gerber (1984, ed.), 219–28. Reprinted in Robbins (2013), 157–66.

Robbins, Emmet I. (2013), *Thalia Delighting in Song. Essays on Ancient Greek Poetry*. Ed. Bonnie MacLachlan. Toronto: University of Toronto Press.

Roberts, W. Rhys (1899), *Longinus on the Sublime*. Cambridge: Cambridge University Press.

Robinson, T. M. (1987), *Heraclitus. Fragments*. Toronto: University of Toronto Press.

Romano, Allen J. and John Marincola (2020, eds), *Host or Parasite? Mythographers and their Contemporaries in the Classical and Hellenistic Periods*. Berlin and Boston: de Gruyter.

Romney, Jessica (2020), *Lyric Poetry and Social Identity in Archaic Greece*. Ann Arbor: University of Michigan Press.

Rotstein, Andrea (2010), *The Idea of Iambos*. Oxford: Oxford University Press.

Roworth, Wendy Wassyng (1988), 'The Consolations of Friendship: Salvator Rosa's Self-Portrait for Giovanni Battista Ricciardi', *Metropolitan Museum Journal* 23: 103–24.

Rutherford, Ian (2019, ed.), *Greek Lyric*. Oxford: Oxford University Press.

Rutherford, Richard (2012), *Greek Tragic Style. Form, Language and Interpretation*. Oxford: Oxford University Press.

de Saussure, Ferdinand (1974), *Course of General Linguistics*. Ed. Charles Bally and Albert Sechehaye. Tr. Wade Baskin. Rev. edn. Glasgow: Fontana / Collins. French original 1916.

Schadewaldt, Wolfgang (1966 [orig. 1928]), *Der Aufbau des pindarischen Epinikion*. Tübingen: Max Niemeyer.

Schadewaldt, Wolfgang (1970 [orig. 1957]), 'Hölderlins Übersetzung des Sophokles', in *Hellas und Hesperien. Gesammelte Schriften zur Antike und zur neueren Literatur*, 2nd edn., 2.767–824. Zurich: Artemis. Repr. in Schmidt (1970) 237–93.

Schechner, Richard (1985), *Between Theater and Anthropology*. Philadelphia: University of Pennsylvania Press.

Schechner, Richard (2013), *Performance Studies: An Introduction*. 3rd edn. London and New York: Routledge.

Schibli, H. S. (1990), *Pherekydes of Syros*. Oxford: Clarendon Press.

Schiller, Friederich (1988–2002), *Werke und Briefe in zwölf Bänden*. Ed. Otto Dann et al. Frankfurt: Deutscher Klassiker Verlag = Frankfurter Ausgabe (FA).

Schmid, M. J. (1998), 'Speaking *Personae* in Pindar's Epinikia', *CFC* 8:147–84.

Schmid, Wilhelm (1929), *Geschichte der griechischen Literatur: Die griechische Literatur vor der attischen Hegemonie*. Vol. 1 Part 1 of Wilhelm Schmid and Otto Stählin, *Geschichte der griechischen Literatur*. Munich: C. H. Beck.

Schmidt, Jochen (1970), *Über Hölderlin*. Frankfurt a.M.: Insel.

Schmitz, Thomas (1993), *Pindar in der französischen Renaissance*. Göttingen: Vandenhoeck & Ruprecht.

Schrijvers, P. H. (2006), 'Silius Italicus and the Roman Sublime', in Nauta, van Dam and Smolenaars (2006, eds), 97–111.

Scullion, Scott (2002), '"Nothing to Do with Dionysus": Tragedy Misconceived as Ritual', *CQ* 52: 102–37.

Seaford, R. A. S. (1984), Cyclops *of Euripides*. Oxford: Oxford University Press.

Segal, Charles (1985), 'Choral Lyric in the Fifth Century', in Easterling and Knox (1985, eds), 222–44.

Seifert, Albrecht (1982), *Untersuchungen zu Hölderlins Pindar-Rezeption*. Munich: W. Fink.

Seifert, Albrecht (1982–83), 'Die Rheinhymne und ihr pindarisches Modell', *Hölderlin-Jahrbuch* 23: 79–133.

Shaw, Philip (2006), *The Sublime*. Abingdon and New York: Routledge.

Shen, Dan (2011), 'What is an Implied Author?', *Style* 45: 80–98.

Shepherd, Simon (2016), *The Cambridge Introduction to Peformance Theory*. Cambridge: Cambridge University Press.

Sider, David (2020), *Simonides: Epigrams and Elegies*. Oxford: Oxford University Press.

Sigelman, Asya C. (2016), *Pindar's Poetics of Immortality*. Cambridge: Cambridge University Press.

Silk, M. S. (1974), *Interaction in Poetic Imagery, With Special Reference to Early Greek Poetry*. Cambridge: Cambridge University Press.

Silk, M. S. (2001), 'Pindar Meets Plato: Theory, Language, Value, and the Classics', in Harrison (2001, ed.), 26–45.

Silk, M. S. (2003), 'Metaphor and Metonymy: Aristotle, Jakobson, Ricoeur, and Others', in Boys-Stones (2003, ed.), 115–48.

Silk, M. S. (2007), 'Pindar's Poetry as Poetry: A Literary Commentary on *Olympian* 12', in Hornblower and Morgan (2007, eds), 177–97.

Silk, M. S. (2009), 'Lyric and Lyrics: Perspectives, Ancient and Modern', in Budelmann (2009, ed.), 373–85.

Silk, M. S. (2010), 'The Language of Greek Lyric Poetry', in Bakker (2010, ed.), 424–40.

Silk, M. S. (forthcoming), *Poetic Language in Theory and Practice: Greek Archetypes and Modern Dilemmas*.

Silk, M. S., Ingo Gildenhard and Rosemary Barrow (2014), *The Classical Tradition: Art, Literature, Thought*. Chichester: Wiley Blackwell.

Slater, Niall W. (2017, ed.), *Voice and Voices in Antiquity*. Leiden and Boston: Brill.

Slater, W. J. (1969a), *Lexicon to Pindar*. Berlin: de Gruyter.

Slater, W. J. (1969b), 'Futures in Pindar', *CQ* 19: 86–94.

Slater, W. J. (1981), 'Peace, the Symposium and the Poet', *ICS* 6: 206–14.

Slater, W. J. (1983), 'Lyric Narrative: Structure and Principle', *ClAnt* 2: 117–32.

Slater, W. J. (1984), '*Nemean One:* The Victor's Return in Poetry and Politics', in Gerber (1984, ed.), 241–64.

Slater, W. J. (2000), 'Gnomology and Criticism', *GRBS* 41: 99–121.

Slings, S. R. (1990, ed.), *The Poet's I in Archaic Greek Lyric*. Amsterdam: VU University Press.

Snell, Bruno (1980), *Die Entdeckung des Geistes*. 5th edn. Göttingen: Vandenhoeck & Ruprecht. 1st edn 1946. Tr. T.G. Rosenmeyer (1953) as *The Discovery of the Mind*. Oxford: Basil Blackwell.

Sommerstein, Alan H. (1989), *Aeschylus:* Eumenides. Cambridge: Cambridge University Press.

Spelman, Henry (2018a), *Pindar and the Poetics of Permanence*. Oxford: Oxford University Press.

Spelman, Henry (2018b), 'Event and Artefact: The *Homeric Hymn to Apollo*, Archaic Lyric, and Early Greek Literary History', in Budelmann and Phillips (2018, eds), 151–71.

Spelman, Henry (2020), 'The View from Olympus: The Muses' Song in the *Homeric Hymn to Apollo*', *CQ* 70: 1–9.

Spelman, Henry (forthcoming), 'Classicising "Pindar"'.

Stafford, Emma (2007), 'Personification', in Ogden (2007, ed.), 71–85.

Stanford, W. Bedell (1936), *Greek Metaphor. Studies in Theory and Practice.* Oxford: Basil Blackwell.

Stehle, Eve (2017), 'The Construction of Authority in Pindar's *Isthmian 2* in Performance', in Bakker (2017, ed.), 8–33.

Steiner, Deborah (1986), *The Crown of Song. Metaphor in Pindar*. London: Duckworth.

Steiner, Deborah (2016), 'Harmonic Divergence: Pindar Fr. 140b and Early Fifth-Century Choral Polemics', *JHS* 136: 132–51.

Steiner, George (1975), *After Babel. Aspects of Language and Translation.* New York and London: Oxford University Press.

Steinrück, Martin (2004), 'Der reihende Prosastil (εἰρομένη) und sein Verhältnis zur Periode', *RhMus* 147: 109–35.

Stoneman, Richard (1981), 'Ploughing a Garland: Metaphor and Metonymy in Pindar', *Maia* 33: 125–38.

Stoneman, Richard (2014), *Pindar*. London and New York: I.B. Tauris.

Sullivan, Shirley Darcus (1995), *Psychological and Ethical Ideas: What Early Greeks Say*. Leiden: Brill.

Sullivan, Shirley Darcus (2002). 'Aspects of the Fictive "I" in Pindar: Address to Psychic Entities', *Emerita* 70: 83–102.

Swift, Laura (2019), *Archilochus: The Poems*. Oxford: Oxford University Press.

Thomas, R., 'Fame, Memorial, and Choral Poetry: The Origins of Epinikian Poetry – An Historical Study', in Hornblower and Morgan (2007, eds), 141–66.

Tissoni, Francesco (2014), 'Pindarus', in Dinkova-Bruun, Hankins and Kaster (2014, eds), 1–125. http://catalogustranslationum.org/PDFs/volume10/v10_pindarus.pdf (accessed 10 May 2021).

Tomory, Peter A. (1971), 'John Hamilton Mortimer and Salvator Rosa', *The Burlington Magazine* 113 no. 818: 276.

Trédé-Boulmer, Monique (2015), *«Kairos»: Là-propos et l'occasion: le mot et la notion, d'Homère à la fin du IVe siècle avant J.-C.* Paris: Les Belles Lettres.

Versnel, H. S. (1990), *Inconsistencies in Greek and Roman Religion 1. Ter unus: Isis, Dionysos, Hermes: Three Studies in Henotheism*. Leiden: Brill.

Versnel, H. S. (1993), *Inconsistencies in Greek and Roman Religion 2. Transition and Reversal in Myth and Ritual*. Leiden: Brill.

Veyne, Paul (1988), *Did the Greeks Believe in their Myths? An Essay on the Constitutive Imagination*. Tr. Paula Wissing. Chicago: University of Chicago Press. French original 1983.

Vogel, Martin (1966), *Apollinisch und Dionysisch. Geschichte eines genialen Irrtums*. Regensburg: Gustav Bosse.

Vöhler, Martin (2005), *Pindarrezeptionen. Sechs Studien zum Wandel des Pindarverständnisses von Erasmus bis Herder*. Heidelberg: Universitätsverlag Winter.

Voigt, Eva-Maria (1971), *Sappho et Alcaeus*. Amsterdam: Polak & Van Gennep.

Voltaire (1769, ed.), *Dictionnaire philosophique. La raison par alphabet*, 6th edn. 2 vols. Geneva: Cramer.

Wackernagel, Jacob (2009), *Lectures on Syntax: With Special Reference to Greek, Latin, and Germanic*. Tr. David Langslow. Oxford: Oxford University Press. German original 1920–24, 2nd edn 1926–28.

Walde, Christine, in collaboration with Brigitte Egger (2012), *The Reception of Classical Literature*. Ed. and tr. Duncan Smart and Matthijs H. Wihier. Leiden and Boston: Brill.

Waller, A. R. (1905, ed.), *Abraham Cowley: Poems*. Cambridge: Cambridge University Press.

Walsh, George B. (1984), *The Varieties of Enchantment. Early Greek Views on the Nature and Function of Poetry*. Chapel Hill and London: University of North Carolina Press.

Ward, Charles E. (1942, ed.), *The Letters of John Dryden*. Durham: Duke University Press.

Węcowski, Marek (2018), 'When did the Symposion Die? On the Decline of the Greek Aristocratic Banquet', in van den Eijnde, Blok and Strootman (2018, eds), 257–72.

Weiskel, Thomas (1976), *The Romantic Sublime*. Baltimore and London: Johns Hopkins University Press.

West, M. L. (1983), *The Orphic Poems*. Oxford: Clarendon Press.

West, M. L. (2007), *Indo-European Poetry and Myth*. Oxford: Oxford University Press.

West, M. L. (2011–13), *Hellenica. Selected Papers on Greek Literature and Thought*. 3 vols. Oxford: Oxford University Press.

West, M. L. (2011), 'The Invention of Homer', in West (2011–13) 1.408–36.

West, M. L. (2013), 'Pindar as a Man of Letters', in West (2011–13) 2.129–50.

Wilamowitz-Moellendorff, Ulrich von (1922), *Pindaros*. Berlin: Weidmann.

Wilamowitz-Moellendorff, Ulrich von (1931–32), *Der Glaube der Hellenen*. 2 vols. Berlin: Weidmann.

Wilamowitz-Moellendorff, Ulrich von (1962), *Kleine Schriften* vol. 4. Ed. Kurt Latte. Berlin: Akadamie-Verlag.

Willcock, M. M. (1964), 'Mythological Paradeigma in the *Iliad*', *CQ* 14: 141–54.

Willcock, M. M. (1995), *Pindar: Victory Odes. Olympians 2, 7 and 11, Nemean 4, Isthmians 3, 4 and 7*. Cambridge: Cambridge University Press.

Williamson, Margaret (2009), 'Sappho and Pindar in the Nineteenth and Twentieth Centuries', in Budelmann (2009, ed.), 352–70.

Wilshire, Bruce (1982), *Role Playing and Identity: The Limits of Theatre as Metaphor*. Bloomington: Indiana University Press.

Wilson, Adrian (2004), 'Foucault on the "Question of the Author": A Critical Exegesis', *MLR* 99: 339–363.

Wilson, Penelope (1974), *The Knowledge and Appreciation of Pindar in the Seventeenth and Eighteenth Centuries*. Diss. Oxford. https://ora.ox.ac.uk/objects/uuid:31023cda-7015-45b5-a5c4-0d27808bad69 (accessed 28 April 2021).

Wilson, Penelope (1980), 'Pindar and his Reception in Antiquity', *PCPS* 26: 97–114.

Wilson, Penelope (1989), '"High Pindaricks upon Stilts": A Case-Study in the Eighteenth-Century Classical Tradition', in Clarke (1989, ed.), 23–41.

Wilson, Penelope (2012), 'Pindar and Eighteenth-Century English Poetry', in Agócs, Carey and Rawles (2012a, eds), 157–68.

Wollstonecraft, Mary (1989), *The Works of Mary Wollstonecraft*. Ed. Janet Todd and Marilyn Butler. 7 vols. London: William Pickering.

Woodbury, Leonard E. (1955), 'The Tongue and the Whetstone: Pindar *Ol.* 6.82–83', *TAPA* 86: 31–9. Reprinted in Woodbury (1991), 72–9.

Woodbury, Leonard E. (1991), *Collected Writings*. Ed. Christopher G. Brown, Robert L. Fowler, Emmet I. Robbins and Philippa M. Wallace Matheson. Atlanta: Scholars Press.

Wright, George T. (1974), 'The Lyric Present: Simple Present Verbs in English Poems', *PMLA* 89: 563–79.

Wright, Matthew (2012), *The Comedian as Critic. Greek Old Comedy and Poetics*. Bristol Classical Press: London.

Young, David C. (1968), *Three Odes of Pindar. A Literary Study of* Pythian *11,* Pythian *3, and* Olympian *7*. Leiden: Brill.

Young, David C. (1987), 'Pindar and Horace against the Telchines (*Ol.* 7.53 & *Carm.* 4.4.33)', *AJP* 108: 152–7.

Young, David C. (1993), '"Something Like the Gods": A Pindaric Theme and the Myth of *Nemean* 10', *GRBS* 34: 123–32.

Zanker, Andreas T. (2019), *Metaphor in Homer. Time, Speech, and Thought.* Cambridge: Cambridge University Press.

Zellmann-Rohrer, Michael (2014), 'A Greek Inscription in a Portrait by Salvator Rosa', *Metropolitan Museum Journal* 49: 187–92

# Index of Passages

Aeschylus *Agamemnon* 82: 215 n.162.
126–55: 171. 456: 130. 839: 215
n.162. 928: 121. 938–9: 130.
1535–6: 217 n.22. *Choephori*
306–12: 217 n.22. 909–11: 217
n.22. *Eumenides* 130: 219 n.31.
956–67: 218 n.22, 218 n.25.
1045–6: 217 n.22. *Persians*
571–4: 212 n.140. *Prometheus*
*Bound* 366–72: 203 n.2. 516: 217
n.22. 545–52: 118. *Seven Against*
*Thebes* 975–7: 217 n.22.
*Suppliant Women* 697: 222 n.85.
742: 210 n.109. fr. 154a.9: 215
n.165. fr. 399: 118.
Alcaeus fr. 298: 172.
Alcman *PMGF* 1.50–1: 110. 3: 78, 112.
13(a).9: 209 n.104. 16.2: 209
n.104. 39: 67, 208 n.86. 64: 217
n.17. 145: 208 n.91.
Anaximander *Vors.* 12 B1: 148.
Apollonius of Rhodes 4.1730: 215 n.172.
Archilochus fr. 16: 148. fr. 19: 87. frr.120–1:
205 n.49. fr. 128: 121. fr. 131:
121. fr. 295: 90.
Aristides *Oration* 3.191: 216 n.1.
Aristophanes *Acharnians* 410–13: 208
n.84. 480–8: 113. 633–40: 2.
*Birds* 904–53: 2. 1321: 154.
*Clouds* 526: 210 n.115. 535: 210
n.115. *Frogs*: 91. 674: 210 n.115.
780: 99. 882: 99. *Knights*
1323–30: 2. *Peace* 799: 99.
*Thesmophoriazusae* 148–70: 208
n.84. *Wasps* 1049: 210 n.115. fr.
694: 208 n.84.
Aristotle *Poetics* 4 p.1448b11: 133. 21 p.
1457b7: 184. *Rhetoric* 3.9
p.1409a24–b12: 41–2.
Athenaeus *Professors at Dinner* 2.13 p. 40f,
13.17 p. 564d: 3.
Auden, W.H. 'September 1, 1939': 87.

Aulus Gellius *Attic Nights* 17.10.8: 195
n.11, 203 n.2.

Bacchylides
*Epinicians 1* 1: 222 n.85. 51: 212 n.137.
53: 212 n.137. *2* 205 n.39. 9: 212
n.137. *3* 9: 205 n.39. 13–21: 219
n.35. 38: 168. 63–6: 158. 85–7:
98. 85–98: 211 n.118. 98: 211
n.118. *4* 4–10: 205 n.39. 7: 222
n.85. 8: 211 n.118. *5*: 80. 1–31:
211 n.118. 3–6: 210 n.110. 11:
211 n.118. 11–16: 99. 187–90:
214 n.154. 195: 213 n.154. *6* 10:
222 n.85. *8* 20–1: 213 n.154. *9* 3:
211 n.116, 211 n.118. 103–4: 206
n.52, 206 n.54, 212 n.140, 213
n.151. *10* 10: 211 n.118. 39: 210
n.113. 51–2: 214 n.154. 52–6:
206 n.52, 212 n.140, 213 n.151.
*11* 12–13: 206 n.52, 206 n.54.
17–21: 205 n.39. *12* 1: 210 n.113.
3: 212 n.132, 212 n.137. 37: 205
n.39, 206 n.54. *13* 74: 206 n.52,
206 n.54. 190–202: 206 n.64, 212
n.140. 201: 212 n.140. 204: 210
n.113. 221–31: 211 n.118. 224:
205 n.44. 231: 213 n.151. *14* 20:
214 n.154. *14B* 10: 222 n.85.
*Dithyrambs* 15 (*Dith. 1*) 24: 210 n.113.
47: 214 n.157. *16* (*Dith. 2*) 13:
212 n.136. *17* (*Dith. 3*) 66: 222
n.85. 130–1: 203 n.5. *19* (*Dith. 5*)
8–11: 213 n.153. 11–14: 99. *20*
(*Dith. 6*) 8: 222 n.85. *29a* 1: 222
n.85.
*Fragments* 5: 97. 5.1: 210 n.113. 14.3:
210 n.113. 20B.1: 213 n.145.
20C.15: 205 n.39, 206 n.54.

*Carmina Popularia PMG* 871.1: 220 n.45.
Choricius *Oration* 29.48: 216 n.1.

Cicero *On the Ends of Good and Evil*
    2.115: 194 n.3. *The Orator* 4: 194
    n.3.
Coleridge, Samuel Taylor *Biographia*
    *Literaria* 18: 196 n.20.
Critias *Vors.* 88 B44: 90.

Demetrius *On Style* 36–127: 4. 100: 53.
    240–304: 194 n.8. 283: 53.
Democritus *Vors.* 68 B26: 224 n.104.
Derveni Papyrus col. 47.9 §21 Janko /
    Kotwick: 209 n.106.
Dionysius of Halicarnassus *Demosthenes*
    22: 53. 38: 194 n.6. 38–9: 194 n.7.
    *Lysias* 13: 194 n.7. *On Imitation*
    6.2: 3. *On the Composition of*
    *Words* 22: 3, 41.
Dryden, John *Love Triumphant* IV 1.83–6:
    196 n.19.

Empedocles *Vors.* 31 A29: 146. B11: 214
    n.159.
Epicharmus fr. 100: 154.
*Etymologicum Magnum* p.11.32 Gaisford:
    215 n.173.
Euripides *Alcestis* 962: 99. *Andromache*
    745: 215 n.162. *Helen* 560: 148.
    *Medea* 1086: 99. 1224: 215 n.165.
    *Phoenician Women* 1543–5: 215
    n.162. 1722: 215 n.162. *The Mad*
    *Heracles* 112–13: 215 n.162. fr.
    25.1: 215 n.162. fr. 494.18: 218
    n.22. fr. 509: 215 n.162.
Eustathius on Homer *Il.* 20.66 p.1196.37:
    194 n.4. *Preface to Pindar*
    3.298.9 Drachmann: 216 n.1.

Gorgias *Vors.* 82 B11.10: 203 n.4.

Hecataeus fr. 19 *EGM*: 66.
Heraclitus *Vors.* 22 A10: 146. A22: 208
    n.86. B10: 146. B32: 224 n.104.
    B42: 208 n.86. B48: 224 n.104.
    B49a: 119. B50: 146. B56–7: 208
    n.86. B62: 224 n.104. B65: 224
    n.104. B67: 224 n.104. B88: 119.
    B104: 208 n.86.
Hermogenes *On Kinds of Style* 1.6: 195
    n.11.

Herodotus 1.5: 221 n.71. 1.29–33: 121. 1.60:
    220 n.47. 2.29: 110. 3.52.5: 129.
    6.105–6: 220 n.47. 6.127.3: 166.
Hesiod
    *Theogony* 147. 1: 109. 22: 91. 27: 91.
    36–52: 123. 135: 155. 360: 217
    n.17. 371: 155. 488: 214 n.159.
    901–2: 148. 905: 217 n.21.
    *Works and Days* 91. 40: 214 n.159.
    90–105: 141. 167–73: 142.
    287–92: 148. 456: 214 n.159.
    654–9: 208 n.86. 1
    *Fragments* 306: 209 n.104.
Hipponax frr. 32.4, 36.2, 37, 79.9, 117.4:
    208 n.86.
Hölderlin, Friedrich 'As when on a
    holiday': 188. 'Bread and wine':
    42–3, 49. 'Fragment of
    Philosophical Letters': 35–6.
    '*Frankfurt Aphorisms*': 32–3, 41.
    *Hyperion*: 32, 36–7. '*My resolve*':
    36. *Night-Songs*: 32. 'When the
    poet gains mastery of his spirit':
    33. Translations of Pindar:
    37–41.
Homer
    *Iliad* 1.8: 214 n.157. 1.34: 220 n.50.
    1.286: 223 n.103. 1.349–50: 220
    n.50. 2.23: 220 n.52. 2.38: 214
    n.159. 2.455–84: 185. 2.484: 214
    n.157. 2.488–90: 182. 2.761–2:
    214 n.157. 5.304: 156. 5.406: 214
    n.159. 5.703: 115. 8.273: 115.
    9.524–99: 171. 11.218: 214 n.157.
    12.309–28: 164. 14.508: 214
    n.157. 15.697: 110. 16.433–42:
    149. 19.87: 149. 20.127: 149.
    20.233–5: 142. 23.59–62: 220
    n.50. 23.69: 220 n.52. 23.787:
    210 n.109. 24.49: 149. 24.209–10:
    149. 24.407: 223 n.103. 24.527–
    33: 121, 141.
    *Odyssey* 1.1: 109. 1.10: 109. 1.323: 140.
    1.337: 203 n.4. 2.260–1: 220
    n.50. 3.254 = 16.61: 223 n.103.
    4.266: 223 n.103. 4.475: 149.
    4.804: 220 n.52. 5.40: 149. 5.345:
    149. 7.197: 149. 8.74: 93.
    8.497–8: 93. 9.408: 120. 9.460:

120. 9.515: 120. 10.495: 117.
11.207: 117–18. 11.222: 117.
11.298–304: 166. 11.507: 223
n.103. 18.136–7: 121. 19.592:
149. 20.76: 149.
*Homeric Hymn to Aphrodite* 223: 214
n.159.
*Homeric Hymn to Apollo* 31: 213 n.145.
149–52: 206 n.62. 166–73: 93,
208 n.86. 189–93: 123. 202: 122.
483: 209 n.104.
Horace *Epodes* 16.66: 195 n.17. *Odes*
1.1.35–6: 8, 195 n.17. 2.20: 2.
3.1.45–6: 2. 3.25.1: 8. 4.2: 2.
4.2.10: 8. 4.6.44: 195 n.17.

Ibycus S151.23: 209 n.104. S151.48: 208
n.86.

Keats, John *Endymion* ii.739: 70.

Libanius *Oration* 64.13: 216 n.1.
*Life of Pindar* 1.2.2, 1.5.10, 1.9.9
Drachmann: 216 n.1.
Longinus *On the Sublime* 1.3: 50–1. 1.4: 10,
50, 51. 5: 177. 7.2: 55. 8.1: 51. 9.2:
51. 9.9: 51. 9.10: 53. 10: 48. 10.5:
53. 26: 110, 213 n.141. 30.1: 51.
32: 184. 33: 4, 13, 194 n.3. 33.2:
51. 34.4: 51, 53. 35.3–4: 10. 35.4:
4, 60. 36.1: 10, 51. 36.3: 52. 36.4:
52. 39–42: 42. 39.2: 61. 39.3: 61.
Lucian *Encomium of the Fly* 5: 194 n.4.
Lucretius *On the Nature of Things*
2.639–702: 203 n.2.

Macrobius *Saturnalia* 5.17.8: 195 n.11.
Mimnermus fr. 6: 66.

Old Testament *1 Kings* 19:13: 165. *Exodus*
3: 165. *Genesis* 1:3: 51. *Genesis*
22: 165.
Ovid *Metamorphoses* 5.346–56: 203 n.2.

*Palatine Anthology* 7.34, 9.571, 16.305: 3.
Parmenides *Vors.* 28 B8.5–6: 146.
B8.38–41, 53–4: 224 n.104.
Pausanias *Description of Greece* 2.11.4: 218
n.22. 2.29: 220 n.46.

Petronius *Satyricon* 2.4: 194 n.3.
Pherecydes of Syros *Vors.* 7 B1: 148.
Philostratus *Images* 2.12: 216 n.1.
Pindar
*Olympians*
*1* 80. 1–7: 10–11, 49, 107, 111, 113,
210 n.109. 5: 213 n.153. 8–11: 98.
10: 205 n.45. 14: 80. 16: 212
n.138. 17–18: 64, 68, 76, 113, 212
n.130, 213 n.142. 23–5: 49. 26:
218 n.23. 28–34: 223 n.101. 29:
223 n.89. 33–4: 218 n.26. 52: 114.
67–87: 164. 97–100: 215 n.171.
100–3: 114, 209 n.100. 110: 194
n.1. 111: 205 n.45. 112: 194 n.1,
214 n.158. 114: 213 n.142, 220
n.43. 115–16: 97.
*2* 82, 142, 146, 159. 1–2: 107, 111,
113, 179. 10: 150, 218 n.28. 13:
203 n.5. 17: 218 n.26. 18–22: 218
n.27. 21: 218 n.23. 25–30: 219
n.39. 31–4: 110. 33: 212 n.139.
35: 218 n.23. 47: 78, 205 n.37. 53:
223 n.89. 54: 125. 68–83: 224 n.2.
70: 73. 78–9: 158. 83: 194 n.1.
83–8: 98–9, 182, 197 n.41. 85:
209 n.106. 86: 3. 88: 194 n.1. 89:
111, 113, 194 n.1, 213 n.153. 92:
223 n.101. 98: 182, 214 n.159.
*3* 70–3, 156. 4: 214 n.158. 5: 68. 6:
79. 7: 213 n.152, 213 n.154. 8:
211 n.130. 32: 73, 224 n.2. 34:
204 n.33. 38: 213 n.154. 42: 210
n.109. 45: 213 n.154.
*4* 2: 205 n.45, 209 n.102. 4: 209
n.100. 9: 77, 206 n.55. 16: 126.
17: 213 n.154, 223 n.101.
*5* 19: 205 n.45, 212 n.130. 21: 223
n.89. 24: 111, 143, 213 n.142, 220
n.43.
*6* 76–7. 1–4: 102, 114, 188. 7: 128. 21:
112, 214 n.158, 223 n.101. 22–7:
203 n.16. 27: 114. 42: 218 n.23.
46–7: 224 n.2. 52–5: 194 n.1.
57–66: 164–5. 82–3: 180, 182,
185–6, 213 n.154. 85–92: 213
n.150. 86: 209 n.98. 87–92: 206
n.64. 90: 96, 204 n.20. 91: 214
n.158. 97: 218 n.27. 98: 206 n.55.

*7* 173–7, 204 n.34. 1: 211 n.123. 1–6: 80. 1–14: 102–5, 106, 188. 7: 214 n.158. 8: 209 n.101. 11–13: 211 n.130. 13–14: 76. 16: 213 n.154. 21: 221 n.70. 33–7: 171. 61–70: 176, 224 n.2. 64: 218 n.23. 93: 80.

*8* 10: 79, 203 n.11, 206 n.55. 15: 217 n.19. 28–9: 218 n.27. 30: 220 n.46. 67: 153. 74: 114. 86: 219 n.43.

*9* 1–4: 205 n.39. 5: 194 n.1, 214 n.158. 6: 213 n.142. 11: 194 n.1, 213 n.142. 13: 212 n.130. 14: 213 n.142. 22: 4, 194 n.1, 215 n.171. 25: 150, 209 n.101. 29: 214 n.159. 36: 213 n.153. 36–48: 110. 38: 97, 124. 60: 218 n.28. 81: 114, 194 n.1, 213 n.154. 82: 205 n.44, 209 n.102. 83: 205 n.45, 209 n.100. 98: 203 n.1. 100: 3. 111: 213 n.142. 112: 73.

*10* 1–6: 108, 110, 112, 114, 183, 210 n.113, 212 n.140. 7–8: 151. 9: 194 n.1. 12: 212 n.132. 52: 218 n.23. 55: 218 n.26. 60: 115. 73–7: 205 n.39. 77: 205 n.37. 78–85: 213 n.150. 85: 209 n.98. 85–90: 112. 91–3: 106. 93–105: 105–7, 114. 98: 194 n.1.

*11* 205 n.39. 8: 212 n.139. 10: 210 n.112, 210 n.112. 14–16: 112–13, 212 n.140. 16–19: 213 n.151. 17: 214 n.158. 39: 216 n.178.

*12* 151–3. 6: 141. 10–12: 218 n.27.

*13* 165. 2: 128. 11–12: 213 n.154. 16–17: 218 n.28. 18–22: 115. 25: 219 n.43. 29: 79, 205 n.37, 206 n.55. 44–6: 96. 46: 182. 47–9: 124, 223 n.99. 48: 216 n.178. 49: 96. 91: 112. 91–5: 213 n.154. 93: 194 n.1. 96: 214 n.158. 97: 205 n.45. 114: 207 n.65, 213 n.142.

*14* 74. 7: 210 n.112. 9: 207 n.65. 13: 122. 16: 206 n.55. 17: 207 n.65.

*Pythians*
*1* 1–4: 68–9, 81, 212 n.130, 213 n.145. 1–26: 59–63, 122, 224 n.2. 41: 209 n.105. 42: 210 n.112. 44: 194 n.1, 223 n.101. 46: 218 n.27.

51: 209 n.100. 55: 150. 58: 214 n.158. 61–6: 130. 70: 126. 81–100: 127–32. 82: 216 n.178. 86: 186. 90: 219 n.35. 92: 209 n.100. 97–8: 81. 99: 206 n.52, 220 n.43.

*2* 3: 209 n.98. 4: 205 n.45, 209 n.102. 52: 114. 52–6: 90. 54: 209 n.105. 68: 209 n.101. 71: 212 n.130. 72: 216 n.183. 82: 128.

*3* 172. 1–3: 108–9, 114, 210 n.112. 23: 141. 36: 172. 38–44: 224 n.2. 40–1: 212 n.132. 59–60: 220 n.43. 60: 212 n.139. 61: 111, 213 n.153. 61–2: 143, 219 n.42, 220 n.43. 63–9: 109, 209 n.100. 65: 212 n.132. 68: 128, 205 n.45. 68–77: 96, 204 n.20. 71: 128. 73: 77, 205 n.45. 76: 205 n.45. 78: 209 n.98, 216 n.1. 81: 141. 86: 217 n.19. 90: 115. 109: 209 n.105, 220 n.43. 113: 97. 114: 212 n.138.

*4* 1: 69. 2–3: 205 n.51, 214 n.158. 27: 212 n.132. 28: 220 n.49. 66: 221 n.58. 67–72: 115. 102–19: 38, 224 n.2. 105: 200 n.100. 110: 212 n.132. 138: 210 n.113. 145: 218 n.25. 150: 212 n.132. 248: 210 n.112, 216 n.178. 277–99: 100. 279: 183, 214 n.158. 286: 125, 216 n.178. 296: 126. 297: 128. 299: 96, 204 n.20, 209 n.98.

*5* 206 n.63. 3: 217 n.19. 22: 206 n.55, 206 n.64. 24: 75. 25: 217 n.13. 27–9: 148. 45: 4, 194 n.1, 215 n.171. 72–81: 101. 76: 218 n.23. 80: 212 n.138. 93–8: 75. 80: 73. 95: 158. 100: 205 n.51. 103–4: 206 n.64. 122–3: 221 n.58.

*6* 1: 110. 1–4: 80. 46–9: 219 n.35. 52–54: 80.

*7* 5: 214 n.159.

*8* 1–20: 125–6, 154. 33: 213 n.152. 34: 209 n.105. 5: 206 n.55. 20: 206 n.55. 29–33: 213 n.154, 216 n.178, 223 n.99. 31: 212 n.130. 32: 220 n.43. 34: 194 n.1. 53: 153. 56–60: 140, 220 n.49. 71: 219 n.43. 88–100: 116–23. 90: 141.

95–6: 117, 214 n.159. 97: 218 n.28. 98: 100.

*9* 172. 26–65: 224 n.2. 62–5: 219 n.39. 73–5: 112, 213 n.150. 76–9: 98, 124–5, 223 n.99. 89: 205 n.51. 90: 215 n.171. 92: 209 n.105. 95–6: 128. 103–4: 213 n.154.

*10* 1–6: 96, 125, 206 n.64. 4: 213 n.154. 6: 205 n.37. 9: 213 n.152. 19–31: 156–9. 20: 219 n.43. 27–9: 220 n.43. 31–40: 224 n.2. 38: 207 n.65. 39: 211 n.130. 43–4: 159, 219 n.43. 45: 71. 46: 73. 51: 213 n.142. 51–4: 180. 53: 78, 205 n.37. 55–8: 206 n.64, 209 n.98, 212 n.140, 213 n.150. 62: 220 n.43. 64: 205 n.44, 209 n.100. 65: 114, 194 n.1.

*11* 74. 38: 209 n.100, 212 n.140. 38–41: 114, 213 n.154. 50–8: 219 n.43. 51: 220 n.43. 62: 166.

*12* 5: 206 n.55. 30–2: 218 n.27. 19: 212 n.130. 27: 207 n.65.

Nemeans

*1* 7: 78, 194 n.1, 205 n.37. 13: 213 n.142. 18–22: 75–6, 125. 31–2: 219 n.35. 46: 151. 61–72: 171, 224 n.2. 69: 151.

*2* 7: 179. 8: 218 n.28. 24–5: 77, 205 n.51. 25: 113, 213 n.151.

*3* 161–3. 1–12: 112, 206 n.64. 3–5: 203 n.11. 5: 205 n.51. 9: 212 n.132. 11: 209 n.98. 12: 211 n.130. 26–31: 213 n.153. 27: 194 n.1. 28: 115. 31: 111. 40: 3. 41–3: 197 n.41. 47–9: 224 n.2. 64: 215 n.171. 73: 212 n.139. 75: 218 n.28, 220 n.43. 76: 209 n.100. 77: 209 n.101. 79: 211 n.130. 80–2: 194 n.1.

*4* 1–8: 78–9. 3: 203 n.4. 4: 153. 7: 153. 11: 78. 11–12: 79, 206 n.55. 33: 216 n.178. 33–5: 213 n.154, 223 n.99. 36–8: 96. 37: 212 n.139, 213 n.142. 42: 217 n.19. 43: 218 n.26. 44: 212 n.130, 213 n.145. 49: 158. 61: 150. 69: 213 n.142. 69–72: 182, 184, 213 n.154. 74: 205 n.45, 209 n.100. 77: 212 n.132.

*5* 1–5: 108, 111. 2: 194 n.1. 3: 213 n.145. 14–21: 213 n.154. 21: 194 n.1. 23: 115, 207 n.65. 50–4: 213 n.142, 213 n.151.

*6* 1–8: 120, 169, 212 n.139. 6: 217 n.19. 24: 153. 27: 216 n.178. 28: 214 n.158, 223 n.101. 32: 78, 205 n.37, 214 n.158. 37–8: 205 n.39, 215 n.171. 53–7: 213 n.154. 55: 220 n.43. 57b: 205 n.45.

*7* 100, 223 n.100. 1: 218 n.23. 4: 212 n.139. 5: 212 n.139. 11–16: 16. 12: 194 n.1. 14: 212 n.139. 22: 209 n.105. 23: 97, 182. 34: 205 n.45, 213 n.142. 44: 150. 50–3: 223 n.99. 54: 212 n.139. 57: 218 n.23. 58: 125. 61: 209 n.100. 61–9: 223 n.101. 62: 194 n.1. 65: 205 n.44, 209 n.100. 67–8: 218 n.27. 69: 205 n.45. 70–9: 181. 71: 194 n.1. 75–81: 213 n.142. 77: 214 n.158. 85: 101. 87: 212 n.139.

*8* 74. 13–16: 181, 184. 19: 207 n.65. 38: 128. 35–42: 220 n.43. 40–2: 194 n.1. 50: 78, 205 n.37, 221 n.68.

*9* 1–3: 77, 203 n.11, 205 n.51. 1–10: 213 n.149. 6–10: 213 n.154. 8: 211 n.130. 10: 112. 33: 213 n.154. 44–7: 220 n.43. 50: 77, 213 n.142. 52: 179, 222 n.88. 53–5: 77, 96, 194 n.1, 213 n.151, 214 n.158.

*10* 165–9, 204 n.34. 7: 158. 18: 158. 18–22: 213 n.154. 19: 182. 20: 216 n.178. 21–2: 203 n.11, 212 n.130, 213 n.142. 23: 73. 26: 214 n.158. 29–30: 221 n.58. 33–5: 205 n.39, 205 n.51. 35–6: 177. 52: 73. 82: 220 n.45. 83–90: 219 n.39.

*11* 82, 206 n.63. 3: 206 n.55. 13–16: 220 n.43. 18: 180. 44: 212 n.139.

Isthmians

*1* 1: 209 n.98. 1–6: 213 n.154. 1–10: 206 n.64. 7: 206 n.65. 41–6: 114. 45: 210 n.112. 52–7: 213 n.154. 62: 216 n.178. 62–3: 213 n.154, 223 n.99. 64–5: 194 n.1. 67–8: 219 n.35.

*2* 74, 82, 206 n.63. 2: 114, 194 n.1.
18: 221 n.58. 22: 125. 30–2: 206
n.52. 35: 194 n.1. 37: 128. 47: 96,
204 n.20, 209 n.101, 213 n.151.
48: 209 n.100.

*3* 4–5: 221 n.58. 7–8: 77, 114, 205
n.51. 15: 212 n.140. 18: 218 n.28.

*4* 204 n.34. 2: 209 n.105. 13: 213
n.142. 35: 212 n.140. 37–9:
182–3. 43: 194 n.1, 214 n.158,
215 n.171. 55: 158. 62: 73, 212
n.138. 72: 205 n.51. 74: 77, 213
n.151.

*5* 160. 1–16: 154–6, 178. 12–15: 206
n.52, 220 n.43. 14: 143. 21–2: 76,
205 n.45, 209 n.102. 24: 213
n.142. 27: 211 n.130. 28: 97. 34:
213 n.142. 38–9: 213 n.142.
39–42: 115. 51: 213 n.142. 53:
217 n.13, 221 n.58. 62–3: 213
n.142, 213 n.151. 63: 194 n.1,
209 n.101.

*6* 160–1. 1–7: 160, 188. 10–13: 206
n.52, 220 n.43. 18: 218 n.23.
19–21: 213 n.154. 21: 205 n.45,
209 n.102. 23: 184. 46: 212 n.132.
52–4: 161, 224 n.2. 57: 77, 114,
205 n.45. 58: 205 n.51. 58–9: 213
n.154, 223 n.99. 74–5: 188, 209
n.98, 213 n.151, 214 n.158.

*7* 18: 97. 19: 194 n.1. 20: 205 n.51,
213 n.142. 23: 194 n.1, 215
n.171. 39–42: 219–20 n.43. 41:
150, 218 n.28. 42: 212 n.139. 44:
143, 220 n.43. 49: 212 n.138.

*8* 1–4: 203 n.11, 212 n.140. 1–8: 213
n.149. 4: 205 n.51. 5: 104, 213
n.154. 6: 209 n.98, 214 n.158. 8:
212 n.138. 10: 212 n.138. 12: 220
n.43. 14: 218 n.28. 16: 209 n.98,
213 n.154. 31–5a: 150. 35a: 171.
47: 97. 61: 114, 194 n.1. 62: 212
n.140.

*Dithyrambs* 1.14: 214 n.158. 2.23–5: 97,
214 n.158.

*Paeans* 1.6: 218 n.28. 2.27: 218 n.27.
2.73–5: 171, 221 n.61. 4.32–5:
220 n.43. 4.40–53: 221 n.61.
4.50: 213 n.153. 6: 223 n.100. 6.6:

99, 144. 6.9: 205 n.45. 6.92–5:
150. 6.122: 212 n.140. 6.128:
212 n.136. 6.132: 217 n.13.
7b.10–20: 203 n.16. 7b.13–14:
114. 7b.16–17: 97. 8a.14–23: 221
n.61. 12.17: 218 n.23. 18.3: 210
n.112.

*Partheneia* 1.11: 209 n.100. 2.6–16: 213
n.149. 2.31: 223 n.89. 2.39: 205
n.45.

*Fragments* 29.7: 212 n.136. 30: 218 n.23.
31: 122–3, 206 n.62. 33: 218 n.26.
38: 153. 39: 153. 40: 152–3. 41:
152. 71: 203 n.16. 75.1: 82. 76: 2.
78: 148. 85: 203 n.16. 89.1: 212
n.136. 94c: 82. 95–100: 137.
107a.3: 212 n.140. 109: 126. 115:
203 n.16. 122: 206 n.64. 122.6:
212 n.136. 123.2: 111, 213 n.153.
124a–b.2: 209 n.101. 126.2: 218
n.28. 127.4: 111, 213 n.153. 128c:
203 n.16. 129: 143. 131: 143, 218
n.28. 133: 143. 140b: 203 n.16.
140d: 146, 217 n.13. 141: 217
n.13. 150: 144, 211 n.116. 159:
218 n.26. 191: 68. 227: 194 n.1.

Plato *Laws* 652a–660a: 203 n.2. 653c–d:
81. 700a–701c: 203 n.2. *Republic*
398c–99e: 203 n.3. *Symposium*:
34, 37. 179e–180a: 168.

Plato Comicus fr. 96: 210 n.115.

Pliny *Natural History* 2.54: 2.

Plutarch *Moralia* 1103A: 216 n.1. *Numa*
4.8: 216 n.1.

Porphyry on Horace *Odes* 4.2.27–8: 2.

Proclus on Plato *Timaeus* 1.64: 194 n.4.

Quintilian *Institutes of Oratory* 8.6.71: 194
n.3. 10.1.61: 2.

Rosa, Salvator *Satires* 2.37–42: 138. 5.550:
216 n.2.

Sappho. fr. 1 ('Hymn to Aphrodite'): 48. fr.
2: 187. fr. 2.13–16: 103. fr. 16:
44–8. fr. 31: 48. fr. 55: 208 n.86.
fr. 56.2: 209 n.104. fr. 58A: 67. fr.
65: 67, 208 n.86. fr. 118.1: 213
n.145. fr. 147: 67. fr. 168B: 87.

Scholia on Pindar *O*.4.7h: 207 n.66.
P.3.139a: 216 n.1. P.8.99a: 207
n.66.
Scholion on Sophocles *Ajax* 124–5: 119,
215 n.165.
*SEG* 30.326: 218 n.22.
Seneca *Epistles* 79.7: 203 n.2.
Simonides T71a Poltera: 217 n.16.
*IEG*² fr. 11.15–18: 93. fr. 11.17: 223
n.103. fr. 19: 93. fr. 20.9: 214 n.159.
fr. 20.15: 217 n.16. fr. 88.1: 148.
*PMG* 511 fr. 1(a).5 = fr. 7a.3 Poltera:
222 n.85. 531.5 = fr. 261 Poltera:
217 n.16. 541.3-5 = fr. 256.3–5
Poltera: 210 n.109. 542 = fr. 260
Poltera: 208 n.86. 564 = fr. 273
Poltera: 66, 93. 579 = fr. 257
Poltera: 148. 581 = fr. 262
Poltera: 208 n.86.
Solon fr. 6.3: 148. fr. 13.52: 209 n.104. fr.
20: 66, 208 n.86. fr. 36.3: 148.
Sophocles *Ajax* 125–5: 119, 215 n.162.
*Antigone* 1170: 215 n.162, 215

n.165. *Electra* 474: 99. *Oedipus
at Colonus* 110: 215 n.162.
1627–8: 165. *Oedipus the King*
1528–30: 121. *Philoctetes*
946–7: 215 n.162, 215 n.165.
fr. 13: 215 n.162, 215 n.165.
fr. 895: 219 n.32. fr. 945.2: 215
n.162.
Statius *Silvae* 1.3.101: 194 n.3. 4.7.5–8: 194
n.3.
Stesichorus fr. 4: 66, 93. fr. 91a: 208 n.86.

Thales *Vors.* 10δ.17: 129. 11 A22: 217 n.11.
Theognis 19–23: 67, 92–3, 96, 209 n.104.
237–54: 92. 266–84: 203 n.5.
490: 211 n.123. 770: 209 n.104.
790: 209 n.104. 820–80: 203 n.6.
995: 209 n.104.

Virgil *Aeneid* 3.570–82: 203 n.2. 6.78: 8.

Xenophanes *Vors.* 21 A29–36: 146.
B10–12: 208 n.86. B23: 146

# Index of Names and Subjects

Addison, Joseph 9, 14
Adorno, Theodor 42–3, 49–50, 134,
    201 n.105
Aegina 100–1, 117
Aeschylus x, 110, 149–50, 179
aesthetics 19–31, 94, 123, 132–5, 190
aetiology 171, 173–4
Agócs, Peter 77
*aiglā* / αἴγλα (gleam) 122
Aion / Αἰών (Lifetime) 148, 150, 179,
    218 n.28
*alātheia* / ἀλάθεια (truth) 183
Alcaeus 83
Ankersmit, Frank 70
apostrophe 68–9, 111
Arcesilas of Cyrene 131
Archilochus 43, 90, 203 n.16
Aristeas 203 n.16
*arrhēta* / ἄρρητα (secret teachings)
    209 n.106
'arrival' motif 75, 96
*astoi* / ἀστοί (citizens) 128, 130
audience(s), *see* Pindar, and audience(s)
Auerbach, Erich 165
*aulos* / αὐλός (double pipe; 'flute') 106
Austin, J. L. 85
author, implied 89
author-function 91–4

Bacchylides
    compared with Pindar by Longinus 4
    and the *kōmos* 74–5, 79
    and performance 66
    unique words in 179, 222 n.85
    use of direct speech 170–1
    use of first-person pronoun 100,
        109–10; use of second-person
        pronoun, 110
Bakker, Egbert 92
Barrett, Spencer 105–6
Baudelaire, Charles 187
Benjamin, Walter 200 n.96

Bloom, Harold viii
Boileau-Despréaux, Nicolas 10–14, 18, 52,
    189
Booth, Stephen 69
Booth, Wayne 89
'break-off' points 111, 114, 115
Budelmann, Felix 46, 95
Bundy, Elroy 86, 112–13
Burke, Edmund 19–24, 51–3, 62, 133,
    184
Butler, Shane 186–7

Carey, Christopher 80, 123
Carne-Ross, David x
*charis,* Charites (Graces) 77, 103, 105–7,
    219 n.37
choral 'I' 84, 100, 109
chorus(es), choral performances 61–2,
    81–3, 99
Chronos / Χρόνος (Time) 148, 150–1
Clement of Alexandria 146
closure 40, 77–8, 168, 170
Cologne cathedral 23
Congreve, William 9–10, 196 n.22
Cowley, Abraham 7–10
Critias 90
Croesus 121, 128, 130, 158, 168
Culler, Jonathan 48, 68, 87, 111
Currie, Bruno 158, 168
Cyclops 119–20

D'Alessio, Giovan Battista 112, 114
daemon 17, 29–30
    *see also Geist*
deixis 68–9, 73, 79
'*dexai*'-motif 79
Diagoras of Rhodes 131, 177
Diderot, Denis, *Encyclopédie* 14–15, 26
Dionysius of Halicarnassus 3–4, 41
Dioscuri 70–3, 165–9
Dorian, Dorians 68, 130
Dryden, John 9–10, 14

*elpis* / ἐλπίς (hope) 141, 153
Empedocles 146
*enargeia* / ἐνάργεια (vividness) 164–5, 176
encomia, in Alexandrian sense 82
*enkōmios* / ἐγκώμιος (in the *kōmos*) 78
Enlightenment, the 5, 23
enthusiasm 7, 14–15, 24, 26, 32–3, 51
envy, *see phthonos*
*epāmeros* / ἐπάμερος (ephemeral) 118,
    121, 214 n.159
epic, Greek, as genre 44, 183
epinician, as compensation for labour 177
epinician, as genre 50, 79, 93, 104, 115,
    143–4, 173, 183
epiphany 163–9, 170
Erinyes 149–50
Etna, Mount 4, 60
*euphrosunā* / εὐφροσύνα (good cheer)
    78–9
event 68, 79
exemplarity 104, 106–7, 113, 156, 171
    *see also* 'I', exemplary
extratextual and intratextual 77, 104
    *see also* Pindar, his persona in the text

Fate, *see* Potmos; Moira(i)
Ferrari, Franco 75
'fidelity' and 'farewell' 104–7, 130
Finley, Moses 132
first-person pronoun 100; singular vs
    plural, 108–10
Fortune, *see* Tyche
Foucault, Michel 91, 93–4
Fränkel, Hermann 43, 155
future, epinician or performative 77, 111–12

*galimatias* (gibberish) 10, 13–14, 32,
    197 n.31
*Geist* (spirit) 17–18, 31, 33
    *see also* daemon
genealogy 143, 147
genius 6, 15–17, 26
Gentili, Bruno 117–18
gods, Greek, nature of 138–42
Goethe, Johann Wolfgang von 18–19
Gontard, Susette 37
Graces, *see charis*, Charites
Gray, Thomas 2, 10
Greene, Roland 95

Halliwell, Stephen 52–3, 123
Hamburger, Käte 85, 94
*hapax legomena* / ἅπαξ λεγόμενα (unique
    words) 71, 78, 79, 103, 178–9,
    223 n.89
*harmoniā* / ἁρμονία (tuning, harmony)
    61–3, 82
Hegel, Georg Wilhelm Friedrich 30–1
Heidegger, Martin 201 n.105
Helios 176
Hellingrath, Norbert von 41
*hen kai pan* / ἓν καὶ πάν (One and All)
    145–6
Heracles 56, 71–3, 151, 153, 158, 161–3
Heraclitus 146
Herder, Johann Gottfried 15–19
hero-cult for athletes 158
heroes 138–44
Hesiod 91, 142, 147, 203 n.16
*hēsuchiā* / ἡσυχία (peace) 63, 125–7, 154
Heyne, Christian Gottlob 37
Hieron of Syracuse 61–2, 80, 108–9,
    127–31, 158, 172
*hīlaos* / ἵλαος (gracious, propitious) 72,
    103
*hīlaskomai* / ἱλάσκομαι (propitiate; 'pray
    good cheer') 103
historicism 5
Hölderlin, Friedrich 30–44, 144–6, 188
    his 'change of tones' 34, 36–7, 46, 132,
        145
    and myth 31, 35–6
    theory of genres 34–6
    translations of Pindar 37–41
Homer 51, 66, 79, 97, 109, 110, 113, 115,
    117, 120, 124, 143, 149, 164, 170,
    171, 182, 183, 185, 188, 190,
    203 n.16
    as author 92–3
    gods in 141–2
Homeridae 93, 203 n.16
Hope, *see* elpis
Hopkins, Gerard Manley x–xi
Horace 2, 8
Horae / Ὧραι (Seasons) 148, 218 n.28
hospitality as theme 75, 84, 96, 155
Hubbard, Thomas 157–8
*hymnos* / ὕμνος (song of praise) 78, 111
Hyperboreans 71, 73, 157–8

'I', exemplary 88, 110
    *see also* exemplarity
'I', the speaking in the odes, *see* Pindar, his
    persona in the text; choral 'I'
*iainei* / ἰαίνει (cheers) 62
iambus 90
immortality 142, 156–63, 177
immortality, conferred by poet 17, 54, 56,
    75, 92, 97, 98, 156, 158, 169
inconstancy of fortune as theme 118,
    120–1, 141, 220 n.43
Isles of the Blessed 142, 158–9, 162, 191

Jauss, Hans Robert 134
Johnson, Samuel 9, 14
Jonson, Ben 7
juxtaposition 43–7, 49–50, 122, 170, 178, 188
    *see also* parataxis

*kairos* / καιρός (fitting time, due measure)
    50, 123–7, 131, 135, 169, 190
Kant, Immanuel 21–31, 33, 35, 52, 54, 70,
    122, 132–4, 145, 147, 159
Kirichenko, Alexander 183
Klopstock, Friedrich 15
Köhnken, Adolf 158
*kōmos* / κῶμος (revel) 64, 73–83

Lachesis 176
*lexis eiromenē* / λέξις εἰρομένη ('strung-on'
    style), *see* parataxis
Longinus, *On the Sublime* 4, 13–14, 42, 48,
    50–6, 168, 189–90
*lutron* / λύτρον (recompense) 177
Lyotard, Jean-François 6, 20
lyre(s) 36–7, 61, 68, 81–2, 106, 130, 179,
    193 n.1, 213 n. 145, 222 n.85
lyric 'now' 68–70, 73, 122
Lyric Age of Greece, so-called 43
lyric, archaic Greek, as genre 43–4
lyric, as transhistorical genre 5, 48, 68,
    193 n.1

*makares* / μάκαρες (blessed ones) 73
Maslov, Boris 66–7, 79, 93–4, 155–6, 178,
    183, 190
mentalizing 95
metaphor, *see* Pindar, metaphor in;
    sublime, the, and metaphor

Miller, Andrew 123
mimesis, mimetic 28, 34, 64, 81, 86, 94, 99,
    109, 124, 161, 170, 206 n.58
Moira(i) / Μοῖρα(ι) (Fate(s)) 148–50, 159,
    163, 176
Muse(s) 79, 103, 114, 115–16, 122–3,
    214 n.158
music, in Greek life 61
myth, and Greek religion 138–44

*nemesis* / νέμεσις (natural order) 159
Niagara Falls 23, 57
Nünlist, René 180

occasion, *see* Pindar, and audience(s);
    Pindar, text and performance
'Oldest Systematic Programme of German
    Idealism' 30–1, 34
Olympus (poet) 203 n.16
One and All, *see hen kai pan*
'oral subterfuge' 123–4
orality of Greek culture 65–6
Orpheus 142, 203 n.16

Pan 137–8
pantheism 17, 145
parataxis 41–5, 71, 95
Parmenides 146, 203 n.16
Pater, Walter 134
patrons and patronage of poet 2, 63, 84, 92,
    96, 131, 143
Pavlou, Maria 171
Payne, Mark 104
performance, *see* Pindar, and audience(s);
    Pindar, text and performance;
    reperformance
performativity 85–92, 95, 101, 104, 111,
    113
Perrault, Charles 10–13
personifications 147–56, 169
*phantasiā* / φαντασία (imagination)
    190–1
*phthonos* / φθόνος (envy) 25, 53–4, 128,
    158–9, 190
Pillars of Heracles 56, 71–2, 104, 130, 161,
    184, 190, 220 n.43
Pindar *passim*
    aesthetics of surprise 50, 71
    Alexandrian edition 82

and audience(s) 63–8, 71, 73, 76, 78, 83, 99, 104–5, 115, 189–90; *see also* Pindar, text and performance
and beginnings 172–3
and dithyrambs 8
early modern editions of 7
and enthusiasm 7–8
and first occasion, *see* Pindar, and audience(s); Pindar, text and performance
and gods 144–69
on inborn talent, nature 98, 149, 182
on language 182–3
as literature 66–7, 73, 79
metaphor in 61, 71, 75, 76, 111, 129, 153, 159, 160, 177–88; mixed, 153, 181–2, 185–6
and myth 49, 144–77, 188
his persona in the text 83–116, 124, 190
and poetic tradition 56, 66, 100, 183
and politics 128–35
programme of the epinician 50
and prophecy 17, 144, 161, 170–2
and the *Psalms* 12, 15
style x, 1–4, 7–9, 37, 41, 100, 111, 117, 129, 153, 162, 171; use of relative pronoun to introduce myth, 49, 71, 170; unique words in, *see hapax legomena*
text and performance 62, 64–5, 67, 73–83, 103–4, 109, 124, 130; *see also* Pindar, and audience(s)
use of direct speech 170–1
Plato 17, 29–30, 34, 37, 69
*poikiliā* / ποικιλία / *variatio* (variation) 49, 111, 125
Polymnestus 203 n.16
Pope, Alexander 14
Porter, James 50
Potmos / Πότμος (Fate) 148–9
present tense, in English 87
priamel 45, 49, 185
*prokōmion* / προκώμιον (prelude to the *kōmos*) 78
prophet, poet as 5, 8, 15, 16–17, 99
Purves, Alex 186–7
Pythagoras 142–3, 146

Quarrel of the Ancients and Moderns 10–14

Raphael, *The School of Athens* 177
relative pronoun, *see* Pindar, style
religion, Greek 138–44
reperformance 49, 66–7, 74, 113
Robbins, Emmet x
Romanticism vii, 6, 42, 50, 56–7, 118, 140, 142, 144, 146, 189, 199 n.80
Rosa, Salvator 137–9

Sacadas 203 n.16
Sappho 48, 87, 115, 172, 190
Schadewaldt, Wolfgang 50
Schelling, Friedrich 30–1
Schiller, Friedrich 26–30, 32, 37
*Schwärmer, Schwärmerei, see* enthusiasm
second-person pronoun 110–11, 129
self-address 88, 111, 113–14
'sending' motif 96
Sigelman, Asya 180
Silk, Michael x, 179, 185
Slater, William 64, 77
Snell, Bruno 201 n.114
*sophiā* / σοφία (wisdom, poetic skill) and cognate words 96–100
Spelman, Henry 63–4
Spinoza, Baruch 145
Stesichorus 93, 170
Stockhausen, Karlheinz 24
sublime, the *passim*
　and apostrophe 68
　and art 25–30, 32–7, 133–4
　and cognition 19–21, 51–2, 189
　and divinity 6, 20; and Pindar's gods, 144–69
　a 'domesticated Gallicism' 14
　and fear 19, 24, 53
　and gender 20–1, 52
　'historical' 70, 183
　and incommensurability 107, 122, 168
　and language 20, 25–6, 52
　and limits of comprehension 10, 20, 25, 29, 185
　and metaphor 182, 185–6
　and morality and politics 23–5, 27, 132–4
　and nature 21–3, 27–8

and objects ix, 19, 21, 28, 68, 82, 165
and reason vs emotion 14–15, 18–23, 27
and suffering 24–5, 133
and the beautiful 19, 21–2, 27–9, 31, 133
and the erotic 70, 105, 107
and the grotesque 186
and transcendence 6, 23, 29–37, 40, 57, 104, 144–7, 155, 169, 177
*sumphōniā* / συμφωνία (consonance) 61–3
Symbolists 186–7
symposium 62, 69, 74, 77, 80–1, 130
synaesthesia 180, 181, 185, 187
*sundikos* / σύνδικος ('supporting advocate') 203 n.1

Telchines 174
Terpander 203 n.16
Theagenes of Rhegium 66, 93
Theia 154–6, 178
Theognis 69, 83, 91–2
theoxenia 70, 73, 80, 166
Theron of Acragas 70–3, 131

Thucydides 24–5
time, temporality 76, 106, 113, 156, 161, 168, 170–7, 188
    *see also* lyric 'now', Chronos
tradition, nature of 67, 94
tragedy, Attic and occasion 67
Tyche / Τύχη (Fortune) 148, 151–4, 159, 176
Tyndaridae, *see* Dioscuri
Typhos 60, 62, 126, 172

variation, *see poikiliā*
*vates* (prophet), *see* prophet, poet as
Voltaire 14

Wackernagel, Jacob 109
Wilamowitz-Moellendorff, Ulrich von 86, 140
Winckelmann, Johann Joachim 39–40
Wollstonecraft, Mary 21, 57
Wordsworth, William 95

Xenophanes 142, 146

Young, Edward 13